Teaching the World's Teachers

Teaching the World's Teachers

Edited by
LAUREN LEFTY
and
JAMES W. FRASER

Johns Hopkins University Press
Baltimore

© 2020 Johns Hopkins University Press
All rights reserved. Published 2020
Printed in the United States of America on acid-free paper
2 4 6 8 9 7 5 3 1

Johns Hopkins University Press
2715 North Charles Street
Baltimore, Maryland 21218-4363
www.press.jhu.edu

Library of Congress Cataloging-in-Publication Data

Names: Lefty, Lauren, 1987– editor. | Fraser, James W., 1944– editor.
Title: Teaching the world's teachers / edited by Lauren Lefty and James W. Fraser.
Description: Baltimore : Johns Hopkins University Press, 2020. | Includes bibliographical references and index.
Identifiers: LCCN 2019040540 | ISBN 9781421438290 (hardcover) | ISBN 9781421438306 (ebook)
Subjects: LCSH: Teachers—Training of—Cross-cultural studies.
Classification: LCC LB1707 .T4474 2020 | DDC 370.71/1—dc23
LC record available at https://lccn.loc.gov/2019040540

A catalog record for this book is available from the British Library.

Special discounts are available for bulk purchases of this book. For more information, please contact Special Sales at specialsales@press.jhu.edu.

Johns Hopkins University Press uses environmentally friendly book materials, including recycled text paper that is composed of at least 30 percent post-consumer waste, whenever possible.

CONTENTS

Preface. Why Look at Teacher Preparation Globally? vii
Acknowledgments xiii

Introduction. Teaching the World's Teachers:
A Long and Global History 1
LAUREN LEFTY

1 Argentina
Continuities and Transformations of Argentina's Teacher Education:
Policies and Reforms since the Mid-Eighties 36
GUSTAVO E. FISCHMAN AND PAULA RAZQUIN

2 Brazil
Teacher Formation in Brazil: *"Old" and "New" Approaches to Teacher Formation Given Today's Challenges for the Teaching Profession* 61
SILVANA MESQUITA AND MARIA INÊS MARCONDES

3 Catalonia-Spain
Preparing Teachers for the Schools We Have or for the Schools We Want?
Challenges and Changes in Catalonia (Spain) 89
EDUARD VALLORY

4 China
Teacher Education Reform and National Development
in China (1978–2017): *Four Metaphors* 111
WEI LIAO AND YISU ZHOU

5 England
Crisis and Opportunity in Teacher Preparation in England 132
RICHARD ANDREWS

6 Finland
Teacher Education in Finland: *Persistent Efforts for High-Quality Teachers*   153
HANNELE NIEMI AND JARI LAVONEN

7 Ghana
Transforming Teacher Preparation and Development in Ghana: *Progress and Prospects*   179
KWAME AKYEAMPONG

8 Israel
From Traditional to Dialogical-Reflective Teacher Training: *The Case of Teacher Education in Israel*   199
ARIE KIZEL AND LILY ORLAND-BARAK

9 Singapore
Teacher Education for a Knowledge-Based Economy: *The Singaporean Case*   226
JASON LOH AND GUANGWEI HU

10 South Africa
Reforming South Africa's Teaching: *The Difficult Dilemmas of Teacher Education Policy Reform Post-1994*   249
AZEEM BADROODIEN AND CAROL ANNE SPREEN

11 United States
Changing Paths and Enduring Debates in US American Teacher Education   281
LAUREN LEFTY AND JAMES W. FRASER

A Concluding Word   301
LAUREN LEFTY AND JAMES W. FRASER

Contributors   307
Index   309

PREFACE. WHY LOOK AT TEACHER PREPARATION GLOBALLY?

This volume owes its initial impetus to a comment Oxford University's long-time teacher educator Harry Judge made to coeditor James Fraser many years ago. Reflecting on an earlier book that Fraser had written on teacher education in the United States, Judge said something along the lines of, "Well, it would have been a much better book if you had offered some international comparisons." As we began our work on the recent—and very contentious—history of developments and changes in teacher education in the United States (*Teaching Teachers: Changing Paths and Enduring Debates*, Johns Hopkins University Press, 2018), we were very mindful of that comment. Initially we had planned two chapters in that work looking at other countries for comparison. What we should have known, and quickly discovered, is that the deeper we examined other nations' experiences with teacher education in the 1980–2017 era, the more complex and significant the story became. The result is this separate volume in which we invited experts on the various countries—almost all based in those places—to analyze teacher education in 11 different nations around the world in the same recent time span—nations of various size, development index, and political system on every continent.

As historians of education we brought the same perspective to this volume as to *Teaching Teachers*. We believe that a careful look at how we got here will help us navigate the future more effectively. History never answers the questions of what is coming next, or should come next. But good history does help us understand context and the why of events, and sometimes answers the question of the possible and even the desirable in a specific context. We believe that viewing a contentious time, as the last few decades have been for all teacher educators worldwide, through the prism of the discipline of history allows us to embrace the complexity and contingency of historical developments and move beyond simplistic good-versus-bad value judgments. One can then begin to understand the historical context—in these chapters especially the national context—that shaped developments as well as unforeseen outcomes that had their own impact. Further, both the positive and negative responses to and effects of the many reforms that have been proposed and changes that have happened help further our analysis. In this book we explore the developments that, taken together, may help us understand the sea change that has taken place in teacher education around the world since the 1980s.[1]

In this volume we seek to show how historical context shapes teacher education, sometimes more than participants in a particular context may understand. We do not write to find the one best system for preparing the next generation of teachers. Indeed, these chapters convince us that any effort to define best practices based on international comparisons is a fool's errand. We are mindful of Maria Teresa Tatto's warning that international comparisons can be "dangerous, especially if teacher policy initiatives are drawn from insufficient empirical data and decontextualized conclusions."[2] We also believe that even with the best of data, finding a single best system of teacher education for China, Israel, Brazil, and Catalonia is simply impossible. On the other hand, studying what teacher educators are doing, and want to do, and what various other actors are prodding them—more gently or less—to do sheds light on the international enterprise.

As we edit this volume, just as with the previous one, we are very aware of how much attention, and contention, focuses on teacher preparation. In the *World Declaration on Education for All* issued in Jomtien, Thailand, in March 1990—and cited by several of our chapter authors—and in many subsequent reports and documents from UNESCO, the OECD, and others, the same core theme has emerged—teaching is essential work if the goal of a basic education for every citizen of the planet is to be met, and this means that teachers need to be well prepared.[3] While there seems to be close to unanimous agreement about the importance of good teaching, and therefore good teacher preparation, we also see that there are many different understandings of just what "good teaching" means. In some places, reform and improvement of teacher education has meant locating it more clearly in university settings than in the past, when normal schools and independent teachers colleges were the norm. In other countries reform has meant just the opposite—creating multiple paths to teacher preparation in and far outside of university settings. In some places national or state governments have the resources and the authority to mandate change, while in other places such resources and authority are lacking and many people begin teaching without the prescribed level of preparation.

A word on the selection of case studies: We have tried to achieve the greatest possible diversity in the chapters that follow. We could certainly have selected other countries that would illustrate their own themes as well as themes in common with those we have discussed. For example, Italy has a similar nationwide approach to setting teacher education policy as do England and Spain. In Italy, however, national policy mandated a significant change in teacher preparation in 1997–1998, when national policy required that the preparation of primary school teachers be moved from upper secondary schools to a university program leading to a baccalaureate degree that generally matched the long-standing programs for middle and secondary school teachers. At all levels these baccalaureate degree programs include a basic academic, disciplinary curriculum plus courses in educational theory, methods, and practice teaching. The national Ministry of Education verifies the "ready to teach" status of aspiring teachers. Given the timing of this move, the emerging Bologna Process negotiations likely played a part.[4]

On the other hand, the tiny Cayman Islands elected to remain a British Crown Colony after separating from the newly independent Jamaica in 1962. As a result of its quasi-independent status, the islands have had to develop a new education policy and teacher preparation plan in the last half century. Prosperous like Singapore, but tiny with 60,000 people spread over three islands, Cayman still imports many teachers but has established a teacher preparation program at its University College of the Cayman Islands following a government-mandated curriculum. After a series of university-based courses followed by intensive school-based student teaching, students receive either a bachelor of science or a postgraduate certificate in education (PGCE).[5] Indeed, there are probably as many different systems of preparing teachers as there are nation-states in the world. Nevertheless, we hope that the eleven here provide a useful glimpse of the diversity we seek to describe.

We are well aware that this is not the first book written attempting to look at teacher preparation in a global context. Stanford University–based scholars Linda Darling-Hammond and Ann Lieberman have given us a most valuable volume in *Teacher Education around the World: Changing Policies and Practices* (New York: Routledge, 2012). Bob Moon from the Open University in England has edited *Teacher Education and the Challenge of Devel-*

opment: A Global Analysis (London: Routledge, 2013). Why another book when we have learned so much from our predecessors? *Teaching the World's Teachers* offers a different, and we hope complementary, approach. While the Darling-Hammond and Lieberman book is an excellent look at the current state of teacher education in many different nations, it is especially concerned with those that might be international models for the United States. On the other hand, we are equally concerned to learn from those that may not stand as exemplars at all in terms of specific practices because different contextual circumstances demand different approaches. We hope that scholars from all over the world can find insight here for teacher education in their home countries, not by adopting this or that model wholesale, but by paying attention to what is most needed at any specific time in their own context. While like others, we look at recognized international models, including Finland and Singapore, our volume also includes nations in Latin America, Africa, and places like China and Israel that are not included in the Darling-Hammond and Lieberman book. On the other hand, Moon's book offers rich detail on countries in the developing world, but it does not look at those in the developed world. Moon's book, like this one, looks at Brazil and China, but not at the Industrialized North. Yet we believe this division between the "developed" and "developing" world often creates unnecessary boundaries between scholars who could benefit and learn from one another in a multidirectional conversation that crosses borders and moves beyond old imperial hierarchies. And perhaps most important, in adding a new perspective to the existing literature, we asked our chapter authors to look at developments in their context historically. What changed since the 1980s? When and why did changes happen? What else in the national context led to such changes? What are the contending forces that shaped teacher preparation in the nation? As we have noted above, as historians we believe deeply that understanding change historically can shed a different perspective on the issues than other approaches. Finally, we have taken the time to compile this book because we believe that multiple approaches to understanding the global context in which teacher education is being shaped are warranted and that teacher educators in many places can learn from all three volumes.

After considering several different ways to list the chapters, we have decided that alphabetical is the best. While we considered organizing chapters by certain characteristics—more centralized versus less centralized, more focused on universities versus many alternative programs—we found that each country is unique and imposing these groupings does not work. While China may be the most highly centralized nation under consideration, China also has both a government-sponsored alternative route to teaching and a branch of Teach for All—the international branch of Teach for America. And while England's government has long sponsored alternative routes to teaching outside of universities, university programs still provide the majority of teachers for English schools. In considering the best organization of the chapters, we were reminded once again that national context and national history shapes education policy and practice and needs to be considered in its own specificity without the blinders that being grouped create. Hence, the alphabetical list that follows. In the conclusion to this volume we offer some thoughts on how the diverse national stories tie together and draw out some similarities, differences, and themes from the various case studies.

NOTES

1. James W. Fraser and Lauren Lefty, *Teaching Teachers: Changing Paths and Enduring Debates* (Baltimore: Johns Hopkins University Press, 2018), 5.

2. Maria Teresa Tatto, "Introduction: International Comparisons and the Global Reform of Teaching" in Tatto, ed., *Reforming Teaching Globally* (Charlotte, NC: Information Age Publishing, 2009), 7.

3. See Nhlanganiso Dladla and Bob Moon, "Teachers and the Development Agenda," in Bob Moon, ed., *Teacher Education and the Challenge of Development: A Global Analysis* (London: Routledge, 2013), 5–18, for an excellent overview of the many international reports and proclamations on teaching and teacher education in the last 30 to 50 years.

4. Downloaded from https://education.stateuniversity.com/pages/722/Italy-TEACHING-PROFESSION.html, June 23, 2019, and based on oral interview, Venice, Italy, June 19, 2019.

5. University College of the Cayman Islands catalog, revised January 2015. Oral interview with Terese Parker, Chair Teacher Education, University College of the Cayman Islands, February 18, 2019.

ACKNOWLEDGMENTS

A book is never a solitary endeavor, and this volume is a testament to that truism. Many conversations, collaborations, and cross-border dialogues made this collection possible, which grew from initial research for *Teaching Teachers: Changing Paths and Enduring Debates* (Johns Hopkins University Press, 2018). While we began that book with a plan to include two chapters on international comparisons as part of the story of US American teacher education, we quickly realized that an international look necessitated its own project, which eventually became *Teaching the World's Teachers*.

We the editors of this book would particularly like to thank each and every author who shared their research with us, as well as their patience and good humor with our questions, suggestions for revisions, and deadlines throughout the process. We benefited from your input and learned a great deal about our world and its teachers in the process. New York University, which has been the academic home for both of us through the process of writing this book, has been most generous with support. We could not ask for a better community of scholars of which to be a part. We would also like to thank our editors at Johns Hopkins University Press—Greg Britton, Catherine Goldstead, Kyle Gipson, and their colleagues—for their extraordinary support at every stage of this process.

Lauren Lefty entered the field of education through a fast-track teacher preparation program after studying history at New York University. Frustrated with the meager five-week training, but forever altered by her experience teaching on the Texas-Mexico border and in Brooklyn, New York, she has since devoted her professional life to improving educational equity through engaged scholarship and public humanities work. Before beginning doctoral studies, Lefty also worked in policy planning for the New York City Department of Education. These experiences in teaching and policy work led to a firm conviction in a sociohistorical approach to understanding complex educational issues, as well as a more global outlook on local educational questions. She would like to thank her coeditor Jim Fraser for his continued guidance, generosity, and kindness. A young scholar could not ask for a better mentor. She would also like to thank her ever supportive and encouraging family, Marty, Kathy, and David Lefty, and her life and thought partner Iuri Bauler Pereira. And last but not least, Lefty would like to thank all of her students—from her 7th graders in the Rio Grande Valley to her high schoolers in Brooklyn to her undergrads and grad students at NYU and Columbia—they inspire this work.

Jim Fraser began teaching in the New York City public schools and quickly realized that his teacher education program had not prepared him for engaging with the life experiences, strengths, and issues faced by his students, who represented many parts of the world. Following doctoral work in the history of education at Teachers College Columbia and a career largely focused on teaching and writing in educational history, he again found himself deeply engaged with teacher education policy as special assistant for teacher education to the Massachusetts Chancellor for Higher Education and subsequently Dean of Education at Lesley University and Northeastern University and now vice-dean for Academic Affairs at the Steinhardt School of Culture, Education, and Human Development. I am most grateful to generations of students at P.S. 76 Manhattan, Boston University, the University of Massachusetts–Boston, Northeastern University, and now New York University for support, tough questions, and deep engagement with some of the issues discussed in this book. Lauren Lefty has been a delight to work with, first as a doctoral candidate and now as coauthor/coeditor of our second book. I so appreciate her scholarship and our friendship, and I am most grateful to her for our work together. I am also so grateful to faculty colleagues and administrators throughout my career and especially here at NYU for support in all of my work. And most of all I want to thank my family, especially my wife Katherine Hanson, for support, love, and understanding.

Teaching the World's Teachers

INTRODUCTION

Teaching the World's Teachers
A Long and Global History

LAUREN LEFTY

This introduction presents a brief global history of teacher education from the late eighteenth century to the present. In doing so, it hopes to provide a big-picture narrative for those thinking about the recent history of teacher education around the world, and it offers context for the nation-specific chapters that follow. As a work of historical synthesis, the chapter also aims to highlight common themes across time and space that are useful in analyzing the teacher education enterprise today.

This type of temporally and geographically expansive overview can never be comprehensive. Yet in this pursuit, we join a growing chorus of historians striving to map a more global, connected, and entangled history, and an array of education researchers aiming to take a more sociohistorical approach to contemporary policy issues.[1] By "global" and "entangled" we simply mean analyzing historical phenomena outside the bounds of the nation-state, recognizing connections and power dynamics that exist across borders as well as the simultaneity and connected nature of historical phenomena.[2] This type of analysis draws on the work of a number of scholars, including Diego Olstein's *Thinking History Globally,* in which he outlines four frameworks for approaching global historical analysis: *comparing* (looking at difference across national and regional contexts), *connecting* (highlighting transnational linkages), *conceptualizing* (recognizing broad themes across time and space), and *contextualizing* (analyzing the local dynamics at play with global forces).[3] The following country-specific chapters in this volume engage most directly with the practice of contextualizing in relation to specific national histories, while we hope to do some of the work of comparing, connecting, and conceptualizing in the introduction and conclusion to link these national stories together.

We believe in the value of this type of broad historical thinking generally, and in relation to education policy specifically. Taking a cue from education historians Larry Cuban and David Tyack, we note:

> Anyone who would improve schooling is a captive of history in two ways. All people and institutions are the product of history (defined as past events). And whether they are aware of it or not, all people use history (defined as interpretation of past events) when they make choices about the present and future. The issue is not whether people use a sense of the past in shaping their lives but how accurate and appropriate are their historical maps? Are their inferences attentive to context and complexity? Are their analogies plausible? And how might alternative understandings of the past produce different visions of the future?[4]

In terms of a global historical approach to *teacher education,* this might mean recognizing the context and complexity of how educational innovations arose, and engaging the power dynamics embedded in the spread of educational ideas. For example, anyone who posits that modern educational techniques necessarily originated in Europe and the United States and flowed to the Global South may well be mistaken, as this introduction will demonstrate. Some of the first teacher education institutions in the world originated in ancient China and Mexico, while the Monitorial-Lancaster system, often attributed to the British, in many ways derived from long-used methods of Indian educators and was adopted in the metropole through imperial encounter.[5]

A global approach to the history of teacher education may also challenge historical maps on long-standing ideas such as women being naturally suited for teaching, an enduring idea in the popular imagination.[6] Those who still hear that claim, or see its legacy in teacher workforce statistics, should take a careful look at when and why those tropes originated in the nineteenth century in such varied places as Massachusetts, Buenos Aires, and Beijing, as school systems were ballooning and cheap feminized labor appealed to school administrators, but also as teaching became one of the few careers for women outside the home and therefore defended by women's rights advocates. These types of insights help us make sense of our past but also our present. They challenge Eurocentric narratives of "progress" and "development" and patriarchal claims of teaching as "women's work." Similar historical remapping can also help us navigate the power dynamics and unintended consequences of past and current education reforms, especially through the lenses of race, class, gender, sexuality, empire, and disability.

On an even more basic level, we also agree with Cuban and Tyack that "history provides a whole storehouse of experiments on dead people. Studying such experimentation is cheap (no small matter when funds are short); and it does not use people (often the poor) as live guinea pigs. Many educational problems have deep roots in the past, and many solutions have been tried before."[7] We therefore think anyone navigating their way through the contentious teacher education debates of today should look back—both far back and more recently—to inform their opinions on current policy.

We therefore engage the following thematic questions in this overview chapter and encourage those thinking about contemporary teacher education policy to do the same:

- Through what means do ideas and practices in teacher education spread?
- What power dynamics are embedded in this circulation of educational ideas across international borders?
- What role does teacher education play in the broader society: locally, nationally, and internationally?
- Who has power to set teacher education policy?
- How has the form and content of teacher preparation changed over time?
- What convergences and divergences can be seen in teacher preparation around the world?
- How have various populations (women, racial and ethnic minorities, the working class, LGBTQ+ individuals, etc.) experienced opportunity and/or exclusion within teacher education institutions?
- What has been the relationship between the state, market, and civil society in shaping teacher education?
- What enduring dilemmas exist in teacher preparation that still challenge teacher educators today?

The Long Nineteenth Century: The Birth of "Modern" and "Global" Teacher Education (1749–1914)

While contact and exchange occurred between civilizations for centuries, many early global approaches to teacher education can trace their origins to the long nineteenth century: the period roughly between 1749 and 1914, characterized by Enlightenment-inspired revolutions, the rise of industrial capitalism, the growth of modern empires and nation-states, and the creation of national education systems. Increased travel and communications technologies contributed greatly to the exchange between educational leaders around the world, creating convergences in thought and practice in teacher preparation.[8]

Given the power dynamics of international politics by the late eighteenth century, many of the "modern" methods of education are said to have originated in Europe and North America—though it is crucial to recognize the various non-Western and premodern models of teacher training that existed before Western models gained international ascendance, such as the ancient Chinese teaching school the *shifan* or the educational practices of indigenous communities in Africa and the Americas.[9] It is also crucial to recognize the imperial ideologies that shaped ideas of what was considered "modern." As theorists of empire and postcolonialism have argued, it is impossible to decouple European "modernity," including the development of modern education systems, from the twin development of European imperialism. Often, "modern" technologies, institutions, and knowledge systems were in fact derived through imperial encounters with non-Western peoples and shaped by colonial ideologies.[10]

The most striking example of this phenomenon is the Lancaster-Bell and Madras systems. According to historian Jana Tschurenev, this model of teacher training (sometimes referred to as the monitorial method) became the "first global model of school management and classroom organization," and in many ways the first global model of teacher education.[11] The system relied on competent older students to aid a primary instructor in teaching large numbers of pupils, often in one giant classroom.[12] This type of peer-to-peer tutoring in a large-group setting, enforced through methods of surveillance, examination, and competition for student teacher positions, became a leading source of teacher preparation around the world, as many of the advanced pupils went on to become primary instructors themselves and did much of the teaching while still training.

Although long considered a British innovation, said to have developed simultaneously in Britain by Quaker Joseph Lancaster and in India by Anglican chaplain Andrew Bell, this form of pedagogy, in fact, drew from Indian educational practices that British imperial agents and missionaries then circulated back to the metropole and applied to poor working-class children in London. This South-to-North transmission first occurred through Bell's writings in 1789 and continued throughout the early nineteenth century. Writing in 1814, the Court of Directors of the East India Company noted, for example: "The mode of instruction that from time immemorial has been practised [in India] has received the highest tribute of praise by its adoption in this country [i.e., in England], under the direction of the Reverend Dr. Bell, formerly Chaplain at Madras; and it is now become the mode by which education is conducted in our national establishments . . . This venerable and benevolent institution of the Hindoos [sic] is represented to have withstood the stock of revolutions, and to its operation is ascribed the general intelligence of the people as scribes and accountants."[13]

Civil society organizations such as the Royal Lancaster Society (founded in 1808), and the National Society for the Education of the Poor in the Principles of the Established Church (founded in 1811) contributed to this flow of ideas. These types of civil society organizations as well as religious orders trained teachers at Lancaster's model school in Borough Road before sending them abroad, and they circulated pedagogical information through various manuals, books, and pamphlets. Lancaster himself traveled across Europe and the Atlantic spreading his ideas, as he did to the United States in the early nineteenth century, giving talks to North American school leaders and helping to establish Lancaster schools in North America, such as the one in Philadelphia in 1813.[14]

In this way, global education policy, including policies that related to teacher training, developed through networks connecting colonies and imperial metropoles, though asymmetrical power relations shaped these interactions, as did "civilizing" and "modernizing" discourses based on premises of Euro-Christian superiority.[15] Indeed, only after accruing proper theorization and therefore authority in Europe was the Lancaster-Bell system exported around the world again through British imperial channels, adopted in such varied regions as North and South America, Russia, continental Europe, the Ottoman Empire, and across Africa in addition to other regions of India, the Middle East, and various British colonial outposts.

Yet the appropriation of this form of school organization and teacher training was not simply adopted wholesale in the places to which it was exported. In Latin America, for example, the newly formed republics appropriated the monitorial system, but they adapted it to their own unique needs in the wake of independence from Spain. In 1824, the Lancasterian Company of Mexico City published a manual on the monitorial system of education, citing a number of English-, French-, and Spanish-language sources, and noting that they were "happy to present an essay derived from the best observations made by the wise men of Europe, supported by our own experience."[16] In this way, as historian Eugenia Roldan Vera makes clear, universal models of schooling based on liberal ideas did not simply diffuse from center to periphery but were debated, contested, adapted, and remade to suit local needs. In the Spanish American monitorial system, it was more common to view "order" not as a means to raise a submissive working class, as in Britain, but to inculcate a sense of individual restraint in a republican democracy and transmit knowledge to younger generations. As the chapters in this volume from Argentina and Brazil demonstrate, this type of negotiation with US and European ideas still shapes teacher education across Latin America today, and similar themes can be found in this book's chapters on South Africa, Ghana, Singapore, and Israel.

While the Lancaster-Bell method was arguably the first global model of education, narratives of modern teacher preparation often begin with the École Normale Supérieure. Heralded as the prototype of modern teacher training, the École Normale became the first nonsectarian normal school following the French Revolution ("norm" coming from the word *normale,* or "standard"). Established in Paris in 1794, the institution became a place "where citizens of the Republic already schooled in the usual sciences should be taught to teach."[17] Around this time, the Prussian monarchy had also implemented teaching academies that became widespread across present-day Germany and Austria.[18]

These were not mere coincidences of timing; European societies communicated with one another about their educational systems, spreading ideas across the continent. A professor from the University of Paris, Victor Cousin, for example, was commissioned to visit the Prussian teaching academies, and he wrote an influential and widely circulated report from his time spent in Saxony, Weimar, and Frankfort.[19] Due to this type of intellectual exchange, normal schools sprang up in Spain, Poland, Norway, Hungary, Italy, and across the European continent.[20] The new normal schools aimed to provide a solid grounding of the disciplinary subjects to be taught, instruction in pedagogical philosophy and practice—"how to teach"—and in some cases apprenticeship training in practice or "laboratory" classrooms.

Crucial to modernization and nation-building projects in the Americas and Asia as well, the first normal school in the Western Hemisphere was founded in the United States around 1823, soon followed by Brazil in 1835, Chile in 1842, Argentina in 1852, the Dominican Republic in 1880, and Canada in 1901.[21] Educational leaders Horace Mann, Catharine Beecher, Calvin Stowe, Domingo Faustino Sarmiento, Andrés Bello, and Eugenio María de Hostos were some of the leading advocates of normal schools in the Americas, as they traveled across the hemisphere and across the Atlantic, sharing innovations with one another and reading each other's texts. As historian Paul Ramsey describes:

> Inspired by the favourable reports coming from Europe—including those of Americans such as Henry E. Dwight and William Channing Woodbridge—educational reformers in the U.S. began to set out for the Old World to see its schools firsthand. Henry Barnard, the great public school champion of Connecticut, visited European schools from 1835 to 1837. During his travels, he became convinced that the Prussian model was the best and, therefore, proselytised on its merits in his American Journal of Education. Like Barnard, Alexander D. Bache—kin of Benjamin Franklin—made the voyage to Europe in order to survey its educational activities. Bache, who was taking up the presidency of the Girard College for Orphans in Philadelphia, was equally impressed with the schools in Prussia, and Barnard used and popularised Bache's observations in his own work.[22]

Prominent Yankee educationists such as Calvin Stowe (husband of Harriet Beecher Stowe) and Horace Mann made similar trips. Argentine statesman Domingo Faustino Sarmiento in turn spent time with Horace Mann, his wife Mary, and other US American education reformers in Massachusetts in the 1840s. He also visited European normal school leaders and cited these influences in his influential *De la Educación Popular* (1849) and various other essays, in which he advocated for a mass public education system with professionally trained teachers for Argentina, a legacy that influenced the country's *estado docente* (teaching state), detailed in Fischman and Razquin's chapter (chapter one).[23] Two generations later, the first

US commissioner of education William T. Harris noted in 1891 that the American normal school was, in essence, "a school with a French name and a Prussian curriculum."[24]

The Asian-Pacific world also joined the global bandwagon. Normal schools appeared in Japan in 1872 at the behest of Meiji leaders looking to modernize the Japanese Imperial system, followed by China in 1898 with what was termed the Imperial Capital School of Supreme Teacher Training (now the preeminent Beijing Normal University, a key actor in Liao and Zhou's chapter on contemporary Chinese teacher education, chapter four).[25] In both China and Japan education policy makers fused "modern" and "traditional" institutional forms as they aimed to modernize but also resist Western imposition, and in so doing blurred the lines of those very categories. Beijing Normal University, for example, grew from the education faculty at the Imperial University of Peking, founded in 1898 as part of the Hundred Days' Reforms of Emperor Guangxu, which itself grew from a previously existing imperial university with origins in ancient China. These normal schools, as well as Chinese teaching colleges (a unique Chinese institutional model), grew on the ancient *shifan* tradition. Similarly in Japan, as Kaori Okano and Motonori Tsuchiya note, "the development of Meiji schooling should not be understood as a simple transplantation of Western civilization into feudal Japan, and as a one-sided departure from the indigenous practice of education."[26] Although normal schools grew from the reforms of Meiji leadership attempting to modernize and compete with Western powers, the reforms of the First Minister of Education Arinori Mori drew on ancient Japanese culture and embedded distinctly Japanese nationalist ideals into the curriculum and institutional framework. The Japanese variety of normal school was therefore said to produce a particular "normal school type," a militantly nationalist educator steeped in Japanese mores (though some of these normal school students would later defy Mori and his agenda).

Whether in metropoles or colonies, republics or monarchies, ideas about teacher education remained impressively linked, though far from uniform. Books, journals, and traveling teacher educators housed at these new teacher training institutions spread ideas on teacher preparation, pedagogy, and the nature of the child—particularly given the rise of the field of educational research from bases in expanding systems of research universities. Early on this led to the global uptake of the educational philosophies of Swiss philosopher Jean-Jacques Rousseau, especially his *Émile, or On Education* (1762), fellow Swiss thinker Johann Pestalozzi, and Germans Johann Herbart and Friedrich Froebel.[27] Late nineteenth- and early twentieth-century normal school curriculums were marked by these thinkers, who set the groundwork for the progressive education movement that preached romantic ideas about the nature of the child, object-based learning, and a style of teaching that moved beyond the rote memorization of the Bell-Lancastrian/monitorial days.

In many countries, feminization also became the twin pillar of professionalization in teacher education by the mid- and late nineteenth century, as liberal republican nation-builders mixed romantic notions of women's "natural" role as mothers with the pragmatic demands of ballooning educational systems. While the first normal schools in most countries enrolled only men, by the mid- and especially late nineteenth century, the argument for a professional class of female teachers gained traction. Written in 1835, Catharine Beecher's "An Essay on the Education of Female Teachers for the United States" built her case for more female teachers colleges on the basis of women's innate qualities, as well as the human resource demands in the growing republic. After all, she reasoned:

> When we consider the claims of the learned professions, the excitement and profits of commerce, manufactures, agriculture, and the arts; when we consider the aversion of most men to the sedentary, confining, and toilsome duties of teaching and governing young children; when we consider the scanty pittance that is allowed to the majority of teachers; and that few men will enter a business that will not support a family, when there are multitudes of other employments that will afford competence, and lead to wealth; it is chimerical to hope that the supply of such immense deficiencies in our national education is to come chiefly from that sex. It is woman, fitted by disposition and habits, and circumstances, for such duties, who, to a very wide extent, must aid in educating the childhood and youth of this nation; and therefore it is, that females must be trained and educated for this employment. And, most happily, it is true, that the education necessary to fit a woman to be a teacher, is exactly the one that best fits her for that domestic relation she is primarily designed to fill.[28]

Other liberal education reformers across the world agreed with these basic premises—that women were naturally suited for teaching, and states could pay them less than men, what Steven Palmer and Gladys Rojas Chaves have described in the Latin American context as "a combination of utterly practical needs and profoundly romantic metaphors."[29] Argentine Domingo Sarmiento noted, for example, women *maestras* could be of use in Buenos

Aires and "entrusted with rudimentary education given the greater aptitude of their sex and their more limited salary requirements."[30] Owing to the spread of these ideas amongst liberal educationists, teaching became both professionalized and feminized in the late nineteenth and early twentieth centuries in many parts of the world (though unevenly), two characteristics that would create lasting challenges for the teacher education enterprise, raising issues of status, prestige, and authority in male-dominated societies.[31]

Yet at the same time, as in the case of the Colegio Superior de Señoritas in San Juan, Costa Rica, the Troy Female Seminary in upstate New York, or the normal school in Svres, France, teacher training institutions could also become places of liberation and social mobility for women and hotbeds of feminist politics.[32] This was particularly true for middle-class women clamoring to enter the public sphere but largely denied that opportunity, though poor rural and urban women also took their place in normal schools around the globe.[33] Teaching often remained the only acceptable profession for women, and many made space for creativity, innovation, and empowerment through their training and subsequent teaching careers. In Asia, normal schools for women grew out of early twentieth-century liberal feminist waves and a broader push for girls' education. The extension of schooling for girls and the opening of normal schools for women similarly "forever altered the position of women in Chinese society."[34]

Nineteenth-century nation-building and the feminization of teaching also coincided with the rise of modern European, US American, Russian, and Japanese empires. This undoubtedly impacted teacher preparation in the colonized regions of Africa, the Middle East, Asia, the Caribbean, and Central Europe, as well as for indigenous and African-descended populations in the Americas.[35] Often European and North American teachers, of both genders, were trained in civilizing discourses of the "white (wo)man's burden" and sent to educate those deemed to be members of inferior races and cultures in need of Euro-descended "enlightenment." Reflecting the dominant eugenic and neo-Lamarckian philosophies of the day, however, nineteenth-century teachers were often also taught to provide different types of education for different groups of children, inscribing raced, classed, gendered, and ableist notions of citizenship into national and imperial systems. For example, teachers in the colonies and of nonwhite and working-class populations in the Americas, Australia, and New Zealand were often taught to provide an industrial, vocational education for their pupils while

Figure I.1. Trainee teachers at the college in Salatiga, Java, Indonesia, October 5, 1929. While this photograph shows Indonesian women studying to be teachers, their instructor was Dutch, as Indonesia was under Dutch colonial rule at this time. ("Groepsportret voor de 'Kweekschool voor inlandse onderwijzeressen.'" Source: Tropenmuseum, Wikipedia)

white and upper-class children received classical curriculums imbued with romantic notions of the goodness of the child.

Religious orders played a large role in teaching and therefore teacher training in the colonies, adding to these tropes, and white and upper-class women played an outsized role in day-to-day teaching and teacher education in colonized regions.[36] Yet religious orders and mission schools were often far more willing than colonial governments to provide education for indigenous populations. In South Africa, for example, far more black South Africans attended mission schools than public secular schools, leaving many, like the country's first black president, Nelson Mandela, to reflect back with mixed feelings on his experiences at a British-run Methodist boarding school. He recalled of the Scottish headmaster, "I saw Dr. Kerr less as a benefactor than a not-altogether-benign dictator," though he also fondly recalled the school's academic rigor: "For young black South Africans it was Oxford and Cambridge, Harvard and Yale, all rolled into one," though this memory too reflected the long shadow cast by imperial domination, with the centers of excellence being associated with European and North American metropoles.[37] (See chapter ten for more on the colonial legacy in South African education.)

Communities excluded from nation-building projects, such as slaves, free blacks in the Americas, or the aboriginal peoples of Australia and New Zealand, sometimes provided their own education and teacher training through informal, community-based methods. As in the case of Afro–Puerto Rican educators Rafael and Celestina Cordero, their parents started their own school in their living room when the established educational institutions in San Juan would not accept black students. The Corderos, through this makeshift training, then went on to educate some of the island's leading statesmen, holding classes in their home and a tobacco workshop to students of various races and classes.[38] In the US American South, African Americans pulled funds together and received grants from Northern philanthropies to run their own teacher training institutes and public schools when segregationist local governments would not provide them.[39]

Ultimately, the nineteenth century witnessed the rise of global teacher education models, including the Lancaster-Bell method and normal schools. These models, along with the pedagogical philosophies of figures like Froebel and Pestalozzi, were transfused through various formal and informal networks by statesmen, academics, mission societies, colonial officials, and teachers themselves. Never divorced from national or local contexts, the places where teachers were taught nevertheless reflected global politics and imperial orders, as they would in the next century.

The "Short" Twentieth Century: Professionalism, Politicization, and Increased Global Entanglements (1914–1980)

Global developments in teacher education continued throughout the "short twentieth century," a term historian Eric Hobsbawm has given to the period between 1914 (the First World War) and 1991 (the fall of the Soviet Union, though we begin our volume in 1980, a marker other historians have used to mark the "age of globalization").[40] During this tumultuous era in global politics, various nations took different paths to prepare their teaching workforces. While in many countries teacher education became a university-level pursuit, other nations maintained the two-year normal school tradition, while some held to a diverse system of pathways into the classroom for K–12 educators.[41] In some countries this meant teacher training institutions became valued and fairly prestigious places of learning, as in Finland. In too many others, teaching became a low-status profession, rendering the places where teachers were taught equally maligned.

Despite these divergences, convergences also became a twentieth-century phenomenon, as the "grammar of schooling" (what classrooms looked like and what was taught) felt markedly similar in teacher education programs around the world.[42] In most countries, as we will see, the short twentieth century was a time of increased pressure for uniformity in teacher preparation and often a loss of autonomy, as previously independent normal schools became schools or departments of education in multipurpose universities, and greater government regulation impacted teacher education curriculum.[43]

This convergence was also in large part due to the proliferation of international intellectual and policy networks, as well as the strengthening of state power within national contexts.

As a result of these linkages, greater professionalization and standardization became the norm for the teaching profession across the globe. In many countries, more extensive university-based training was often required for secondary-level teaching, while elementary education demanded less preparation, and lower-level teaching remained, as it does to this day, more feminized. Certification requirements were adopted in a greater number of countries, and accreditation agencies slowly gained traction across the century and across the globe, though it is fair to say that teaching, unlike the professions of law and medicine, rarely to never developed and agreed on the same type of unified body of professional knowledge that could be distilled into a standard curriculum, and teachers never gained the same prestige as their professional peers. As the chapters on Argentina, Brazil, South Africa, England, and the United States explore, low social status has long plagued the teacher education enterprise, though places like Finland after the 1960s and Singapore in the 1990s passed specific education reforms that transformed teaching into a high-prestige and academically rigorous career path (see chapters six and nine, respectively).

In terms of curriculum, debates also ensued about whether or not to embrace classical subjects and pedagogical models, such as rote learning and Latin; progressive, secular, and applied ways of learning in the spirit of John Dewey and Maria Montessori; or curriculums that favored national political projects, as in the case of postrevolutionary Russia or Maoist China. Each model found adherents at various times and places, often imbued by political context.

Despite these debates, ideas about progressive pedagogy traveled widely and became a hallmark of twentieth-century teacher education, impacting curriculums in normal schools and teachers colleges around the globe. US American philosopher John Dewey's extensive writings and personal travel (particularly to Soviet Russia, China, Turkey, and Mexico in the 1920s) fueled this trend, though his ideas on progressive and applied learning also spread through intellectual and institutional exchanges, civil society organizations, and imperial state apparatuses.[44] The University of Chicago and then Columbia University, where Dewey was based, and the London Institute of Education (now the Institute of Education at University College London), became leading sources of educational authority around the globe

Figure I.2. John Dewey of Columbia University on his visit to China between 1919 and 1921. Here he is pictured with Chinese educational leaders. (Source: Columbia Teachers College)

in the early twentieth century, as they remain to this day.[45] As education historian Jonathan Zimmerman notes, "Though born in Europe and the Americas," by the postwar period "progressive education had become a truly global initiative."[46]

In many countries, "visible and relatively invisible" networks connected teacher educators with their peers across the world, as historian Malcolm Vick analyzes in his research on Australian teacher education in the first half of the twentieth century. In some instances, Australian leaders of teachers colleges wrote to North American counterparts directly. In other instances, they traveled to each other's schools on exchanges and fellowships, met through meetings of educational research organizations, or read published materials and reports from various parts of the Anglophone world. These processes, though specific to Australia in Vick's work, elucidate the many ways in which teacher education became even more entangled in the twentieth century as people and ideas moved across borders.[47]

Figure I.3. Brigadistas, as Cuban literacy teachers were called, trained in informal camps on a beach once owned by a private hotel company following the Cuban Revolution in 1959. They then set out to teach fellow Cubans in the countryside basic literacy. Many remained teachers after this experience. (Source: Atlanta Black Star)

Yet alongside professionalization, the twentieth century also saw large pushes for mass literacy, and consequently the rise of community-based educators with little to no formal training. Literacy campaigns sprang up in such varied places as China, Russia, and Nicaragua. As H. S. Bohla notes, the Soviet push to educate the peasantry after the overthrow of the Romanov dynasty was "the ancestor of all modern mass literacy campaigns," though Y. C. James Yen's rural literacy initiative in China in the 1930s, Frank Laubach's "each one, teach one" model in the colonial Philippines in the '40s, Paulo Freire's community-based literacy program in Brazil in the late '50s and early '60s, and Cuba's postrevolutionary peer literacy campaign also exemplified this trend.[48] Often, these mass educational efforts used literate citizens with little to no formal pedagogical training to teach nonliterate citizen peers. While the twentieth century was indeed the era of professionalization and increased standardization, nonprofessional and grassroots initiatives also served as important sites of teacher formation in many parts of the world, complicating narratives of a march toward professionalization everywhere.

As teacher education generally became more professionalized, however, it could also become more exclusionary. In nations with white supremacist ideologies, like the United States, South Africa, and the European colonies, many teacher education institutions barred persons of color from enrolling, maintained racially segregated teacher education institutions, or only allowed teachers of color to teach at the lower grade levels. In places with less explicit segregationist policies but that also held to notions of European superiority, such as Latin America, normal school admissions policies and curriculum could also promote racial and ethnic hierarchies. In Brazil, for example, where leaders rhetorically espoused an ideology of racial democracy, professionalization still led to a whitening of the teaching force. While a fair number of Afro-Brazilian educators taught in Rio de Janeiro's schools in the nineteenth and early twentieth centuries, during the regime of Getúlio Vargas in the 1930s those numbers dwindled. "What happened to Rio's teachers of color?" historian Jerry Dávila asked in his study of race and Brazilian education between 1917 and 1945. "They lost ground to the rising tide of the social sciences, modernization, technicalization, and professionalization."[49] As Marcondes and Mesquita detail in their chapter on Brazil (chapter two), these legacies over the prestige and demographics of the teaching profession still haunt Brazilian teacher educators, as they do in many countries around the world.

In the Southern United States and South Africa, legal segregation barred Afro-descended people and other racial minorities from enrolling in many teacher training institutions. In the American North, while some black Americans were admitted to teacher education institutions, numbers remained limited. Even in a relatively progressive city like New York, laws barred teachers from possessing Southern or Spanish-inflected accents, functioning in practice to exclude African Americans and Latinxs from the profession.[50] Despite these barriers, black teachers like Charlotte Forten attended Salem State University in Massachusetts even before the Civil War, and New York University's first graduating class from the School of Pedagogy included African Americans, showing that some institutions could also lead the charge against societal racism.[51] In the case of the American South, segregated but community-run or philanthropy-funded black normal schools provided opportunities for higher and professional education where few existed in the broader society. At the all-black Alabama State College in Montgomery, for example, students became active in that city's famous civil rights bus boycott, while the Cherokee Female Seminary in

Tahlequah, Oklahoma, prepared Native American women to teach children from their communities. As in the previous century, normal schools and teacher training institutions therefore continued to serve as sites of contestation, negotiation, discrimination, and empowerment for women, the working class, the colonized, and ethnic and racial minorities.[52] As Badroodien and Spreen discuss in their chapter on South Africa (chapter ten), and Lefty analyzes in the chapter on the United States (chapter eleven), legacies of white supremacy and segregation still impact the teaching profession and the content of teacher preparation today.

Teachers colleges and normal schools also served as sites of revolutionary state formation and social change in the twentieth century, as they became swept up in the century's battles between capitalism, communism, socialism, and nationalism. This occurred in such varied settings as Russia, Mexico, China, Cuba, and Mozambique. In Russia, following the 1917 revolution, teacher training institutions were marshaled in service of the new political order and prepared educators to forge a new nation in the principles of state-led communism. The embrace of modern and scientific educational practices, blended with communist ideology, had a profound impact on educational models in Russia, but also in Eastern Europe and around the world, as countries looked to the Soviets as a leading prototype of economic development and educational quality. Soviet approaches to science and mathematics education, as well as child psychology, particularly the work of Lev Vygotsky, proved particularly influential to teacher education programs around the world.[53]

In Mexico, the rural normal schools created in the 1930s following the Mexican Revolution of 1910–1920 also aimed to create school teachers who would go forth and forge a new nation. *Normalistas* underwent training in the latest pedagogical techniques, inspired by Mexican educational philosophers' own ideas about cultural pluralism as well as Deweyan pragmatism (statesman and secretary of education Moises Sáenz studied with John Dewey at Columbia Teachers College). Their goal was to fuse indigenous and European heritage together in a social democratic republic, all the while creating educated citizens incorporated into one national society. While Dewey's work inspired Mexican statesmen, these efforts inspired other Latin American countries and civil rights advocates in the United States working to incorporate rural Native American and Mexican American populations into the national body politic. As historian Ruben Flores notes in his study of these "backroads pragmatists," "This exchange showed not merely how

America's history of cultural difference influenced the history of pluralism in Mexico, but also how Mexico's own melting pot was integral to the history of democracy in the United States."[54] Ideas about teacher education, and the role of teachers and schools in society, therefore flowed across borders—from South to North, South to South, and in all directions.

At midcentury, leaders on the left and right also influenced the education of teachers as they gained political power, often to develop cadres of deeply patriotic and nationalist molders of their nations' youth. This was true in Italy, Spain, Germany, and Japan. In China, many of the leaders of the 1949 Communist Revolution, including Mao Zedong, Cai Hesen, and Xiao Zisheng, were in fact educated at the same normal school, the Hunan First Normal University, which had its origins in the drive for educational improvement in the 1910s. As historian Liyan Liu argues, it was in this teaching school, with its blend of traditional Chinese and "modern" international curriculum, that provided a space to spread new ideas and foment Marxist revolution.[55] These revolutionaries then used teaching institutions themselves as they sought to remake Chinese society completely, schools that Liao and Zhou discuss in their chapter on teacher education in contemporary China (chapter four).[56]

Following the Second World War, newly formed global bodies such as the United Nations and its Educational, Scientific and Cultural Organization (UNESCO), the World Bank, International Monetary Fund (IMF), and the Organisation for Economic Co-operation and Development (OECD) became international institutions that functioned to spread ideas about education across borders, including teacher preparation. Between fiscal year 1962 (when the World Bank began lending for education) and 1984, 52% of the bank's 284 education projects involved teacher education in some way, with Africa being the largest recipient region.[57] The World Bank's first education project, in fact, included the construction of a teachers college in Tunisia.[58] UNESCO began publishing resource materials in the late 1940s related to education, and it hosted multiple international and regional conferences on the topic in the second half of the century. Not surprisingly, even greater global convergences in the way teachers were taught occurred due to these global networks. By 1966, for example, UNESCO and the International Labour Organization (ILO) jointly published an influential and enduring set of guidelines regarding the teaching profession entitled *Recommendation Concerning the Status of Teachers*.[59] In it, a number of suggestions were set forth concerning teacher preparation, including the selection of candidates, purpose of preparation, content of curriculum, and nature of teacher preparation institutions. In regard to curriculum, the report recommended: "Fundamentally a teacher-preparation programme should include: (a) general studies; (b) study of the main elements of philosophy, psychology, sociology as applied to education, the theory and history of education, and of comparative education, experimental pedagogy, school administration and methods of teaching the various subjects; (c) studies related to the student's intended field of teaching; (d) practice in teaching and in conducting extra-curricular activities under the guidance of fully qualified teachers."[60]

Ultimately, the report stressed the importance of teachers and encouraged their professionalization, stating, "Teaching should be regarded as a profession: it is a form of public service which requires of teachers expert knowledge and specialized skills, acquired and maintained through rigorous and continuing study." In that vein, it also became more standard practice for teachers, especially secondary school teachers, to possess a four-year university degree rather than a two-year degree in most parts of the developed world, while at least a secondary education was encouraged in areas with more limited access to higher education. The 1966 UNESCO/ILO report noted that ideally, however, "all teachers should be prepared in general, special, and pedagogical subjects in universities, or in institutions on a level comparable to universities, or else in special institutions for the preparation of teachers."[61]

The entry of these international institutions into global policy occurred within the context of Cold War imperatives. Development aid became a useful tool on the ideological battlefield of the global conflict, as the Soviets and Americans competed for hearts and minds around the world. Both the US and Soviet footprint could be felt across the globe, particularly through aid programs such as USAID, the Peace Corps, Soviet trade programs, and the influence of Cold War American and Soviet universities, which sent researchers and "experts" as technical advisors abroad and invited a number of international scholars to study in the metropoles, including to many normal schools and colleges of education.[62] The United States' Alliance for Progress, for example, poured millions of aid dollars into development programs across Latin America, and the reform of teacher education became an important recipient of that aid. As Gustavo Fischman and Paula Razquin discuss in their chapter on Argentina, however, US influence also extended to support for anticommunist military dictatorships across the region, most of which maintained a firm grip on teacher education from the '60s to the early '80s, promoting conservative curriculums in alliance with the conservative wing of the Catholic Church (chapter one).

The Peace Corps, created in 1961 under the leadership of US president John F. Kennedy, also trained and sent thousands of idealistic young Americans into classrooms across the globe, rendering it an important site of informal teacher formation.[63] The Soviets invited a number of scholars from around the world to study at Soviet universities through a university aid program that began in 1956. By 1973 over 15,000 international students from the developing world and satellite socialist republics received scholarships to study in Soviet universities, creating networks that functioned to spread educational ideas across borders.[64] In Afghanistan, where the Soviets and Americans vied for allegiance, the United States became an influential player in teacher education and curriculum design, producing in the 1980s what became an influential textbook, *Alphabet of Jihad Literacy*, which ironically promoted a violent vision of jihadism in hopes of spurring an uprising against the Soviets—produced by USAID in conjunction with the University of Nebraska at Omaha.[65] Similar to earlier eras, Cold War metropoles and neocolonial regions remained linked through such initiatives, and missionary-like enthusiasm impacted how the "First World" interacted with the "Third World" (terms coined in the 1950s).

The Cold War also coincided with the age of decolonization. Starting in the 1950s, many newly independent nations across the Global South could educate their own teaching force with decolonized and nationalist curriculums for the first time. In some of these new nations, teachers colleges and normal schools became sites of more explicit anti-imperial and nonaligned nationalism. Anticolonial leaders and intellectuals such as Franz Fanon, Jawaharlal Nehru, and Kwame Nkrumah shaped the intellectual milieu of these postcolonial nations, consequently shaping the institutions where teachers were prepared.[66] Brazilian educator Paulo Freire's *Pedagogy of the Oppressed*—which argued in favor of a "consciousness-raising" form of education that challenged power dynamics—found fertile soil in these new nations and took root around the world in the 1970s and beyond while Freire himself was in exile in the United States and Switzerland, influencing the pedagogical style of future educators in both formal education school settings and more informal grassroots education networks across the globe.[67]

Education research on human capital development for economic growth also influenced the form and content of teacher education programs, as education systems ballooned and investment in teacher preparation was seen as a direct investment in the nation's workforce, though material constraints often plagued reform efforts in the developing world. (See chapter nine for more on investments in teacher education for economic growth in the case of postcolonial Singapore.) In postcolonial Ghana, for example, while the Ministry of Education spearheaded a teacher education reform based on progressive pedagogical principles to transcend the old colonial forms of rote learning, political upheaval and lack of funds greatly hampered the success of the reform. "Despite scattered assistance from the West, in money and manpower, Ghana simply *lacked* the money or manpower to change teaching."[68]

Philanthropies and civil society organizations also continued to shape teacher education in the twentieth century, just as they had since the earliest days of European and North American civil society organizations such as the Lancaster Society. The US-based Carnegie Corporation, and the Ford and Rockefeller Foundations became some of the most influential nongovernmental actors influencing educational thought and practice around the world, providing grants and technical assistance to domestic and international institutions to reform their teacher education programs.[69] The result was often a complex interplay between the influence of American and Soviet power, in the form of technical expertise and development aid, and efforts to chart a postcolonial path in the nonaligned countries. As Liu reflects in her study on China, for example, "The development of modern schools and teachers schools in particular, played a part in the two processes that most influenced China's twentieth century transformation: 'localizing the global' and 'nationalizing the local.'"[70] The form and content of teacher education reflected this dialectic process in China but also across the globe.

Ultimately, the twentieth century became a time of increased professionalization but also a time of rapid educational expansion. This meant that hundreds of thousands of new teachers entered classrooms, prepared through a variety of channels and for a variety of purposes amidst global upheavals, drives for economic development, and movements for liberation, however defined.

The Turn of the Twenty-First Century: Globalization, Neoliberalism, and the Technological Revolution (1980–2020)

Before the fall of the Soviet Union in 1990–1991, a new global order was already brewing. Rather than the Keynesian liberalism or Soviet communism of the postwar years, by the mid- and late 1970s a group of economists and intellectuals in the United States and Europe began formulating an ideology now known as neoliberalism. Though its definition is still being debated, neoliberalism can be roughly characterized as a faith in markets, competition, and small government to solve social problems and promote economic growth. This ideology also held specific ideas about education, including a set of practices related to teacher education. Its advocates, such as US Americans Milton Friedman, Chester Finn Jr., John Chubb, Terry Moe, and Rick Hess, suggested moving teacher education outside of professional teacher training institutions and allowing uncredentialed teachers to enter the classroom if they passed certain basic competency tests. The idea was to spur competition with the "university monopoly" and introduce markets into the realm of public education, part of a larger standards and accountability movement and embrace of market logics to fix a supposed educational "crisis." These thinkers also encouraged the private sector (both for- and not-for-profit) to enter the teacher preparation scene. With the fall of the Soviet Union, these free-market ideas gained traction at the turn of the twenty-first century and migrated across borders with profound global effect.[71]

Border-crossing policy makers, philanthropists, and organizations helped spread these new ideas, often through twentieth-century institutions such as the World Bank and IMF, which used the carrot of loans and grants to disseminate and advance the markets, standards, and accountability reform agenda.[72] International conferences and research journals also served as contact zones for education policy makers, many of whom advocated a variety of decentralized pathways into teaching, sometimes challenging and sometimes encouraging a redefinition of the twentieth-century idea of teacher professionalism.[73] Global bodies like the OECD, however, continued to support teacher professionalization, expressing such sentiments at important meetings and through documents such as the *World Declaration for Education for All,* issued in Jomtien, Thailand, in 1990, and in Dakar, Senegal, in 2000.[74]

Nevertheless, countries across the Global South arguably experienced the most extreme effects of the implementation of neoliberalism, often in the context of economic and political crisis. Perhaps the first case of widescale imposition of neoliberal education policy occurred in Chile in 1973 following a US-backed military coup of socialist leader Salvador Allende. Following the coup, a group of University of Chicago–trained economists who worked with Milton Friedman traveled to Chile as technical advisors for the military government and provided recommendations to overhaul the nation's economic and political system along neoliberal lines—including its educational institutions. It was during this time that the *estado docente* (centralized teaching state) was dismantled and teacher education morphed from a field regulated by the state and backed by strong unions to one that faced erratic policy choices within a privatizing system. During the military dictatorship (1973–1990), all normal schools were brought into four-year universities, only to be supplemented a few years later with non-university "Pedagogical Academies." When the democratization process occurred in the '90s, the center-left government brought teacher education back into universities, but the funding and incentive system was and still is shaped by market forces.[75] Chile is well known in the region as a continental laboratory for neoliberal education reforms, which then became the blueprint for initiatives passed in Argentina, Colombia, Brazil, Panama, and Costa Rica, among others.[76]

However, the role of the state, market, and civil society in teacher education varied from country to country at the turn of the century. Not every nation adopted the neoliberal model wholesale, and those who did adopt a neoliberal approach did so in different ways. Local and regional forces were just as important in the development of policy and curriculum as global ones. In some countries such as Finland and Spain (after the end of the Franco era; see chapters six and three, respectively), teacher education remained highly regulated and managed by the state, within the context of education's definition as a public good. In Singapore, where there has only been one teacher education institution, the National Institute of Education, the government "invested heavily in a quality teaching force—to raise up the prestige and status of teaching and to attract the best graduates."[77] In other countries, the state provided teachers with stipends and free or highly reduced tuition for their studies, bolstering the appeal and quality of the profession. This was often the case across Europe, which for the most part retained fairly strong social welfare states throughout the twentieth and into the twenty-first centuries. In other countries, such as Brazil, Argentina, Bolivia, and South Africa, lively anti-neoliberal social movements sprang up, often supported by teachers unions, teacher educators in universities, and social movements, mounting a challenge to dominant neoliberal ideas known as the "Washington Consensus."[78]

In other countries such as England (which bucked the European trend), Israel, and the United States (see chapters five, eight, and eleven, respec-

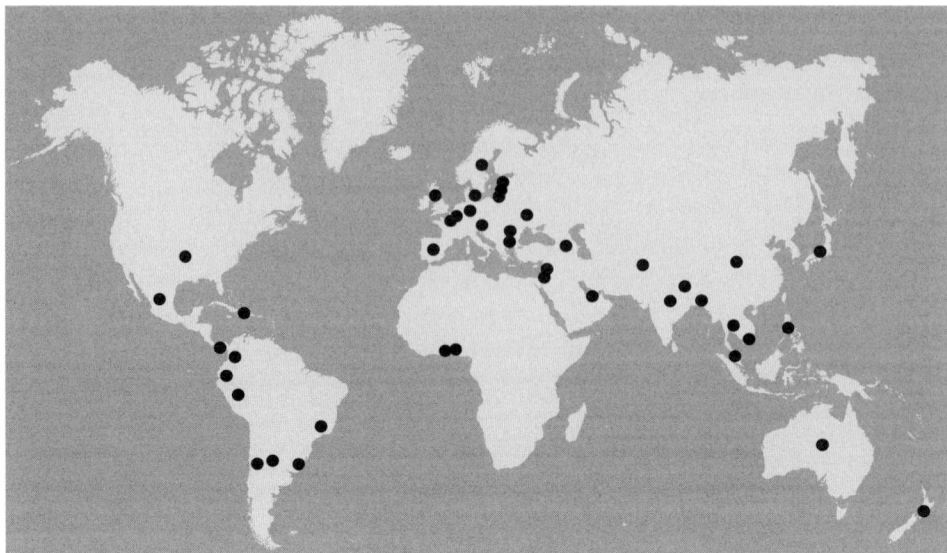

Figure I.4. Teach for All, the global offshoot of the US American Teach for America, operated in 48 countries around the globe as of 2018. (Source: Teach for All, www.teach forall/networkpartners.org)

tively) and Australia, neoliberal education reforms faced less resistance—or at least less successful resistance at the policy-making level. Pathways into teaching became diversified and marketized, managed by public as well as private colleges and institutions, some maintaining no university affiliation at all, and some being for-profit. In each country, debates about what teachers needed to know and be able to do before entering the classroom picked up steam, with some advocating a more professional degree and others dismissing the necessity of professional pedagogical training and focusing instead on competency exams. In the United States, Great Britain, and Israel, non-university-based alternative certification programs like Teach for America (United States), Teach First (England), and Teach First (Israel) attempted to attract top-flight undergraduates to work in some of the country's most impoverished schools, but only after five or so weeks of summer training. Now Teach for All, the global offshoot of Teach for America that opened in 2007, operates in 48 countries across the world, with headquarters in New York, Washington, London, Doha, Pune, and Hong Kong, offering programs such as Teach for Cambodia and Teach for Qatar.[79]

In the Global South, human and financial resources continued to place limits on the quality and reach of teacher education at the turn of the new millennium. Despite calls from global bodies to reform, often teacher preparation institutions remained resource-deprived and resistant to significant change, as they did in the developed world, but with more extreme financial constraints. In much of the Global South, neoliberalism also continued to shape the educational landscape, from India to Mexico to Nigeria. Yet a growing emphasis on social justice and human rights arose in many places, particularly in postconflict and postdictatorship societies, where teachers found themselves on the front lines of political conflict, from standoffs with guerilla forces in Colombia to Islamic militants in Iraq and Afghanistan.[80] Yet global inequality was and still is mirrored in the quality and nature of teacher education. In too many developing countries teacher preparation remains limited, and problems of supply, retention, and working conditions are of utmost concern.[81]

By the turn of the twenty-first century, increased global connections due to free-trade zones and technological innovations—what many call the phenomenon of "globalization"—also impacted teacher education. Although some scholars have described this period as one in which "teacher education—long a very local, even provincial, part of a nation's education sector—is now part of the global conversation,"[82] we note that while these global discourses increased in intensity during this era, they were far from novel, as evidenced by the eighteenth- and nineteenth-century entanglements discussed above in this introduction. Yet it is important to recognize the powerful role of twenty-first-century development agencies, global governance bodies, and their array of published studies, conferences, reports, and initiatives that functioned to shape teacher education in various national contexts. Reports such as the OECD's 2005 *Teachers Matter: Attracting, Developing and Retaining Effective Teachers* functioned in this way, making arguments about the importance of teacher workforce quality to student learning for economic development (see chapter ten for a lengthier discussion of this report's impact in South Africa).[83] Government and nongovernmental entities such as the US Development Bank and the Tinker Foundation impacted education policy in Latin America and around the world in the 1980s through the 2000s.[84] Upon the creation of the European Union in 1993, and the passage of the Bologna Process in 1999, teacher certification policies across the European Union became standardized, impacting teacher education requirements across the region. Similar regional agreements in Latin America and Asia, with MERCOSUR and ASEAN, also impacted certification and licensure requirements for teachers, and spread models of teacher preparation across national borders.[85] ASEAN, for example, publishes a multidisciplinary academic journal on teacher education and offers exchange programs through a teacher education reciprocity initiative. Notably, however, victories in 2016 and subsequent years by antiglobalization leaders in the United States, England, and other countries challenge this open-borders ethos, which may in turn impact teacher education policy in regional zones such as the European Union and the Americas.

Furthermore, while the twentieth century focused on the expansion of education systems and teacher training around the world, in this new millennium access was no longer enough. The focus instead moved to quality, and teacher preparation was believed to play an important role in bringing about high-quality teaching and learning. As teacher education scholar Bob Moon notes, "A child's school success, especially where wider informal community support is scarce, depends crucially on how well teachers teach. The quality of teacher education and training, therefore, becomes fundamental to the development process."[86] International assessments in this era of standards, accountability, and data also meant that nations increasingly compared themselves with one another. The high rankings of Finnish and Singaporean students on the PISA exam, for example (as discussed in this volume in chapters six and nine, respectively), sent researchers flocking to those countries to see what was happening in classrooms and teacher preparation institutions, resulting in much discussion about the teacher education styles of these high scorers.

The conversation about curriculum and pedagogy has also changed in recent years due to this emphasis on quality, along with what type of students teachers should be trained to educate—from rural to indigenous students, to students with disabilities or varying language skills. Discourses of "twenty-first-century skills" and "competencies" for a "knowledge economy" also gained prominence in this era, as did a focus on global citizenship education and multiculturalism, particularly as immigration increased in the developing world, and minority-rights movements gained traction.[87] The rise in technology also brought new questions about the role of technological innovations in the educational process of teachers. New online teacher preparation models have arisen—especially in the United States, home to Silicon Valley and its tech-entrepreneurs looking to "disrupt" the field of teacher preparation—though distance learning through educational television and online programs have also grown in the resource-strapped developing world, as they have since the 1960s.[88]

In the twenty-first century, teacher education continues to be a high-priority field in spurring general improvements to education systems around the world. Countless reports, from the World Bank to the United Kingdom's Department for International Development, continue to call attention to the need for quality teacher preparation. Though the height of neoliberal reforms is arguably over, as decades of decreased professionalization raised significant concerns about quality, and revolts against globalization gained traction on the right and left, the debate continues over the best way to recruit, prepare, and retain educators around the world—in other words, how to teach the world's teachers.

Conclusion

Policy makers and educational researchers should take heed of this long and rich global history of teacher education. Controversies that occupy our present moment, and that are discussed in the following chapters—from curriculum debates, to certification requirements, to the demographics of the teaching force—are questions that have long been discussed in national and, indeed, international contexts for centuries. These conversations, which resulted from the deep wells of local context, also long interacted with global forces. Taking a strictly national framework denies the connected history of teacher education that resulted from the physical movement of people across borders—from nineteenth-century missionaries to twentieth-century World Bank representatives—and the circulation of texts, ideas, and discourses—from Andrew Bell's writings on the monitorial system to the OECD's most recent reports on competency curriculum. Looking only to certain "success stories" and ignoring the history of teacher training in the rest of the world also limits our understanding of the underlying politics of teacher education, and the ways in which power dynamics play out in a world long shaped by hierarchies based on race, gender, and an imperially constructed North-South divide.

The next eleven chapters look to the far more recent history of teacher education around the globe, in the age of neoliberalism, globalization, and technology—and the age of critique of these three phenomena. Each chapter details a specific national story from roughly 1980 to 2020. As the reader will observe, these case studies draw from researchers acting in and outside the field of historical research and often focus on issues of policy rather than historiography, per se. This is deliberate. We aim to place multidisciplinary educational research in conversation with work coming from the discipline of educational history in order to break down the often impossible barriers between these conversations. Nearly all of our chapter authors also hail from the countries on which they write, bringing local and national insight into the conversation rather than imposing an outward gaze upon the world from the United States.

As the reader will see, many of the same themes that appear in this historically minded overview, such as geopolitical power dynamics, the influence of international policy networks, and debates over curriculum, also appear in the following chapters. Though we often toil in isolation, many countries confront similar challenges in preparing their nation's educators, from issues of selection criteria, to curriculum decisions, to where and how long teachers should be prepared and what sort of educational experiences should be part of their preparation. We hope that readers will learn from various national experiences. Yet taking a global perspective also requires us to attend to the ways national and local policy, as well as specific political contexts, impact the teaching profession. Ideas often move across borders, although they are almost always reframed and reanimated in the process of such movement. It is our hope that understanding how these stories fit together, across time and space, can help us rewrite our historical maps and alter our visions of the future.

NOTES

1. In the history of education, see Barnita Bagchi, Eckhardt Fuchs, and Kate Rousmaniere, eds., *Histories of Education: Transnational and Cross-Cultural Exchanges in (Post)-Colonial Education* (New York: Berghahn Books, 2014); Barnita Bagchi, "Connected and Entangled Histories: Writing Histories of Education in the Indian Context," *Paedagogica Historica* 50, no. 6 (2014): 813–821; Peter Kallaway and Rebecca Swartz, eds., *Empire and Education in Africa: The Shaping of a Comparative Perspective* (New York: Peter Lang, 2016). In the field of teacher education research, see Linda Darling-Hammond and Ann Lieberman, eds., *Teacher Education around the World: Changing Policies and Practices* (New York: Routledge, 2012); Maria Teresa Tatto, *Reforming Teaching and Learning: Comparative Perspectives in a Global Era* (Oxford: Symposium Books, 2007).

2. For example, rather than analyzing something like the American Revolution within a strictly US American context, this approach would place that event within a global age of revolutions, the Enlightenment, and the slave trade, and chart the movement of people, texts, and discourses across borders to reveal how the revolution came to be, what it meant

on a local and an international level, and how we should think about it today. See Thomas Bender, *A Nation among Nations: America's Place in World History* (New York: Hill and Wang, 2006).

3. Diego Olstein, *Thinking History Globally* (New York: Palgrave Macmillan, 2015). For distinctions between the various fields of world, international, comparative, transnational, global, and entangled history, see Ian Tyrrell, "Reflections on the Transnational Turn in United States History: Theory and Practice," *Journal of Global History* 4, no.3 (November 2009): 453–474.

4. David Tyack and Larry Cuban, *Tinkering toward Utopia: A Century of Public School Reform* (Cambridge, MA: Harvard University Press, 1995), 6.

5. Xiaoping Cong, *Teachers' Schools and the Making of the Modern Chinese Nation-State 1897–1937* (Vancouver: UBC Press), 2007; Jana Tschurenev, "Diffusing Useful Knowledge: The Monitorial System of Education in Madras, London and Bengal, 1789–1840," *Paedagogica Historica* 44, no. 3 (June 2008): 245–264.

6. For an example of how this topic can be approached through a global historical lens, see Regina Cortina and Sonsoles San Román, *Women and Teaching: Global Perspectives on the Feminization of a Profession* (New York: Palgrave Macmillan, 2006).

7. Tyack and Cuban, *Tinkering Toward Utopia*, 6.

8. For global histories of the long nineteenth century, see C. A. Bayly, *The Birth of the Modern World, 1780–1914: Global Connections and Comparisons* (Malden, MA: Wiley-Blackwell, 2003); Jürgen Osterhammel (author), Patrick Camiller (translator), *The Transformation of the World: A Global History of the Nineteenth Century* (Princeton: Princeton University Press, 2015).

9. Cong, *Teachers' Schools and the Making of the Modern Chinese Nation-State, 1897–1937*.

10. Frederick Cooper and Anne Stoler, eds., *Tensions of Empire: Colonial Cultures in a Bourgeois World* (Berkeley: University of California Press, 1997); Frederick Cooper, *Colonialism in Question* (Berkeley: University of California Press, 2005); Dipesh Chakrabarty, *Provincializing Europe: Postcolonial Thought and Historical Difference* (Princeton: Princeton University Press, 2000); Bill Ashcroft, Gareth Griffiths, Helen Tiffin, eds., *The Post-Colonial Studies Reader* (New York: Routledge, 2006); Enrique Dussel, Mabel Moraña, and Carlos A. Jáurgui, eds., *Coloniality at Large: Latin America and the Postcolonial Debate* (Durham, NC: Duke University Press, 2008).

11. Tschurenev, "Diffusing Useful Knowledge," 245.

12. Paul J. Ramsey, "Toiling Together for Social Cohesion: International Influences on the Development of Teacher Education in the United States," *Paedagogica Historica* 50, no. 1–2 (2013): 109–122; Carl F. Kaestle, *Joseph Lancaster and the Monitorial School Movement* (New York: Teachers College Press, 1973); Tschurenev, "Diffusing Useful Knowledge," 245–264; Eugenia Roldan Vera, "'Learning from Abroad?': Communities of Knowledge and the Monitorial System in Independent Spanish America," in *Books between Europe and the Americas: Connections and Communities, 1620–1860*, L. Howsam and J. Raven, eds. (New York: Palgrave Macmillan, 2011).

13. Quoted in Tschurenev, "Diffusing Useful Knowledge," 262, ellipses mine.

14. Kaestle, ed., *Joseph Lancaster and the Monitorial School Movement*.

15. See also Kallaway and Swartz, *Empire and Education in Africa*.

16. Eugenia Roldan Vera, "Order in the Classroom: The Spanish American Appropriation of the Monitorial System of Education," *Paedagogica Historica* 41, no. 6 (December 2005): 655–675.

17. Reginald Edwards, "Theory, History, and Practice Education: Fin de siècle and a New Beginning," *McGill Journal of Education* 26, no. 3 (1991): 237–266.

18. Jurgen Herbst, *And Sadly Teach: Teacher Education and Professionalization in American Culture* (Madison: University of Wisconsin Press, 1989); Edwards, "Theory, History, and Practice Education"; Paul J. Ramsey, "Toiling Together for Social Cohesion: International Influences on the Development of Teacher Education in the United States," *Paedagogica Historica* 50, no. 1–2 (2013): 109–122.

19. Victor Cousin, *Report on the State of Public Instruction in Prussia*, v–xvii, 62–67, as quoted in Ramsey, "Toiling Together for Social Cohesion," 114–115.

20. Maurits de Vroede, "The History of Teacher Training: Opening Address of the International Standing Conference on the History of Education (Louvain, 24–27 September 1979)," *History of Education* 10, no. 1 (1981): 1–8.

21. Note, various founding dates appear in different sources. These are roughly correct, give or take a few years. See Edwards, "Theory, History, and Practice Education"; Steven Palmer and Gladys Rojas Chaves, "Educating Señorita: Teacher Training, Social Mobility, and the Birth of Costa Rican Feminism, 1885–1925," *The Hispanic American Historical Review* 78:1 (February 1998): 45–82; Patricia Ducoing, "Origen de la Escuela Normal Superior en México," *Revista de Historia de la Educación en América Latina* 6 (2004); José Carlos Souza Araújo, Anamaria Gonçalves Bueno de Freitas, and Antônio de Pádua Carvalho Lopes, eds., *As Escolas Normais no Brasil do Império à República* (Campinas, SP: Alínea, 2008); Maria A. Laubach and Joan K. Smith, "Transatlantic Dialogue: Pestalozzian Influences on Women's Education in Early Nineteenth Century America," *American Educational History Journal* 39:2 (2012): 365–382.

22. Ramsey, "Toiling Together for Social Cohesion," 115.

23. Domingo Faustino Sarmiento, *De la Educación Popular* (Alicante: Biblioteca Virtual Miguel de Cervantes; Buenos Aires: Biblioteca Quiroga Sarmiento, 2007, orig. 1849).

24. "The Inception and the Progress of the American Normal School Curriculum to 1880," in *Report of the Commissioner of Education for the Year 1888–89* (Washington, DC: Government Printing Office, 1891), 278, as quoted in Ramsey, "Toiling Together for Social Cohesion," 111. For more on the influence of European models on the United States, see Ramsey, "Toiling Together for Social Cohesion"; Herbst, *And Sadly Teach*; Henry Geitz, Jürgen Heideking, and Jurgen Herbst, eds., *German Influences on Education in the United States to 1917* (New York: Cambridge University Press, 1995); Jurgen Herbst, "Teacher Preparation in the Nineteenth Century: Institutions and Purposes," in Donald Warren, ed., *American Teachers: Histories of a Profession at Work* (New York: Macmillan, 1989), 213–236.

25. Mark E. Lincicome, *Principle, Practice, and the Politics of Education Reform in Meiji Japan* (Honolulu: University of Hawaii Press, 1995); Yoshio Katagiri, "The Study of the History of Education in Japan," *Paedagogica Historica* 30, no. 2 (1994): 637–644; Cong, *Teachers' Schools and the Making of the Modern Chinese Nation-State, 1897–1939*; Patricia Potts, "Taking Normal Education to China," in *Modernising Education in Britain and China: Comparative Perspectives on Excellence and Social Inclusion* (London: Routledge, 2003).

26. Kaori Okano and Motonori Tsuchiya, "The Development of Modern Schooling,"

in *Education in Contemporary Japan: Inequality and Diversity* (New York: Cambridge University Press, 1999), 15.

27. Julio Ruiz Berrio, Teresa Rabazas, and Sara Ramos, "The Reception of New Education in Spain by Means of Manuals on the History of Education for Teaching Training Colleges (1898–1976)," *Paedagogica Historica* 42, no. 1–2 (2006): 127–141.

28. Berrio, Rabazas, and Ramos, "The Reception of New Education in Spain," 53.

29. Palmer and Rojas Chaves, "Educating Señorita," 49.

30. Domingo F. Sarmiento, "Las Escuelas: base de la prosperidad de la república de los Estados Unidos [1866]," as quoted in Palmer and Rojas Chaves, "Educating Señorita," 49.

31. Palmer and Rojas Chaves, "Educating Señorita"; James C. Albisetti, "The Feminization of Teaching in the Nineteenth Century: A Comparative Perspective," *History of Education Quarterly* 22:3 (September 1993): 253–263; Nany Hoffman, ed., *Women's "True" Profession: Voices from the History of Teaching,* 2nd ed. (Cambridge, MA: Harvard Education Press, 2003); Patrick Harrigan, "The Development of a Corps of Public School Teachers in Canada, 1870–1980," *History of Education Quarterly* 32 (1992): 510.

32. Palmer and Rojas Chaves, "Educating Señorita"; Anne Firor Scott, "The Ever Widening Circle: The Diffusion of Feminist Values from the Troy Female Seminary, 1822–1872," *History of Education Quarterly* 19:1 (Spring 1979): 3–25; Jo Burr Margadant, *Madame le Professeur: Women Educators in the Third Republic* (Princeton: Princeton University Press, 1990).

33. For more arguments regarding the empowering nature of teachers colleges and normal schools for women, see Christine A. Ogren, "A Large Measure of Self-Control and Personal Power: Women Students at State Normal Schools during the Late-Nineteenth and Early-Twentieth Centuries," *Women's Studies Quarterly* 28:3–4 (Fall/Winter, 2000): 211–232; Ogren, *The American State Normal School: "An Instrument of Great Good"* (New York: Palgrave Macmillan, 2005); Geraldine Jonçich Clifford, "Women's Liberation and Women's Professions: Reconsidering the Past, Present, and Future," in *Women and Higher Education in American History,* John Mack Faragher and Florence Howe, eds. (New York: W. W. Norton, 1988); Clifford, "Eve: Redeemed by Education and Teaching School," *History of Education Quarterly* 21:4 (Winter 1981): 479–491; Clifford, "Man/Woman/Teacher: Gender, Family and Career in American Educational History," in *American Teachers: Histories of a Profession at Work,* Donald Warren, ed. (New York: Macmillan, 1989), 293–343; Polly Welts Kaufman, *Women Teachers on the Frontier* (New Haven: Yale University Press, 1984); Anne Firor Scott, "The Ever Widening Circle," 3–25; Dina Copelman, *London's Women Teachers: Gender, Class and Feminism, 1870–1930* (London: Routledge, 1996); Alison Prentice and Marjorie R. Theobald, eds., *Women Who Taught: Perspectives on the History of Women and Teaching* (Toronto: University of Toronto Press, 1991); Alison Oram, *Women Teachers and Feminist Politics, 1900–39* (Manchester: Manchester University Press, 1996); Sabyasachi Bhattacharya, B. M. Sankhdher, Joseph Bara, and Yagati Chinna Rao, eds., *The Development of Women's Education in India: A Collection of Documents 1850–1920* (New Delhi: Kanishka, 2001); Elizabeth Edwards, "The Culture of Femininity in Women's Teacher Training Colleges 1900–50," *History of Education* 22:3 (1993).

34. Cong, *Teachers' Schools and the Making of the Modern Chinese Nation-State, 1897–1937,* 12.

35. For more on the history of education for colonized populations, see John Willinsky, *Learning to Divide the World: Education at Empire's End* (Minneapolis: University of

Minnesota Press, 1999); Kallaway and Swartz, eds., *Empire and Education in Africa;* Clif Stratton, *Education for Empire: American Schools, Race, and the Paths of Good Citizenship* (Oakland: University of California Press, 2016); Solsiree Del Moral, *Negotiating Empire: The Cultural Politics of Schools in Puerto Rico, 1898–1952* (Madison: University of Wisconsin Press, 2014), 58–69; A. J. Angulo, *Empire and Education: A History of Greed and Goodwill from the War of 1898 to the War on Terror* (Baltimore: Johns Hopkins University Press, 2012); Erwin H. Epstein, "The Peril of Paternalism: The Imposition of Education on Cuba by the United States," *American Journal of Education* 96:1 (1987): 1–23; Klaus Dittrich, "The Beginnings of Modern Education in Korea," *Paedagogica Historica* (June 2014): 265–284.

36. Deirdre Raferty, "Teaching Sisters and Transnational Networks: Recruitment and Education Expansion in the Long Nineteenth Century," *History of Education* 44:6 (2015): 717–728.

37. James W. Fraser and Diane L. Moore, "Religion and History of Education," in John L. Rury and Eileen H. Tamura, eds., *The Oxford Handbook of the History of Education* (New York: Oxford University Press, 2019), 445.

38. Del Moral, *Negotiating Empire,* 58–69.

39. Heather Andrea Williams, *Self-Taught: African American Education in Slavery and Freedom* (Chapel Hill: University of North Carolina Press, 2005); James D. Anderson, *Education of Blacks in the South, 1860–1935* (Chapel Hill: University of North Carolina Press, 1988).

40. Eric Hobsbawm, *The Age of Extremes: The Short Twentieth Century* (New York: Vintage Books, 1994).

41. Darling-Hammond and Lieberman, eds., *Teacher Education around the World;* James W. Fraser, *Preparing America's Teachers: A History* (New York: Teachers College Press, 2006); Bob Moon, ed., *Teacher Education and the Challenge of Development: A Global Analysis* (New York: Routledge, 2014).

42. The term "grammar of schooling" was coined by historians David Tyack and Larry Cuban in their work *Tinkering toward Utopia: A Century of Public School Reform,* and refers to the enduring nature of established institutional forms and practices of schooling across the world, such as a self-contained classroom with one teacher at the head, students in desks, and classroom bells.

43. Bob Moon, "Teachers and the Development Agenda," in *Teacher Education and the Challenge of Global Development,* Bob Moon, ed. (New York: Routledge, 2012), 9.

44. John Dewey, *John Dewey's Impressions of Soviet Russia and the Revolutionary World: Mexico, China, Turkey, 1929* (New York: Teachers College Press, 1964); Jessica Ching-Sze Wang, *John Dewey in China: To Teach and to Learn* (Albany: State University of New York Press, 2007); Ruben Flores, *Backroads Pragmatists: Mexico's Melting Pot and Civil Rights in the US* (Philadelphia: University of Pennsylvania Press, 2014).

45. Ronald Goodenow and Robert Cowen, "The American School of Education and the Third World in the Twentieth Century: Teachers College and Africa, 1920–1950," *History of Education* 15:4 (1986): 271–289; Gary McCulloch, "Fred Clarke and the Internationalization of Studies and Research in Education," *Paedagogica Historica* 50, no. 1–2 (March 2014): 123–137.

46. Jonathan Zimmerman, "Money, Materials, and Manpower: Ghanaian In-Service

Teacher Education and the Political Economy of Failure, 1961–1971, Presidential Address," *History of Education Quarterly* 51, no. 1 (February 2011): 1–27.

47. Malcolm Vick, "Australian Teacher Education 1900–1950: Conspicuous and Inconspicuous International Networks," *Paedagogica Historica* 43, no. 2 (2007): 245–255.

48. Andrew J. Kirkendall, *Paulo Freire and the Cold War Politics of Literacy* (Chapel Hill: University of North Carolina Press, 2010).

49. Jerry Dávila, "What Happened to Rio's Teachers of Color?" in *Diploma of Whiteness: Race and Social Policy in Brazil, 1917–1945* (Durham, NC: Duke University Press, 2003), 90–154.

50. Christina Collins, *Ethnically Qualified: Race, Merit, and the Selection of Urban Teachers, 1920–1980* (New York: Teachers College Press, 2011).

51. Brenda Stevenson, ed., *The Journals of Charlotte Forten Grimke* (New York: Oxford University Press, 1988).

52. Williams, *Self-Taught*.

53. For more on the history and historiography of teacher training in the Soviet Union, see Evgenii Mikhailovich Balashov, *Shkola v rossiiskom obshchestve 1917–1927: Stanovlenie "Novogo Cheloveka" [The School in Russian Society, 1917–1927: The Creation of the "New Person"]* (St. Petersburg: Dmitrii Bulanin, 2003). See also, Rita Hofstetter and Bernard Schneuwly, "Knowledge for Teaching and Knowledge to Teach: Two Figures of New Education: Claparède and Vygotsky," *Paedagogica Historica* 45, no. 4–5 (August–October 2009): 605–629.

54. Flores, *Backroads Pragmatists*, 1.

55. Liyan Liu, *Red Genesis: The Hunan First Normal School and the Creation of Chinese Communism, 1903–1921* (New York: State University Press, 2012).

56. Z. L Yang, B. Lin, and W. C. Su, *Teacher Education in the People's Republic of China* (Beijing: Beijing Normal University Press, 1989).

57. Wadi D. Haddad, *Teacher Training: A Review of World Bank Experience*, Report No. EDT21, Education and Training Department, World Bank, November 1985, http://documents.worldbank.org/curated/en/404521468767084496/pdf/multi-page.pdf.

58. Haddad, *Teacher Training*, 9.

59. UNESCO and ILO, *The ILO/UNESCO Recommendation Concerning the Status of Teachers (1966) and the UNESCO Recommendation Concerning the Status of Higher-Education Teaching Personnel (1997), with a User's Guide*, 2008, http://unesdoc.unesco.org/images/0016/001604/160495e.pdf.

60. UNESCO and ILO, *The ILO/UNESCO Recommendation*, 26.

61. UNESCO and ILO, *The ILO/UNESCO Recommendation*, 26.

62. Odd Arne Westad, *The Global Cold War: Third World Interventions and the Making of Our Time* (New York: Cambridge University Press, 2007); Jeffrey Taffet, *Foreign Aid as Foreign Policy: The Alliance for Progress in Latin America* (New York: Routledge, 2007). For an example of the United States' footprint in education and teacher education in formerly Soviet-controlled Afghanistan, see Dana Burde, *Schools for Conflict or for Peace in Afghanistan* (New York: Columbia University Press, 2014).

63. For more on global linkages in education policy during the Cold War, see Lauren Lefty, "Seize the Schools: Que Viva Puerto Rico Libre: Cold War Education in New York and San Juan, 1948–1975," PhD Dissertation, New York University (2019).

64. Tom G. Griffiths and Euridice Charon Chardona, "Education for Social Transformation: Soviet Union Education Aid in the Cold War Capitalist World System," *European Education* 47 (2015): 226–241.

65. Dana Burde, "Jihad Literacy," *Schools for Conflict or for Peace in Afghanistan*. The fact that the United States became global leader of antiterrorism and an opponent of Islamic militancy is a supreme irony in this story, as Burde underscores.

66. Zimmerman, "Money, Materials, and Manpower."

67. Paulo Freire, *Pedagogy of the Oppressed*, 30th anniversary ed. (New York: Bloomsbury, 1968; 2000); Kirkendall, *Paulo Freire and the Cold War Politics of Literacy*.

68. Zimmerman, "Money, Materials, and Manpower," 4.

69. Michael Omolewa, "UNESCO as a Network," *Paedagogica Historica* (2007): 211–221; Vick, "Australian Teacher Education"; Edward H. Berman, "Teacher Education," in *The Influence of the Carnegie, Ford, and Rockefeller Foundations on American Foreign Policy* (Albany: State University of New York Press, 1983), 88–92.

70. Liu, *Red Genesis*, 10.

71. Michael Apple, "Markets, Standards, Teaching, and Teacher Education," *Journal of Teacher Education* 52, no. 3 (2001): 182–196; R. Yinger and M. Hendricks-Lee, "The Language of Standards and Teacher Education Reform," *Education Policy* 14 (2000): 94–106. For a study of how this played out in the US case, see James W. Fraser and Lauren Lefty, *Teaching Teachers: Changing Paths and Enduring Debates* (Baltimore: Johns Hopkins University Press, 2018); and Megan Blumenreich and Bethany Rogers, "TFA and the Magical Thinking of the 'Best and the Brightest,'" *Education Policy Analysis Archives* 24, no. 12–18 (2016): 1–31. For a classic argument in the neoliberal vein, see Fordham Foundation, *Better Teachers, Better Schools* (Washington, DC: 1999).

72. Wayne Au and Joseph J. Ferrare, eds., *Mapping Corporate Education Reform: Power and Policy Networks in the Neoliberal State* (New York: Routledge, 2015).

73. Lynn Paine and Kenneth Zeichner, "The Local and the Global in Reforming Teacher Education," *Comparative Education Review* 56:4 (November 2012): 569–583; Richard Bates, "Teacher Education in a Global Context: Towards a Defensible Theory of Teacher Education," *Journal of Education for Teaching* 34:4 (2008): 277–293. The term "contact zones" comes from Mary Louise Pratt and refers to social spaces where different cultures "meet, clash, and grapple with each other, often in contexts of highly unequal relations of power," usually in the context of empire and slavery. Yet it has also been used to refer to various sites of unequal power relations. Mary Louise Pratt, "Arts of the Contact Zone," *Profession* (1991): 33–40.

74. Moon, "Teachers and the Development Agenda," 7.

75. Beatrice Ávalos, "Chile: Effectiveness of Teacher Education: Contexts, Policies and Practices," *Education in South America*, Simon Schwartzman, ed. (London: Bloomsbury, 2015), 201–220.

76. Varun Gauri, *School Choice in Chile: Two Decades of Educational Reform* (Pittsburgh: University of Pittsburgh Press, 1999); Susana López Guerra and Marcelo Flores Chávez, "Neo-Liberal Educational Reform in Latin America," *Revista Electrónica de Investigación Educativa* 8, no. 1 (2006), http://redie.ens.uabc.mx/vol8no1/contents-lopez.html; Gustavo Fischman, Stephen Ball, Silvina Gvirtz, "Toward a Neoliberal Education? Tensions and Change in Latin America"; Lynne Phillips, "Introduction: Neoliberalism in Latin

America," in *The Third Wave of Modernization in Latin America: Cultural Perspectives on Neoliberalism*, ed. Lynne Phillips (Wilmington, DE: Jaguar Books, 1998).

77. Professor Lee Sing Kong as quoted in Loh and Hu, in chapter nine of this volume, "Teacher Education for a Knowledge-Based Economy: The Singaporean Case."

78. Fischman, Ball, and Gvirtz, "Toward a Neoliberal Education?"; Gustavo Fischman, "Donkeys and Superteachers: Popular Education in Latin America," *International Review of Education* 44:2–3 (March 1998): 191–213.

79. "About," *Teach for All*, https://teachforall.org/about.

80. Raúl Zibechi and Ramor Ryan, *Territories of Resistance: A Cartography of Latin American Social Movements* (Oakland, CA: AK Press, 2012); Kirkendall, *Paulo Freire and the Politics of Cold War Literacy*; Moon, ed., *Teacher Education and the Challenge of Development: A Global Analysis*.

81. Liz Bird, Bob Moon, and Anne Storey, "The Context for Teacher Education in Developing Countries," in Moon, *Teacher Education and the Challenge of Global Development: A Global Analysis*, 19–31.

82. Paine and Zeichner, "The Local and the Global in Reforming Teacher Education," 570.

83. OECD, *Teachers Matter: Attracting, Developing and Retaining Effective Teachers*, OECD Publishing, 2005, http://www.oecd.org/education/school/34990905.pdf.

84. Guerra and Chávez, "Neo-Liberal Educational Reform in Latin America."

85. "AsTEN Journal of Teacher Education," AsTen, http://po.pnuresearchportal.org/ejournal/index.php/asten; *Los Sistemas de Formación Docente en el MERCOSUR: Planes de estudio y propuestas de formación continua* (Buenos Aires, Argentina: Editorial Teseo, 2014), http://oei.org.ar/new/wp-content/uploads/2018/01/Los-Sistemas-de-Formaci%C3%B3n-Docente-en-el-MERCOSUR.pdf.

86. Nhlanganiso Dladla and Bob Moon, "Teachers and the Development Agenda," in Moon, ed., *Teacher Education and the Challenge of Global Development: A Global Analysis*, 18.

87. For reports that evidence the trend of new types of knowledge for a new economy, see Andreas Schleicher, UNESCO, *Rethinking Education: Towards a Global Common Good?* (Paris, France: UNESCO, 2015), http://unesdoc.unesco.org/images/0023/002325/232555e.pdf; OECD, *Preparing Teachers and Developing School Leaders for the 21st Century: Lessons from around the World* (Paris: France, OECD Publishing, 2012), https://www.oecd.org/site/eduistp2012/49850576.pdf; OECD, *The Knowledge-Based Economy* (Paris, France: OECD Publishing, 1996). For examples of reports that focus on training teachers for multicultural student populations, see OECD, *Where Immigrants Succeed: A Comparative Review of Performance and Engagement in PISA 2013* (Paris, France: OECD Publishing, 2013), and OECD, *Educating Teachers for Diversity: Meeting the Challenge* (Paris, France: OECD Publishing, 2010).

88. Fraser and Lefty, *Teaching Teachers*.

CHAPTER ONE

Continuities and Transformations of Argentina's Teacher Education
Policies and Reforms since the Mid-Eighties

GUSTAVO E. FISCHMAN AND PAULA RAZQUIN

Argentina has a long tradition of extreme ideological and cultural polarization, and recent history is no exception. Antonymic positions are pervasive in all areas of the society, and consequently it is uncommon that scholars from opposing political and ideological perspectives reach a consensus when interpreting educational problems. One of those exceptional coincidences is the centrality assigned to the intimate and entrenched relationship between the state, especially at the federal level, and the Argentinean Teacher Education (hereafter TEd) system.[1]

The literature points to two key historical dynamics that still resonate and are evoked in contemporary processes framing the structure, quality, status, and cultural understandings surrounding TEd. The first and oldest dynamic emerged since the beginning of the consolidation of Argentina as a nation-state when teaching was seen as a *profession of state* (Estado Docente).[2] For more than a century, the federal state kept a dominant role in the definition, regulation, governance, and management of TEd and the teaching profession. The relationship between the state and teachers' organizations fluctuates between collaboration and dependence on conflicts and contradictions, depending on the economic conditions and political context. The second dynamic framing TEd emerges from the multiple ideological and pedagogical debates about who could and should be a teacher and which institutions should be in charge of TEd. These debates have been tensioned by multiple conflicts with intersecting economic, political, religious, cultural, and social dimensions.[3]

In this chapter, we examine teacher education policies and reforms in Argentina since the mid-eighties. We argue that understanding the continuities and transformations of Argentina's TEd requires considering how the two dynamics noted above have simultaneously coalesced and manifested around the professional status of teachers and, consequently, of the institutions and programs designated to educate them.

A caveat about our use of the notion of "profession" throughout this chapter is needed here. Broadly speaking, professions are accepted, established, and recognized as having developed high levels of specialized knowledge that cannot be acquired informally, and for that reason are self-regulated. A profession's specialized knowledge is structured to be recognized and reproduced by the professionals in the field. As in other countries,[4] teaching in Argentina is not organized around a research-based, categorized and shared corpus of knowledge that could support a reliable system of quality control as expected in other professions. Given the enormous variations and inconsistencies when teaching the same content found in Argentina's classrooms, even within a single school, it may be more appropriate to refer to teachers as "semi-professionals."[5] We believe that teaching is a profession and that there are many educators in Argentina who are outstanding professionals. But it is important to acknowledge that, during the period analyzed, the working conditions, training, and levels of codification of the pedagogical knowledge needed to strengthen the recognition of teaching as a profession are still insufficient. In other words, we use the term *professionals* in the field of teaching as an expression of an aspiration, not as an accurate categorization.[6]

We organize this chapter into three sections. In the first section, we provide a brief historical contextualization of the evolution of TEd and, particularly, the legacy of the military dictatorship that concluded in the early 1980s. The second section presents changes and continuities in the governance and structure of teacher training since the mid-1980s, presented around two political periods. The third section examines the changes in the socioeconomic profile of TEd students, and the final section concludes the chapter by highlighting the lack of substantial transformations in spite of three decades of policy efforts and reforms.

A Brief History of Teacher Education and the Legacy of Authoritarian Times

Before addressing the legacy of the military dictatorship, it is worth providing a brief history of teacher education in Argentina. In 1869, President Domingo Faustino Sarmiento (1868–1874) established the first public institution of formal teacher training and for almost a century—until 1969—any Argentinean who wanted to become a teacher was required to attend a normal school.[7] The normal schools were secondary education schools that offered a teaching credential for primary education or preschools; they were independent from, yet coexisted with, the other modalities of secondary education. Training for secondary education teaching, on the other hand, was provided at the tertiary level, initially by the national universities. Teaching was considered a feminine occupation, and socially appropriate for young middle-class Catholic women, who brought a particular and somewhat homogenous social and cultural capital to the teaching profession. These early pioneers accepted the demands of the state that, as the dominant employer (a quasi-monopoly if it was not for the few private schools), offered low wages but plenty of formal praise, coupled with high social prestige vis-à-vis the majority of the population, often considered uncivilized and unintelligent by the political and commercial elites. Normal schools remained at the secondary school level until 1969, when teacher education "moved up" to a tertiary level. This shift increased the years of study needed to become a teacher and made the normal schools part of a non-university higher education system. Training for secondary school teachers continued at the tertiary level and, by the late 1960s, private teacher training institutions had also spread.

In the late 1970s, the country initiated a process of political and structural rearrangement of the highly hierarchical and centralized education system, leading to the decentralization of education.[8] The process began with the decentralization of elementary education in the late 1970s, during the most brutal and criminal dictatorship, and concluded in the mid-1990s during a recovered democratic government with the decentralization of secondary and tertiary education, including TEd. In both periods, schools were transferred from the national to the 24 provincial governments (including the federal district of Buenos Aires). It is important to highlight that the military government had a political pedagogical component conceptualized as an "Authoritarian Educational Project," which persecuted, jailed, tortured, and disappeared hundreds of educators and students.[9] As part of a systematic plan of imposing terror on the population, the Authoritarian Educational Project imposed a very rigid and ideologically hyperconservative curriculum, censored publications, and closely scrutinized the functioning of schools, universities, and cultural spaces.

The emphasis upon the decentralized governance implied that the national state lost the quasi-monopoly it had over the employment of primary school teachers. The main aspects of teacher training and teacher contracts with the provincial governments remained essentially unaltered, except for the greater variations encountered in teacher salaries and salary scales.[10] Overall, during the military dictatorship, TEd curriculum remained under the national state's control. It was strongly influenced by the most conservative sectors of the Catholic Church, with the main goal of guaranteeing greater control and discipline in education while emphasizing the state's subsidiary role.

Teacher Education since the Mid-1980s: Changes and Continuities

In December 1983, with the elected president Raúl Alfonsín (from the centrist liberal party, the Radical Civil Union), Argentina transitioned to a period of sustained democratically elected governments. In education, it signaled the beginning of a renewed period of pedagogical optimism: schools and teachers regained a special role in the process of political, social, and educational redemocratization.[11] There was a public recognition that for the education sector to be a vital part of the process of democratization it was key to improve the TEd systems as well as the working conditions, salaries, and professional status of teachers. These expectations, however, soon faced the limits imposed by a context in which a still traumatized society and its weak democratic institutions were confronted with threats of military uprisings, rampant inflation, the financial burden of a ballooning external debt, and economic instabilities related to the fragile position of the country's economy in a moment of accelerating globalization.[12]

In 1988, after seven small strikes, the national confederation of teachers launched a 47-day strike, which culminated in a massive demonstration called La Marcha Blanca (the White March), demanding better salaries and working conditions. After an initial period of popular support, the striking Argentinean teachers did not fare very well in defending their salaries and improving working conditions.[13] By the end of the teachers' strike, negative opinions about public school teachers were frequently expressed in numerous newspaper and magazine articles, and some commentators related the noticeable decline in enrollment in teacher education programs with these negative opinions.[14] In sum, by the mid-1980s till the early 1990s, the pedagogical optimism and much-awaited changes in education were relegated to a secondary place.

Teacher Education in Neoliberal Times (1989–2001)

From 1989 (when President Carlos Menem from the Justicialist Party took office) until an economic and political collapse suffered in 2001, Argentina went through several packages of IMF- and World Bank–sponsored and supervised structural adjustment programs.[15] The country became a leading example of what was defined as a neoliberal reform movement, implementing in a short time a wide-ranging program of privatization of government-owned companies and restructuring of the role of the state.[16] This neoliberal reform, as it happened with the reform of the 1970s, was justified as the best path for the "modernization" of the country.

Education and TEd policies mirrored broader political debates. A neoliberal education framework equated the economic structural adjustment program, although it restructured the role of the state in education through fiscal decentralization more than privatization policies. The neoliberal framework was defined between 1992 and 1995 and emerged from the following laws: the Transfer Law (1992), the Federal Education Law (1993), and the Higher Education Law (1995).[17] The laws were accompanied by federal agreements developed within the framework of the Federal Council of Culture and Education (CFCyE). Together, they constituted a new discursive and regulatory framework for strategies, programs, and projects for the transformation of teacher training.[18]

As noted earlier, Argentina went through a decentralization process that began in the late 1970s with the transfer of elementary schools from the national to the provincial governments. In 1991–92, the second stage in the process of decentralization, the government transferred nationally administered secondary education schools and tertiary (non-university) education to the provincial administrations, including TEd institutions. Similar to the decentralization of elementary schools, financial motivations and ideological blindfolds were significant components of this educational reform, and once again, pedagogical and educational matters were not the driving motivation.

The 1993 Federal Education Law and the 1995 Higher Education Law established new foundations for the governance and management of teacher education, in the context of a major restructuring of the education system.[19] The two laws regulated the rights and obligations of teachers, established the roles of the national and provincial governments for TEd, and created the Permanent Federal Teacher Education Network (RFFDC). To organize teacher education, CFCyE and the National Ministry of Education passed general and specific rules, formalized in a series of documents known as "agreements." The objective was to ensure the development of new procedures for the institutional reorganization, the curricular transformation, a national system of accreditation of TEd institutions, and the national validity of teaching credentials.

The documents characterized TEd as continuous and established the following levels: (a) initial education leading to a teaching credential; (b) in-service TEd; (c) training of teachers for new professional roles; and (d) pedagogical training of professionals without teaching certification. The RFFDC represented the institutionalization of policies toward teacher education to develop an educational structure capable to be national in its scope, thereby establishing criteria for pedagogical quality. This institutionalization allocated resources and defined strategies to increase the prestige and relevance of teacher education in the overall educational system.

Some negative consequences for teacher education were already visible by the end of the 1990s, not necessarily due to the new normative framework per se but mostly due to poor implementation and lack of state intervention and regulation.[20] First, what was a historically nationally unified system of teacher education for primary school teachers turned into a diversified system with a disjointed, fragmented, and segmented landscape of institutions that included private institutions and universities.[21] Institutions generally operated in isolation and, in some cases, badly articulated with the actual schools that received practitioner teachers. Second, policy making and management of teacher training were generally placed together with secondary schools in the provincial administrations, undermining the identity of TEd and often putting it down on the priority list. Third, teacher education planning and curriculum development were weak, in part because of the poor capacity of the provincial teams that were previously in charge only of primary education. Fourth, not all public institutions followed the same TEd curriculum (even within the same province), undermining the validity of the teaching credentials nationally and limiting the mobility of teachers and, in some cases, even students.

Finally, the restructuring of lower-secondary education (middle schools) led to a relocation of teachers to courses and students they were not prepared for.[22] In some provinces, secondary education teachers took over teaching in the last grade of primary; in other provinces, primary education teachers assumed the responsibility of middle school teaching. The preparation mismatch created a surge in the demand for in-service teacher training.[23] However, left to the individual decisions of teachers, in-service training resulted in an unarticulated supply of courses in some cases unresponsive to the needs of schools and with limited capacity to promote improvements in instructional practices.[24]

Overall, the weak technical and financial capacity of the provincial governments added more challenges to adequately address the transfer in such a short period. The national government found itself "without schools" for the first time since the origins of public education and experimenting with the model "governing at a distance,"[25] which required forging a new identity and generating the necessary institutional and normative framework conducive to governing the newly instituted federal system of teacher education.

Teacher working conditions also worsened in the 1990s. In the wake of the new century, real salaries were at their lowest point since the mid-1970s; they were lower than the mean salaries and 24% lower than mean salaries in the public administration.[26] There were wide salary disparities across the provinces related to differences in the regional economies and education spending. Because of the lack of funds, some provincial administrations had even stopped paying teachers altogether.[27] The situation of teachers was not unique. Economic and political conditions worsened, reaching a turning point in December of 2001, when the federal government entered into a highly unstable period, with four changes of presidents, the declaration of the default of servicing Argentina's external debt, and numerous restrictions for the population to access their savings and checking funds.

The first years of the twenty-first century in Argentina have to be understood as a phase of traumatic transitions. In 2001 all major indicators of the country's welfare deteriorated dramatically, with high levels of poverty, unemployment, malnourishment, health-related problems, and the like. During this critical period, public schools, especially those located in areas with high unemployment and higher levels of poverty, became a refuge for many children and their families. In a dramatic way, schools and teachers once again were tasked with caring for the poor and in many cases relegating the pedagogical dimension to a secondary place, after the distribution of food, and other welfare services.[28]

In May 2003, a new government took office (President Néstor Kirchner, Justicialist Party), initiating a period of political game-changing disruption. The economy recovered between 2003 and 2005 and inflation decreased, although it remained relatively high. The federal government implemented important packages of assistance to the poor and economic policies that were significantly different from the previous governments, ushering in a new framework for understanding TEd. This led, in education, to an assessment of the 1990s reforms, to another wave of structural reforms, and to the passing of new regulations and national plans that would recover the strategic role teacher education once had.

Another Era for TEd within a New Governance Framework and National TEd Policies for a Federal System (2005–2015)

In 2006, the National Education Law (26,206) introduced a very important reform to the structure of the teacher education system, the second since its origins in 1870.[29] Other definitions around governance, policy, teachers' work, and identity also served to distinguish a new era for teacher education. As explained earlier, preservice teacher training originated in the normal schools (secondary education level), and in 1969 it was moved to tertiary, non-university institutions, with a duration of two years. The 2006 law extended initial TEd for early childhood and primary education from two to four years and introduced various forms of pedagogical residency.[30,31]

The law also restated national goals and functions for early childhood and primary teacher education and reinforced the position of TEd within the broader subsystem of higher education. The goals emphasized five aspects of a newly defined identity for TEd: professional autonomy, a link with contemporary culture and society, work in teams, a commitment to equality, and trust in the learning capacities of pupils (Art. 71). Two innovative functions of TEd stressed in the law are the pedagogical support of schools and education research, in addition, of course, to the already established functions of initial and continuous training of future and in-service teachers (Art. 72).

The other definitions of the 2006 law include establishing a new governance framework for a federal system, delineating nine goals for a national TEd policy, and creating a national TEd agency. First, TEd had already been decentralized in the early 1990s, cementing a federal system for the provision of teacher education. Yet, the lack of an institutional federal framework had resulted, as mentioned previously, in the diversified provincial systems and the institutional segmentation of TEd, adding to the lack of recognition of teaching credentials across the provinces. The law entrusted a federal state agency (the CFCyE renamed CFE) with reaching agreements on initial TEd policies and plans, guidelines for the organization and administration of TEd, quality guidelines for common standards, and on the concrete actions that would guarantee the right to free professional development (Art. 74).

The new governance framework was accompanied, second, by nine emerging guidelines or goals for a national policy for TEd (Art. 73). The intentionality of the policy stressed: (a) revamping of teacher education as a key element for quality improvements; (b) the development of knowledge and skills useful for teaching; (c) the promotion of research and innovation on teaching, experimentation, and systematization of lessons for reflecting on and renewing practice and instruction; (d) the supply of varied options and devices for professional development; (e) an emphasis on articulating with the universities for professional development; (f) planning and development of a national system for teacher initial and continuing education; (g) the accreditation of teacher training institutions, programs, and alternative trajectories; (h) a coordination between teacher training institutes, universities, and other education research institutions; and (i) granting national validity to the many types of teaching credentials. In another section, the law makes an explicit statement about improving the quality of teacher education (Art. 85c).[32] For Mónica Pini and Jorge Gorostiaga, some of these goals were seen as a qualitative leap, provided they were to be implemented in a collaborative manner, involving teachers, students, and schools.[33]

Finally, establishing a new governance framework and guidelines for a national TEd policy had immediate practical implications. The law created the National Institute of Teacher Education (INFD, or Instituto Nacional de Formación Docente), an agency within the national Ministry of Education commissioned to plan and implement the TEd policy guidelines as agreed federally (Art. 76).[34] In addition, the INFD was charged with the monitoring and evaluation of policy implementation; development of training plans, curriculum, and even TEd materials; implementing an incentive fund for developing and strengthening a system of teacher trainers; and promoting and developing research on TEd. The INFD was tasked with the organization of federal meetings to guarantee the participation and consultation with provincial higher education officials to reach technical agreements on the policies discussed at the federal agencies (Art. 139). The national Ministry of Education retained the main role of developing and implementing policies for teacher education assessment, presumably through the INFD (Art. 85).

In the preceding paragraphs, we described various components of the reforms in TEd introduced by the 2006 law. However, the law also regulates other aspects affecting teacher education indirectly, although some of them have already been instituted in previous laws.[35] One of the most important innovations was that, in light of the many different provincial arrangements for the teaching career typical of the 1990s, the law charges a federal education agency with establishing a national and common structure for the teaching career.[36]

Another innovation introduced in the 2006 law would have potentially affected the demand for teachers and, indirectly, teacher education—were these innovations actually implemented. For instance, the law calls for achieving universal early childhood education starting from age 4 (Art. 19), it extends the primary school day from part-time to a full day (Art. 28), and it makes secondary education compulsory.[37] Also, the law revisits the structural reforms introduced in 1993. Addressing the lack of cohesion and fragmentation resulting from the earlier reform, it reinstates the structure that has traditionally organized the education system, reverting the three-cycle model of basic education introduced in 1993 (primary, lower-, and upper-secondary) to a unified structure of two cycles, primary and secondary. This would assure a cohesive arrangement for a federal system, a better articulation between the education levels, and a national validity to the diplomas issued by the provinces (Art. 15).

Flavia Terigi, a well-known and influential scholar in the field, identified four distinctive stages during the 12-year period of the Kirchner government:[38] an initial moment of attending to the crisis of the educational system; a transitional period marked by the approval of the National Education Law; a third instance signed by the extension of compulsory school; and a final phase focusing on the idea of "educational inclusion." Terigi notes various achievements of the Kirchner period worth highlighting, such as the sanction of the laws of Professional Technical Education, the Guarantee of the Teaching Salary, and—in particular—Educational Financing (which was designed to invest 6% of GDP in education, science, and technology), in addition to the creation of the National Institute of Teacher Formation (INFD), and the implementation of programs such as *FinEs* (Plan de Finalización de Estudios Primarios y Secundarios, an alternative for youth and adults to finish primary or secondary school), or Conectar Igualdad (in English, Connect Equity, the first state initiative to universalize the incorporation of ICT—information and communication technology—into the school system). Roxana Perazza, another researcher with policy-making experience at the national and state level, also identified as an educational debt of the Kirchner period the lack of attention given to the much-needed regulations of the teaching career.[39] Most jurisdictions follow the Statute of the Teacher (Law 14473), a national standard adopted in 1958. In short, the paths for teachers and professors to increase their professional perspectives, capabilities, and recognitions are still quite narrow and antiquated.

In sum, the reforms introduced by the 2006 law served to declare teaching as a state policy, consolidated the role of the government as the guarantor of the right to education, and, implicitly, proclaimed teaching as a *public good*.[40] Needless to say, changes at the legal and political level are never mechanically transferred to schools and classrooms. But it is important to acknowledge that perhaps the major regulatory definitions in the 2006 education law are those at the level of the political-pedagogical imagination, once again emphasizing the role of the federal government in education and education policy, in comparison with the deregulation policies of the previous decade.

Before concluding this section it is important to introduce a caveat. As noted before, the political parties or coalitions governing Argentina between 1985 and 2015 oscillated between applying neoliberal-oriented policies and attempts to consolidate the public sector. The 2006 law was implemented during a period of a relative ideological alignment between the federal government and teachers' unions (and supposedly the authorities of TEds), which nonetheless was marked by a significant amount of conflict and teachers' strikes. Given the prominent financial, social, and political space that public education has in the country, and not less relevant the size of the teachers' union (one of the largest unions in the country), the centrality of the conflict around teachers and TEd programs during this period is not surprising.[41] A team that has been studying the incidence of teachers' strikes in the national political landscape concludes: "The strikes in Argentina are mainly limited to the educational sector and practically hegemonized by the teaching staff of public schools, even after supposedly significant salary increases and promoted laws guaranteeing minimum days of class. In Argentina, to speak of strikes is to speak, mainly, of strikes in educational institutions."[42]

Changing Socioeconomic Profile of Teacher Education Students

In Argentina as in other countries, many people look at schools and teachers with nostalgia, and the school of yesterday was always better than today's. What is distinctive in the Argentinean case is the perception that it is not the "pedagogical quality" (e.g., how much teachers know or how well they are trained) that has changed but the type of people who choose to become teachers. In 2015, 491,405 students were enrolled in 1,248 TEd institutes, 80% of them in public TEds.[43] There were 957,275 teaching personnel, in this case for the year 2014.[44]

According to media reports, and from the perspective of some Argentinean researchers, the teaching profession appears to be in the grip of cultural change: a "social descent" that seemingly began back in the late 1970s, accentuated in the 1990s, and believed to be have reached a point of "crisis" in the mid- to late 2010s.[45] The process is evidenced, in part, by the apparent changes in the social composition of students enrolling in TEd programs and joining the teaching ranks. Three dimensions of the "social descent" are addressed here: the class and SES (socioeconomic status) background, the gender composition, and educational trajectories, or human capital, background of TEd students and appointed teachers.

First, there is the issue of class, SES background, and social prestige more generally. Educational historians and sociologists agree that the social composition of teachers is now different from what it was historically. While some argue that the social mix of aspiring teachers has been increasingly more *homogeneous*,[46] others claim that the mix of actual appointed teachers has progressively turned more *heterogeneous*.[47] Although this is apparently contradictory, it can be said that both groups point to the same phenomena: that the teaching profession has been systematically losing its attractiveness for upper middle-class groups, and therefore aspiring teachers are, from a class perspective, a less diverse group or, on the other side of the same coin, that teaching is gaining attractiveness among students from working-class groups and therefore teachers are becoming more heterogeneous socially, economically, and in their cultural capital.

Teaching is a job that historically ranked low compared to other professional jobs requiring a university degree.[48,49] However, in its origins, the belief that it was an honorable, cultivated, and skilled occupation was one reason that attracted young women from rich families (mainly in the big cities), who viewed in teacher training and especially all-girl normal schools a legitimate and liberating path away from traditional roles for women in society.[50,51] The fact that it was a source of upward social mobility was another element for teacher training that persuaded other social groups as well, for example, boys and girls from lower middle classes.[52] Many were able to attend teacher training secondary schools thanks to government scholarships, particularly in the City of Buenos Aires (the country's capital), and many others were the first generation in the family in making it to secondary education.[53]

Notwithstanding some regional differences in the social class composition, educational historians agree that one main commonality of aspiring teachers was that they constituted a socially heterogeneous group.[54] Broadly speaking, up to the 1970s teacher education programs attracted a mix of social groups, including foreigners, children of immigrants, and students from middle classes as well as working-class households. Teacher education enjoyed a somewhat high social image, respect, and symbolic recognition among the social groups with low cultural capital, and among wealthy and cultivated women despite the meager economic recognition it offered. Boys from wealthy families, though, preferred secondary education tracks leading to liberal professions.[55] The social prestige of the normal school TEd option ranked quite low for them.

In the second decade of the twenty-first century, TEd is still seen as a source of social mobility among certain groups, with a high proportion of first-generation students entering into the higher education system.[56] While a century ago women from upper middle classes used to be part of the TEd programs, as a way out of traditionally restrictive roles—social, cultural, economic, and political changes that opened more professional opportunities for these women grew steadily—their interest in teaching for this group has clearly decreased.

The process of decline in the prestige of teaching and consequently of TEd programs is a phenomenon that started to acquire more media visibility and research in the late eighties and continued into the late nineties.[57] A study of the profile of TEd students in the early nineties shows that less than 20% of trainees had parents who finished university, and between 9% and 12% of trainees had professional parents.[58] Still, TEd students prominently came from the middle and lower middle class, although with a shifting tendency toward the inclusion of new social groups.[59]

Research for the 2000s reinforces the evidence on the new social configuration of aspiring teachers. Except in the City of Buenos Aires, parents of more than 50% of TEd students have not even finished high school, and a nationally representative sample shows that about half of the students are in TEd programs seeking opportunities for social mobility and do not mention teaching as their "vocational" option.[60] In a way, teaching seems to be just another job, losing some of its traditional social and cultural markers of a quasi-sacred vocationally determined profession.[61]

The perceived SES of aspiring teachers is more varied than actual parents' educational background. A bit more than a third of the 3,091 respondents in a nationally representative sample of TEd students[62] identified as having a high SES, and another third identified as belonging to the working class. Much of the perceived high SES might be caused by early childhood education TEd students and to students in the City of Buenos Aires, for whom the proportion of those who identify themselves with having a high SES is superior.[63] On the other hand, a majority of aspiring primary and secondary education teachers (non-university track) are perceived to have a low SES, and to a certain extent so do those in the northern part of the country.

As mentioned, and contrary to those examining the social composition of aspiring teachers, other scholars highlight the *increasing* heterogeneity of the actual teaching force as a demonstration of the "social descent" of the profession. Donaire, for example, argues that teachers are still a middle-class group.[64] But there is a higher representation of the lower middle class, a reflection both of the generalized pauperization of the Argentinean middle class that began in the nineties and of the decline in teacher salaries.[65] The author uses the 2001 census data and focuses on married teachers, a bit less than half of all women.[66] He examines the social adscription of spouses / chief of household to three different social groups: the haute bourgeoisie (the highest echelons of society), petit bourgeoisie (including the upper middle and middle class), and the working or proletarian group. The author finds that 54% of female teachers are in middle-class or petit bourgeoisie households and 18% are in the poorer middle class. The percentage of teachers in working-class households was 38% back in 2001, and the richer class represented only 1.4% of married teachers.

It is important to highlight that the lack of longitudinal or historical data is a key limitation of the available empirical research on the overall prestige and changing social class or SES background of TEd students and teachers. The available studies take a cross-sectional view,[67] and although they argue for changing trends their actual findings portray only a picture. Since the 1990s, the federal Ministry of Education has been surveying teachers all over the country (census data) to gather information on their sociodemographic background, among other teacher employment characteristics. Preliminary findings of the 2014 census indicate that only less than 15% of school personnel (classroom and teachers in other roles, and other school staff as well) have parents who have more than a secondary education degree.[68] The three rounds of census data have not been analyzed longitudinally. That said, data for 2004 showed an apparent similar landscape: an average of only 18% of teachers (this time classroom teachers only) have fathers who have completed a higher education degree.

Gender is another relevant dimension in the socioeconomic profile of TEd students and teachers. Research indicates that this has slightly changed, although generally speaking women still are the vast majority.[69] Teacher education has always had a high proportion of female candidates, but in the last part of the nineteenth century it also recruited boys from lower middle classes looking for a vocational secondary education and a stable job. The share of female TEd students has increased over the years, even though there are still regional variations. A study for the Greater Buenos Aires shows that by the mid-nineties, 90% of aspiring teachers were women.[70] Recent research portrays a slightly more varied national picture: TEd students are preponderantly women, but in some regions of the country the share of male students can climb to 35%.[71]

Population and occupational census data for 2001 show that a bit more than 80% of teachers are women and a bit less than half of them are married.[72] Teacher census data for 2014 give 76% of female teachers in all levels, from early childhood to secondary education, a percentage declining slightly from previous decades and confirmed by studies analyzing household surveys from 2003 to 2011.[73] Botinelli explains that the slight decrease in female teachers might be due to the expansion in secondary and higher education enrollments, the two levels where men teachers are more represented.[74]

A third and final issue in the socioeconomic composition of aspiring and practicing teachers is the educational trajectory, or human capital, background. There is not much research on how academically sound aspiring teachers were historically. In a study of the very first teacher training institutes back in the late 1880s to early 1900s (when teacher training for primary education was at the secondary education level), Alliaud mentions that many students did not pass the final exams. The number of failing teacher candidates was particularly high in the first and third years, before the fourth and fifth years, where the actual work for the credential was done. Primary school TEd students had a limited cultural capital, at the time sufficient to embark on the specific job of teaching primary education.[75]

Since the 1990s several studies have provided enough clues to suspect that teacher training might not be attracting the top educational performers. Using the student achievement survey of 2000 (applied countrywide), where high school students in their last year were asked about their expectations for the future, Kisilevsky shows that the lower the test score in language and math, the higher the expectation to consider TEd or non-TEd tertiary, which at the time was much shorter than university degrees.[76] The percentage of those who would choose shorter options like TEd increases for students who have repeated one or two grades and is much lower for those who have never repeated. Kisilevsky also reviews the very few qualitative papers published, all with similar arguments: aspiring teachers have cultural deficiencies, poor linguistic competency, lower analytical and synthesis skills, and they do not master the basic concepts of the discipline. In a TEd institute in Bariloche, a city in a southern province, 19% of incoming teachers were admitted, conditionally until they approved some pending high school courses. Writing and reading comprehension problems were already documented in a study of TEd students in the City of Buenos Aires.[77]

Nowadays, it appears that there is a consensus around the idea that the majority of students joining TEd programs seem to have been exposed to a declining schooling experience and, consequently, arrive with impoverished educational trajectories. It is important to highlight that there are no data to support the idea that the educational trajectory of aspiring teachers improved or worsened over the years. Pineau and Birgin show an increase in groups coming from deteriorated schooling and, although cultural practices are varied, the cultural practices of students in TEd were far from those expected for entering into the teaching profession.[78] Nationally, a fourth of TEd students have some academic problems.[79]

In sum, although some scholars look at the representation of the wealthier and others at the poorer groups in teaching, all seem to point to the same description: TEd and teaching attracts mostly middle-class and poorer groups, and its prestige is linked to the social mobility it promises for those with lower human and social capital. The historically low salaries, the bad working conditions, and the relative lack of professional prestige that traditionally constrained teaching and TEd have proved persistent traits, even after the many changes in the institutional location of teacher training and the apparent increase in salaries that teachers received in the 2000s. Yet, one thing seems to have changed over a century and a half. The social image and symbolic recognition the profession once enjoyed appear to be breaking apart.[80] Teacher training and tertiary non-university options are in no position of privilege compared to the university studies, and there is a widespread perception that the new, incoming TEd students are inadequately prepared for the tasks of teaching. A caveat is due: intensive and in-depth analyses of the broad trends in the socioeconomic composition of TEd students are lacking, and so are approaches that intend to increase our understanding of the possible forces that explain the why and how of these trends.

Concluding Remarks

In this chapter, we discussed changes and continuities in TEd and sociocultural representations related to the professional status of teachers in Argentina's postdictatorship period. In terms of continuities, in spite of all the legislative changes, institutional reorganizations, budgetary changes, curricular modifications, and seemingly constant strikes in the public education sector, taken as a whole TEd appears to be very resilient and resistant to change. The proposed changes have not altered the long-standing institutional profile of this specific educational sector. TEd has not changed its mission, structure, or the profile of the candidates that it attracts into the profession. A similar trend can be used to describe the social representation about the professional status of teachers. In other words, TEds and teachers occupy a great deal of attention in the debates about education in this period and were foci of political and legislative action and conflicts, but the empirical evidence about significant changes remain unclear.

This lack of substantial transformation, in spite of a great deal of effort and attention, is a question that requires further research. As we have argued before, teaching in Argentina cannot be understood without considering it as a *profession of state* and consequently recognizing the central role of the federal government in the definition, regulation, governance, and management of TEd and the teaching profession. As expected, during the period analyzed, the relationships between the state, TEd, and teachers in general fluctuated depending on the political party or coalition of parties leading the federal government. When the governments implemented neoliberal-oriented policies framing public education as an expenditure that needed to be reduced, teachers, mainly through their unions, and TEd programs showed a great deal of political capital and institutional capacity to resist some of the most drastic measures, and to some extent mobilize public opinion, especially when framing the conflict as a defense of "good quality public education."

Resistance to changes, especially when the changes were perceived to diminish the always elusive notion of "publicness" of public education, characterizes the main continuity in the teaching profession during this period. However, the almost permanent state of conflict between teacher unions and the government, as well as the highly visible and polarized political debates about education, coupled with the real and/or imagined demographic changes in the social composition of the students attending TEd, seem to have increased social levels of skepticism about teachers' sense of altruism, consolidating already high levels of mistrust about teachers' professional expertise.

Changing social perceptions about teachers' professionalism is perhaps one of the biggest challenges for Argentinean teachers in the always difficult road to a substantial improvement of public schooling. To improve the professional standing of teaching, it is important but not sufficient to continue with the just demands for adequate funding of public schooling, teacher education, and social policies to reduce the inequalities that affect student achievement. Teachers and the programs educating future teachers also need to work as hard, demonstrating with their daily pedagogical actions the legitimacy of their claims to be defenders of the public good.

NOTES

1. See, among others, the works of Inés Aguerrondo and Cecilia Braslavsky, *Escuelas Del Futuro En Sistemas Educativos Del Futuro: ¿Qué Formación Docente Se Requiere?* (Buenos Aires: Papers Editores, 2003); Alejandra Birgin, "La Docencia Como Trabajo: La Construcción De Nuevas Pautas De Inclusión Y Exclusión," in *La Ciudadanía Negada: Políticas De Exclusión En La Educación Y El Trabajo*, ed. Pablo Gentili and Gaudêncio Frigotto, *Colección Grupos De Trabajo* (Buenos Aires: Consejo Latinoamericano de Ciencias Sociales, 2000); Inés Dussel and Marcelo Caruso, *La Invención Del Aula: Una Genealogía De Las Formas De Enseñar* (Ciudad Autónoma de Buenos Aires: Santillana, 1999); Myriam Feldfeber and Analía Ivanier, "La Descentralización Educativa En Argentina: El Proceso De Transferencia De Las Instituciones De Formación Docente," *Revista Mexicana de Investigación Educativa* 8, no. 18 (2003); Daniel Filmus, ed., *Los Condicionantes De La Calidad Educativa* (Ciudad Autónoma de Buenos Aires: Novedades Educativas, 1995); Daniel Friedrich, "Historical Consciousness as a Pedagogical Device in the Production of the Responsible Citizen," *Discourse: Studies in the Cultural Politics of Education* 31, no. 5 (2010); Juan José Llach and Federico Schumacher, "La Segregación Social En La Educación Primaria

Argentina," in *El Desafío De La Equidad Educativa: Diagnóstico Y Propuestas*, ed. Juan José Llach (Ciudad Autónoma de Buenos Aires: Granica, 2006); Mariano Narodowski, "La Inclusión Educativa. Reflexiones Y Propuestas Entre Las Reflexiones, Las Demandas Y Los Slogans," *REICE: Revista Electrónica Iberoamericana sobre Calidad, Eficacia y Cambio en Educación* 6, no. 2 (2008); Pablo Pineau, "¿Por Qué Triunfó La Escuela? O La Modernidad Dijo: 'Esto Es Educación' Y La Escuela Respondió: 'Yo Me Ocupo.'" in *La Escuela Como Máquina De Educar: Tres Escritos Sobre Un Proyecto De La Modernidad*, ed. Pablo Pineau, Inés Dussel, and Marcelo Caruso (Buenos Aires: Paidós, 2001); Adriana Puiggrós and Sandra Carli, *Sociedad Civil Y Estado En Los Orígenes Del Sistema Educativo Argentino*, vol. 2 (Buenos Aires: Editorial Galerna, 1991); Juan Carlos Tedesco, "Profesionalización Y Capacitación Docente" (Buenos Aires: UNESCO–Instituto Internacional de Planeamiento de la Educación, 2001); Juan Carlos Tedesco and Emilio Tenti Fanfani, "La Reforma Educativa En La Argentina. Semejanzas Y Particularidades," in *Las Reformas Educativas En La Década De Los 1990: Un Estudio Comparado De Argentina, Chile Y Uruguay*, ed. Martin Carnoy, Gustavo Cosse, and Cristian Cox (Buenos Aires: Akian Gráfica Editora, 2004); Flavia Terigi, *Viii Foro Latinoamericano De Educación. Saberes Docentes: Qué Debe Saber Un Docente Y Por Qué* (Buenos Aires: Santillana, 2013).

2. Moreover, by the end of the nineteenth century, the national state itself was even characterized as an *Estado Docente*, or a teacher-state. Several researchers argue that the institutionalization of TEd preceded, and was a necessary condition for, the organization and expansion of the country's public schools system. See Andrea Alliaud, *Los Maestros Y Su Historia: Los Orígenes Del Magisterio Argentino*, ed. Biblioteca Política Argentina, vol. 1: Estudios Sobre Educación (Buenos Aires: Centro Editor de America Latina, 1993); Mariano Narodowski, *Ser Maestro En La Argentina* (Buenos Aires: Sindicato Unico de los Trabajadores en Educación de la Provincia de Buenos Aires, 1990).

3. We want to highlight that the feminization of the profession and related gender regimes are particularly relevant for framing the ideas and ideals of who could be a "good teacher" in Argentina; see Gustavo E. Fischman, *Imagining Teachers: Rethinking Teacher Education and Gender* (Boulder, CO: Rowman and Littlefield, 2000); "Persistence and Ruptures: The Feminization of Teaching and Teacher Education in Argentina," *Gender and Education* 19, no. 3 (2007); Graciela Morgade, "Quiénes Fueron Las Primeras Maestras?," *Revista del Instituto de Ciencias de la Educación* 2, no. 2 (1993); *Mujeres En La Educación: Género Y Docencia En Argentina, 1870–1930* (Buenos Aires: Miño y Dávila, 1997).

4. Jal Mehta, "From Bureaucracy to Profession: Remaking the Educational Sector for the Twenty-First Century," *Harvard Educational Review* 83, no. 3 (2013).

5. Dan C. Lortie, "The Balance of Control and Autonomy in Elementary School Teaching," in *The Semi-Professions and Their Organization: Teachers, Nurses, Social Workers*, ed. Amitai Etzioni (New York and London: The Free Press, 1969).

6. Argentinean sociologists of education refer to teaching as a "quasi-profession." See Emilio Tenti Fanfani, "Profesionalización Docente: Consideraciones Sociológicas," in *El Oficio De Docente: Vocación, Trabajo Y Profesión En El Siglo Xxi*, ed. Emilio Tenti Fanfani (Buenos Aires: Siglo XXI, 2006); Emilio Tenti Fanfani and Cora Steinberg, "Hacia Un Mayor Conocimiento De Los Docentes En America Latina: Características Sociodemográficas Y Posición En La Estructural Social De Los Docentes De Argentina, Brasil Y México" (Buenos Aires: UNESCO–Instituto Internacional de Planeamiento Educativo, Sede Regional Buenos Aires, 2007).

7. Every year for the anniversary of his death, September 11, Sarmiento is still remembered and honored with a national holiday as the "schoolteacher of the nation," "the father of the classroom." *El Día del Maestro (sic),* or "Male Teacher's Day." A well-known joke says that the poor state of schools is not surprising because the system "has a dead father and no mother to take care of it."

8. Jeffrey Puryear and José Joaquín Brunner, *Education, Equity and Economic Competitiveness in the Americas: An Inter-American Dialogue Project,* vol. 2 (Washington, DC: Organization of American States, 1994).

9. Juan Carlos Tedesco, Cecilia Braslavsky, and Ricardo Carciofi, eds., *El Proyecto Educativo Autoritario: Argentina, 1976–1982* (Buenos Aires: Facultad Latinoamericana de Ciencias Sociales, 1983).

10. Paula Razquin, "El Salario Relativo De Las Docentes En Chile, Argentina Y Uruguay," in *Las Reformas Educativas En La Década De Los 1990: Un Estudio Comparado De Argentina, Chile Y Uruguay,* ed. Martin Carnoy, Gustavo Cosse, and Cristian Cox (Buenos Aires: Akian Gráfica Editora, 2004).

11. Pablo Gentili, *Proyecto Neoconservador Y Crisis Educativa* (Buenos Aires: Centro Editor de América Latina, 1994).

12. Gustavo E. Fischman, Stephen Ball, and Silvina Gvirtz, "Towards a Neo-Liberal Education? Tension and Change in Latin-America," in *Education, Crisis and Hope: Tension and Change in Latin-America* (New York: Routledge-Falmer, 2003).

13. Martin Carnoy and Carlos Alberto Torres, "Educational Change and Structural Adjustment: A Case Study of Costa Rica," in *Coping with Crisis: Austerity, Adjustment and Human Resources,* ed. Joel Samoff, A Project of the ILO-UNESCO Task Force on Austerity, Adjustment and Human Resources (Paris: CASSELL-UNESCO, 1994).

14. Alejandra Birgin, *El Trabajo De Enseñar. Entre La Vocación Y Los Mercado: Las Nuevas Reglas Del Juego,* Serie Flacso Acción (Buenos Aires: Troquel, 1999); María Cristina Davini and Andrea Alliaud, *Los Maestros Del Siglo Xxi: Un Estudio Sobre El Perfil De Los Estudiantes De Magisterio,* ed. Maria Cristina Davini, vol. Tomo I, Investigaciones Sobre Formacion Docente (Buenos Aires: Miño y Dávila Editores, 1995).

15. Fischman, Ball, and Gvirtz, "Towards a Neo-Liberal Education?"; Lynne Phillips, "Introduction: Neoliberalism in Latin America," in *The Third Wave of Modernization in Latin America: Cultural Perspectives on Neoliberalism,* ed. Lynne Phillips (Wilmington, DE: Jaguar Books, 1998).

16. David Hursh, "Neoliberalism and the Control of Teachers, Students, and Learning: The Rise of Standards, Standardization, and Accountability," *Cultural Logic* 4, no. 1 (2000).

17. Argentina Congreso de la Nación, "Ley N° 24409: Ley De Transferencia De Los Servicios Educativos" (Buenos Aires: Boletín Oficial de la República Argentina, 1992); "Ley N° 24.195: Ley Federal De Educación" (Buenos Aires: Boletín Oficial de la República Argentina, 1993); "Ley N° 24.510: Ley De Educación Superior" (Buenos Aires: Boletín Oficial de la República Argentina, 1995).

18. The CFCyE comprises the provincial ministers of education.

19. The compulsory years of schooling were extended from 7 to 10 years, to include preschool and middle schools, and the structure was reformulated to include a lower-secondary cycle (like the middle schools) when till then the system had been organized in just two cycles: primary and secondary schools.

20. Argentina Ministerio de Educación, "La Formación Docente En Cifras: Argentina

2014" (Buenos Aires: Ministerio de Educación, Instituto Nacional de Formación Docente, 2015).

21. Argentina Comisión Federal para la Formación Docente Inicial, "Informe Final" (Buenos Aires: Ministerio de Educación, Ciencia y Tecnología, 2005).

22. Argentina Ministerio de Educación, "Informe De Investigación. El Tercer Ciclo Desde La Mirada Docente: Avances Y Desafíos Frente a La Extensión De La Obligatoriedad Escolar," ed. Unidad de Investigaciones Educativas (Buenos Aires: Ministerio de Educacion de la Nación, 2000).

23. Daniel Galarza and Dora González, "El Trabajo Docente En El Tercer Ciclo De La Egb" (Buenos Aires: Ministerio de Educacion, Secretaria de Educacion Basica, Subsecretaria de Educacion Basica, Unidad de Investigaciones Educativas, 1999).

24. Argentina Comisión Federal para la Formación Docente Inicial; Argentina Congreso de la Nación, "Ley N° 24409: Ley De Transferencia De Los Servicios Educativos"; "Ley N° 24.195: Ley Federal De Educación"; "Ley N°24.510: Ley De Educación Superior."

25. Nikolas S. Rose, *Governing the Soul: The Shaping of the Private Self* (London: Taylor & Frances/Routledge, 1990).

26. Claudia Giacometti and Susana Lumi, "Análisis Sobre La Estructura Salarial Y El Gasto Educativo: Síntesis Y Estado De Avance" (Buenos Aires: Ministerio de Cultura y Educación, Dirección Nacional de Planificación Educativa y Programación Presupuestaria, 1995).

27. Alfredo Iñiguez, "El Salario Docente: Un Síntoma Del Estado De La Educación Argentina," in *Serie II: Congreso Educativo Nacional Aportes para la Discusión* (Buenos Aires: Confederación de los Trabajadores de la Educación de la República Argentina, 1999); Marta Maffei, "Sobre La Situación De Los Docentes En La Argentina," in *Políticas, Instituciones Y Actores En Educación,* ed. Graciela Frigerio, Margarita Poggi, and Mario Giannoni, Colección Reflexión Y Debate (Buenos Aires: Centro de Estudios Multidisciplinarios/Ediciones Novedades Educativas, 1997).

28. Sarah A. Robert and Heather Killelea McEntarfer, "Teachers' Work, Food Policies, and Gender in Argentina," *Anthropology & Education Quarterly* 45, no. 3 (2014).

29. The law elaborates on previous proposals presented by a Federal Commission for Initial Teacher Training (Comisión Federal para la Formación Docente Inicial), which had been created in June 2005; see Argentina CFCyE, "Resolución Cfe N° 241/05" (Buenos Aires: Consejo Federal de Cultura y Educación, Secretaría General, 2005). The commission was to propose a specific federal agency for teacher education, delineating its missions, functions, strategies, and an initial work plan. A final report was presented in December 2005, Argentina Comisión Federal para la Formación Docente Inicial. It offers an assessment of the status of teacher education in Argentina and advances six recommendations and guidelines, including a work plan.

30. Argentina Congreso de la Nación, "Ley N° 26.206: Ley De Educación Nacional" (Buenos Aires: Boletín Oficial de la República Argentina, 2006), Art. 75.

31. Since then, teacher education is organized in two cycles: a basic/common education cycle—centered on the fundamentals of the profession, knowledge, and reflection about the education—and a specialized cycle focused on the teaching of curricular contents.

32. A previous law passed in the same year (Law of Educational Financing, 26,075) approved an increment in education investment, a portion of which would be used to improve the quality of initial and in-service teacher education. See Argentina Congreso de la

Nación, "Ley N° 26.075: Ley De Financiamiento Educativo" (Buenos Aires: Boletín Oficial de la República Argentina, 2006).

33. Mónica E. Pini and Jorge M. Gorostiaga, "Reforming Teacher Education in Latin America and the USA," in *Reforming Teaching and Learning: Comparative Perspectives in a Global Era,* ed. Maria Teresa Tatto and Monica Mincu, Comparative and International Education: A Diversity of Voices (Rotterdam/Boston/Taipei: Sense Publishers, 2009).

34. The creation of the INFD was one of the main recommendations posed in the final report presented by the Federal Commission for Initial Teacher Education created in 2005, *Resolución Cfe N° 251/05.*

35. The law reinforces other national regulations that have already been elaborated in the education law of 1993. For example, the 2006 law says that teachers have the right to participate in ongoing and free professional development, to decide freely on their instructional practices, to participate in the development of the school's institutional project, to enjoy decent working conditions, tenure, salary, and other benefits, to participate in education policy making, and to national and provincial collective bargaining mechanisms; see Argentina Congreso de la Nación, "Ley N° 26.206: Ley De Educación Nacional."

36. The proposed common teaching career structure would admit at least two options: classroom teaching and principals/supervisory roles; see Argentina Congreso de la Nación, "Ley N° 26.206: Ley De Educación Nacional," Art. 69. The continuous training is one of the basic dimensions for career advancement.

37. In 1993, kindergarten (for 5 years old) and middle school years (ending at age 14) were added to the already compulsory primary school years; "Ley N° 24.195: Ley Federal De Educación."

38. Flavia Terigi, "Políticas Públicas En Educación Tras Doce Años De Gobierno De Néstor Kirchner Y Cristina Fernández" (Buenos Aires: Fundación Friedrich Ebert, 2016).

39. Roxana Perazza, "La Norma Laboral Docente En Argentina: Entre La Historia Y Los Retos Futuros" (Tesis de Maestría, Facultad Latinoamericana de Ciencias Sociales, 2015).

40. These were the considerations that led to the creation of the Federal Commission for Initial Teacher Training, whose proposals were incorporated in the writing of the law; see Argentina CFCyE, "Resolución Cfe N° 241/05."

41. Roxana Perazza and Martin Legarralde, "El Sindicalismo Docente En Argentina," in *Sindicatos Docentes Y Reformas Educativas En América Latina: Argentina,* ed. Peter Fischer-Bollin (Rio de Janeiro: Fundación Konrad Adenauer, Programa Regional Políticas Sociales en América Latina, 2008).

42. Mariano Narodowski, Mauro Moschetti, and Silvina Alegre, "Radiografía De Las Huelgas Docentes En La Argentina: Conflicto Laboral Y Privatización De La Educación" (Ciudad Autónoma de Buenos Aires: Universidad Torcuato Di Tella, Área de Educación, 2013).

43. Argentina Ministerio de Educación y Deportes, "Datos Formacion Docente 2015_Pedido24 07 2017" (Ciudad Autónoma de Buenos Aires: Ministerio de Educación y Deportes, Instituto Nacional de Formación Docente, Área de Investigación, Unidad de Información, 2017).

44. "Cenpe 2014: Censo Nacional Del Personal De Los Establecimientos Educativos. Datos Generales," ed. Dirección Nacional de Información y Estadística Secretaría de Innovación y Calidad Educativa (Buenos Aires: Presidencia de la Nación, Ministerio de Educación y Deportes, 2015).

45. Mónica Beltrán, "Radiografía De Los Maestros: Desafíos De Una Profesión En Crisis," *El Cronista,* 4 abril 2014; Ricardo Donaire, "Extracción Social Y Condiciones De Vida De Los Docentes En Argentina," *Propuesta Educativa* 39, no. 22 (2013): 24; "El Reclutamiento De Los Docentes En Argentina: Una Aproximación a Partir De La Ocupación De Sus Cónyuges," *Educação & Sociedade* 34, no. 122 (2013): 122.

46. Alejandra Birgin, "La Docencia Como Trabajo: La Construcción De Nuevas Pautas De Inclusión Y Exclusión," *Cuaderno de Pedagogía Rosario* 4, no. 7 (2000); Pablo Pineau and Alejandra Birgin, "Esos Raros Peinados Nuevos: ¿Qué Traen Los Futuros Docentes?," in *Políticas Educativas Y Trabajo Docente: Nuevas Regulaciones, ¿Nuevos Sujetos?,* ed. Myriam Feldfeber and Dalila Andrade Oliveira (Buenos Aires: Novedades Educativas, 2009).

47. Davini and Alliaud, *Los Maestros Del Siglo Xxi,* Tomo I; Donaire, "Extracción Social Y Condiciones De Vida De Los Docentes En Argentina"; Silvia Llomovatte, "Estado Del Arte Sobre Condiciones Laborales Docentes En Argentina," in *El Sistema Educativo Como Ambito Laboral,* ed. Graciela Frigerio et al., Coleccion Cea-Cbc (Buenos Aires: Programa del Area de Investigacion sobre Trabajo y Empleo, 1995); Narodowski, *Ser Maestro En La Argentina.*

48. Alliaud, *Los Maestros Y Su Historia: Los Orígenes Del Magisterio Argentino,* vol. 1; Birgin, *El Trabajo De Enseñar. Entre La Vocación Y Los Mercado: Las Nuevas Reglas Del Juego;* Juan Carlos Tedesco, *Educacion Y Sociedad En La Argentina (1880–1945),* ed. Gregorio Weinberg, Dimensión Argentina (Buenos Aires: Ediciones Solar, 1986).

49. Since the beginning of the national system of education and the institutionalization of teaching as a "profession of state" (end of the nineteenth and beginning of the twentieth centuries), teacher salaries were low and comparable to salaries for daily farm laborers; see Andrea Alliaud, *Los Maestros Y Su Historia: Los Orígenes Del Magisterio Argentino,* ed. Biblioteca Política Argentina, vol. 2: Estudios Sobre Educación (Buenos Aires: Centro Editor de América Latina, 1993). Pay schedules could be irregular, especially outside the country's capital city, and teachers could go months without getting paid. The normal (secondary) schools were designed to attract mainly women. Because of their vocational nature, they were perceived as being of lower quality than the Colegios Nacionales, a secondary general education track that offered direct access to the university and was preferable among boys from rich families.

50. Alliaud, *Los Maestros Y Su Historia: Los Orígenes Del Magisterio Argentino,* vol. 1; *Los Maestros Y Su Historia: Los Orígenes Del Magisterio Argentino,* vol. 2.

51. In the interior, the gender composition of aspiring teachers was more balanced. See Birgin, *El Trabajo De Enseñar. Entre La Vocación Y Los Mercado: Las Nuevas Reglas Del Juego;* Alliaud, *Los Maestros Y Su Historia: Los Orígenes Del Magisterio Argentino,* vol. 1; *Los Maestros Y Su Historia: Los Orígenes Del Magisterio Argentino,* vol. 2.

52. Alliaud, *Los Maestros Y Su Historia: Los Orígenes Del Magisterio Argentino,* vol. 2; Tedesco, *Educacion Y Sociedad En La Argentina (1880–1945).*

53. Birgin, *El Trabajo De Enseñar.*

54. Alliaud, *Los Maestros Y Su Historia: Los Orígenes Del Magisterio Argentino,* vol. 2; Birgin, *El Trabajo De Enseñar. Entre La Vocación Y Los Mercado: Las Nuevas Reglas Del Juego;* Pineau and Birgin, "Esos Raros Peinados Nuevos."

55. Alliaud, *Los Maestros Y Su Historia: Los Orígenes Del Magisterio Argentino,* vol. 2.

56. Birgin, *El Trabajo De Enseñar.*

57. Llomovatte, "Estado Del Arte Sobre Condiciones Laborales Docentes En Argen-

tina"; Sarah A. Robert, "(En)Gendering Responsibility: A Critical News Analysis of Argentina's Education Reform, 2001–2002," *Discourse: Studies in the Cultural Politics of Education* 33, no. 4 (2012).

58. Davini and Alliaud, *Los Maestros Del Siglo Xxi,* Tomo I.
59. Birgin, *El Trabajo De Enseñar.*
60. Gabriel Noel, "Los Estudiantes De Los Institutos De Formación Docente," in *Estudiantes Y Profesores De La Formación Docente: Opiniones, Valoraciones Y Expectativas,* ed. Emilio Tenti Fanfani, Serie Estudios Nacionales (Buenos Aires: Ministerio de Educación de la Nación, 2010).
61. Fischman, *Imagining Teachers;* "Persistence and Ruptures."
62. The 3,091 TEd students surveyed represent less than 10% of the students nationwide; Emilio Tenti Fanfani, ed. *Estudiantes Y Profesores De La Formación Docente: Opiniones, Valoraciones Y Expectativas,* Serie Estudios Nacionales (Buenos Aires: Ministerio de Educación de la Nación, 2010).
63. In the City of Buenos Aires, for example, over 60% of students self-identified with a high SES; see Noel, "Los Estudiantes De Los Institutos De Formación Docente."
64. Donaire, "Extracción Social Y Condiciones De Vida De Los Docentes En Argentina."
65. Birgin, "La Docencia Como Trabajo: La Construcción De Nuevas Pautas De Inclusión Y Exclusión"; Cecilia Braslavsky and Alejandra Birgin, "Quiénes Enseñan Hoy En La Argentina," in *Las Transformaciones De La Educacion En Diez Años De Democracia,* ed. Guillermina Tiramonti, Cecilia Braslavsky, and Daniel Filmus (Buenos Aires: Tesis-Norma, 1995); Narodowski, *Ser Maestro En La Argentina.*
66. In the 2001 census, about 81% of all teachers, excluding university professors were women; see Donaire, "Extracción Social Y Condiciones De Vida De Los Docentes En Argentina."
67. Birgin, "La Docencia Como Trabajo: La Construcción De Nuevas Pautas De Inclusión Y Exclusión"; Davini and Alliaud, *Los Maestros Del Siglo Xxi,* Tomo I; Donaire, "Extracción Social Y Condiciones De Vida De Los Docentes En Argentina"; Pineau and Birgin, "Esos Raros Peinados Nuevos"; Razquin, "El Salario Relativo."
68. Argentina Ministerio de Educación y Deportes, "Cenpe 2014: Censo Nacional Del Personal De Los Establecimientos Educativos. Datos Generales."
69. "Relevamiento Anual 2015," in *Relevamiento Anual,* ed. Red Federal de Información Educativa Dirección Nacional de Información y Evaluación de la Calidad Educativa (Ciudad Autónoma de Buenos Aires: Ministerio de Educación y Deportes de la Nación, 2016); Noel, "Los Estudiantes De Los Institutos De Formación Docente."
70. Davini and Alliaud, *Los Maestros Del Siglo Xxi,* Tomo I.
71. Noel, "Los Estudiantes De Los Institutos De Formación Docente."
72. Donaire, "Extracción Social Y Condiciones De Vida De Los Docentes En Argentina."
73. Argentina Ministerio de Educación, Ciencia y Tecnología, "El Perfil De Los Docentes En La Argentina: Análisis Realizado En Base a Los Datos Del Censo Nacional De Docentes 2004," in *Boletín DINIECE* (Ciudad Autónoma de Buenos Aires: Ministerio de Educación, Ciencia y Tecnología; Dirección Nacional de Información y Evaluación de la Calidad Educativa, 2007); Argentina Ministerio de Educación y Deportes, "Cenpe 2014: Censo Nacional Del Personal De Los Establecimientos Educativos. Datos Generales."

74. Leandro E. Bottinelli, "El Empleo Docente En La Argentina: Tendencias En La Posconvertibilidad (2003–2011) Y Aportes Para Su Estudio a Partir De La Encuesta Permanente De Hogares" (Maestria, Universidad Nacional de Tres de Febrero, 2015).

75. Alliaud, *Los Maestros Y Su Historia: Los Orígenes Del Magisterio Argentino,* vol. 2.

76. Marta Kisilevsky, "Condiciones Sociales Y Pedagógicas De Ingreso a La Educación Superior En La Argentina," in *Dos Estudios Sobre El Acceso a La Educación Superior En La Argentina,* ed. Marta Kisilevsky and Cecilia Veleda (Buenos Aires: UNESCO–Instituto Internacional de Planeamiento de la Educación, Sede Regional Buenos Aires, 2002).

77. Davini and Alliaud, *Los Maestros Del Siglo Xxi,* Tomo I.

78. Pineau and Birgin, "Esos Raros Peinados Nuevos."

79. Noel, "Los Estudiantes De Los Institutos De Formación Docente."

80. Birgin, "La Docencia Como Trabajo: La Construcción De Nuevas Pautas De Inclusión Y Exclusión"; Pineau and Birgin, "Esos Raros Peinados Nuevos."

CHAPTER TWO

Teacher Formation in Brazil
"Old" and "New" Approaches to Teacher Formation Given Today's Challenges for the Teaching Profession

SILVANA MESQUITA AND MARIA INÊS MARCONDES

The purpose of this chapter is to give background information on the formation[1] of teachers in Brazil over the last three decades. It will be seen that in the Brazilian context, the formation of teachers is associated with the growing need to recruit new teachers, in the face of the expansion of student numbers in schools. However, there are two obstacles to an effective response to this demand: one, the low level of attractiveness of the teaching career, due to the social undervaluation of teaching; and two, the practical difficulties teachers face in the schools, which are insufficient to meet the demands of the population that needs to use them, due to problems with working conditions, mainly in the free, public sector.

In view of the above and in order to provide elements for understanding this educational scenario, this text is organized around three leading questions:

1. How has the basic formation of teachers been structured in the last 30 years in Brazil?
2. What are the new demands on teachers and their work in the face of the "schools crisis"?
3. What initiatives have been implemented through national public policies?

The Brazilian educational scene, starting in the 1970s, has been characterized by a progressive expansion of basic education, seeking to guarantee access to school at all levels of education for increasingly inclusive sectors of society, in order to bring about the so-called democratization of education. In the 1990s, the total number of students in elementary school, which had previously lasted for a period of eight years, as well as being compulsory and free of charge, reached almost universal levels, with an increase in completion rates.

As pointed out by Oliveira,[2] this process began to generate a demand for expansion of the entire education system, especially the stages after elementary school. High school has also experienced great expansion in recent years, and higher education has been growing significantly.

Historically in Brazil, the desire to increase, or not, access to basic education for the majority of the population was associated with the political shifts that were changing the National Constitution and the legislation that regulated the educational system. During the period of military government (1964–1985), LDB 5,692 (the 1971 Law of Guidelines and Bases for National Education)[3] mandated compulsory eight-year elementary education free of charge from 7 to 14 years of age. With the end of the military dictatorship, the process of redemocratization began and a new "LDB" (Law 9,394 of 1996) during the government of President Fernando Henrique Cardoso was introduced. This law allowed for a period of mandatory elementary education of nine years, from the age of 6 years, to be provided free by the state. However, it only came into force effectively during the government of Luis Inácio Lula da Silva ("Lula") government in 2006, with a deadline of 2016 for its full implementation.

Since 2009, still during the Lula government, through an amendment to the LDB 9,394, basic education has become compulsory and free from 4 to 7 years of age, with the state also being obliged to provide free education to children up to 5 years of age. In Brazil, basic education comprises early childhood education, elementary school, and high school. Early childhood education, the first stage of primary education, is offered in daycare for children up to 3 years of age and in preschools for children aged 4 to 5 years. Elementary school lasts at least nine years and is divided into two phases, initial series (formerly primary) and final series (formerly gymnasium). High school, the last stage of basic education, is for students from 15 to 17 years of age, offering a general education and guaranteeing continuity of studies into higher education (table 2.1).

TABLE 2.1
Organization of the education system in Brazil

Duration	Basic education	Age	Legislation
2–5 years	Early childhood education		
	Day care	0–3	Free
	Preschool	4–5	Free and compulsory
9 years	Elementary school		
	Initial series (formerly primary)	6–10	Free and compulsory
	Final series (formerly gymnasium)	11–14	Free and compulsory
3 years	High school	15–17	Free and compulsory

Duration	Higher education	Management
2–3 years	Vocational	Public or private
3–5 years	Bachelor	Public or private
3–4 years	Teacher education program (*licentiate*)	Public or private

Duration	Postgraduate	
1–2 years	Lato sensu	Public or private
2–4 years	Stricto sensu (master and doctorate)	Public or private

However, even after the deadline for its implementation in 2016, the universalization of early childhood education and high school is far from being achieved. In 2015, about 2.5 million children and youngsters aged 4 to 17 were still not in school. Of these, approximately 1.5 million are young people aged 15 to 17 who are expected to be in high school. In addition, of the total number of young people enrolled in schools, about 33% of the total, are still in elementary school. Age-grade distortion[4] is a problem in Brazil, due to the high rates of failure to pass the year and children simply leaving school. In terms of nine-year elementary school, attendance rates for the population aged 6 to 14 years are at an advanced level when compared to early childhood education and high school, reaching a percentage of 97.7% in 2015 for students enrolled in this age group.

As for the schools that Brazilians attend, the country has 186,000 basic education schools. It can be seen that the educational networks in the country differ between public institutions, which are the responsibility of the Brazilian government, the states, the federal districts and the municipalities, and private schools, maintained and administered by individuals or legal entities. As a result, the largest network of basic education in the coun-

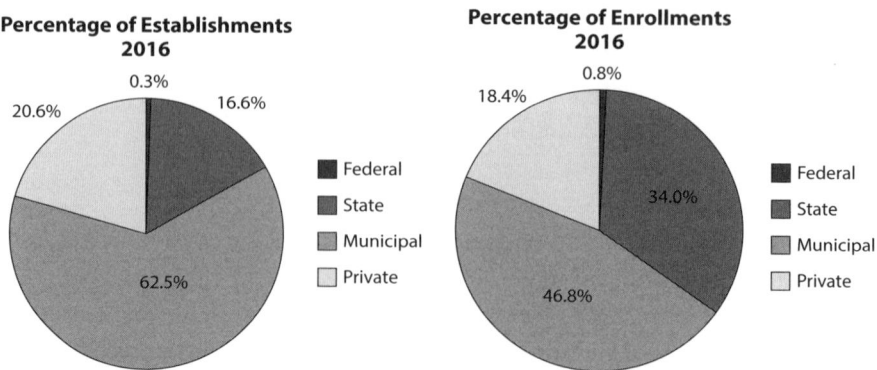

Figure 2.1. Distribution of schools and enrollments per administrative segment, 2016. (Source: "School Census of Basic Education 2016," Ministry of Education / Institute of Educational Studies and Research (Brasilia: Mec/Inep, February 2017).

try is under the responsibility of the municipalities, concentrating about 2/3 (114,700) of the schools in Brazil (fig. 2.1).

In Brazil, public schools, mainly municipal and state schools, are responsible for 80.8% of enrollments in basic education and serve the majority of the popular classes. However, they present a series of problems related to the infrastructure and the quality of education offered, evidenced by the low performance of their students in the national standardized tests (PROVA BRASIL, Saeb). Federal public schools are exceptions, with performance indicators above the national average, but they maintain only 0.8% of enrollments. Given this scenario, private schools are seen as alternatives with better school outcomes and are driven by a portion of the population that can afford the costs. However, it should be noted that the country's private schools show significant differences between them, in terms of the attending public itself, the tuition values, the infrastructure, and the quality of teaching offered to the students. Of the 18.4% of basic education students enrolled in the private network, only a small portion attends the so-called "elite" private schools, aimed at the highest classes of the population, with good indicators of teaching quality. There is another part of private schools that is aimed at the lower middle classes, with lower costs for families, but with problems similar to those presented by public schools.

In relation to teachers, a great majority move between the different networks, except those who work in the federal network, because they can't work in other schools. The initial formation of teachers, whether at the upper or middle level, as discussed in the second part of this chapter, allows the teacher to work in both public and private networks. However, the processes of entering the networks are different. In the public network there is a public exam for teachers mandated by current legislation, based on theoretical and/or practical evidence, and may or may not include an analysis of a candidate's academic/professional qualifications. It is worth mentioning that the preparation and execution of public exams for teachers are managed by each local entity for which they are intended, with variations in structure and organization. Teachers entering through this route become public servants and acquire job stability, something very much desired among Brazilian workers. In private schools the hiring process is quite varied. Candidates can be given internships or be hired based on their CVs, or in very few cases given a theoretical exam, as in the public networks. However, portions of the private schools designed for the elites, and the small number of elite federal schools, offer better working conditions and benefits and therefore recruit teachers who were educated in the best universities and who have higher levels of academic training, like master's and doctoral degrees (although these qualifications are not a requirement for the teaching profession in Brazil).

Working conditions also vary in both public and private networks, as well as the intensity of working hours and the infrastructure of schools, including the organization of school time and paid wages. For example, the country's regional differences, the economic differences between municipalities and the various private schools for different social classes are responsible for the significant wage variations among teachers. However, it is possible to affirm that among the OECD nations, Brazil is one of the countries with the lowest average wage paid to teachers of basic education. Given that pay and working conditions are important in attracting, developing, and retaining qualified teachers, this is a major problem for the formation of new teachers in the country.

The expansion of schooling in Brazil after the period of military dictatorship (1964–1985), was a reality both in terms of the growth of the number of new schools and in terms of increased enrollments in the different segments. The process of political redemocratization that ran through governments with neoliberal, progressive, or conservative ideals was marked by their belief in the value of increased schooling, as discussed throughout this chapter.

As a result of the investment in educational expansion, the teaching profession grew significantly in Brazil. According to data from the 2016 school census, 2.2 million teachers were working in basic education. The profile of these teachers is characterized by an average age of 40.1 years, with a standard deviation of 9.9 years. The data show that 78.3 of the teachers work in one school, 84.3% work in urban schools, and 80% are female. It is a professionally heterogeneous category from a cultural and socioeconomic point of view, stemming from multiple training processes.

How Has Basic Formation for Teachers Been Structured in the Last 30 Years in Brazil?

In the last few decades, as a result of the process of expansion and democratization of opportunities for basic education for the entire population, there was an increase in the demand for the recruitment of new teachers and investment in initial formation. However, the need for an increase in the number of teachers created a process that reduced the academic demands of initial training, favoring the maintenance of teacher formation at the high school level (normal school or teachers college)[5] and an emphasis on distance learning for further education and the consolidation of complementary courses in multiple establishments, with few regulatory strategies by government agencies. The teaching profession is undergoing rapid expansion, but it is fragmented, heterogeneous, and diversified, and blighted by precarious working conditions and low social prestige.

Historically, teachers who work in basic education are in two distinct groups in terms of the nature of their work, formation, and salaries. There are the so-called *multipurpose teachers* who work in early childhood education and elementary school initial series (corresponding to primary education), teaching all the different subjects for students of these first grades, with each class having only one teacher. The second group comprises *specialist teachers* who teach a specific subject area for elementary school final series and for high school. In this case, in one class there is normally one teacher for each discipline that composes the curricular structure of these teaching segments. With regard to teacher training, each group has distinct historical trajectories that mark the professional culture of each one and explain the entrenched processes for professional development for teachers in Brazil today.

From Lay Teachers to the Rise of University Formation Programs (Universitarization) for Multipurpose Teachers

The Federative Republic of Brazil is composed of 27 political units, of which there are 26 states and one federal district, distributed over an area of

TABLE 2.2
Number of teachers in the initial grades by level of schooling and regional distribution, year 2016

Geopolitical regions	Total number of teachers	Lay teachers	Teachers with high school	Teachers with higher education
Brazil	1,339,163	4,822	382,787	951,554
		0.4%	28.6%	7.0%
North	105,988	476	36,681	68,831
Northeast	355,823	1,942	160,177	193,704
Southeast	557,398	1,192	121,668	434,538
South	221,040	908	49,311	170,821
Center-West	98,986	304	14,954	83,728

Source: "School Census of Basic Education 2016," Ministry of Education / Institute of Educational Studies and Research (Brasilia: Mec/Inep, February 2017).

Note: This includes early childhood education and elementary school initial grades.

8,514,876 km². These 27 units are distributed in five macroregions: North, Northeast, Central West, Southeast, and South. However, the regions have very different levels of economic and social development. In the educational field, mainly in the North and Northeast regions, they have used a significant number of lay (untrained) teachers for several decades, who received no specific training for teaching and in some cases have not even completed their own basic schooling.

In 1996, the current LDB was passed, which established the need for all teachers in the country to have a university education. The new law, coupled with higher-education policies, has led to a significant increase in the number of teachers with higher education in the country to have a university education. In 2016, of the 2.2 million teachers who worked in basic education, 77.5% had a higher education qualification and another 6.5% were studying. The greatest impact of this legislation was on primary or multipurpose teachers, whose formation for many years was only at the normal school (teachers college) or elementary school, as in the case of lay teachers (table 2.2). According to Louzano et al.[6] in the year of the introduction of the law, one-third of primary school teachers in the North and Northeast had not achieved high school education. However, by 2016, less than 1% of teachers in this region could be considered lay. In Brazil as a whole, the rate of teachers in the initial series with higher education has reached 71%; with intermediate level it is around 28%, while the lay rate does not reach 0.5%.

This progression in the process of universitarization of the teachers' level of education is the result of a series of policies implemented initially in the government of President Fernando Henrique Cardoso (1995–2003) of the

PSDB (Partido da Social Democracia Brasileira) considered to have neoliberal tendencies. However, such policies gained further impulse under the progressive governments of the PT (Workers' Party) presidents, Lula (2004–2011) and Dilma Roussef (2012–2016).

In this process, the implicit purpose of the law creating university-level education for teachers was directly related to the need to establish higher status for them based on their professionalization through higher education. It was understood that the upgrading of the levels for training of primary teachers would strengthen the existence of specific knowledge sets in this phase of teaching, contributing to the prestige of this type of professional and recognition of their specific skills. As Gatti et al.[7] argue, teacher training goes beyond improvisation, beyond the status of missionary or talented amateur, and should eliminate any doubts as to their role as valued and necessary professionals.

The path taken toward primary teacher training programs at a higher level has been a long and halting one throughout. It began in 1998 with the institution of the Normal Superior[8] undergraduate program in the newly created Educational Institutes,[9] in order to specifically train initial series teachers, with an average length of three years. However, the Normal Superior course was not carried through, mainly because of the institutes' distance from the universities, and in the end it became a program to train in-service teachers who did not have the qualifications required by the new law.

In 2006, a new national standard was set to regulate the formation of early childhood education teachers and elementary school initial series teachers at the higher level. From this moment until the present day, pedagogy courses are being restructured and are beginning to use this new demand as a central pillar of their program. Prior to 1996, pedagogy courses mainly prepared teachers to work in a normal school (teachers college) and formed school principals, supervisors, educational counselors, and pedagogical coordinators.

However, according to the legislative changes proposed, higher education courses in pedagogy became the responsibility of teacher formation for early childhood education and the initial years of elementary school, as well as for high school in the form of normal schools, in those states where these courses existed (table 2.3), as well as the training of school managers and staff. Today, pedagogy courses have expanded throughout the country and are offered by higher education institutions, in person or as distance learning programs, in the public or private network. They are considered the locus

TABLE 2.3
Number of enrolled in intermediate teacher formation courses (normal schools), by region and administrative network, 2016

	Total	Federal	State	Municipal	Private
Brazil	102,797	143	95,711	2,836	4,107
North	994	—	407	—	587
Northeast	13,454	—	10,725	1,716	1,013
Southeast	53,118	143	50,605	651	1,719
South	33,115	—	31,904	423	788
Center-West	2,116	—	2,070	46	—

Source: "School Census of Basic Education 2016," Ministry of Education / Institute of Educational Studies and Research (Brasilia: Mec/Inep, February 2017).

of training for elementary school teachers, although they are not the only institutions offering training for these teachers, since the normal schools were not abolished.

However, the promise of university degrees for primary teachers has not yet been fully implemented in Brazil. As can be seen, the data in table 2.3 show that depending on regional differences, the number of teachers working in early childhood education and initial grades of basic education with intermediate-level education is still an expressive reality (28.6%), despite the number of lay teachers having been reduced to minimum levels.

Despite the expansion of pedagogy courses throughout the country and incentive policies, such as PARFOR (National Plan for the Training of Teachers in Basic Education) in 2007, the deadline for all teachers to have a higher education degree was not fulfilled and the law was amended. Today, the LDB of 1996 allows for the maintenance of a minimum specific level of teacher formation, at the high level (normal school), for teachers working in early childhood education and the initial series of basic education, despite maintaining it as a priority formation at a higher level: "Art. 62. The training of teachers to work in basic education will be carried out at a higher level, in a full university course, allowing for the minimum training required for the exercise of teaching in early childhood education and in the first five years of basic education to be the intermediate level, in the modality known as 'Normal.'"[10]

It can be noted that the formation of new basic education teachers at the intermediate level (normal school), is still a reality in Brazil. Data from the 2016 census indicate that of the 27 Brazilian federation units, only five do not offer this mode of teacher training. There are 102,797 enrolled students in normal schools throughout the country, offered mostly by state networks. This demonstrates a reality that is far from being replaced by complete university formation, in the face of both the demands of the states for new teachers and the demands of the population for this level of formation, and given the need for early entry into the labor market.

From the "Recognized Expertise" of Other Professions to Graduate Courses for Specialist Teachers

Historically, the role of secondary education teachers[11] in Brazil was structured around the knowledge of professionals in the liberal professions or self-taught professionals from different disciplines with recognized expertise in mathematics, physics, chemistry, history, biology, and geography, among others. There was no specific teaching formation for these teachers until the 1930s, their knowledge in the chosen discipline being the only requirement to become a teacher.

As Dias states: "Until the 1930s, there were no national public policies for vocational formation of secondary school teachers or legal requirements to be fulfilled by those who practiced teaching in this branch of education. People came from other professions, such as the military, members of religious brotherhoods and congregations, graduates from schools of higher education, and self-taught individuals."[12]

The process of professionalization of secondary school teachers in Brazil has historically had two important milestones: the creation of the teachers' register in 1931 and in 1939 the Faculty of Philosophy, Science and Letters, the first institution supporting the formation of teachers at a higher level for candidates for secondary school teaching. The creation of this institution was based on the recognition of the need for the specific formation of the secondary school teacher who had all the required knowledge for the exercise of teaching.

It should be noted that this period, politically, between the years 1930 and 1945, was strongly influenced by the government of Getúlio Vargas, which instituted the so-called Estado Novo (New State). It was a type of dictatorship based on the ideals of nationalism, populism, and the fight against communism. In the educational field, the Escola Nova (New School) movement developed, aiming at supplanting traditional teaching with what was termed modern teaching, with an emphasis on the formation of new teachers.[13]

The initial teacher formation model for secondary education in undergraduate courses comprised two phases, the bachelor's degree, with a duration of three years dedicated to the scientific knowledge of each area, and the one-year licentiate, which included the course for specific pedagogical knowledge. This form of organization of the courses became known as the "3 + 1" scheme, which was in force until 1968, but it still has repercussions today, as we describe below.

Today, the registers of secondary school teachers are no longer needed, having been replaced by the diplomas of the Teacher Education Program (*licenciate*)[14] issued by the institutes of higher education. The current formation of secondary school teachers seeks to overcome the fragmented model of the "3 + 1," proposing a greater connection between the epistemology of each subject area of the bachelor's degree with the pedagogical knowledge necessary for teaching. It seeks to overcome the dichotomy between theory and practice, between an excessive focus on content and having the degree course only as a complement. In the debates about the formation of secondary teachers, there is a need to overcome fragmentation and the strong disciplinary tradition that has shaped the formation of new teachers and given teaching its provisional character.

The search to overcome these dichotomies in the formation of secondary school teachers also speaks to the need to value their professionalism in order to make professionalization of teaching a reality. As Gatti states when referring to the studies of Ramalho, Nuñez, and Gauthier,

> Professionalism is the set of characteristics of a profession that bring together the rationalization of the knowledge and skills necessary for the proper exercise of that profession; the professionalization of teachers requires the definition of an autonomous space, proper to their professionalism, with a value clearly recognized by society. There is no adequate professionalization without the constitution of a solid base of knowledge and defined methods and procedures. With these concepts, we begin to move away from the improvised, amateur, "missionary" teacher, from the private tutor, the self-taught teacher, the "hobby" teacher, towards the conception of a professional who is able to deal with complex and varied problems, with the capacity to build solutions in their everyday teaching role, mobilizing their cognitive and affective resources.[15]

Current legislation requires that all teachers who work in secondary education, the so-called *specialists,* have a Teacher Education Program (*licen-*

tiate). The 2016 census data show the expansion of teacher formation in this segment in the country, which in 2016 reached about 80% with a Teacher Education Program (*licentiate*).

However, in addition to the questions about the curricular designs of these courses and growth in the level of formation, there is also a shortage of specialist teachers in some disciplines. The expansion in enrollments in high school with a growth of more than 100% began to fuel a demand for greater numbers of specialist teachers.[16]

Studies identify[17] a shortfall of about 235,135 teachers in basic education in 2007, which is a worrying fact in view of the educational goals of expanding high school, since about 1.5 million young people between 15 and 17 were still outside this segment of education in 2016. Moreover, data from 2016 show that, although most secondary school teachers have a higher education degree, only 53% of teachers have formation compatible with the discipline they teach. What we can see is that teachers are teaching different disciplines from their qualifications, especially in those disciplines with a greater deficit of teachers with the appropriate formation. In the final series of elementary school, only 32% of art teachers have adequate formation, whereas in high school, only 28.7% of sociology teachers have specific formation. Disciplines such as physics, chemistry, philosophy, and foreign literature also have teacher formation adequacy indexes of around 50%.

Faced with this scenario of inadequacy in the formation of teachers working in these segments of education, in 2005, the federal government implemented the "pro-licenciature" program, focused exclusively on distance-learning for initial formation for teachers in service, in order to correct part of this educational gap. However, this is still a long way from happening, as the data for 2016 show.

The government has been seeking to increase access to initial formation courses, and it has also encouraged teachers already working to obtain a second degree. However, the fact that most undergraduate courses are outdated has been pointed out by Gatti et al.[18] as a difficulty in the initial formation and preparation of teachers to deal with the current demands of young people and of contemporary society itself. As stated by Kuenzer,[19] it is not enough to increase the incentives for initial formation; it is necessary to improve the structure of the teaching career, wage policies, a sense of dignity, and adequate working conditions.

The data of the study by Gatti and Barretto[20] based on the socioeconomic questionnaire of the National Exam of Courses, ENADE-2005, covering 137,001 respondents, help to reflect on the low attractiveness of the teaching career in Brazil and its scarcity. According to the research of these authors, only 30% to 40% of the graduates in Teacher Education Programs (*licentiates*) will work as teachers. When asked about the main reason that led them to opt for the degree, 65.1% of pedagogy students attribute the choice to the fact that they want to be a teacher, whereas this percentage drops to approximately half (48.6%) among the other graduates. The choice of teaching as a kind of "unemployment insurance," that is, as an alternative in case there is no possibility of another activity, is relatively high (21%), especially among graduates of areas other than pedagogy.

Since the enactment of the current LDB, there has been concern about the standardization of the different types of formation for teachers and the encouragement of the implementation of common curricular guidelines for the formation of specialist teachers. The different institutional forms, however, are still evident in undergraduate courses of teacher formation. We can note a proliferation of Teacher Education Programs (*licentiates*), mostly promoted by private colleges and independent of each other, without the desired common standard or structure. According to the curricular guidelines, the pedagogical projects of the different degrees should be comparable, avoiding the traditional fragmentation that has been common in Brazil. According to Bernadete Gatti and Elba Barretto, "The prevalence of the historical idea of offering formation in the specific disciplinary area, with a high number of disciplines and class hours, practically without integration with the pedagogical disciplines, can be seen in courses for specialist teachers. These have a reduced total number of class hours or activities."[21]

Their research[22] has uncovered a lack of standardization regarding teacher formation and its internal fragmentation in terms of curriculum, which seems to be caused by diverse institutional interests, such as the existence of crystallized institutional niches, or by the lack of prospects for teachers, and also by cost reduction.

This brief overview of the initial formation of new teachers in Brazil points to a scenario of shortage and lack of standard and high-quality formation, which are associated with the problems of the attractiveness of the teaching profession, explained not only by the devaluation of the profession since its origin, but above all by the conditions of work to which teachers are submitted in their day-to-day experiences in schools.

What Are the New Demands on Teaching in the Light of the "Schools Crisis"?

Schools in various parts of the world are accused of being in "crisis." However, from a historical approach, it is possible to observe that the word *crisis* can also be understood as "transition" or "change." The expansion of formal education, the consolidation of school as a locus for the formation of children and young people from all walks of life, and changes in the processes of social interaction with the advance of technologies and the globalization of knowledge are some examples of the processes of reorganization that society and institutions are going through today. The need for ruptures, innovations, and rethinking of the processes of socialization and education is a reality schools are also experiencing. Rather than simply stating that schools are in crisis, we need to highlight the new demands being placed on them in order to gradually reveal their complexity.

In the case of Brazil, two important findings characterize the main challenges for the formation of new teachers, referencing the context of the school where they will work. First is students' lack of learning in school. Second is the lack of adequate working conditions for teachers in the face of the new demands that affect Brazilian schools in the new expanded educational scenario. There have been low rates of achievement and little progress in recent years, especially in secondary education.

The expansion of school access is not associated with satisfactory levels of learning. The data show a stagnation over the years with little progress in the results. Taking as an example the results of the Brazil Test[23] in 2015, only 14% of the young people enrolled in the ninth year of public school have achieved sufficient levels of mastery in mathematics and only 30% in the Portuguese language. Students, even after at least nine years of schooling, are not acquiring basic levels of proficiency in Portuguese and mathematics. If we compare students' performance in the different Brazilian states, these results become more alarming, since in the states of Amapá and Maranhão only 3% and 5%, respectively, of students learn what is expected for their grade. These results configure what we can call the nonquality of the school education offered, marked by exclusions and social inequality; limits to the free education offered; successive grade-level repetitions; lack of resources; and the discontinuity in policies, resulting in the departure of students with no mastery of learning, little cognitive development, and much disenchantment. We go from "exclusion from school to exclusion in school."[24]

TABLE 2.4
Brazilian IDEB per segment of education, 2009–2015

	2009		2011	
	Public schools	Private schools	Public schools	Private schools
Elementary school (initial series)	4.4	6.4	4.7	6.5
Elementary school (final series)	3.7	5.9	3.9	6.0
High school	3.4	5.6	3.4	5.7
	2013		2015	
	Public schools	Private schools	Public schools	Private schools
Elementary school (initial series)	4.9	6.7	5.3	6.8
Elementary school (final series)	4.0	5.9	4.2	6.1
High school	3.4	5.4	3.5	5.3

Source: "School Census of Basic Education 2016," Ministry of Education / Institute of Educational Studies and Research (Brasilia: Mec/Inep, February 2017).

Note: IDEB (basic education development index) combines the results of the students' effort grades in their evaluations (Brazil Test Brasil / Saeb—Basic National Evaluation System) with the rate of approval/pass grades with grades calculated on a scale from 0 to 10, where the higher the grade, the better their performance.

Even with increasing schooling time, the student who attends public school in Brazil does not learn, either because the student is not interested in school, or because the content of the classes does not connect with reality, or because of a lack of human and pedagogical resources—in other words, due to the inadequate format of the school. Today we are undergoing a search for quality school education in order to offer better learning opportunities for students and decrease the number of repeated years and truancy. There is a unanimity of opinion that the school needs to redeem its role as a developer of new generations, by guaranteeing basic knowledge that allows them to socialize and reduce social inequality.

Part of the explanation for the low learning outcomes of the students is that, with the universalization of teaching and the entry of the working classes into schools, a conflict of interests exists between the students and the objectives of the school, which triggers contradictions, a scenario present mainly among adolescents and young people who attend secondary school.

Historically, the school was not created for these new students from poorer and less privileged backgrounds. What has resulted is a new social morphology and new cultures that are coming into conflict with school traditions and with the teachers themselves. This type of school reality is sometimes called "schooling for the masses," characterized by Formosinho[25] as schools with enormous student and contextual heterogeneity, heterogeneity of teachers, and organizational complexity that require structural and pedagogical changes.

The arguments of two authors help us to interpret this reality, Dubet[26] with his thesis of "institutional decline" and Charlot[27] with the debate about "the meanings of school." For Dubet,[28] the deterioration of both the institutional program and the clear definition of the roles played within the school (teacher's role, student's role, role of the administration or director, etc.) allows for the questioning of the socialization power of institutions, as well as their methods and models, and it points out that those actors involved (mentioned above) are an important part of this new process.

In this study, students who entered the public secondary school, intended for lower socioeconomic groups, have divergent relations with the knowledge legitimized by schools over the years.[29] Unlike the country's "heirs," that is, elite students and even middle-class students, who value the preparatory character of the high school, the young people of the working- or low-income class come to question the validity of the forms of knowledge being taught. These are divergent perspectives on the future they seek and their own self-esteem.

According to Dubet,[30] the function of the school is no longer the same as when it was first created. In the golden age[31] of school in the early twentieth century, the underlying ideology of the school sought to transform values into norms, and these norms into well-defined roles in the mold of classical society, contributing to the distribution of social positions and the socialization of a common national culture. It was in these ways that the expectations of teachers, the state, students, and families were oriented.

However, at the same time, we are experiencing an age of mass schooling—the "opening up of schooling"—and the breakdown of this stratified orientation. Values are no longer unique and social roles are no longer so defined. There are, in fact, a multiplicity of roles played by the same subject. Not because the school has lost its legitimacy, because families and society as a whole still believe in its value, but because of the way its subjects view it and the roles they attribute to it, since they are no longer given in a unified form. We can see an increasing distance between the social expectations placed on the school and the possibilities of their realization.

In this context, the various manifestations of students' apparent refusal to learn take various forms, such as absenteeism, indiscipline, dispersiveness, and abandonment.[32] Yet what Charlot's and Canário's[33] studies corroborate is the idea that, for students to study and learn, school needs to make sense, that is, to have meaning for them, because the student learns when he or she builds meaning and takes in knowledge in all circumstances. To identify the meaning of school we must first reflect on the relationship of young people to knowledge.

Students become resistant or passive to most of the content taught and considered by them without practical meaning and without applicability in their daily life. This relationship to knowledge causes serious conflicts with the school and even with the teachers, who label them as uninterested young people with no future prospects. For Galvão and Sposito,[34] the question of the loss of attachment to school is related to the instrumental view of the students in relation to their studies, which makes it impossible for them to become involved in the process of acquiring school knowledge.

According to Fanfani,[35] young people and their families are becoming aware that the so-called social ascension through a higher level of schooling is no longer achieved through diplomas alone. Besides this difference of age between teacher and student, there are also differences of language and goals between individuals who are obliged to coexist in the confined space of a classroom. Thus the practice of teaching is faced with this conflict between the valorization of knowledge and the teacher-student relationship.

In their classrooms Brazilian teachers deal with a scenario of dispersion on the part of students. This is responsible for difficulties with classroom management, and is associated with the crisis of teaching authority that results from the lack of the profession's prestige and the accountability for the poor academic results that ensue.

According to teachers[36] the most serious problems in the teaching process in the school are linked to the students, due to the low levels of learning, uninterest, and dispersion. This scenario causes a relational crisis and great differences in the results of the teachers who can manage the challenge of teaching in these conditions. Issues such as crisis of authority, respect, stress, and indiscipline mark the teachers' discourse with students and the difficulties of classroom management. It is practically a unanimous criticism among teachers that it is not possible to teach people who do not find any meaning in schools or what is taught there. What differs between teachers is how they deal with these difficulties associated with the working conditions provided.

The pedagogical theory of Paulo Freire[37] can help us understand the work with these students and has been developed in the initial training courses of teachers throughout Brazil. However, the problems with the working conditions of teachers in Brazil, such as the lack of equipment and infrastructure in schools, low salaries, long working days, and the multiplicity of tasks that face them in order to deal with the diversity of the students, intensify the issues already facing the Brazilian teaching profession.

What Does the School Expect from a Teacher in Brazil? Dilemmas of Teacher Formation

If the students lack an interest in learning because of conflicts with the type of knowledge that is valued by the institution, how can teachers relate this scientific and scholarly knowledge to the knowledge the students have, awakening in them a desire to learn? The students themselves seem to give the answer: "Only the teacher can make me interested in knowledge."[38]

A need has been identified to search for new teaching strategies and even to redesign the role of the teacher in the classroom. The reality of the school demands the expansion of social/academic functions and consequently of teaching. However, due to the unfavorable working conditions that are offered to teachers, these professionals are limited in what they can do to develop a reflexive, innovative, and committed practice with the new students who come to the school.

Faced with the students' appeals for more attractive classes and the incorporation of technological advances in society, the present infrastructure of schools is too precarious to develop a teaching method based on the integration between science, technology, and work, since access to libraries, laboratories, and the internet is restricted. Salaries are low, compared to other professionals with the same level of educational qualification, and the profession is subject to temporary employment contracts with negative salary variations. The category of teacher is one of the most numerous in Brazil, but it has a heterogeneity of career plans, daily rates, and salaries, since the different states and municipalities adopt their own forms of teacher regulation.

Schools in Brazil, since 1996, have adopted a school year of 200 days. Most students go to school Monday through Friday on a part-time basis. Due to this part-time study, both multipurpose teachers and specialists work in more than one class or school in order to boost salaries. Thus, it is common knowledge that Brazilian teachers work in more than one school, with a workload of more than 30 hours, exclusively in the classroom, with little time for formation and planning. The specialist teachers also have a large variety of classes with an average of 40 students each, and a small number of hours weekly in each class. They deal with a high number of students and tasks, which intensifies the teaching load and compromises the processes of continuous development.

In the context of an exhaustion of the "institutional program" which no longer makes sense, teachers must move from understanding their role as sole transmitters of knowledge, toward the need to construct a new sense of work done at school.[39] We see the need to appeal to new teachers based on the expansion of their academic formation as well as professional and financial recognition associated with better working conditions. We see the need for the development of a new teaching professional capable of communicating the rationale for knowledge, someone with the skills necessary for the exercise of the profession as well as for recognizing teaching as a process of construction and ongoing adaptation to the working context.

This complexity of school reality and teachers' working conditions points to the need to restructure initial teacher education in order to attract and train new teachers to act in this scenario in a more conscious and efficient way. Thus, in the third part of this chapter some programs developed in Brazil in search of new teacher preparation alternatives are presented. They allow for a dialogue between the demands of the new students and the professionalization of the teacher, supporting the combination of theory and practice and how to use both appropriately.

What Initiatives Are Being Implemented through National Public Policies?

In this section[40] we present the *National Curricular Guidelines for Initial and In-Service Teacher Education for Basic Education Professionals*[41] in Brazil, which guide universities and higher education institutions to organize their curricula. This document was created during the progressive governments of the Workers' Party in 2015 and is structured within the context of the policies implemented to increase the training for teachers and show its merit, with the support of the academic community.

Teacher education programs in Brazil prepare teachers to work in basic education, which includes preschool, elementary school, high school, young adults' and adult education, education for people with special needs, technical schools, indigenous education, country/rural education, *quilombola*[42] education, and distance education.

The National Curricular Guidelines define the principles, teaching and learning conditions, and educational procedures that must be attended to by the higher education institutions when making their curricula. The document argues that initial teacher education must take place through theoretical-practical studies, research and critical reflection. The guidelines propose a research attitude through which student teachers must read and analyze educational research throughout their courses, trying to develop their critical thinking skills and capacity to observe the evidence produced in the research. The student teachers must also participate in research groups (scientific initiation), and they must present a final assignment, usually a monograph.

By emphasizing these principles—theory-practice, research, and critical reflection—the document seems to acknowledge that initial teacher education programs have not overcome the challenge to integrate theory with practice in their curricula yet. Thus, to overcome this challenge, the National Curricular Guidelines, in paragraph 12, propose that an initial teacher education curriculum integrates study with research in three curricular units distributed into 2,200 hours.

The first unit is dedicated to basic studies that allow the student teachers to study: (a) basic education and basic education management; (b) philosophical, historical, political, and sociological aspects of education; (c) children and adolescents' development and learning in their social, psychological, and cultural aspects; and (d) "research and study of the relations between education and work, education and diversity, human rights, citizenship, environmental education, among other issues."[43]

The second curricular unit is for deepening and diversifying studies in their subject areas, being constituted by specific and pedagogical content, such as: (a) objectives formulation, choice of methods of teaching, and pedagogical tools that allow for the construction of adequate pedagogical practices based on the principles and tenets of basic education; and (b) study and research of pedagogical knowledge and fundamentals of education, didactics and teaching practices, educational theories, educational policies, funding policies, assessment and curriculum.

The third curricular unit proposes that higher education institutions promote seminars, curriculum studies, projects of scientific initiation and initial teacher education projects.

Therefore, these three units are clearly concerned with research throughout initial teacher education.

Another proposal to integrate theory with practice in the National Curricular Guidelines refers to the curricular component called "practice as curricular component," in which the student teachers will have the chance to know and analyze pedagogical situations (though indirectly) through other teachers' oral narratives, case studies, simulated situations, and basic education students' materials, among others. Four hundred hours are to be dedicated to this component throughout the program.

Moreover, the guidelines suggest that 200 hours should be developed in theory-practice activities to deepen specific subject matters of the interest to the student teachers, such as: (a) scientific initiation; (b) teacher education initiation; (c) extension; (d) tutorials; and (e) any other activity that each higher education institution might consider consistent with its curriculum.

Finally, the National Curricular Guidelines suggest that initial teacher education programs allow 400 hours for supervised practicum in each subject area (education, mathematics, and physics, among others). As the student teachers join a school for their practicum, they will have the opportunity to engage in a professional community and to become familiar with the school where they are placed, with the socioeconomic-cultural situation of the pupils, and the physical conditions of the school itself. Meanwhile, the student teachers will be able to discuss with their teacher educators and supervisors, as well as with the school teachers, the possibilities of action, the working conditions, and any other relevant issue that might come to discussion. Together all these professionals and the student teachers will be able to analyze, investigate, and try out solutions and educational procedures for the observed and experienced practices during their practicum, which is an essential feature of the extended professional orientation aimed at in the program curriculum.

Therefore, from the 3,200 hours that should be dedicated to academic work in initial teacher education, according to the National Curricular Guidelines, 1,000 hours are to be used to integrate theory with practice in the curricula. It does not mean, though, that all initial teacher education programs will in fact attend to this recommendation, since each higher education institution performs a recontextualization of the proposal based on its own political pedagogical project[44] and its contextual reality.

Government Grant Program for Initial Teacher Education—PIBID
PIBID was created by Coordination for the Improvement of Higher Level Personnel—CAPES,[45] in 2009, and implemented by Ordinance no. 72, in April 2010. PIBID has as its main objectives to stimulate and value teaching

as a career, and to improve the process of teacher education for basic education in all regions of the country, especially public education. It is mainly achieved by improving and stimulating the education of student teachers enrolled in higher education institutions nationwide.

The institutions that formally participate in PIBID are CAPES, public higher education institutions (HEIs), and basic education school systems. The initial PIBID proposal was intended to promote the partnership between public higher education institutions and basic schools, trying to connect academic and school knowledge. PIBID deals with teaching projects designed and proposed by each participant HEI, which are then developed by student teachers in public schools under the supervision of both basic education teachers and university supervisors (teacher educators). In order to develop the projects, CAPES provides financial support to the program by funding academic activities, as well as by giving grants to these students, to the school teachers who supervise them, and also to the HEI's coordinators. The student teachers have the opportunity to integrate theory with practice from the very beginning of their university programs, since they may take part in PIBID from their first academic term on, as well as the opportunity to experiment with teaching situations and environments in real-world contexts. The dialogue and interaction among student teachers, supervisors, and coordinators create a dynamic, virtuous movement of reciprocal education and continuous professional growth.[46]

Amongst PIBID objectives, the program contributes to initial teacher education by promoting teacher education connected with basic education schools; by encouraging public basic school systems to stimulate their teachers to act as coeducators (supervisors) of preservice teachers, and thus making them leaders in initial teacher education processes; and by contributing to the integration of theory into practice, indispensable to teacher education, which raises the quality of academic production in undergraduate programs.

When PIBID was launched, the priority areas were physics, chemistry, biology, and mathematics at the high school level, due to the lack of teachers in these specific subjects. Nevertheless, as the first positive results of the program started to appear, and with the growth of demand and new educational policies related to enhancing teaching, the program has started to comprise all basic education levels, including adult education, education to Brazilian indigenous peoples, country/rural education, and education in *quilombos*. It has been the participant HEI's responsibility to determine the levels of education and also the priority areas to be attended to. Such choices are made in accordance with the educational systems, taking into account the social and educational demands of the place or region.

Since 2013, private not-for-profit HEIs all over the country have been integrated in PIBID as well, which is a new regulation hallmark in the program. Another new feature is the fact that student teacher beneficiaries of the University for All Program (ProUni, in Portuguese) are now also eligible to participate in PIBID. With these actions, PIBID started to recognize a broader range of HEIs (196 HEIs in 2013), school teachers, teacher educators, and student teachers. According to an official report,[47] 90,254 grants were given under the aegis of this program in 2013.

It should be noted that ProUni was created in 2004, under the Lula government, as one of the policies to increase access to higher education for the low-income population, mainly from the country's public schools. It is an educational inclusion program with the purpose of providing scholarships from 50% to 100% for students who cannot afford the tuition fees for private colleges (which are a majority in Brazil). The scholarship is valid for the entire course and is funded by the federal government, provided that the student meets the established criteria for scholarship eligibility and achieves the required grades throughout the course.

Nevertheless, the grants awarded by CAPES/PIBID have no relation to the regular curricular practicum of the student teacher in his/her course; they are different categories of practicum. PIBID is an optional program, which depends on the acceptance of the student teacher into the program by the programs' own rules; it broadens the opportunities for the student teachers, but it does not include the total amount of teacher educators or student teachers, whereas regular curricular practicum is compulsory to all higher education students who intend to become teachers.

PIBID has indeed shown positive results and received positive feedback. It has also provided some student teachers, though not all, with experience in public school reality from the very beginning of their teacher education programs.

The grants have made it possible for teacher educators, and basic school teachers, to get involved in the education of the student teachers, supporting and guiding them both in planning and supervising their lessons. Consequently, the student teachers have had the opportunity to experience a teacher education course based on a collaborative culture and teamwork. Such experience comes close to what some researchers[48] believe to be the type of professional education and learning that should take place. It does not mean that this kind of education is solely based on practice or purely technical but rather, as Nóvoa[49] puts it, this kind of education is based on theoretical proposals built within the profession, within the actual classroom, "and appropriate to what is needed after reflection about the teachers on their own work."

Grants are a strategy used by CAPES to allow the student teachers to remain in their programs without needing to find other kinds of jobs. This diminishes the drop-out rates. However, receiving these grants is a privilege available to few student teachers, which may divide and differentiate the quality of the teacher education course among students within the same program and in the same institution.

According to Gatti,[50] PIBID contributed to teacher education courses by promoting a reflection on the curricular organization in relation to how to connect knowledge, academic participation, and critical thinking about learning processes. Besides, it contributed to: "a) the appreciation, empowerment and revitalization of teacher education programs and the teaching career; b) remarkable shared actions between student teachers, school supervisors and higher education coordinators, in a collaborative, participatory framework; and c) the reduction in drop-out rates and the increase in student teachers remaining in their courses, and attracting other new student teachers."[51]

Hence, PIBID has brought a series of positive aspects to initial teacher education. Nonetheless, a point to be made now is that the program is based on grants, and those are not enough for the totality of student teachers, teacher educators, and school teachers. A financial assistance that cannot be given to all creates uneven opportunities among those involved in the educational process. Another important aspect is that the program is supported by government funding, which can be interrupted at short notice, depending on the government's priority choices.

Final Considerations: What Sort of Professional Formation Do We Want for the Teaching Profession in Brazil?

The presentation of this brief scenario of the complexity of the education and formation of teachers in Brazil requires the consolidation of a process of professionalization of teaching that will contribute to the recognition of the value of this profession and to greater investments in working conditions and the attainment of professional autonomy. The recognition of elements of new teaching professionals who combine theory and practice brings specificity to teaching and allows for the improvement of their professional status. Policies for the formation of new teachers must be underpinned by investments in better salaries, better working conditions, and the development of career plans in line with the level of university education demanded from these professionals.

More than thirty years ago the debate about the process of professionalization of teaching began. The quest to elevate teaching from being just a vocation or an activity analogous to a trade, and to raise it to the status of a skilled profession, may allow, according to Tardif,[52] for improvements in raising the prestige of teachers, giving their work value in the face of public opinion, and increasing their autonomy, but also ensuring better working conditions, especially pay. Defending the professionalization of teaching could well be one of the most substantial transformations necessary in education today.

NOTES

1. We have used the word *formation* and not *training* to designate the development process for new teachers.

2. Romualdo Portela Oliveira, "Da universalização do ensino fundamental ao desafio da qualidade: uma análise histórica," *Educação & Sociedade* 100 (2007).

3. Brasil, "Lei de Diretrizes e Bases da Educação Nacional," *Ministério da educação*, 1996. In Brazil, the Law of Guidelines and Bases for National Education (LDB–No. 9394 of 1996), regulates on a centralized basis the organization of Brazil's schools, including the professional formation requirements for teachers.

4. Brasil, "Censo Escolar,"*Instituto Nacional de Estudos e Pesquisas Educacionais Anísio Teixeira* (2016). The age-grade distortion rate is a flow indicator that represents the percentage of students who are not enrolled in a stage that is compatible with their school age. In 2014, the rate in elementary school starting grades was 14.1%, in the final grades 27.3%, and in secondary grades 28.2%.

5. The formation of high-level teachers, after elementary school, occurs in the so-called normal schools, or *teacher colleges*, based on the French model of the Écoles Normales of the seventeenth century.

6. Paula Louzano et al., "Quem quer ser professor? Atratividade, seleção e formação docente no Brasil," *Estudos de Avaliação em Educação*, v. 21, n. 47 (2010).

7. Bernadete Gatti et al., *Políticas docentes no Brasil: um estado da arte* (Brasília: UNESCO, 2011), 93.

8. The Normal Superior course is a Teacher Education Program that was created in Brazil to train teachers of elementary school initial grades and early childhood education at the higher level. When creating the Normal Higher course, the institutes of higher education were created, specifically to train teachers, but unrelated to universities.

9. These are specific institutions to train teachers at a higher level, but outside universities.

10. Text taken from Law No. 13,415 of 2017.
11. This comprises the initial series of elementary school and high school for young people aged 11 to 17 years.
12. Amália Dias, *Apostolado cívico e trabalhadores do ensino: História do magistério do ensino secundário no Brasil (1931–1946)* (Niterói: Universidade Federal Fluminense, 2008), 10.
13. Manoel Bergström Lourenço Filho, *Introdução a Escola Nova* (São Paulo: Melhoramento, 1978).
14. Teacher Education Programs (*licentiate*) are courses offered by institutions of higher education: universities, colleges, and university centers, with the objective of training teachers for the different stages of basic education.
15. Bernadete Gatti, "Formação de professores no Brasil: Características e problemas," *Educação& Sociedade* 31, n. 113 (2010): 1.360.
16. In 1991, the number of enrollments in intermediate school was 3,772,339, and in 2016 it was 8,113,040.
17. Antonio Ibañez Ruiz and Mozart N. Ramos e Murilio Hingel, *Escassez de professores no Ensino Médio: soluções emergenciais e estruturais* (Brasília: Câmara de Educação Básica, 2007).
18. Bernadete Gatti et al., *Políticas docentes no Brasil: um estado da arte* (Brasília: UNESCO, 2011).
19. Acacia Zeneida Kuenzer, "A formação de professores para o ensino médio: Velhos problemas, novos desafios," *Educação &Sociedade* 32, no. 116 (2011).
20. Bernadete Gatti and Elba Barretto, *Professores do Brasil: impasses e desafios.* (Brasília: UNESCO, 2009).
21. Gatti and Barretto, *Professores do Brasil,* 21.
22. Gatti and Barretto, *Professores do Brasil,* 21.
23. Test Brazil, also known as the National Assessment of School Achievement (Anresc), is an evaluation created in 2005 by the Ministry of Education. It composes the National System of Evaluation of basic education (Saeb), and it is one of the components for the calculation of IDEB (basic education development index). It is held every two years, and all students who attend urban public schools from the fifth to the ninth year of schooling and third year of high school classes with more than 20 students, take part. The evaluation is divided into two tests: Portuguese language, which assesses the ability to read, interpret texts, and retain the message. And the mathematics test, which evaluates logical reasoning and applied mathematical concepts.
24. Romualdo Portela Oliveira, *Estado e Política Educacional no Brasil: desafios do século XXI* (São Paulo: Universidade de São Paulo, 2006).
25. João Formosinho, *Formação de professores. Aprendizagem profissional e acção docente* (Porto: Porto Editora, 2009).
26. François Dubet, *El declive de la institución: profesiones, sujetos e indivíduos en la modernidad* (Barcelona: Gedisa, 2002).
27. Bernard Charlot, "Relação com o saber e com a escola entre estudantes de periferia," *Cadernos de Pesquisa,* no. 97 (1996).
28. Dubet, *El declive de la institución,* 28.
29. Dubet, *El declive de la institución,* 28, 29, and Ana Karina Brenner and Paulo Cesar

Rodrigues Carrano, "Os sentidos da presença dos jovens no ensino médio: representações da escola em três filmes de estudantes," *Educação & Sociedade* 35, no. 129 (2016).

30. François Dubet, *A Sociologia da Experiência* (Lisboa: Porto, 1994).
31. Dubet, *A Sociologia da Experiência*, 28. Dubet makes use of this expression to refer to the school that dominated society and legitimized policies. This school was not responsible for social exclusion, as graduates could find jobs corresponding to their training.
32. Isabel Lelis, "O trabalho docente na escola de massa: desafios e perspectivas," *Sociologias* 14, no. 29 (2012).
33. Bernard Charlot, "Relação com o saber e com a escola entre estudantes de periferia," *Cadernos de Pesquisa* n. 97 (1996); Rui Canário, *A escola tem futuro? Das promessas às incertezas* (Porto Alegre: Artmed, 2006).
34. Izabel Galvão and Marília Sposito, "A experiência e as percepções de jovens na vida escolar na encruzilhada das aprendizagens: a indisciplina, a violência e o conhecimento, *Perspectiva* 22, no. 2 (2004).
35. Emílio Tenti Fanfani, "Aqueles que colocam o corpo. O professor do ensino médio na Argentina hoje," *Educação e Revista* no. 1 (2010).
36. Silvana S. A. Mesquita,*O exercício da docência no ensino médio: a centralidade do papel do professor no trabalho com jovens da periferia* (Pontifícia Universidade Católica do Rio de Janeiro, 2016).
37. Paulo Freire, *Pedagogy of the Oppressed* (New York: Herder and Herder, 1970).
38. Freire, *Pedagogy of the Oppressed*, 38.
39. Freire, *Pedagogy of the Oppressed*, 28.
40. This part of the text is an adapted version of Maria Inês Marcondes, Vânia Finholdt Angelo Leite, and Rosane Karl Ramos, "Theory, Practice and Research in Initial Teacher Education in Brazil: Challenges and Alternatives," *European Journal of Teacher Education* 40, no. 3 (2017).
41. Brasil, "Diretrizes Curriculares Nacionais para a Formação de Professores da Educação Básica, em nível superior" (Brasília: Ministério da educação, 2015).
42. For those Afro-slave descendants who live in protected communities called *quilombos*.
43. Brasil, "Diretrizes Curriculares Nacionais para a Formação de Professores da Educação Básica, em nível superior," 43.
44. The political pedagogical project is a document created by each educational institution, whether basic school or higher education institution, which presents the mission, aims, and main pedagogical and political aspects of each individual institution.
45. Coordenação de Aperfeiçoamento de Pessoal de Nível Superior. CAPES is one of the major Brazilian government agencies to foster scientific and scholarly research and projects.
46. Brasil, "Regulamento do programa institucional de bolsa de iniciação à docência" (Brasilia: CAPES), https://www.capes.gov.br/images/stories/download/legislacao/15042016-Portaria-46-Regulamento-PIBID-completa.pdf
47. Brasil, *Relatório de Gestão PIBID 2009–2013*. Brasilia: CAPES. Management Report, PIBID, 2013, p. 43, http://www.capes.gov.br/images/stories/download/bolsas/1892014-relatorio-PIBID.pdf.
48. Rui Canário,"Um processo estratégico de mudança—Projeto ECO 1986–1992,"*Ex-

periências e Reflexões (Lisboa: IIE, 1994); Antônio Nóvoa,"Nada substitui um bom professor: propostas para uma revolução no campo da formação de professores,"in *Por uma política nacional de formação de professores,* Bernadete Gatti et al., eds. (São Paulo: Editora Unesp, 2013); Maurice Tardif, *Saberes docentes e formação profissional* (Petrópolis: Vozes, 2002).

49. Antônio Nóvoa, "Nada substitui um bom professor," 50.

50. Bernadete Gatti, "Formação inicial de professores para educação básica: pesquisas e políticas educationais," *Estudos em Avaliação Educational* 25 no. 57 (2014).

51. Gatti, "Formação inicial de professorespara educação básica, 104.

52. Maurice Tardif, "A profissionalização do ensino passados trinta anos: dois passos para a frente, três para trás," *Educação & Sociedade* 34, no. 123 (2013).

CHAPTER THREE

Preparing Teachers for the Schools We Have or for the Schools We Want?

Challenges and Changes in Catalonia (Spain)

EDUARD VALLORY

> As formal teaching and training grow in extent, there is the danger of creating an undesirable split between the experience gained in more direct associations and what is acquired in school. This danger was never greater than at the present time, on account of the rapid growth in the last few centuries of knowledge and technical modes of skill.
> —*John Dewey, Democracy and Education (1916)*

> The teacher should now be a guide who enables learners, from early childhood throughout their learning trajectories, to develop and advance through the constantly expanding maze of knowledge . . . We must, therefore, rethink the content and objectives of teacher education and training.
> —*Rethinking Education, UNESCO (2015)*

An education system cannot be reshaped without also reshaping the way teachers are trained. In Catalonia, an autonomous community within Spain (with a self-government that includes a Parliament and government bodies responsible for public education, under Spanish basic rules), this has been a clear concern; one that became more acute with the 2009 adoption of the Catalan Education Act, which called for a competency-based education system. Since then, several prominent initiatives have contributed to advancing that change, including the Program for Improvement and Innovation in Teacher Training (MIF), launched jointly by the government of Catalonia and 10 universities in 2013; and the three-years civil society-led initiative

Escola Nova 21: Alliance for an Advanced Education System, which indirectly influence teacher training by reconsidering the role of the educator in the learning environment.

The last UNESCO report, *Rethinking Education* (2015), summarizes in a single sentence what are at the same time the two main reasons for educational change and the two main elements that must be changed: "Rethinking the purpose of education and the organization of learning has never been more urgent."[1] Any reflection on teacher preparation must be situated in this context.

First, we should *rethink the purpose of education,* because it can no longer be conceived as the simple transmission of knowledge; instead, as the report tells us, "Education is the deliberate process of acquiring knowledge and developing the competencies to apply that knowledge in relevant situations."[2] Recognizing that the context in which these "relevant situations" will occur is also profoundly altered—evolving global challenges, exponential technological growth—the body of necessary competencies must also be revised in a wide competency-based curriculum.

The *Incheon Declaration "Education 2030,"* adopted by the more than one hundred governments attending the World Education Forum (UNESCO and UN System) in May 2015, states this clearly: "Quality education fosters creativity and knowledge, and ensures the acquisition of the foundational skills of literacy and numeracy as well as analytical, problem solving and other high-level cognitive, interpersonal and social skills. It also develops the skills, values and attitudes that enable citizens to lead healthy and fulfilled lives, make informed decisions, and respond to local and global challenges through education for sustainable development and global citizenship education."[3]

Second, we must *rethink the organization of learning,* because most education systems and schools were designed to facilitate the transmission of facts and concepts by rote learning—memorizing and repeating back the words of the teacher and the contents of the textbook. To this end, diverse elements of education systems have been designed to serve that goal of transmission. Teacher training, teacher selection, the physical environment of the school, curriculum contents, learning practices, and assessment tools have been designed in a way that research now shows can neither develop needed competencies, nor properly support the acquisition of related knowledge—that is, information, understanding, skills, attitudes, and values.

To rethink the purpose of education and the organization of learning also requires rethinking the desired profile and competencies of teachers and the characteristics of their training. On this subject, the 2015 UNESCO report states: "The missions and careers of teachers must constantly be recast and reconsidered in the light of new requirements and new challenges to education in a constantly changing globalized world."[4]

Conceiving of teachers as *guides* is quite different from casting them as repositories of information for rote learning. This is equally important for the school as it is for the university, as Harvard Professor Alfred North Whitehead observed in 1919: "So far as the mere imparting of information is concerned, no university has had any justification for existence since the popularization of printing in the fifteenth century."[5]

To read thinkers like Dewey and Whitehead a century later illustrates that this is not new territory; we have not managed to change either the conception of school or teacher training in one hundred years. And, all of this means that we still face a parallel challenge in teacher training: to redefine the competencies a teacher must have within the new paradigm of education, to change the way we learn and teach at the university level, and to create programs capable of developing those competencies and assessment systems that can adequately measure them.

The struggles to reform university-level teacher training in Catalonia and in Spain have been highly conditioned by this parallel challenge, which we will explore in depth in this chapter. First, I will explain the constraints created by the highly bureaucratic and centralized public education system. Second, I will describe the past and present of teacher training in Catalonia and in the broader Spanish context. Third, I will connect that experience with the limits of universities in competency-based education. Finally, I will review actions being taken, both in teacher training and in the education system, toward a common goal.

What School Are We Training Teachers For? A Question for Catalonia
The design for the universalization of public education in nineteenth-century Spain followed the Prussian and French bureaucratic, centralized models. The public school was conceived as an extension of the state which managed the transmission and acquisition of facts through rote learning (memorization and mechanical repetition). In this centralized model, schools were designed to work from a prescriptive standardized curriculum concretized in the textbook, and thus, the teacher played the role of a transmitter of the same basic standardized curriculum, regardless of the pupils' context.

Based on these assumptions, the entirety of the public education system was designed to facilitate this transmission, and many of these design characteristics persist:

— *Low educational autonomy of schools.* Based on a transmission model, schools did not need to act with autonomy. They acted as a bureaucratic delegation of the state to implement the curriculum.
— *External supervisors, no educational leadership.* The role of the school principal was purely bureaucratic, without any requirement for educational leadership. State supervisors or *inspectores* (inspectors) monitored the school, ensuring that it was performing according to standards.
— *Teachers are civil servants.* Access to the position of public school teacher is achieved through an official standardized examination (*oposiciones*), with no competency-based element, besides practices in a random school; once the examination is passed, the candidate becomes a civil servant for life and "owns" his or her position without any additional accountability.
— *Teachers belong to the system, not to a particular school.* The teacher conceived as a transmitter of facts is interchangeable; therefore, while the position of the teacher's tenure is linked to a particular school, the teacher belongs to a body of civil servants (*cuerpo de funcionarios*), categorized into three groups: elementary/primary school teachers; secondary school teachers; and inspectors.
— *Teacher seniority defines precedence for mobility.* Salary increases for public school teachers (civil servants) depend fundamentally on seniority, not on assessed performance; in addition, because they belong to the centralized body of civil servants, each year teachers can apply to transfer competitions (*concursos de traslado*) to change school. Individual seniority establishes precedence, so school principals have very limited capacity to select their own staff based on their educational project.
— *Narrow rote-based assessment systems.* Just as is the case with the examinations used to fill public school teacher positions, assessments for students are primarily based on information recall and regurgitation, asking learners to merely repeat information they have retained in the short term, without asking them to make sense of it, explain it, or apply it.

The structure of public schooling in Spain, many rules related to public education, and the basis of teacher training, are still founded on obsolete nineteenth-century assumptions: the assumption that the acquisition of encyclopedic knowledge is a sign of culture and intelligence, in contrast with manual labor; "the notion that some subjects and methods and that acquaintance with certain facts and truths possess educational value in and of themselves";[6] the assumption that therefore the school should be a transmitter of those pieces of knowledge, selected and structured according to the age of children, who learn in the same way and at the same speed; and the assumption that assessment serves to support secondary education in its role as mainly a preparatory period to gain access to higher education; the "smartest" have the best grades and the best can go to university; the less smart have worse grades or fail and will develop studies and careers of lower status.

At the end of the nineteenth century and beginning of the twentieth, as in many other societies, Catalonia and Spain saw several movements that proposed to radically change the education system from the transmission-based model to a learner-centered approach. The "Institución Libre de Enseñanza," established in Madrid in 1876 by university professors expelled for ideological reasons—in a dogmatic, religious, and traditional context—began to promote a new educational approach and to import international theories and concepts of education. In the first third of the twentieth century, several Catalan initiatives started to work for change in the education system, including Francesc Ferrer i Guàrdia's "Escola Moderna." All those initiatives of progressive education, linked to the ideas of Dewey, Montessori, Freinet, or Decroly, among others, were later called the "Escola Nova" (New School) movement—as Ferrière's "école nouvelle."

Throughout the twentieth century, the several restorations of self-governing institutions in Catalonia (1914, 1931, and 1977) have been linked with a focus on improving education. In 1914, the Catalan aggregation of provincial councils became a first step toward self-government—the Mancomunitat de Catalunya, established the same year, which created a summer school to bring teachers trained in official state programs up to date. The summer school was directed by a Catalan graduate of the University of Chicago, who introduced John Dewey's theories and Maria Montessori's educational methodologies to the program. In 1915, the Mancomunitat created the first Montessori schools outside of Italy, five of them as public schools. All were closed in 1923, when the Mancomunitat de Catalunya was dismantled by the dictatorship of General Primo de Rivera in Spain (1923–29). In addition, in 1916, the Barcelona city council had started to develop municipal schools with the excuse of addressing health issues; they were empowered to select their own teachers and employed active learning methodologies. These schools remained open during the dictatorship of the 1920s.

In 1931, when the Spanish Republic was settled and the King of Spain abdicated, Catalonia obtained self-government status, the Generalitat, with an executive government and a Parliament. Catalan institutions resumed work for educational change and promoted learner-centered developments in the curriculum, structure of schools, teacher training, and teacher selection, in parallel to similar changes underway through the Spanish Republican government. Unhappily, the coup d'état and the long military dictatorship of General Francisco Franco (1939–77) terminated these efforts for change and returned Spain to the nineteenth-century model of rote learning and transmission of facts. An example of that model came at the beginning of the dictatorship, when in order to cover positions vacant in consequence of ideological purging and exile, the new regime decided that some fascist soldiers who had been disabled in the 1936–39 civil war could obtain a civil servant position as a teacher or education inspector without having had any training in education: ideology was enough.

When the mid-1960s saw a tentative relaxation of the military dictatorship that allowed for the creation of private schools, Catalan cooperative schools, which were formed by teachers or parents and which emulated prewar active education efforts, flourished. Nevertheless, this movement was not strong enough to overcome the inertia of the nineteenth-century education system when, after Franco's death, democracy was reestablished in all of Spain in 1978.

And thus today, when we review assumptions that were disputed a century ago by the New School movement, we must recognize that they are still at the foundation of what defines our schools. Although since 1990 official government rules and acts use the language of the "competency-based curriculum," subjects are still the effective unit within the school system, textbooks still constitute the actual curriculum, and teachers still function as transmitters of facts and concepts.

Over the last four decades, Spanish education legislation has certainly evolved. Influenced by international approaches, like those described in the 1972 UNESCO report *Learning to Be: The World of Education Today and Tomorrow*,[7] the 1990 Spanish Act LOGSE (General Organization of the Education System Organic Act) introduced in the Spanish education system a first approach of a competency-based education. It defined curricular contents beyond information, including understanding, procedures (skills), and attitudes and values, indicating that knowledge should be constructed instead of merely transmitted, and thus indicating the need for formative evaluation processes.

During the 1990s, several international initiatives delved into the competency-based educational approach: the UNESCO Delors Report *Learning: The Treasure Within* (1996), which established the four pillars of learning (to know, to be, to do, to live together); the 1997 OECD initiative DeSeCo (Definition and Selection of Competencies); and the US National Research Council work *How People Learn: Brain, Mind, Experience, and School* (1999). Nevertheless, necessary structural changes in the system and essential investments in the training of education professionals were not made to support the implementation of the LOGSE. This has led to a system that lives with an important gap between discourse and practice. It uses the language of competencies but thinks in subjects; it talks about competency-based contents but finds the actual contents in textbooks; it refers to formative and competency-based evaluation but mostly implements tests, written exercises, and examinations of rote learning.

This gap between discourse and reality is not unique to Catalonia or Spain. Although there exists an international consensus that we must move school curriculums and the whole education system from the transmission of facts to the development of competencies,[8] which implies a relevant change in the role of the teacher, most of the indicators we use to assess our work and our approach to teacher training continue to respond to the old paradigm. In this regard, there is a strong relationship of dependency between the model of school and the profile of teacher. Teacher training is highly conditioned by the accepted model of school; any change in the former must be coordinated with changes in the latter.

This underlines the importance of using knowledge generated through research to make systemic updates in educational practice. "In the field of learning, the past quarter century has been a period of major research advances," states the 1999 US National Research Council report; "these developments in understanding how humans learn have particular significance in light of changes in what is expected of the nation's education systems."[9]

Relevant education reports from international organizations lead us in the same direction. In 2010, the OECD published the research report *The Nature of Learning*,[10] which indicates the ILE (Innovative Learning Environments) seven principles of learning that should underpin all education practices. Similarly, the UNESCO report *Rethinking Education* states very clearly the consequences for this transformation in teacher training: "We must rethink the content and objectives of teacher education and training. Teachers need to be trained to facilitate learning, to understand diversity, to be inclusive, and to develop competencies for living together and for protecting and improving the environment. They must foster classroom environments that are respectful and secure, encourage self-esteem and autonomy, and use a wide range of pedagogical and didactical strategies."[11]

Educational transformation proposes a double challenge: to overcome our inheritance of the transmission-based model and to move beyond indicators of quality primarily based on quantifiable knowledge. Even the PISA tests (Programme for International Student Assessment), which are competency-based, are widely interpreted as tests of basic knowledge by popular media: the equivalent of level in the former subjects of language, math, and science. For that reason, changes in teacher training must be framed within the reformulation of the entire education system. Moving from the academic, transmission-based, and selective school to the inclusive school that is centered on learning, competency-based, and focused on guiding students to pursue their own potentials and interests, requires a profound transformation of all components that contribute to the education process: the initial and continuing training of teachers, teaching methods and practices, organization of contents, monitoring of student progress and indicators of evaluation, resources, and materials, management and structure of teaching teams, social organization of the classroom, models for living together and conflict resolution, use and characteristics of space, time management, and so on.

Teacher Training in Spain and Catalonia, and Its Limitations

The transformation of educational practices in Spain and Catalonia, both in schools and in universities, to generate useful and significant learning experiences has advanced in many areas thanks to the work of professionals at all levels. Even so, there continues to be a general assumption that real learning is defined by rote learning, which still influences the school at all levels, including the role of teachers, teacher training, and university education.

In that respect, two main limitations have deeply affected teacher training in Spain as a whole and in Catalonia, as they have in other countries. The first limitation is the assumption that the age of children determines the relevance of their education and, therefore, how much training their teachers should be required to receive. The second limitation is the lack of the competency-based approach in universities, which tends to lead to a primarily theoretical teacher training experience.

The First Limitation: How Much Training Is Needed to Be a Teacher?
Several elements that influence teacher training have evolved in parallel. One is the long tradition of regarding teaching as a low-status profession. Another is the separation between primary and secondary education, and as a consequence, the different professional categories and training that teachers of primary and secondary students receive. And finally, is the unfinished education reform in Spain, started in 1990, which maintained and even formalized the separation between primary and secondary education.

From the origin of teacher training schools (Escuela Normal) in Spain in the mid-1800s until the 1970s, the official degree required to enter the profession in compulsory (primary) schooling was non-university, equivalent to a high school diploma (with the exception of the years of the 2nd Republic: 1931–39). In 1972, teacher training schools became university schools, although this change was not properly implemented until 1983. Since then, an official Spanish university degree has been a compulsory requirement to become a teacher in Spain, and thus only universities—since only they grant the degrees—could provide the needed training to become a teacher.

An act adopted in 1970, in the last years of Franco's dictatorship, made education compulsory between the ages of 6 and 14. Secondary education (ages 14 to 18), either through the academic baccalaureate or vocational training, remained noncompulsory. Thus, in public schooling, primary and secondary education were housed in different buildings and carried out by two distinct bodies of civil servants. Likewise, the university undergraduate teaching degree was meant only for primary school teachers. Secondary school teachers were required to obtain a university degree in their discipline, and in addition, complete a short (three-month) university course on teaching/education.

The assumption that the school was primarily a place for the transmission and memorization of facts and concepts helped to bolster the outdated preconception that the older the child, the more knowledge can be transmitted. Thus, secondary education teachers had higher salaries and were required to have more years of training than their primary school counterparts, even though their training only extended to their discipline: practically no knowledge of how people learn or how to develop learning strategies was provided or required.

The LOGSE Act of 1990 changed the structure of compulsory education, breaking it into two phases: a primary education remained compulsory from ages 6 to 12; and a newly designed compulsory secondary education from ages 12 to 16. For ages 16 to 18 (instead of 14 to 18 as has been the case until this point), noncompulsory secondary education remained available through both academic (baccalaureate) and professional (vocational training) paths.

The implementation of the 1990 reform perpetuated the separation of primary and secondary school teachers. Rather than extending primary education by two years, creating comprehensive schools for ages 6 to 16, and updating teacher training, it was decided that now-compulsory secondary education (ages 12 to 16) would be moved to high schools and carried out by teachers trained in disciplines, with practically no training in learning methods or practices. Secondary school teachers are therefore selected primarily for their knowledge of a discipline, like history, physics, math, or biology.

In practice, this approach has translated into a huge leap between primary and secondary school, with the result that, at the age of 12, children must change schools and, typically, enter into an experience even more centered on rote learning. It should be noticed that Spain has one of the highest levels of early school leaving and educational failure in the European Union (between 30% in 2006 and 20% in 2018, according to Eurostat),[12] to which the poor transition from primary to secondary contributes.

Until the 2000s, the difference between primary and secondary school teacher training was significant:

—A primary school teacher was required to be a "Diplomado" in primary teaching (a three-year university undergraduate degree).[13]

—A secondary school teacher was required to be a "Licenciado" in a discipline (a four- or five-year university degree), plus complete a three-month (120-hour) "course of pedagogical aptitude" (CAP), composed of 80 hours of theory and 40 hours of practical training.

As a result, a large number of teachers currently working in the system are a product of this model of preparation. After the early 2000s, this marked

Preparing Teachers for the Schools We Have or for the Schools We Want?

TABLE 3.1
Changes in teacher certification following 1990 by grade level

Until 1990		Currently	
Primary Ed.	Secondary Ed.	Primary Ed.	Secondary Ed.
Compulsory, for ages 6–14	Noncompulsory for ages 14–18	Compulsory, for ages 6–12	Compulsory (ages 12–16); non-compulsory for ages 16–18
Teachers must hold a "Diplomatura" (3-year university teaching degree)	Teachers must hold a "Licenciatura" (5-year university degree in their discipline) plus a 120-hour education course (CAP)	Teachers must hold a "Grado" (4-year university teaching degree)	Teachers must hold a "Grado" (4-year university degree in their discipline) plus a 1-year master's degree in secondary school teaching.

difference between the training of primary and secondary school teachers was slightly reduced for two reasons:

— First, the implementation of the Bologna Process[14] (2007) in Spain transformed primary school teacher training into a four-year university degree: a BA (Grado) in teaching.
— Second, in 2009 the 120-hour CAP was replaced with a one-year master's degree, so that secondary school teachers were required to have a four-year university degree in a discipline plus a one-year master's degree in secondary school teaching.

It continues to be true, therefore, that in Spain the training required to be a kindergarten teacher, a primary school teacher, or a secondary school teacher, increases with the age of the children taught, as do the corresponding teacher salaries. This is tantamount to suggesting that a pediatrician requires less training than a geriatrician and should be paid a smaller salary. In keeping with this approach, primary public school teachers belong to a lower body of civil servants.

The Second Limitation: Specialized, Non-Competency-Based University Degrees

Aside from the structure of school education in Spain, and the consequent profiles and requirements defined for teacher training, the way universities approach learning entails its own limitations, which strongly influences teachers' preparation.

First, we find a high level of specialization in university degrees. Despite the process leading to the European Higher Education Area, which attempted to create a mechanism for translation among European university degrees, undergraduate university degrees in Spain are still very particular, and many times universities operate on an assumption of scholarly excellence that is often distant from—and disregards—expertise at practice. That creates limitations both for (elementary/primary) teaching degrees and for the undergraduate studies undertaken previous to the master's degree for secondary school teachers. It also has the effect of limiting teachers' competency to employ holistic, interdisciplinary learning practices.

As an illustration, in Spain to be a lawyer you must take a four-year undergraduate university degree in law. That means that when entering the university at the age of 18, young people must effectively choose their professional path: biologist or architect, physician or philosopher. In this system it would be quite improbable to find the cases made possible by the Anglo-Saxon liberal arts model, in which a 29-year-old history PhD could feasibly return to graduate school and become a lawyer.

Specialization has implications for the teacher training debate, because many people with a specialized undergraduate degree in philosophy, history, literature, biology, physics, chemistry, or math, who do not find a career opportunity with their degree, can decide to take the one-year master's degree program and exit as a fully qualified secondary school teacher.

To these structural characteristics must be added the reality that universities are themselves still very poor at developing competencies. The educational shift from the transmission of facts and concepts to the development of competencies has not been properly achieved either in schools or at the university level and, thus, university teacher training is not preparing candidates in this sense. Given UNESCO's assessment that "education is the deliberate process of acquiring knowledge and developing the competencies to apply that knowledge in relevant situations,"[15] and accepting that the development of competencies requires learning processes other than rote learning,[16] we can see that this weakness at the university level will impact teaching in schools.

Nevertheless, professional competencies to develop complex learning processes, or competency-based education, even at a superficial level, are not a requirement to become a university professor of education in Spain, and few people think that it should. As a professor from the School of Education of the Complutense University (Madrid) stated in a press interview: "In the University (worldwide), specific training for university teaching is occasional and voluntary. What is important is the knowledge."[17]

Universities' limitations in competencies development are also linked to assessment. Here, the Spanish education system remains mostly focused on retention of facts (memorization) and does very poorly in assessing competencies (mostly mechanical, not functional). This approach extends to university exams and evaluations, the entry examination for university, and secondary school assessments. Likewise, to become a university professor in a Spanish public university a candidate must just defend a topic of his/her selection in front of a committee, in addition to demonstrating a body of published research and previous teaching experience.

A proper competency-based education requires a profound change in the measurement of learning achievement. In their deep critique of achievement tests, James Heckman et al. have shown the limitations of the assessment tools currently used in the educational system.[18] What we currently assess are pieces of knowledge that have been memorized, at least in the short term. This can provide us with very little insight into learning, as rote learning itself fails as a building block for relevant competencies like complex problem solving, critical thinking, creativity, and communication.

Finally, we encounter another limitation in the growing consensus that teacher training should be primarily residential (clinical), like the training designed for physicians. If we pursue this approach, it is essential that we identify schools that can serve as the equivalent of teaching hospitals, whose directors and staff are exemplars and mentors to those entering the profession, and whose practice reflects the newly imagined role of the teacher in the development of fundamentally competency-based learning experiences.

However, in 2018, the Spanish Congress rejected a proposal to establish a clinical residence model for prospective school teachers. The main limitation of the initiative was that it copied the model of a government-led centralized memorization-based examination that medical doctors carry out before their clinical residency. That sort of examination, in addition to going against the competency-based model, could introduce systems of ideological control depending on the exam questions. At the same time, the initiative generated strong resistance from trade unions, which said that challenging the current selection model called into question the competencies of current teachers.

At present, the practical aspect of teacher training in Spain is quite unbalanced: it represents 21% of total training time for primary school teachers, and just 7% of total training time for secondary school teachers. Aside from the number of hours, there is the question of the relationship between the practicum to the rest of the teacher training program: "When students take courses before rather than during clinical practice, those courses all too often seem irrelevant once the student is in a school for the practicum experience."[19]

Achieving a balance of practical experience for trainee teachers is even more relevant when they will be asked to act as reflective strategists for learning, instead of implementers of a static curriculum. It is not only the disjunction between theory and practice that makes it difficult to apply theoretical knowledge to real-life situations but also the rote learning practices that many trainee teachers will observe during their practicum, generating a counterproductive learning experience.

The dilemma we face when deciding if we will prepare teachers for the school we have, or for the school we want, becomes even more evident in this practical or clinical phase of training. Educational systems in which clinical residency is central for teacher training, as is the case in Finland and in Estonia, make use of exemplar schools that serve the double purpose of training educators and developing and testing innovative learning practices. Here, teacher candidates rely on the supervision of educators who have the competencies that they want to develop. This guarantees that the training of future teachers is focused on the schools they want, more than those that they have.

In contrast, in the Catalan and Spanish context, the schools that serve as locations for practical training are not selected on the basis of excellence in learning practice, but rather on the basis of student test results, or even simple capacity to take on trainees.

With this we close the circle of challenges to overcome for teacher training in Catalonia: inherited models that assume that teachers of young children require less training; access to jobs based on tests of rote learning; highly specialized university education with too much rote learning; assessment systems linked to rote learning; and the absence of standards to ensure that teacher candidates carry out their practical work in exemplar schools.

Actions Being Taken to Enhance Teacher Training

In the Catalan context, the past five years have seen diverse initiatives designed to revise and improve the university-level training that constitutes the only existing path to becoming a teacher. In fact, although initial teacher training is regulated by Spanish legislation, which establishes the number of credits and the minimum number of hours to be dedicated to specific contents and to the practicum, there is room for movement in terms of methodology and model, in establishing access requirements to training programs and, in the mid- to long term, for advancing new legislation relevant to teacher preparation.

Access to university studies in Spain depends on the grade achieved on a single examination (Selectividad) that all students who wish to enter university must take. The minimum grade required to enter a particular degree program reflects only the relationship between supply and demand. As the minimum grade required to enter teaching studies has been low, in 2012 one first step taken was to reduce the overall number of seats available in teaching degrees, leading to a slight increase in the grade required to enter. At the same time, a double undergraduate teaching degree (a five-year program combining elementary and primary school undergraduate teaching degrees, which are two separate programs of four years each) was created with the purpose of attracting top candidates through a high-grade requirement for entry.

In order to monitor the progress of these two initiatives, and to promote broad improvement of elementary and primary teacher training in Catalonia, the government of Catalonia and 10 universities created in 2013 the Program for the Improvement and Innovation in Primary School Teachers Training (MIF Program), with a board composed of the university deans of education, other faculty, and representatives of the government. The program does not deal directly with secondary teacher preparation.

Since then, the MIF has developed several lines of action. The first and most important is the analysis and debate of a new university model for training teachers, led by a group composed of university scholars, school principals, and members of the public administration. The work of the group has opened up a needed space for reflection on teacher education, allowing important issues to be raised, including: the necessity to balance the educational requirements for primary and secondary school teachers; the value of a practicum period in the form of a clinical residency for the development of competencies for teacher students; and the importance of reviewing competencies of university professors of education in order to improve the level and rigor of university teacher training.[20] The goal of this debate is to help create consensus on changes to teacher training that could be undertaken through an agreement among universities and the Catalan government, and also to promote legislative changes at the Spanish level, where the overall content and structure of teacher training is decided.

Seven other thematic groups, where school teachers are also represented, are working on issues like assessment of the new teacher degrees created with the European Higher Education Area, the development of the new double undergraduate teaching degree, prospects and challenges of the clinical residency, linguistic and digital competencies of teachers, and the filter to access the university programs.

On that last issue, a relevant action of the MIF has been the establishment of a joint entry common aptitude test for the undergraduate elementary and primary teacher programs for all Catalan schools of education, intended to assess communication skills, mathematical logic, and reasoning skills, in addition to the single general examination (Selectividad). The exam was done for the first time in June 2017, for all universities (public and private), and it resulted in a reduction of 30% of selected applicants.

In addition, the MIF has promoted specific research on interdisciplinary and competency-based teacher training through competitive research grants, involving around 400 university researchers. It also makes connections with teacher training research already underway in other countries through short-term international travel grants for university professors to study initiatives, experiences, or innovations in initial teacher preparation and to channel this research into the improvement of the teacher training model in Catalan universities.

Last, but not least, the MIF program has been working to increase educational opportunities for teaching students. It has created a study abroad support program, which has already offered 120 scholarships for teaching students to study in other European countries or in North America. The program aims to develop the international profile of future educators, as well as their ability to use research to improve their practice and to continually develop their own competencies.

Another relevant initiative which could impact teacher training in Catalonia has been the three-year program Escola Nova 21: Aliança per un sistema educatiu avançat[21] (New School 21: Alliance for an Advanced Education System), launched in 2016 by three nonprofit institutions and one university,[22] together with 25 innovative Catalan primary and secondary schools. The program's objectives were to generate social awareness of the need for a transformation of the Catalan education system toward a fully competency-based one, leading to social pressure for system reforms, and to systematize and develop the knowledge and processes necessary to make that change possible. An open call in April 2016 for voluntary participation in the program brought together in just three months 481 schools, representing around 16% of the Catalan education system.

Escola Nova 21 has been highly focused on the "school that we want," which is to say, on the basic characteristics that all schools must have today, which have been synthesized into a framework of four elements: (a) an educational *Purpose* committed to the development of competencies for life in the context of the knowledge society (the Four Pillars of Learning as described by UNESCO,[23] including the twenty-first-century competencies); (b) learning *Practices* that are personalized and holistic, based on existent research into how humans learn (the ILE 7 principles of learning, as described in Dumont et al.).[24] (c) holistic *Assessment* of all competencies, directed at the development of self-regulation and autonomy and at the improvement of learning; and (d) *Organization* in service of learning, with the three characteristics of an innovative learning environment:[25] capacity to innovate, assess and improve its pedagogical core; becoming formative organizations with learning leadership; and openness to partnerships and engagement with the communities.

In adopting this framework as a shared horizon for the whole education system, Escola Nova 21 sought to define and generate during its three years (2016–19) public demand for the "school that we want" through four main actions: consolidating advancements that have already been made in individual schools and in the overall system; generating and experimenting with protocols designed to facilitate systemic transformation of schools; developing collaborative work through extensive networks for educational change; and constructing alliances with public administrations that promote shared responsibility for change.

The first action, focused to support normative change toward competency-based learning and evaluation practices, worked to highlight the existence of Catalan schools that are already properly competency-based—including Escola Nova 21's 25 initial innovative schools—and grow their public educational reputation. These 25 reference schools, public and charter, practice a diversity of methodologies but share the four key elements of the framework. Learning at these schools is no longer dependent on subjects or on the individual work of teachers but is developed through co-teaching in cooperative schoolwide teams, competency-based approaches like project-based learning, and other strategies to develop holistic and interdisciplinary educational experiences. Thus, the main goals of the action were both to facilitate an ongoing grounding of these educational projects and to progressively introduce these schools as references for the system, including for the purposes of teacher training.

The second action of the program has been to develop and test a three-year protocol for intensive and systematic school transformation using a representative[26] sample of 30 schools. The goal of this work was to generate procedures through which all schools in Catalonia could be systematically transformed with the support of the appropriate public entities, once Escola Nova 21 has run its course. Key elements of this protocol were the month-long training residencies undertaken by teachers from the 30 schools of the representative sample at the initial 25 innovative schools, which played the role of reference schools that showed a potential to follow for the university-based teacher training.

The third action on collaborative work was based in a critical mass needed to launch the broad movement for change, found in the nearly 500 primary and secondary schools that voluntarily joined the Escola Nova 21 program. The three-year intervention was developed through more than 60 local networks of between 6 and 10 schools each, constituted with the support of local city halls, and employing the Spiral of Inquiry methodology[27] to adapt the process of education change to each school's zone of proximal development.

Finally, the fourth action on building alliances for the proposed change to become generalized throughout the system, was made through the work of an Escola Nova 21 team to facilitate and ensure that the Catalan government's Department of Education take on the responsibility for the initiatives for change promoted by Escola Nova 21 and to extend education change within all schools in the system.

Escola Nova 21's four-point framework (Purpose, Practice, Evaluation, and Organization) has facilitated the identification of the 25 initial innovative schools that are leaders in Catalan educational innovation and has enhanced our understanding of which profile should have the reference schools that, in the future, should host the clinical residencies for trainee teachers. The intervention proposed by the program was intended to increase the number of schools that meet these characteristics and, thus, could help meet demand for practicums in competency-based school environments. Indeed, the mobility of teachers within the system and their eminently transmission-based training has made the continuity of the innovative educational projects developed by these schools difficult to maintain. For this reason, Escola Nova 21 has sought to raise the profile of the schools and to develop their public reputations with the idea of gathering support for their long-term survival and growth.

A point of connection between the MIF program's efforts to update teacher training in universities, and the Escola Nova 21 Alliance to transform Catalan schools, could be found in the Mid-career Master's degree in Elementary and Primary School Teaching Improvement (Màster en Millora dels Ensenyaments d'Educació Infantil i Primària), which started in February 2017 as an innovative two-year part-time program endorsed by the Catalan Ministry of Education and co-organized by the University of Vic and the Open University of Catalonia (UOC). The master's program, whose design and implementation I was commissioned to supervise, has been promoted by the Catalan government as part of an effort to update the training of primary school teachers already placed in schools, using a competency-based approach. The desired outcome is that graduates will become reflective strategists for learning, as well as agents of change in their schools.

That master's program is the first university teacher training program to adopt a case-based approach in that system, using competency-based modules, instead of subjects, and using a subset of Escola Nova 21's reference schools as case studies. Two pilot editions of the master's (2017–19) have tested the program before being launched for the entire Catalan education system. The master's competency-based model experience is also contributing to the existing work to redevelop the Master for Secondary School Teachers by the Pompeu Fabra University (UPF) and the UOC in a competency-based model, a step which reinforces teacher-training change throughout Catalonia.

Furthermore, in 2017 the Catalan government created the Margalida Comas Program for the Improvement of Teaching and Learning at the university, in order to extend to the university system as a whole the updating of teaching and learning methods and the competency-based assessment, thus going beyond to the improvement of the teachers' training.

Conclusion

In Catalonia and Spain, as in many other countries, the crisis in teacher training is linked to our continuing use of the industrial school model, conditioned by nineteenth-century assumptions on the purpose of education and of what and how we should learn and teach. Although the discourse of our educational legislation has changed, in a practical sense this has not translated into real educational reform.

The transformation of the education system and of teacher training are two inseparable and necessary processes, both of which must go forward if we are to achieve "the school we want." In this school of a competency-based curriculum system, the teacher is a guide and a learning strategist, a role that requires vastly different competencies from that of the implementer of a traditional prescriptive rote-learning curriculum. But even as we begin to clearly define the school that we want, our systems largely continue to train teachers for the school that we have, keeping us locked in a vicious cycle of rote learning at all levels of the system.

Escaping this educational inertia will require concerted efforts at many levels: from administration, to schools, to universities. Many of these efforts are underway in Catalonia, through the approaches to reform teacher education at the undergraduate and postgraduate levels, the prospects to implement clinical residencies for teaching students at university, and the definition of a framework for the school we want, through a civil society–driven initiative for education change, which might allow the many actors at work today on behalf of systemic change to concentrate and magnify their efforts.

NOTES

This chapter is based on a paper prepared for "The Crisis in Teacher Preparation: A Look at the U.S., England and Spain," a symposium in celebration of the 125th anniversary of the Steinhardt School of Culture, Education and Human Development, New York University, March 2, 2016.

1. UNESCO, *Rethinking Education: Towards a Common Goal?* (Paris: UNESCO, 2015), 10.
2. UNESCO, *Rethinking Education*, 79.
3. UNESCO, *Incheon Declaration and Framework for Action: Towards Inclusive and Equitable Education and Lifelong Learning for All* (Paris: UNESCO Publishing, 2016), 8.
4. UNESCO, *Rethinking Education*, 55.
5. Alfred North Whitehead, "Universities and Their Function," in: *The Aims of Education and Other Essays* (New York: The Free Press, [1929] 1967), 92–93.
6. John Dewey, *Experience and Education: An Introduction to the Philosophy of Education* (New York: Touchstone, [1938] 1997), 46.
7. "We are now entitled to talk of a change in the learning process, which is tending to displace the teaching process. New theories of learning highlight the principle of contiguity and the importance of needs and motivations, of choice of content, of the hierarchic nature of learning, the interrelationship between educational content and environment, etc." UNESCO, *Learning To Be: The World of Education Today and Tomorrow (Report to UNESCO*

of the International Commission on the Development of Education) (Paris: UNESCO, 1972), 130.

8. Mmantsetsa Marope, "Reconceptualizing and Repositioning Curriculum in the 21st Century: A Global Paradigm Shift" (Geneva: International Bureau of Education–UNESCO, 2018).

9. National Research Council, *How People Learn: Brain, Mind, Experience, and School,* expanded ed. (Washington, DC: National Academy Press, 2000), 4.

10. Hannah Dumont, David Istance, and Javier Benavides, eds. *The Nature of Learning: Using Research to Inspire Practice* (Paris: Center for Educational Research and Innovation, OECD, 2010).

11. UNESCO, *Rethinking Education,* 55.

12. "Europe 2020 Education Indicators in 2018," Eurostat News Release, April 26, 2019, https://ec.europa.eu/eurostat/documents/2995521/9751510/3-26042019-AP-EN.pdf/49c38a50-52b5-4f97-95f7-483a570fbb36.

13. Since 1970, undergraduate university degrees in Spain were of two varieties: three-year "Diplomaturas" and five-year "Licenciaturas." In 1987, it was ordered that most Licenciaturas (including psychology and pedagogy) were to be shortened to four years. In 2007, in the context of the new European Higher Education Area, the Spanish government decided that all undergraduate degrees (now called "Grados") were to be of four years—whereas in most European countries they were of three years. The former Diplomaturas were extended from three years to four—as was the case of the Diplomatura in teaching degree. This decision was modified in 2014, so that some Grados of three years are now accepted, but this change has not affected teaching degrees.

14. Established in 1999 by 29 European governments, the Bologna Process encompassed a series of agreements to ensure comparable quality and standards in higher education qualifications in Europe. It culminated with the creation of the European Higher Education Area in 2010.

15. UNESCO, *Rethinking Education,* 79.

16. We adopt the UNESCO definition of knowledge: "The information, understanding, skills, values and attitudes acquired through learning." UNESCO, *Rethinking Education,* 11.

17. "En la Universidad (en todo el mundo), la formación específica para docentes es ocasional y voluntaria. Lo importante son los conocimientos," statement of Prof. Julio Carabaña, quoted in "Cómo aprende a enseñar el docente" [How the university professor learns teaching], *El País,* November 14, 2016.

18. James J. Heckman, John Eric Humphries, and Tim Kautz, eds., *The Myth of Achievement Tests: The GED and the Role of Character in American Life* (Chicago: University of Chicago Press, 2014).

19. James W. Fraser and Audra M. Watson, "Why Clinical Experience and Mentoring Are Replacing Student Teaching on the Best Campuses" (Princeton, NJ: The Woodrow Wilson National Fellowship Foundation, 2014), 12.

20. Miquel Martínez, Enric Prats, and Ana Marín "La millora de la formació inicial de mestres: El Programa de Millora i Innovació en la Formació de Mestres, MIF," *Revista Catalana de Pedagogia* (2016), 9, 37.

21. Eduard Vallory, "Rethinking Education in Catalonia: The Escola Nova 21 Alliance"—

A Case Study. UNESCO Education Research and Foresight Working Papers 23 (March) (Paris: UNESCO, 2019).

22. The Escola Nova 21 Alliance was convened by the Center for UNESCO of Catalonia; the Jaume Bofill Foundation, an education think tank; the Open University of Catalonia (the first online university worldwide, 1995); and the "la Caixa" Foundation. Later on, the Diputació de Barcelona (the Provincial Government of Barcelona) joined the previous four as promoter.

23. UNESCO, *Learning: The Treasure Within (Report to UNESCO of the International Commission on Education for the Twenty-First Century)* (Paris: UNESCO, 2016); UNESCO, *Rethinking Education*.

24. Dumont, Istance, and Benavides, *The Nature of Learning*.

25. UNESCO, *Rethinking Education*.

26. The representation reproduces the percentages in Catalonia of public/charter, geographical distribution, socioeconomic profile, primary/secondary, and rural and large city profiles.

27. Helen Timperley, Linda Kaser, and Judy Halbert, "A Framework for Transforming Learning in Schools: Innovation and the Spiral of Inquiry," Seminar Series Paper, 234 (Victoria: Centre for Strategic Education, 2014).

CHAPTER FOUR

Teacher Education Reform and National Development in China (1978–2017)

Four Metaphors

WEI LIAO AND YISU ZHOU

This chapter reviews the history of China's teacher education over the past four decades (1978–2017). Different from previous work on the same topic,[1] this review explores an important relationship that has been scantly examined in the existing literature: how teacher education has been shaping and is being shaped by the national development discourse. Drawing on policy documents, statistical data, and research literature, this chapter contends that teacher education has played varying roles in supporting China's national development during different historical periods. Specifically, teacher education has served as a *cornerstone* for national reconstruction (1978–1992), an *engine* for boosting economic growth (1992–2004), an *equalizer* for harmonizing the society (2004–2012), and a *window* for envisioning a global agenda (since 2012). On the one hand, the national development discourses continually drive the teacher education system to reform its goals, structure, and practices for preparing educators. On the other hand, the development of teacher education in return supports national development.

In the remainder of this chapter, we elaborate on the interactive relationships between teacher education and national development within four specific periods of China's national development. These are: (1) reconstructing a broken society left by the Cultural Revolution (1978–1992); (2) focusing on economic development (1992–2004); (3) constructing a harmonious society (2004–2012); and (4) aiming to rise as a global power (since 2012). Before we dig into each period, two caveats should be mentioned. First, for the purpose of this work, and as informed by previous studies,[2] we use key historical events (e.g., the birth of the "Reform and Open Door" policy in 1978) to organize the past four decades into the aforementioned four chronological periods. However, we by no means intend to suggest that how we segment the history is the only or best way. Neither do we mean to imply the four periods are neatly separate from one another. Rather, we believe history is a continuous flow of time and events. Therefore, we devote special efforts to show how each period relates to the ones before and after it. Second, we use a metaphorical approach[3] to try and capture the key role(s) that teacher education plays in each of the four national development stages. However, we acknowledge that teacher education may concurrently play multiple roles in a given period. Thus, in addition to characterizing the dominant role in each period, we also discuss how these metaphorical roles sustain or transform over time.

1978–1992: Teacher Education as a *Cornerstone* for Reconstructing the Nation

Before the Cultural Revolution,[4] China had already successfully improved the basic conditions of education with two decades of concerted effort since modern China was founded in 1949. By 1965, net enrollment for primary education reached 80%, up from 50% in 1953.[5] Yet, the graduation rate was low, and year-to-year enrollment fluctuated. The education sector was systematically destabilized when the Cultural Revolution brought upheaval across the country. This 10-year-long movement (1966–1976) had also seriously damaged the sociopolitical, economic, and cultural foundations of Chinese society.[6] When facing the broken society left by this movement, the former Chinese leader, Deng Xiaoping, and his leadership team formulated and enacted the "Reform and Open Door" policy in 1978, hoping to restore social order and refocus the society on economic development. The birth of this policy also marked the beginning of a period of nationwide reconstruction. The reconstruction lasted 14 years, until Deng's South China Tour[7] in 1992, an event regarded as a catalyst for China's rapid economic growth in the following years.[8]

Teacher education was considered a *cornerstone* for reconstructing the nation during this period. Two slogans, first established in the 1980s, thor-

TABLE 4.1
Key policies/legislations about teaching and teacher education

Year	Policies/legislations	Impact on teaching and teacher education
1978	Strengthening and Developing Teacher Education	Set the goal of rebuilding the closed, three-level teacher education system.
1985	Decision on Setting Every September the 10th as Teacher's Day	Increased the prestige and respect of teaching and teacher education.
1986	Suggestions on Strengthening and Developing Teacher Education	Outlined the specific reform objectives of each of the three-level teacher education institutions.
1993	Teachers' Law of People's Republic of China	Guaranteed the legitimate rights of teachers.

Notes: Though Teachers' Law was passed in 1993, we still include it here as evidence of the state's emphasis on teaching and teacher education because the formulation of this law primarily occurred during the national reconstruction period (1978–1992).

For a comprehensive review of policy and legislative documents about teacher education, please refer to Jun Zhou and Lynda Reed, "Chinese Government Documents on Teacher Education since the 1980s," *Journal of Education for Teaching* 31, no. 3 (2005): 201–213.

oughly illustrated the foundational role that teacher education was expected to play in the national reconstruction: "Education is the foundation of a 100-year [national development] plan,"[9] and "Teacher education is the machine tool for the education enterprise."[10] Because of its high visibility on the national development agenda, the teacher education system underwent a series of legislative, administrative, and financial reforms. As China's governance system is fairly centralized, a series of policies and regulations were set at the national level to reform teacher education. Table 4.1 lists several key policies and legislative acts that demonstrate the state's strong emphasis on teaching and teacher education during this period.

These policies and legislation have significantly improved the teacher education enterprise. Particularly, they have helped reestablish the closed, three-level teacher education system that already existed before the Cultural Revolution.[11] *Closed* means that teachers were exclusively prepared by teacher education institutions, and these institutions also focused on the initial preparation and continuous development of teachers. The three-level teacher education institutions refer to secondary-level teacher schools (*zhongshi,* 中师), three-year normal colleges (*shizhuan,* 师专), and four-year normal universities (*shida,* 师大). In this hierarchical system, *zhongshi* was mainly responsible for preparing kindergarten and primary school teachers (grades K–6), *shizhuan* for preparing middle school teachers (grades 7–9), and *shida* for preparing high school teachers (grades 10–12).[12] Such a closed and highly structured teacher education system supported the national reconstruction in several ways.

First, this system guaranteed the sufficient supply of school teachers. A key strategy was the rapid expansion of elementary and middle school education.[13] In order to ensure that every school-aged youth—a society's future human resource—could receive the required minimum years of education, the Chinese government passed the Compulsory Education Law in 1986, mandating that every child was entitled and obliged to receive nine years of compulsory education.[14] Aided by this law, the enrollment in primary and middle schools sharply increased during this period. As a result, a large number of new teachers were needed to educate the expanding student population. Benefiting from the centralized governance structure, the closed teacher education system had successfully met the growing need of teachers within a short period of time. This was achieved by expanding teacher education institutions, incentivizing students to apply for teacher education programs (e.g., providing financial support and guaranteeing job placement), and using institutional power to channel teacher education graduates to targeted high-need schools. As Zhou argues, "It can be seen that the policy of resetting the teacher education system directly addressed the shortage of teachers in the 1980s and ensured an adequate supply of teachers to schools."[15]

Second, the three-level teacher education system sustained the traditional assumption of knowledge.[16] An underlying belief of the leveled system is that the teachers who teach at a higher grade level need to possess more specialized content knowledge, thus they need to receive longer and more intensive professional preparation. Such a hierarchical conceptualization of knowledge is deeply rooted in Confucianism, which says that knowledge should be placed at the center of teaching and learning, learning is a process of accumulating a preexisting body of knowledge, and students should respect the authority of teachers and their knowledge and work hard to acquire knowledge.[17] From a 1980s viewpoint, this ideology did contribute to the quick expansion of compulsory education, because knowledge-centered pedagogy could be efficiently taught in teacher education programs and then carried out in public schools, where the class sizes were usually very large.

Third, the development of teacher education made people value education again. The stigmatization of education was one of the most seriously damaging consequences of the Cultural Revolution.[18] Many school teachers, scholars, and intellectuals were publicly humiliated and punished because the then-authorities perceived the educated person as a defender of the "outdated" traditional culture as well as a threat to their regime. However, during the national reconstruction, the government reinstated teacher education at the center of its reform agenda, leading to the significant development of teacher education. Coupled with this developmental agenda were improved work conditions and new benefits for the teaching profession. These reforms rekindled people's interests in pursuing a career in education. For instance, many high-performing middle school graduates, especially those from poor rural families, chose to become a teacher through attending *zhongshi* programs because of generous financial aid from the state, shorter time of preparation, and stable job placement.[19]

In brief, during the 14 years following the Cultural Revolution, China strived to drag society back on track for economic development and modernization. Guided by this national development agenda, teacher education reestablished the closed, three-level system. This system provided foundational support to national reconstruction by feeding schools with sufficient educators, sustained the traditional educational beliefs that contributed to the rapid universalization of compulsory education, and helped to nurture a societal discourse of respect and value toward education.

1992–2004: Teacher Education as an *Engine* for Boosting Economic Growth

After Deng Xiaoping's South China Tour in 1992, China embraced a period of rapid modernization by further transforming the planned economy to a market economy.[20] The marketization reform had also penetrated higher education; universities and colleges were granted greater autonomy, for example, but the reforms also necessitated competition among institutions for students and resources in a freer market.[21] Teacher education as a component of higher education was also influenced by the marketization movement. While the teacher education system continued to play a cornerstone role in preparing a sufficient number of teachers for schools, the closed, three-level teacher education system had started to transform (fig. 4.1).

Specifically, the teacher education system had significantly changed in two respects. First, the three levels of institutions started to merge into two levels. The secondary-level teacher schools, *zhongshi,* which prepared middle school graduates to become preschool and primary school teachers through two- to three-year programs, had significantly contributed to the universalization of public education during the mid-1980s and 1990s. Nevertheless, with the focus of national development shifting from restoring social order

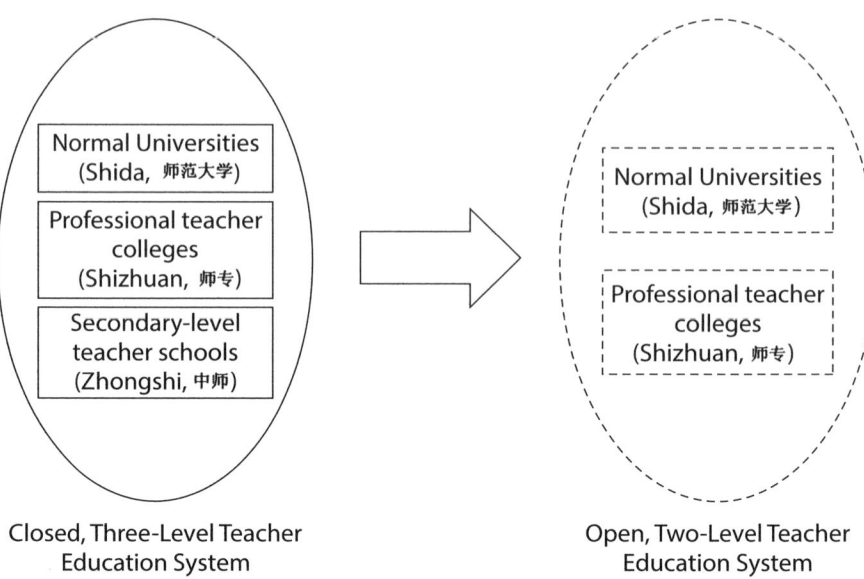

Figure 4.1. The structural shift of China's teacher education system

to boosting modernization and economic growth, it was viewed that the secondary-level teacher schools could no longer produce high-quality teachers. As a result, many were shut down while others actively sought reform by strengthening their programs (e.g., elongating the program length) and elevating themselves to achieve post-secondary-level status.[22] Figure 4.2 shows the numbers of the secondary-level teacher schools (*zhongshi*) and normal colleges/universities (*shizhuan* and *shida*) from 1978 to 2011. As shown in this figure, the number of normal colleges and universities remains stable over time, but the number of secondary-level teacher schools plummeted from 1,064 (as of 1978) to 132 (as of 2011), with the steepest section of the curve between 1992 and 2004.

Another change was the opening of a once-closed teacher education system. Two national policies issued by China's Ministry of Education triggered this shift, the "Suggestions on the Reforms and Development of Teacher Education (1996)" and the "Suggestions on the Adjustments of Distribution and Structure of Teacher Education Institutions (1998)." Both policies state that normal colleges and universities were allowed to offer nonteacher education programs, and comprehensive colleges and universities were now allowed to participate in teacher preparation. After almost two decades of development since 1978, the teacher education system was no longer strug-

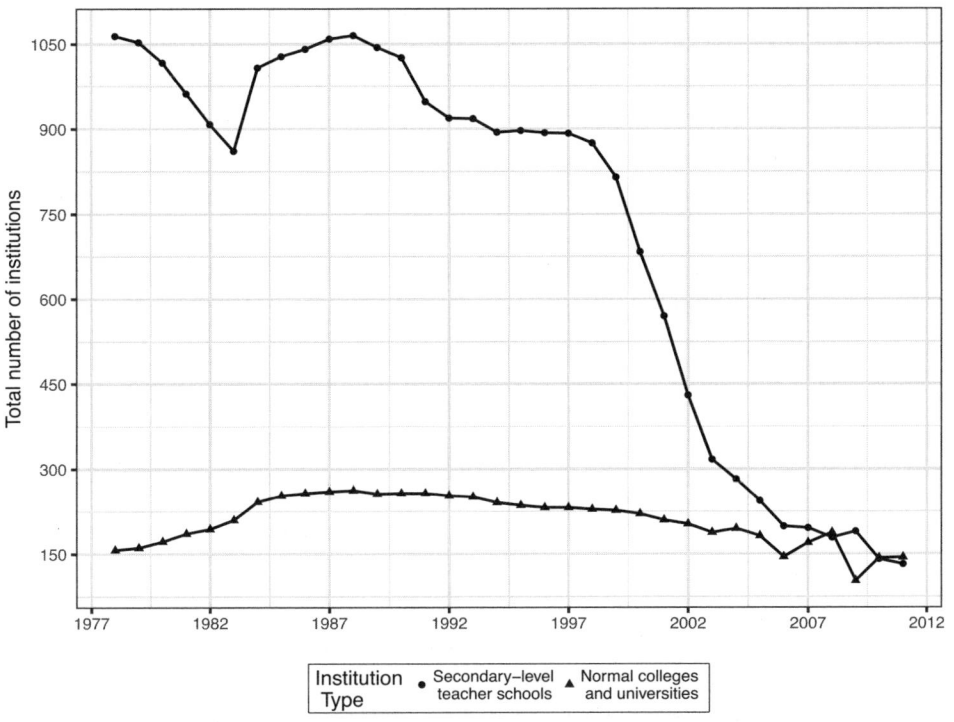

Figure 4.2. The number of secondary- and post-secondary-level teacher education institutions. Data from 1978 to 2007 are from Xudong Zhu and Yan Hu, *China's Education Reform in the Past Three Decades: The Volume on Teacher Education* (Beijing: Beijing Normal University Press, 2009, 112), and data from 2009 to 2011 are from the website of the Ministry of Education (MOE): http://www.moe.gov.cn/jyb_sjzl/moe_364/. Starting from 2012, the MOE stopped publishing the numbers of teacher education institutions. Secondary-level teacher schools = *zhongshi* (中师); normal universities and colleges = *shida* (师大) + *shizhuan* (师专). In certain years, the data about *shizhuan* and *shida* are reported separately, but in other years they are lumped together. In this figure, we report the total of *shida* and *shizhuan* in order to maintain consistent data structure across different years.

gling to prepare a sufficient number of teachers. Rather, the primary challenge in the 1990s became the quality of preparation instead of the quantity of educators produced.

Influential academia claimed that teacher education in many developed countries all pointed to an open system that facilitates competition between normal colleges/universities and comprehensive universities, as such a setup could help improve the overall quality of teacher education programs.[23] This argument fueled the structural shift in teacher education. Furthermore, this shift was also contextualized in the massification of China's higher education beginning in 1998.[24] In order to capitalize on the growing needs of higher education, many normal colleges and universities repositioned themselves as comprehensive colleges or universities and started to offer nonteacher education programs in order to compete for high-caliber students and more resources. As a result, teacher education was gradually marginalized inside normal colleges and universities.[25] A typical example of teacher education becoming peripheral in teacher education institutions is the shift of Southwest Normal University (SWNU) to Southwest University (SWU). SWNU was a normal university located in the prominent city of Chongqing, exclusively preparing educators for the southwestern regions of China from 1950. Influenced by the massification movement in higher education, in 2005 SWNU merged with Southwest Agricultural University to form a new comprehensive university called Southwest University (SWU). Teacher education became only one of many academic units inside SWU.

While the social discourse around economic development from 1992 to 2004 enabled the teacher education system to reform, the resulting transformations have in turn contributed to economic growth. The teacher education system during this period served as an *engine* for boosting the economic growth as viewed by the public. Similar to the functions of an engine, the revised teacher education system (open, two-level) sustained the development of the economy and was reflected in two distinct aspects.

First, compared to the closed, three-level teacher education system, the open, two-level system was able to feed Chinese elementary and secondary schools with higher-quality teachers. Teacher quality is a complex concept. Researchers have proposed a range of indicators to measure teacher quality, such as educational attainment, certification status, classroom teaching performance, and student learning outcomes.[26] While in academia there are still widespread debates on whether and to what extent these indicators can reflect the quality of a teacher, these indicators have been widely used in teacher education policy and practice. Using a teacher's educational attainment as a proxy, figures 4.3 through 4.5 demonstrate the increasing quality of primary and secondary school teachers. For instance, in 1992, only 0.1% of primary school teachers held a bachelor's degree or above, yet this number climbed to 4.6% in 2004 and 50.4% in 2016. Similar patterns are present in the data about middle and high school teachers. Another noticeable change is that the numbers of middle and high school teachers have drastically in-

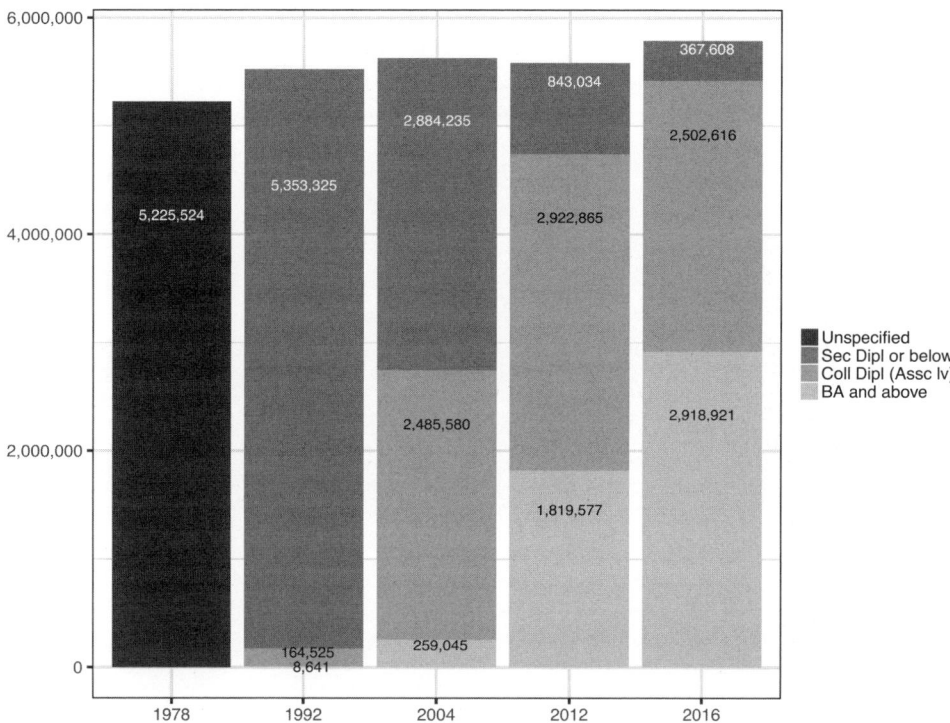

Figure 4.3. The number and educational attainment of *primary* school teachers. Data sources: *Educational Statistics Yearbook of China* (1978, 1992, 2004, 2012, 2016). Beijing: People's Education Press. Teachers' educational attainment was not reported in the 1978 yearbook, but it has the numbers of teachers in primary, middle, and high schools. We still include the 1978 data in these figures in order to show the changes in the numbers of schoolteachers.

creased, climbing from 2,564,987 and 576,145 in 1992 to 3,487,789 and 1,733,459 in 2016, respectively. Taken together, these changes suggest that the teacher education reforms have improved both the *quantity* and *quality* (using educational attainment as a proxy) of teachers in China's primary and secondary schools.

Furthermore, the relaxed structure of the teacher education system has nurtured the explorations of new models for preparing educators. In Shi's influential book, *Knowledge Transformation and Education Reform*,[27] he argues that the traditional understanding of knowledge—something fixed, hierarchical, and accumulative—could no longer fit the learning needs in the postmodern era, where knowledge is fragmented, constructive, and elu-

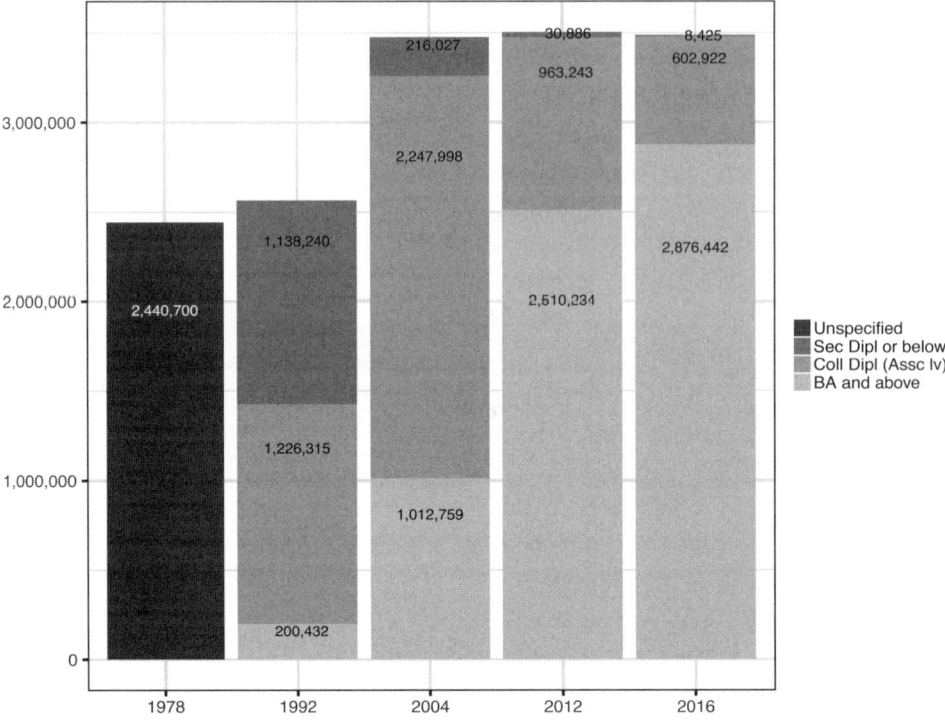

Figure 4.4. The number and educational attainment of *middle* school teachers

sive. Thus, the call for a new version of teaching and teacher education has become emphatic. Both the traditional teacher education institutions (i.e., normal colleges and universities) and the new players in this field (comprehensive colleges and universities that participate in teacher education) started exploring new models for preparing high-quality teachers for the new era. For instance, Beijing Normal University—one of the leading teacher education institutions in China—started piloting the "4 + 2" model of preparing teachers. In the first three years of this model, students receive education in subject areas (e.g., mathematics, history, chemistry) along with other students majoring in the same subject areas. By the end of the third year, students who are interested in teaching are enrolled in teacher education programs. After one year of coursework (the fourth year) that transitions the students from learning in subject areas to pedagogy, and from undergraduate level to graduate level, the students receive master's level education in teacher education in their last two years in the program. During their graduate

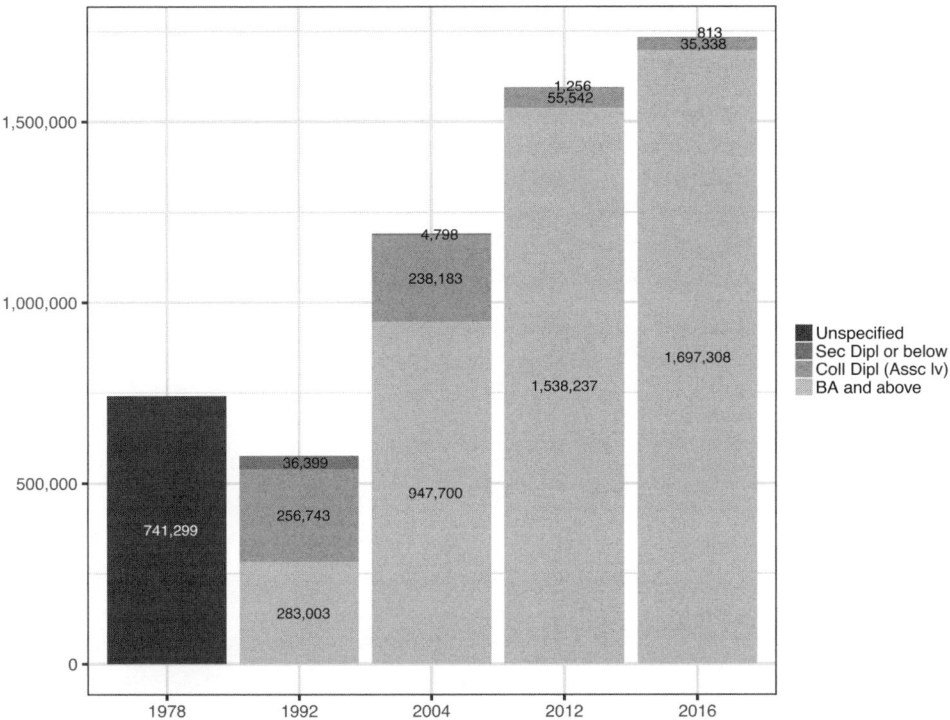

Figure 4.5. The number and educational attainment of *high* school teachers

studies, they receive intensive preparation in the most cutting-edge pedagogical ideas and strategies.[28]

In short, from 1992 to 2004, the national development discourse around economic development interplayed with the field of teacher education. On the one hand, the demands for higher-quality human resources for a developing economy had transformed the teacher education system to be an open, two-level system. In return, the reforms in teacher education guaranteed the supply of sufficient teachers with higher educational attainment and more rigorous preparation in both content and pedagogy, which further contributed to economic growth during this period.

2004–2012: Teacher Education as an *Equalizer* for Harmonizing Society

Overall, China achieved rapid economic growth from 1992 to 2004, with the annual gross domestic product (GDP) growth rates ranging from 7.7%

to 14.2%.[29] The trend of economic growth even continued thereafter. However, Chinese society was also becoming increasingly unequal. People living in rural regions, working in lower-rank professions, and from ethnic minority groups benefited much less from the national development than their counterparts in urban regions, those working in high-paying professions, and those in the mainstream Han group.[30] For instance, China's Gini coefficient—a commonly used indicator of a society's degree of inequality—was very low in the 1980s, when the economic reform just started. The low Gini coefficient indicates that the nation was poor, but the income distribution was relatively even among the residents. However, the Gini coefficient steadily climbed to very high levels (in the range of 0.53–0.55) in 2005, as estimated by many researchers.[31] Similarly, primary and secondary school students' access to quality teachers was also becoming increasingly unequal due to the marketization process taking place in education and society.[32]

In order to tackle the widening social inequalities, the Chinese government started a new national development agenda in 2004 called "Constructing a Harmonious Society." This agenda aimed to harmonize the emerging "disharmonies" (i.e., the growing inequalities) by equalizing public services across different regions and populations.[33] Education as an important public resource, especially access to quality teachers, was again placed at the center of the reform agenda during this period. While the teacher education system continued to aim at preparing enough quality teachers, the question of how to distribute teachers more equally across different regions and student populations became a top priority during this time. To address this issue, the Chinese government formulated and enacted three equality-oriented teacher polices.

In 2006, the Chinese government started implementing the *Tegang* policy, roughly translated as Special Teaching Position (STP). The goal of STP was to use alternative hiring routes to staff China's most underresourced rural schools. Effectively, STP deregulates the entry barriers into teaching by making those who graduate from nonteacher education programs, but who hold a bachelor's degree or higher, eligible to apply as teachers. STP initially hires teachers on a three-year fixed-term contract. By the end of the third year, STP teachers with satisfactory performance reviews are eligible for renewing their contracts to become tenure-stream educators.[34] This policy was developed during a time when teaching and teacher education were marginalized during the massification of higher education beginning in 1998.

First, STP was viewed as a solution to addressing unemployment issues for college graduates. Second, teaching as an occupation had lost its appeal for job seekers because of the low incomes and increasingly demanding environments, especially for schools located in underdeveloped rural regions, where very few teachers were willing to go and teach. As of 2016, over 500,000 STP teachers have been recruited and placed into more than 30,000 rural schools located in the most underdeveloped rural regions of China, significantly alleviating the teacher shortages facing those schools. Furthermore, according to a national survey conducted by *China Education Daily* in 2015, over 90% of STP teachers chose to stay in the teaching profession after their first three years of teaching.[35]

It is worth mentioning another program called Teach for China (TFC). TFC is the Chinese partner of Teach for All, a global network for improving teacher quality in hard-to-staff schools. As of 2018, the network has 48 partner organizations, including Teach for America in the United States, and Teach First in the United Kingdom. TFC shares the same goal of STP (i.e., channeling high-quality teachers to China's rural schools), but TFC's approach to achieving this goal is different. While STP is a formal educational policy designed and led by the central government, TFC uses a grassroots-based approach to bettering China's rural teacher workforce. In particular, TFC recruits student volunteers from China's selective universities, provides them with a few weeks of intensive pedagogical training, and then sends them to teach in hard-to-staff rural schools for two years. Since its launch in 2008, TFC has placed about 1,500 teachers into 270 rural classrooms. Though TFC has been playing a positive role in the efforts at addressing teacher quality disparities between China's urban and rural schools, its impact is hard to assess. The actual size of TFC is considerably smaller compared to the total number of elementary and secondary school teachers in China (i.e., about 11 million as of 2016).

The second policy that aimed to equalize the teaching workforce is the Free Teacher Education program (FTE). Starting in 2007, six national normal universities[36] were tasked to prepare highly qualified teachers for Chinese schools, especially those located in underdeveloped provinces and regions. The central idea of FTE was to use incentives to attract high-performing high school graduates, with a focus on those who were in need of financial support for college education, to join teacher education programs.[37] During the massification process of higher education, many teacher education institutions started to offer nonteacher education programs, which led to a steady loss of quality candidates to what students saw as more promising majors and departments. The national government attempted to use the FTE policy and its administrative power over the six most prominent normal universities to refocus teacher education institutions on preparing teachers. According to its design, FTE participants can receive a generous package of benefits, including a waiver of tuition and free housing, a monthly stipend, and a guaranteed civil servant teaching position (equivalent to a tenure-track teaching position in other contexts) after they graduate. Upon completion of study, FTE graduates must return to their home provinces and commit to teaching for at least 10 years. If the graduates default on their promise, they are liable for refunding all educational costs, paying a penalty, and being blacklisted in the Credit Record Archives, established by the educational authorities.[38] As of 2015, over 100,000 high school graduates have been recruited into FTE programs, and over 95% of FTE graduates went on to teach in their home provinces after graduation.[39] However, because of the conflict between FTE's value of educational equality and the participating teachers' intrinsic motivation for individual mobility, many FTE teachers have suffered from severe professional disorientation or even burnout.[40]

The third policy initiative, *Guopei,* or roughly translated as the National Professional Development Plan (NPDP), was another policy that aimed to enhance the quality of the rural teaching workforce. The implementation of NPDP started in 2010. NPDP provides diverse, tailored, and recursive professional development programs to in-service rural school teachers. Typical NPDP programs include several days of intensive face-to-face trainings on relevant topics (e.g., use of technology in teaching), semester-long online training, and one-year-long off-job professional learning in normal universities or colleges.[41] As of 2015, over one million primary and secondary school teachers have participated in NPDP programs. Over 95% of the participating teachers come from rural schools.[42]

Briefly, under the influence of the national development discourse around social equality since 2004, China's teacher education system has been serving as an *equalizer* for harmonizing the society. Particularly, the three policies—FTE, STP, and NPDP—respectively target the preservice preparation, initial recruitment, and in-service development of the teacher preparation pipeline, with the shared goal of equalizing students' access to quality teachers. While STP and NPDP seem to have helped enhance the quantity and quality of teachers working in high-need rural schools, the impact of FTE on the teaching workforce is mixed. More time and additional empirical evidence are still needed for concluding whether, and to what extent, the three teacher policies have contributed to China's broader agenda of narrowing social inequalities.

Since 2012: Teacher Education as a *Window* for Envisioning a Global Agenda

The inauguration of the sitting president Xi Jinping in 2012 marked the beginning of a new national development stage. Different from his predecessors, Xi and his leadership team have outlined a more globally oriented agenda for national development. For instance, the Belt and Road Initiative aims to strengthen the connectivity and cooperation between Eurasian countries. It also intends to increase China's power in influencing global affairs.[43] Similarly, in the field of education, a growing number of Confucius Institutions are dedicated to enhancing China's soft power in the world of politics.[44] Both the population of Chinese students studying abroad and international students coming to study in China have expanded in recent decades. Taken together, these new trends demonstrate China's ambitious agenda of becoming a globally influential power. To construct this agenda on the ground entails the efforts from almost every sector of society, including teacher education. As a response to the new direction of national development, the teacher education system has lately been undertaking three major reforms. These are: expanding preparation goals, innovating preparation approaches, and setting professional standards.

The first recent reform is expanding the preparation goals. In the past, China's teacher education system was primarily dedicated to preparing educators for schools in China. However, as China continues to unfold its global agenda, certain teacher education institutions and programs have started preparing teachers for schools outside China. A manifestation of this trend is the sharp growth in the Teaching Chinese as a Foreign Language (TCFL) programs. Chinese is becoming a popular language around the world. As a result, the need for Chinese teachers is also rapidly increasing.[45] In order to address the shortage of Chinese language teachers, a growing number of teacher education institutions have started preparing Chinese language teachers for "other" schools.

China's teacher education system has also been exploring how to prepare globally minded educators. Because of the ongoing trend of globalization, the communication and collaboration between Chinese schools and schools in other countries are becoming more frequent and intensive. Benefiting from their strong international partnerships, some leading teacher education institutions in China have started exploring innovative approaches to preparing globally minded and competent teachers. For instance, Beijing Normal University and Michigan State University have formed a partnership of exchanging teacher education students. This partnership explores how to use short-term study abroad programs to enhance future educators' global-mindedness and their competency for teaching in global contexts.[46] Similarly, starting in 2009, East China Normal University has been sending 20 to 30 teacher education students per year to study for one month in several prestigious overseas universities, such as Columbia University, University College London, and National University of Ireland. The purpose of this program is to broaden participating students' horizons and help them become excellent teachers in global contexts.[47] While at present only a few well-resourced and pioneering institutions are experimenting with how to prepare globally competent educators, more institutions and programs are expected to be joining them in the near future.

Another reform is the standardization movement. Sponsored by the Ministry of Education, a research panel at Beijing Normal University conducted a comparative study of teacher education standards in several developed countries, such as the United States, United Kingdom, Japan, Germany, and Australia.[48] The research panel concluded that, as suggested by international experiences, establishing professional standards is crucial for ensuring the quality of teaching and teacher education.[49] This research provides conceptual and empirical support to the publication of two national standards. The first is the "Teacher Education Curriculum Standards,"[50] and the other is the "Professional Standards for Preschool, Elementary and Secondary School Teachers."[51] The two standards introduce several new concepts to the teacher education system. These are "learner-centered, practice-oriented and teacher lifelong learning."[52] While the actual impact of the two standards on teaching and teacher education is still unclear, the standardization movement is another illustration of how China's teacher education system dynamically interacts with the national and global discourse around development, quality, and excellence.

To summarize, as China is aiming to step further into the center of the global stage, it also asks more from teacher education in order to support this ambitious agenda. The teacher education system has been quickly responding to this call with several new initiatives, such as starting to prepare Chinese language educators for the schools of other countries, exploring innovative teacher preparation approaches through international partnerships, and using professional standards to control the quality of teaching and teacher education. These reforms have opened up several windows for envisioning a broader and more ambitious future of Chinese education and society. However, since these reforms are still at the beginning stages of implementation, it is too early to conclude whether, to what extent, and in what ways these teacher education reforms have shaped China's most recent national development agenda centering on global engagement.

Conclusion

Drawing on various forms and sources of literature, this chapter provides a narrative of the relationships between teacher education reform and the national development in China over the past four decades. We conclude that teacher education reform and national development interactively influence each other. One the one hand, the discourse on national development shapes the goals, structures, and practices of the teacher education system. On the other hand, the achievements of the teacher education reforms have contributed to the development of China from a broken, poor society to an increasingly prosperous and influential member on the global platform. This Chinese experience resonates with the widely held assertion that teacher education is pivotal for a nation and its continuous development.[53] Furthermore, this chapter proposes four metaphorical roles (i.e., cornerstone, engine, equalizer, and window) about the specific ways in which teacher education can support national development. Future studies on China's teacher education can refine these roles and fill them with concrete meanings and connotations. These roles could also be used as a conceptual reference for exploring the relationships between teacher education and national development in other national contexts.

While China's teacher education system and the nation as a whole have significantly developed since 1978, the changing domestic and global circumstances are posing new challenges, such as how to reform education to be more learner-centered,[54] how to make education and society more equitable,[55] and how to move beyond the nation-state logic of development in the postmodern era, where the national, social, and cultural boundaries are becoming increasingly blurred.[56] These questions are beyond the scope of this chapter, but they should be worth exploring in future studies.

NOTES

1. John Chi-Kin Lee and Huan Song, "Teacher Education in the Greater China Region: Status, Issues and Prospects," in *Quality and Change in Teacher Education*, eds. John Chi-Kin Lee and Christopher Day (Gewerbestrasse: Springer, 2016), 39–57; Jun Zhou, "Teacher Education Changes in China: 1974–2014," *Journal of Education for Teaching* 40, no. 5 (2014): 507–523; Defeng Li, "Modernization and Teacher Education in China," *Teaching and Teacher Education* 15, no. 2 (1999): 179–192.

2. Michael Pettis, "The Four Stages of Chinese Growth," *China Financial Markets*, June 18, 2014, http://carnegieendowment.org/chinafinancialmarkets/55947; Xudong Zhu and Yan Hu, *China's Education Reform in the Past Three Decades: The Volume on Teacher Education* (Beijing: Beijing Normal University Press, 2009), 1–6.

3. Bart McCandles, "The Use and Misuse of Metaphor in Education and Education Reform," *Education* 132, no. 3 (2012): 538–547; Lynn Paine, "Teacher Education in Search of a Metaphor: Defining the Relationship between Teachers, Teaching and the State of China," in *The Political Dimension in Teacher Education: Comparative Perspectives on Policy Formation, Socialization and Society,* eds. Beverly Lindsay and Mark B. Ginsburg (London: Falmer Press, 1995), 76–98.

4. The full name of the Cultural Revolution is "the Great Proletarian Cultural Revolution." It was a political movement launched by Mao Zedong, the supreme leader of the Chinese Communist Party (CCP). Its goal was to rectify the overbureaucratization of the CCP since it took power in 1949, but it eventually evolved into factional fights and social turmoil (see Lili Wu, "Cultural Revolution," in *The Wiley-Blackwell Encyclopedia of Social and Political Movements,* eds. David A. Snow, Donatella Della Porta, Bert Klandermans, and Doug McAdam (Oxford: Wiley, 2013), 305–311.

5. Chris Bramall, "Out of the Darkness: Chinese Transition Paths," *Modern China* 35, no. 4 (2009): 439–449.

6. Wu, "Cultural Revolution."

7. "South China Tour" refers to Deng Xiaoping's visits to several southern cities in early 1992. During this tour, Deng made important speeches that have formed the conceptual framework for China's reform and opening-up as well as the socialist modernization process (source: http://www.china.org.cn/china/CPC_90_anniversary/2011-04/19/content_2239 2494.htm).

8. John Wong, "The Economics of the Nanxun," in *The Nanxun Legacy and China's Development in the Post-Deng Era,* eds. John Wong and Yongnian Zheng (Singapore: World Scientific, 2001), 35–50.

9. "百年大计,教育为本。It was discussed and set as the guiding principle for education reform at the 13th National Congress of Communist Party of China in October 1987.

10. "教师教育是教育事业的工作母机。It was discussed at the National Conference on Teacher Education in 1980.

11. Zhou, "Teacher Education," 507–523.

12. Jun Zhou and Lynda Reed, "Chinese Government Documents on Teacher Education since the 1980s," *Journal of Education for Teaching* 31, no. 3 (2005): 201–213.

13. Bramall, "Out of the Darkness," 439–449.

14. Ministry of Education, *Compulsory Education Law of People's Republic of China*

(Beijing: Ministry of Education, 1986), http://www.npc.gov.cn/wxzl/gongbao/2000-12/06/content_5004469.htm.

15. Zhou, "Teacher Education," 510.

16. Zhou, "Teacher Education," 507–523.

17. Sally Chan, "The Chinese Learner—A Question of Style," *Education + Training* 41, no. 6/7 (1999): 294–305, https://doi.org/10.1108/00400919910285345.

18. Wu, "Cultural Revolution," 305–311.

19. Zhu and Hu, *China's Education Reform*, 46.

20. Wong and Zheng, *Nanxun Legacy*, 3–18.

21. Rui Yang, "Toward Massification: Higher Education Development in the People's Republic of China since 1949," in *Higher Education: Handbook of Theory and Research*, ed. John C. Smart (Dordrecht: Springer, 2004), 311–374.

22. Zhu and Hu, *China's Education Reform*, 88–91.

23. Xudong Zhu and Xue Han, "Reconstruction of the Teacher Education System in China," *International Education Journal* 7, no.1 (2006): 66–73.

24. Yang, "Toward Massification," 311–374.

25. Zhu and Hu, *China's Education Reform*, 54–57.

26. Michael Strong, *The Highly Qualified Teacher: What Is Teacher Quality and How Do We Measure It?* (New York: Teachers College Press, 2011), 12–17.

27. Zhongying Shi, *Knowledge Transformation and Education Reform* (Beijing: Educational Science Publishing House, 2001), 143–160.

28. Zhu and Hu, *China's Education Reform*, 136–138.

29. World Bank, *The World Bank GDP Growth Dataset* (Washington, DC: World Bank, 2017), https://data.worldbank.org/indicator/NY.GDP.MKTP.KD.ZG?locations=CN.

30. Martin King Whyte, *One Country, Two Societies: Rural-Urban Inequality in Contemporary China* (Cambridge: Harvard University Press, 2010), 16: 1–26.

31. Yu Xie and Xiang Zhou, "Income Inequality in Today's China," *Proceedings of the National Academy of Sciences* 111, no. 19 (2014): 6928–6933; Ricardo Molero-Simarro, "Inequality in China Revisited: The Effect of Functional Distribution of Income on Urban Top Incomes, the Urban-Rural Gap and the Gini Index, 1978–2015," *China Economic Review* 42 (2017): 101–117.

32. Eryong Xue and Tingzhou Li, "Policy Evaluation of Urban and Rural Balanced Allocation of Compulsory Education Teaching Staff," *Educational Research* 36, no. 8 (2015): 65–73; Yisu Zhou and Dan Wang, "Understanding the Constraints on the Supply of Public Education to the Migrant Population in China: Evidence from Shanghai," *Journal of Contemporary China* 25, no. 100 (2016): 563–578.

33. Bangguo Wu, "The Guidelines for Constructing a Socialistic Harmonious Society," *People's Daily,* October 20, 2006, http://cpc.people.com.cn/GB/64093/64094/4937731.html.

34. Ministry of Education, *The Plan of Implementing the Special Teaching Position Programs in Compulsory Education Rural Schools* (Beijing: Ministry of Education, 2006), http://www.moe.gov.cn/srcsite/A10/s7058/200605/t20060515_81624.html.

35. Jia Liu, "A Review, Reflection and Prospect of the Implementation of the Specially Contracted Teachers Plan over the Past 10 Years," *Modern Education Management,* no. 2 (2017): 79–84.

36. These are: Beijing Normal University, East China Normal University, Central China Normal University, Northeast Normal University, Shaanxi Normal University, and Southwest University. They are regarded as the leading teacher education institutions in China.

37. Ministry of Education, *The Guidelines for Implementing Free Teacher Education Programs at the Ministry of Education Affiliated Normal Universities (Trial)* (Beijing: Ministry of Education, 2007), http://www.gov.cn/zwgk/2007–05/14/content_614039.htm.

38. Dan Wang and Manman Gao, "Educational Equality or Social Mobility: The Value Conflict between Preservice Teachers and the Free Teacher Education Program in China," *Teacher and Teacher Education* 32 (2013): 66–74.

39. Wei Liao and Rui Yuan, "Understand an Emerging 'Failure' of an Equality-Oriented Teacher Policy in China: A Job Search Perspective," *International Journal of Educational Research* 81 (2017): 71–82.

40. Liao and Yuan, "Understand," 71–82; Wang and Gao, "Educational Equality," 66–74.

41. Ministry of Education, *The Notification of Implementing the National Professional Development Plan for Primary and Secondary Teachers* (Beijing: Ministry of Education, 2010), http://www.gov.cn/zwgk/2010–06/30/content_1642031.htm.

42. Ministry of Education, *The Achievements of the National Professional Development Plan after 5-Year Implementation* (Beijing: Ministry of Education, 2015), http://www.moe.gov.cn/jyb_xwfb/s3165/201511/t20151117_219522.html.

43. Michael D. Swaine, "Xi Jinping on Chinese Foreign Relations: The Governance of China and Chinese Commentary," *China Leadership Monitor* 48 (2015): 1–13.

44. Su-Yan Pan, "Confucius Institute Project: China's Cultural Diplomacy and Soft Power Projection," *Asian Education and Development Studies* 2, no. 1 (2013): 22–33.

45. Yinghui Wu, "On the Dynamic Development and National Differences of the Need of Chinese Teachers as a Second Language," *Educational Research* no. 11 (2016): 144–149.

46. Wei Liao, Margo Glew, and Huan Song, "Principals of Designing the 'Global and Future Educators Program,'" *Teacher's Journal*, no.5 (2017): 15–19.

47. Jijun Cao and Weiqi Yan, "Preparing Excellent Future Educators: East China Normal University's Innovative Approaches for Preparing Teachers," *Guangming Daily*, July 7, 2014, http://epaper.gmw.cn/gmrb/html/2014–07/07/nw.D110000gmrb_20140707_8–06.htm?div=-1.

48. Xudong Zhu and Qiong Li, *The Research on Teacher Education Standards System* (Beijing: Beijing Normal University Press, 2011), 24–42.

49. Zhu and Lu, *Research on Teacher Education Standards System*, 42–44; Zhou, "Teacher Education," 507–523.

50. Ministry of Education, *Teacher Education Curriculum Standards (Trial)* (Beijing: Ministry of Education, 2011), http://jsjy.110161.com/upload/file/20170605/20170605153100_3576.pdf.

51. Ministry of Education, *Professional Standards for Preschool, Elementary, and Secondary School Teachers (Trial)* (Beijing: Ministry of Education, 2012), http://www.gov.cn/zwgk/2012–09/14/content_2224534.htm.

52. Zhou, "Teacher Education," 520.

53. Linda Darling-Hammond, "Teacher Education and the American Future," *Journal of Teacher Education* 61, no. 1–2 (2010): 35–47.

54. Wei Liao and Sihua Hu, "Chinese Teachers' Perceptions of Academically Oriented Teacher Preparation," *Journal of Education for Teaching* 43, no. 5 (2017): 628–633.

55. Xue and Li, "Policy Evaluation," 65–73.

56. Yongbing Liu and Yanping Fang, "Basic Education Reform in China: Globalization with Chinese Characteristics," *Asia Pacific Journal of Education* 29, no.4 (2009): 407–412.

CHAPTER FIVE

Crisis and Opportunity in Teacher Preparation in England

RICHARD ANDREWS

Crisis

There is a crisis in teacher supply in England, and part of the picture is uncertainty in routes into teaching. The principal experience in teacher preparation in universities is one of flux and increasing diversification. Such fragmentation goes back to the early 1990s with the shift to more formal partnerships between schools and universities and skepticism, if not suspicion, on the part of right-wing governments about the role of "theory" in universities in teacher preparation. In order to understand the crisis, it is necessary to look at the teacher shortage question, then at the routes into teaching, and subsequently to consider why the picture for teacher preparation is so fragmented. The factors that create the current situation are many and interrelated.

Teacher Shortage

The shortage in quality teachers is an international problem. In the late 1990s, concern was expressed in 13 of the then 15 European countries, in the United States, Canada, Australia, and New Zealand. Cockburn and Haydn[1] report that "as early as 1974, OECD research on teacher supply moved beyond an emphasis on teacher numbers towards an analysis of factors impacting on teacher quality. Recent DfES [Department for Education and Science, now the Department for Education] and ministerial rebuttals of the idea that there are teacher shortages have tended to focus on numbers rather than quality issues."[2]

The UK government has been trying to deny the issue of teacher shortages in England[3] for some time, largely because such a shortage of high-quality teachers affects parents and their children, and therefore is a voting issue. There have been warnings of a crisis for some time, particularly as the demographic bulge or baby boom in England, currently affecting primary/elementary schools, will soon move into the secondary/high schools. Overall numbers of school students are rising, with the secondary/high school population "projected to increase by 15% between 2018 and 2025."[4]

Part of the demographic picture is net migration to the United Kingdom. (Immigration to the United Kingdom was a key issue in the debates that preceded the Brexit referendum vote in June 2016 and at time of writing, still is—couched in terms of the free movement of workers across Europe. At the extreme end of the spectrum, immigration was and is confused with ethnicity and race. The bulk of the "leave" vote in England, however, was based more on class differentiation; a sense of exclusion from economic benefits; and resistance to overarching bureaucracy.) In November 2015, the Office for National Statistics reported that 336,000 more people came into the country than left the country in the year to June 2015: the highest total ever.[5] This migration was largely economic, and from within Europe. Since then, migration from within Europe has decreased and migration from the rest of the world increased; and overall net migration has remained fairly stable since 2016. The population of the United Kingdom was 63,843,856 in 2015 and rises by about 0.5% per annum. It is forecast to reach over 73 million by 2050. In terms of spatial size, England is about the same as Oregon or Arizona: 40 times smaller than the United States, whose population is about 322 million. In terms of population density according to Eurostat figures for 2012, the United States has 88 people per square mile; the United Kingdom has 681, but England's is 1,062: the highest in Europe and second only to the Netherlands. More recent figures (2019) put the UK as a whole (720 per square mile—an increase on 2012) as the third highest in Europe after the Netherlands and Belgium.

These figures provide a background to the question of teacher supply and teacher shortage. The implication is that more teachers are needed; and we know from research that the biggest single factor in a child's education, after social class, is the quality of his or her teachers. More teachers have been recruited in the last few years but such increases in the teaching workforce do not mask the fact that there is a shortage in primary/elementary schools at present, and already a shortage in key subject areas in secondary/high schools. The prediction of the government's own School Teachers' Review Body is that there will be 17% more secondary school pupils by 2023;[6] and the Department for Education calculates that England will need 570,000 extra secondary school places by 2025.

Types of School in England

To understand the context for initial teacher preparation, it is necessary to list the different types of school that are currently available in England. The range of types suggests not only variety but fragmentation in the system, which is discussed later in the chapter.

There are at least ten types of school:

- comprehensive (mostly secular) state schools (funded by local authorities, e.g., Birmingham)
- state schools that are affiliated with religions, e.g., Church of England schools, other faith schools (cofunded by local authorities and faiths)
- state grammar schools (selective schools which are government funded)
- private and/or independent schools (the most elite of which are called "public schools")
- academies and academy chains (funded direct from government)
- free schools (funded direct from government)
- teaching schools and clusters of schools (akin to teaching hospitals)
- city technology colleges (funded direct from government)
- university technology colleges (ditto, but sponsored by universities)
- specialist schools, e.g., Specialist Mathematics Schools

The key determinants of which school you might end up going to are parental income and postcode/zipcode, that is, where you live. Parents and children in some parts of the country have far less choice because of the economy and population density in that region; London, on the other hand, has examples of all these schools within reachable distance, though the economic factor still pertains.

Main Routes into Teaching

In the period between 1945 and the late 1960s in England, local education authorities (mapped on to counties as administrative regions within England)

TABLE 5.1
The main routes into teaching in England

Postgraduate Certificate of Education (PGCE)	Employment-based routes	Teach First
• Launched in the 1970s, the PGCE is a one-year postgraduate professional training course, mostly run and awarded by universities. Followed by a year's experience in a first job as a newly qualified teacher (NQT), it leads toward Qualified Teacher Status (QTS), which is awarded by the government's Department for Education. Since the 1970s, the PGCE and QTS have been a requirement for teachers working in the state system. • Two-thirds of the course takes place in practice settings (schools). • The PGCE qualification is worth a third or half of the credits toward a master's. Entrants to the PGCE need to have a First or 2.1 or 2.2 degree.	• Introduced by the government in 2010, these routes are led and managed by consortia of schools or by "training schools" (the analogy is with "training hospitals"). Schools can "buy in" expertise from universities where they need it. One version, School Direct, *can* lead to the PGCE qualification and then on to a master's. • There is no specific academic requirement for entry to the School Direct route. • An earlier version, still operating, were School-Centred Initial Teacher Training consortia (SCITTs), outside university control.	• Started in the UK in 2002, Teach First takes graduates with First or 2.1 Honours Degrees (i.e., the top grades) and after an intensive six-week summer training course, puts them in challenging schools. There is continuing professional development support, often with university help, leading to qualifications (e.g., a master's in leadership, part-time, over two years). • Emphasis is on working in socially and economically deprived areas, and on leadership. There is less of an emphasis on pedagogy.
• In 2016, 54% of teacher preparation trainees came through this route.	• In 2016, 42% of teacher preparation trainees came through this route (SCITTs 12%, School Direct 30%).[2]	• In 2016, 4% of teacher preparation trainees came through this route.
• 90% of all trainees via this route are still in the profession a year later, and 72% are still in teaching after five years.	• 90% of all trainees are still in the profession a year later, and 72% are still in teaching after five years.	• The commitment required is to stay in teaching for two years minimum. 54% trained via Teach First were still teaching, but over 70% were still working in education-related fields (2014 figures).[3]

1. Universities and other "providers" differ in the amount of master's level credit they offer for the one-year PGCE course. A master's course consists of 180 credits. Some universities award 60 credits for the PGCE; others award 90.
2. I am grateful to Chris Husbands, vice-chancellor of Sheffield Hallam University, for these figures.
3. Taken from https://www.teachfirst.org.uk/blog/how-many-our-teachers-stay-classroom.

were the main framework within which teachers were recruited, trained, and supported. The grammar schools for the "top" 20% of state school students and the independent schools did not see much need for training; qualification for teaching the "secondary modern" schools was optional. In the 1970s, teaching became a fully graduate profession with the establishment of the postgraduate certificate in education (PGCE), a one-year intensive pedagogic program run by universities to prepare graduates for the profession in state schools. In 1999, the Bologna Process (a series of meetings and initiatives to work toward compatibility between academic and professional qualifications in Europe) added the possibility that teaching qualifications in one country could be used to teach in another within the European Union. (The June 2016 referendum result and Brexit negotiations in the United Kingdom could mean that the Bologna Process will no longer apply, which will mean there will be reduced movement of teachers in both directions between the United Kingdom and the rest of Europe.) In the early 2000s, the category of "teaching assistants" came to the fore: a nonqualification route to helping in the classroom. There are now pathways to move from teaching assistant to qualified teacher.

The PGCE route, as it's called, is actually a university-based teacher preparation program that leads toward the qualification of PGCE. PGCE is a qualification, not a course. It has *kudos* as well as currency because of its postgraduate status, which could lead through credit accumulation to a master's. PGCEs were established in the 1970s as one-year academic/professional qualifications for what became a graduate profession. In other words, you had to have a first degree to enter teaching as a career. For twenty years or so, they operated largely free from government control, though the Department for Education monitored teacher supply needs across the country and allocated course numbers to universities and other higher education providers.

In the early 1990s, recognition that early career teachers needed a more practical education and less theoretical one came to dominate government thinking. However, the balance (and interaction) between theory and practice had been part of the fabric of PGCE initial teacher preparation since the 1970s. In the 1990s, the more formal establishment of partnerships between schools and universities specified that a third of the time should be spent in universities and two-thirds in schools, so the PGCE courses could hardly be defined as ideological or theory-based, as often labeled by right-wing politicians. More accurately, PGCEs could be said to be research- and pedagogically based. The advantages of a PGCE course are: you learn in a cohort of students, rather than individually, so there tends to be more sense of being a professional; you learn from lecturers who may have been out of the classroom for a while, but who are experienced and understand (if not practice) research and who work closely with mentors and practitioners in schools; and you learn pedagogical variation. The disadvantages are that: you might get a university tutor who is badly out of date; you might end up preferring theory to practice (though that's rare); and you might be seriously out of pocket by the time you start teaching (it now costs £9,250, like each year of an undergraduate degree, though many bursaries are available). The other two routes—School Direct and Teach First—tend to pay an entry-level wage.[7]

School Direct, as the principal employment-based route, came in with the Coalition UK government of 2010, driven by a suspicion about university-based training and its closely associated qualification, the PGCE. Again, the suspicion was against intellectualism, or "theory." The Coalition (center-right) Party, like the Thatcher government of the late 1970s to early 1990s, distrusted "ideas" and what it termed "ideology," seeing them as part of a left-wing subversion of order, and as stemming from the social revolutions of the 1960s in San Francisco, London, and Paris. In fact, many of the government ministers looked to the eighteenth century for their models—a period of supposed stability before the French Revolution. As noted above, however, teacher preparation in England via the PGCE in the period from the 1970s to the 1990s, and to the present day, has hardly been driven by a radical social justice agenda.

Rather, it could be said to be research-based, pragmatic, and highly supportive of schools. However, the School Direct movement gave *schools* the lead and a degree of autonomy in coordinating teacher preparation. Gradually more schools of all kinds have become involved, especially through consortia, "teaching schools," and "academy chains," which are run like businesses, with chief executives ("executive headteachers"). They can choose to buy in university help if they want it, but many choose not to. If they want their training course to lead toward a teaching qualification—the PGCE—they have to collaborate with universities, which retain the power to award such qualifications. There are two routes within School Direct: the tuition fee route, which tends to be associated with universities; and the "salaried" route, which can be associated with universities but is relatively more autonomous. As a result, both numbers of students, and therefore the government money that goes with them, have moved away from universities and toward schools. The policy commitment of the government is for 51% of new teachers to come through the school-led routes by 2020. Such a percentage indicates government agency allocation rather than actual uptake. Critically for university-based routes, the monies would not be there to support sustained staffing in university departments and schools of education if School Direct (salaried), School-Centred Initial Teacher Training (SCITTs), and other school-based apprentice routes into teaching increase. However, as Wilson[8] states, "If you look at the actual uptake you will see that university-led programmes are still dominating, and that's quite significant." The pendulum might well swing back to universities, especially if schools themselves wish universities to play a coordinating role in a region in terms of recruitment, teacher preparation, retention, and continuing professional development.

The most recent manifestation of employment-based routes is the idea of degree apprenticeships. At time of writing, standards for undergraduate and postgraduate teaching were being debated and finalized. Few universities have launched such degree apprenticeships, and the employers, who lead the process, are skeptical about the scheme on financial grounds and because they wish to have freedom in selecting their teachers, once initially trained. The apprenticeship scheme assumes the apprentice will become employed in the school, academy, or academy trust.

Teach First was based on the model of Teach for America (1990) and began life in the United Kingdom as London First. A group of business leaders, disappointed with standards of teaching in London, invited McKinsey & Co. to London to advise, and subsequently Brett Wigdorz was appointed CEO to launch London First. Teach First, and Teach First Cymru (Wales) have now expanded to create Teach for All (2007) and to cover a wider international spread. It is hard to determine exactly what proportion of the teaching workforce is prepared through Teach First, but the figures range from 4% to 7%. It is not the solution to the teacher shortage problem, whether we look at the shortage in regional and/or subject terms, but it is an injection of a different style of teacher preparation approach into the system. It has helped the other two main routes to define more clearly what their distinctive characteristics are. Its advantages are that: it takes the highest proportion of students with the highest grades of degree; it takes dynamic achievers who have a potential for leadership; it goes into difficult social areas into schools in challenging circumstances and tries to make a difference. The disadvantages are: six weeks is not enough for professional training; it is very demanding on its trainees, often leading to burnout; there is no pedagogical model that underpins its ideology—it assumes that bright students will make good teachers; and it has the highest dropout rate and the lowest retention rate of the main routes into teaching. Although the intention of Teach First was for bright graduates to spend two years in teaching and then take their experience elsewhere, the additional burnout and dropout means that only 40% of Teach First trainees are still in teaching after five years, compared to 72% in the other routes into teaching.

A recently formed charity, Now Teach,[9] provides a gateway for those who would like to enter teaching in their forties (or older) and who have already had a career in another field and/or parenting responsibilities. Now Teach is currently government-supported and works in partnership with teacher education providers.

The State of Play

Late in 2015, a cross-party Education Select Committee of the UK government called for written evidence on teacher shortages. The remit of the committee was to determine:

- whether there was a "crisis" in the recruitment and retention of teachers, including at senior levels of the profession, at a regional level, and by subject, and how the situation might develop
- what the root causes of the current situation with regard to the supply of teachers were
- what further action should be taken by the government to tackle teacher shortages

The evidence[10] that came in was telling. At a meeting in December 2015 (which can be viewed on video)[11] several key points arose.

A Systemic Problem

The principal problem was seen to be systemic, in that there was a lack of a national joined-up strategy on teacher supply. Developments over the last seven or eight years had led to a more piecemeal, market-driven system, with some subjects in oversupply (physical education) and some subjects and regions suffering a shortage. Also there was a lack of medium- and long-term thinking by successive governments. One of the policy decisions by the Coalition and Conservative governments had been to "remove the cap" on teacher trainee recruitment, thus marketizing the system and giving up responsibility for managing it ("shrinking the state" is a mantra of the present government). That means that the larger, more successful universities increased numbers, often at the expense of smaller and less successful universities. As the government's schools minister put it: "What we want to do is to move the power, the decision making and the discretion to schools. We want schools to have the ability to recruit directly the graduates that they seek, and we want schools to have a greater say in the composition of the training, because there were concerns that some teachers were leaving the universities without training in things such as behaviour management that the schools wanted."

Data

There were some telling data about the problems faced by schools in recruiting high-quality teachers. The government's teacher supply model was not sufficiently accurate. To compound the problem, some of those training for a teaching qualification used their training in private and independent schools (where there is no absolute need for it) or work in continental Europe or globally. According to Howson,[12] "In some subjects we are now [in 2015/16] in the third year . . . where the figure set by the teacher supply model, which one might regard as the Department's baseline for what is necessary to staff the school system, has not been met." The head of the National Association of Headteachers[13] noted that when teacher recruitment was sampled in November 2015, schools had already taken measures to fill the vacancies, but that may have meant appointing a nonspecialist teacher to a subject, appointing an unqualified teacher or appointing a long-term supply teacher as well. He added: "You cannot have an empty classroom." To compound the problem, there were three further factors: more than half (54%) of headteachers in schools with a large proportion of disadvantaged students found attracting and retaining good teachers "a major problem," compared with 33% in other schools. The number of teachers leaving the profession has increased by 11% over the last three years.[14] And, from a Teach First perspective, the improving economy had attracted graduates into other sectors and away from teaching.

The University and College Union (UCU)[15] cited a National Audit Office report[16] stating that the targets for teacher recruitment had been missed in each of the previous four years, and that higher education institution initial teacher education providers had performed best at filling recruitment places, "having filled 85% of their allocations in the 2015–16 cycle, compared to 65% for SCITTs and 58% for School Direct." The briefing further notes that a centralized governmental approach to teacher supply could have taken account of regional supply and demand, whereas the localized nature of School Direct could not.

Routes into Teaching and the "Academy" Effect

The Teach First route into teaching has considerable publicity but was never seen as a major route into teaching. Freedman[17] notes that "we have never positioned ourselves or seen ourselves as a solution to the whole issue of teacher recruitment [. . .] some City firms are now paying £65,000 starting salaries and that is what we are competing against. That is where the challenge is for us." Neither has the School Direct route attracted the numbers that were expected, as table 5.1 shows, though this number is increasing in line with UK government pressure. The School Direct route takes various forms, but essentially School Direct courses are designed by schools, either in SCITTs or in collaboration with universities. Often schools in a region with a long-standing relationship with a university will look to that university for leadership and coordination. However, some universities have left the system, and the government has not fully tracked the impact of these departures on trainee and teacher supply. A major new entrant into the field of initial teacher preparation is the multi-academy trust (MAT). These trusts, supported by the government wish that "every school should become an academy," have eroded the power of local education authorities, and they often work independently from universities, wishing to train their own staff. "Academization" was in 2016 a flagship government policy.[18] Academies were first launched in the early 2000s, but were scaled up (without appropriate infrastructure) in 2010 with a view by 2016 that they would revolutionize the whole education system via the basic principle of increased "autonomy." Autonomy, in itself, has not delivered. Research by Hutchings et al. suggests that academies, in relation to mainstream schools, have lower inspection grades. There is considerable variation within the academy movement, with some academies and academy chains performing relatively well in relation to improvement for disadvantaged students, and others performing badly. Longitudinal analysis suggests exacerbation of this trend. Overall, "when analysed against a range of Government indicators on attainment, a majority of the [academy] chains analysed still underperform the mainstream average on attainment for their disadvantaged pupils."[19]

Regional Variation

Few training providers (universities, various school consortia, and Teach First) operate in areas of the country which are becoming known as "cold spots" or "isolated, coastal and disadvantaged areas,"[20] for example, the Essex and Kent coastal areas, or the fenland area between Norfolk, Suffolk, Cambridgeshire, and Lincolnshire. These areas are economically challenged, with ageing populations. Not without coincidence, they also happen to be the areas of most intense resistance to European integration, and registered the highest proportion of voters wishing to leave Europe in the June 2016 referendum. They are unattractive to young teachers, who tend to want to work in the inner city and/or the leafy suburbs or the countryside. The same is true of doctor (general practitioner) supply.

The regional disparities are heightened in relation to London. House prices in London have become unaffordable for young teachers, as public sector wage rises are around 1%[21] per annum, compared to 4% in the private sector. House prices had risen by 20% in London in the year to May 2014. By September 2015, the rise per annum had dropped to 7.2% and has dropped further since 2016. The average house price in London was in the region of £531,000 in 2015, and in June 2016 it rose to above £600,000 for the first time.[22] In the rental sector, rents increased by 4.2%. (The London economy has grown by 21% since 2009, whereas the rest of the United Kingdom has grown by 8%.) Such disparity between the capital city and the regions partly fueled the discontent that led to the June 2016 EU referendum result: the protest vote was as much about dissatisfaction with a London "elite" and metropolitanism as it was with the European Union.

Subject Shortages and Retention

The news stories and the general public concern tend to be around the supply of quality secondary subject specialists, especially in design and technology (only 41% of places filled at the initial teacher education stage) and business studies; and also in English and modern foreign languages. Shortages were also revealed by the National Audit Office report in biology, drama, religious education, geography, classics, music, computing, and art and design. But there is also a shortage in primary schools of English and mathematics specialists.[23] The latest figures from the National Audit Office show that 28% of physics teachers have a qualification no higher than Advanced level (school level at 18).

Indicative of the problem is the case of the supply of mathematics teachers. Pope[24] refers to a snapshot produced in 2014 by the Advisory Committee for Mathematics Educators[25] but indicates that the 2016 picture showed a worsening trend. In 2014, over 20% of mathematics lessons for pupils aged between 11 and 18 were taught by teachers with no post–A level (the highest qualification available in schools in England) qualification. In the context of a need for more secondary school mathematics teachers by 2025, the higher wastage rate for mathematics teachers (12% as opposed to 10% in other subjects) is worrying. It is good to know that there is currently a government initiative to train and upskill an additional 17,500 mathematics and physics teachers by 2020.[26]

Cockburn and Haydn[27] warned of the coming crisis in the *retention* of teachers, and a 2016 survey by *The Guardian* newspaper (March 22, 2016) revealed that 43% of teachers were planning to leave in the next five years, principally based on the fact that 98% felt under increasing pressure, 82% said their workload was unmanageable, and only 12% said they had a good work-life balance. The survey shows that the staff recruitment and retention crisis, described by ministers as "scaremongering," is a reality, based on a number of contributing factors: workload; high-stakes accountability; rapid government reform of the curriculum and the qualifications system; deprofessionalization; and confusion about the multiple routes into teaching as a career. Finally, the government is acknowledging the crisis, and recognizing that the management and reduction of teacher workload is a key factor in recruitment and retention of teachers to the profession.[28]

Dissatisfaction and a Lack of Morale

There are other factors that bear upon the crisis of teacher supply and retention. One is related to teacher morale, itself the result of a number of contributing factors. Northcott,[29] head of the National Association of Teachers/Union of Women Teachers, one of the largest teaching unions, addressed the problem thus:

> Why is there this dissatisfaction, this expression that people are contemplating leaving teaching? I think it boils down to a number of important issues . . . One is increasing workload. Another is that pay in real terms for teachers has declined relative to other graduate occupations. I think the way sometimes that teaching is portrayed does not help. Sometimes the teaching profession is demeaned in some quarters and that is found by teachers to be unattractive. I also think the

extent to which teachers are able to concentrate on teaching and leading teaching and learning in their working lives is another issue.

Another head of a teaching union, the National Union of Teachers, agreed: "Teachers believe the dominant narrative from politicians is of school failure, coasting schools and locating that blame with teachers. We think that narrative has passed its sell-by date. We are all in favour of school improvements but you have to do that with the profession; the narrative has to change and that applies to trusting teachers about accountability and workload."[30]

Government Position

As noted earlier, up to 2018 the government appeared to be in denial of the crisis in teacher supply and teacher retention. The unions, in particular, believed the government position to be based on a weak understanding of the situation. The Select Committee also interviewed the minister of state, Department for Education: "We have at the moment 454,900 teachers and that is an all-time high and [. . .] that is 5,200 more teachers this year than last year and 13,000 more teachers than 2010. There are also record numbers of returners to the profession. Some 14,000 more returners joined the profession again last year compared to 11,000 a few years before that, so the idea there is some view prevailing that teaching is not a profession that people want to join is simply not true."[31] But this position failed to take into account that "just because a situation is improving does not necessarily mean that it is not still in crisis. There were 2,300 shortages in 2014–15, coupled with the fact of the baby boom."[32] Factors that continue to concern headteachers include not only what they see as a myopic and short-term approach from government but regional variation, the quality of teachers, and retention.

The UCU, which represents many lecturers and teachers in higher and further education, noted in response to the government's paper, *Educational Excellence Everywhere*,[33] that although there was acknowledgment of the role of higher education institutions in providing initial teacher education (ITE), the government seemed intent on pressing ahead with more school-led ITE. UCU's briefing suggests "[the government] also recognises problems in teacher recruitment and supply but does not make the connection between the reforms implemented so far and their role in exacerbating the problem."[34]

A key government document, published in early 2019, signals a potential change in policy direction. David Foster's *Teacher Recruitment and Retention in England*[35] discusses government initiatives to encourage teacher recruitment and retention; a strategy for recruitment and retention; teacher workload; and cites a range of further reports on teacher supply and retention. Whether this report is translated into policy is yet to be seen and will be discussed further in the following section on opportunities in the field.

Why Is the Picture So Fragmented?

Fragmentation of provision has led to a crisis in teacher preparation. There are also other factors: any form of economic upturn; the patchiness of the supply/demand position (in both subject and geographical terms); the lack of a properly coordinated national system; disputes about data; perceptions by teachers and those outside the profession of work overload; a top-heavy assessment regime; perceptions of "difficult" children; and the lack of sufficient long-term thinking in government. Government has not helped: particularly since 2010 it has replaced what it sees as left-wing ideology with a right-wing ideology of the free market, and a distrust of theory and even of ideas. The quality of leadership and management in the government's Department for Education appears to have dropped. The reluctance to forge a single national system of teacher preparation has a deeper, characteristically English (perhaps British) reason: the distrust of systems per se. Deep in the English psyche is a celebration and defense of freedom, of individualism. It may be partly to do with the island mentality, and certainly contributed to the EU referendum result in June 2016. Its advantages are that it promotes creativity, liberalism, and diversity; its disadvantages are that it continually restructures, disposes of systems, and thus eats away at fairness and equality of provision. However, the situation is not intractable.

Opportunity

There are opportunities to address these problems. In the short term, these appear to be most promising for entrepreneurs in education. In the longer term, there are challenges for governments with regard to the system as a whole.

Entrepreneurs

I include in the category of entrepreneurs everyone from opportunists to genuinely creative people who have the interests of children and young people at heart. Opportunists, who include private individuals and organizations, charities, and headteachers, have exploited the current government's encouragement for diversity and choice within the education system. A clear example is the burgeoning of different types of school, like academies, teaching schools (e.g., teaching hospitals) and free schools, referred to earlier in the chapter.

The point with regard to teacher preparation is that academy chains and teaching schools (again, like teaching hospitals) are large enough to organize their own training. There are now executive headteachers who look after a consortium, or cluster, of schools. As there is a degree of autonomy in these schools, not all teachers are now required to have qualified teacher status, so these schools and chains can, in effect, take someone who expresses an enthusiasm for teaching and train them. Such chains and teaching schools are also large enough to have the resources to commission universities to assist in the training if they wish to or not. The move has been part of a movement to deregulate and deprofessionalize teaching. Anyone who has the enthusiasm, the will and the organizational skills to set up a free school can do so, though these tend to be smaller and more niche than academies or teaching schools. Those who can do so include charities, businesses, community and faith groups, teachers, parents, independent schools, and universities. Interestingly University College London's Institute of Education, the United Kingdom's (one of the world's) largest trainers of teachers, put detailed plans into the Department for Education for a new free school to serve the people of Camden, a central London borough, and for it to act as a laboratory school for the training of teachers and the honing of new methods of teaching. The bid was turned down by the government, seemingly for political reasons. Although some universities (e.g., Birmingham, Cambridge) have opened free schools, others (e.g., Oxford, the University of East Anglia) have held back from doing so, believing that the role of the university is not to design, run, and be accountable for schools and their performance but to work closely with all schools in a region to maintain and raise standards in the education of teachers.

The System as a Whole

Teaching, and training to become a teacher, are not organized by nation, but by jurisdiction. So far, the jurisdictions for education in the United Kingdom follow the constituent countries of the nation: England, Scotland, Wales, and Northern Ireland. Training in one jurisdiction does not equip you or credit you to teach in another—at least until the Bologna Agreement.

Theoretically, since the agreement in 1999 a trainee teacher in England could go and teach in Barcelona in Catalonia, in Dubrovnik in Croatia, or Helsinki in Finland. It doesn't happen much, because the education systems, the curricula, and the assessment regimes are different—but not so much that the differences and commonalities cannot be understood and overcome where necessary. However, the United Kingdom's decision to leave the European Union would mean such mobility will be curtailed.

Reforming the English system alone, with its ten types of school and three main routes into teaching—thus giving (again theoretically) at least 30 different routes into teaching within England—is probably unrealistic. Unless there is a government of extraordinary vision and force in implementing systemic change, such centralized integration will not happen. Ideally, there would be a situation in which there was no distinction between private and public education; in which all children and young people went to school in their own neighbourhood, irrespective of class or parental wealth, and learned alongside each other in a nationally run education system that was well resourced by the government and thus by the taxpayer. Such a system would have teachers trained—or better, educated—in practice, theory, research, and pedagogy by universities and schools in partnership.

Such an ideal is unlikely to be realized, but there is a middle way between the grassroots opportunism and creativity on the one hand, and large-scale systemic reform on the other.

Regionalism

About half of the 132 universities or higher education institutions in England and Wales are involved in initial teacher education. The actual number is 65. There is no commonly agreed upon regional map for England, but it has been recently divided into eight regions for the purposes of the governance, development, and academization of schools: the East Midlands and the Humber; the South-West; Eastern England and NE London; the South-East and South London; the West Midlands; NW London and South Central England; the North; and Lancashire and West Yorkshire. Each region is led by a regional schools commissioner reporting to a national schools commissioner as part of the Department for Education. The original brief of these regional schools commissioners was to have a responsibility to help create academies; to intervene in failing academies; and to encourage the development and governance and accountability of multi-academy trusts. They do not cover school improvement, curriculum, or assessment issues, but their brief has widened as the academization has reached a degree of maturity to include improving underperforming maintained schools and helping them to find an appropriate sponsor.

Nevertheless, such regionalism is a step forward in working toward a coherent, fit-for-purpose system. Further moves need to take place to embed the new structures but also to work in collaboration with universities to provide a world-class system.

The eight regions have an average of 12 or so universities within each of them. For the sake of argument, it could be the case that four to six of these universities per region were interested in taking forward major responsibility for coordinating initial teacher education. We would then have about 40 universities specializing in teacher education across England controlled by 40 teacher education boards consisting of schools, parents, teachers, university representatives, and other interested parties (businesses, faiths, charities, etc.).

There are considerable advantages in such a system based on regions. These include:

- recognition that about 60% of those trained in a region tend to stay teaching in that region
- reasonable traveling arrangements for those trainees who (as now is the case) need to experience at least two types of school in the preparation period
- complementarity between universities and schools, rather than the tensions and territorial battles that currently take place in a free market
- monitoring of teacher supply, so that those schools in coastal, disadvantaged, and remote regions do not find themselves without teachers
- governance by partnership boards consisting of all interested parties who can work together for the benefit of children and young people in the region
- the opportunity for long-, medium-, and short-term planning on teacher supply

There would be no constraint within such an arrangement on trained teachers moving outside their region, though in order to maintain economic balance with the countries or jurisdictions as a whole, there may need to be some checks and balances, for example, a requirement that the first two years of teaching through to qualified status are undertaken in the region in which you are trained.

Teacher trainers and trainees could still work within a nationally recognized framework, and toward a master's, thus making teaching a master's profession. There is also the possibility of a more coherent continuing professional development (CPD) framework with the option of a license to teach having to be renewed every 10 years or so, as in some other professions.

If the Bologna Process via which teacher qualifications are transferable will no longer be an option for England and the United Kingdom, thus allowing free movement of teachers within Europe, there is the possibility of a drive toward a globalized framework. Such a framework would allow freedoms for jurisdictions to meet local, contextual needs. These freedoms would be for starting-out teachers, for experienced teachers, and for schools to ensure a highly qualified, professional workforce. Such a framework, interpreted on a regional basis, would also ensure (with appropriate checks and balances) reasonable supply and demand. Above all, such a move may help to inspire talented young people to enter teaching and stay in it, and more experienced teachers to renew their energy and commitment to the teaching profession and to the education of children and young people.

The other hopeful sign, though not specifically related to initial teacher preparation, comes from a Department for Education response to consultation on strengthening qualified teacher status and improving (early) career progression for teachers.[36] The framework of early career progression[37] proposes to build on and complement initial teacher preparation; mentoring becomes a more recognized service and pathway for beginning teachers; and qualified teacher status, as now, will be awarded on the completion of a program of initial teacher education, with the difference that statutory induction will be extended from one to two years. It is hoped that such a framework will, in due course, lead to teaching as a master's level profession. It will also help to encourage more flexible working for teachers, including part-time and job-sharing opportunities; and, crucially, in the light of the confusing plethora of routes into teaching, a one-stop service for applications to initial teacher education.

Conclusion

This chapter has tried to provide a snapshot of a fast-moving period in teacher preparation in England, set against its historical background and the context of a crisis in teacher supply and retention. In particular, it has emphasized the increasing fragmentation of the school systems and their governance, as well as the varied routes into teaching.

Given the increasing mobility of students worldwide for undergraduate and postgraduate education, plus the global market for high-quality teachers and the likelihood that serial careers in teaching will involve international experience, some degree of transferability of qualifications and expertise might be necessary. To an extent, that already happens in limited ways through international school networks, teacher exchanges, and in private/independent education. The bigger problem, globally, is not how the elite will be educated but how high-quality education will be made available to those children and young people who are most in need. Gordon Brown[38] (ex-UK prime minister and an advocate for the retention of the United Kingdom within Europe, as well as United Nations envoy for global education) notes that by 2030 half of the world's children will not get a full education and 12% (200 million) will receive no formal schooling at all.

Such a prospect suggests that not only comparative studies in teacher preparation, supply and retention are critical, as in the present volume, but that concerted action is needed on an international level to address fragmentation, quality of teachers, and an increasing differentiation in education opportunities.

NOTES

This chapter is based on a paper prepared for *The Crisis in Teacher Preparation: A Look at the U.S., England and Spain,* a symposium in celebration of the 125th anniversary of the Steinhardt School of Culture, Education and Human Development, New York University, 2 March 2016.

1. A. C. Cockburn and T. Haydn *Recruiting and Retaining Teachers: Understanding Why Teachers Teach* (London: Routledge Falmer, 2004), 12.

2. OECD, *Recent Trends in Teacher Recruitment* (Paris: Organisation for Economic Co-operation and Development, 1974).

3. England has a different jurisdiction for schooling and teacher supply from Scotland, Wales, or Northern Ireland—these four countries currently make up the United Kingdom.

4. House of Commons Library Briefing paper no. 7222, *Teacher Recruitment and Retention in England,* February 12, 2019, 4.

5. The September 2015 figure is 323,000. In May 2016, the figure stood at 333,000.

6. *School Teachers' Review Body 29th Report,* July 22, 2019, https://www.gov.uk/government/organisations/school-teachers-review-body.

7. In 2016/17, the entry-level salary for unqualified teachers was £16,461 outside inner London, and £20,701 within inner London; for qualified teachers, the starting minimum salaries were £22,467 and £28,098, respectively.

8. E. Wilson, "Routes into Teaching: Initial Teacher Training Post-Carter Review," paper given at Westminster Education Forum (2016), 7, Westminster Education Forum,

Initial Teacher Training in England: Developing a Core Content Framework, Improving Course Quality and Support for Trainee Teachers (Berkshire: Bracknell, 2016).

9. See https://nowteach.org.uk/ (accessed April 4, 2019).

10. Evidence to the Select Committee on teacher shortages, 2015/16, available at https://www.parliament.uk/business/committees/committees-a-z/commons-select/education-committee/inquiries/parliament-2015/supply-of-teachers-15–16/ (accessed July 29, 2016).

11. Found at http://parliamentlive.tv/Event/Index/d4cbc273-0b52-4101-9949-04105bac1e75.

12. J. Howson, Evidence to the House of Commons Education Select Committee on Teacher Shortages (2015), 6.

13. R. Hobby, Evidence to the House of Commons Education Select Committee on Teacher Shortages (2015).

14. Found at http://www.theguardian.com/education/2016/feb/10/teachers-are-leaving-as-government-falls-short-on-recruitment-nao-finds.

15. University and College Union (2016) Parliamentary briefing on teacher training implications of the Department for Education's *Educational Excellence Everywhere* white paper.

16. National Audit Office (2016), https://www.nao.org.uk/report/training-new-teachers (accessed July 29, 2016).

17. S. Freedman, Evidence to the House of Commons Education Select Committee on Teacher Shortages (2015).

18. Post-Brexit, Prime Minister Theresa May has proposed the return of grammar schools to the English education system, further exacerbating fragmentation within the system. Grammar schools served an elite 20% of the school population in their heyday in the 1960s. They do not promote social mobility and are more disadvantageous to the general population than advantageous.

19. M. Hutchings, B. Francis, and P. Kirby, *Chain Effects 2015: The Impact of Academy Chains on Low-Income Students* (London: The Sutton Trust, 2015), 4.

20. Found at http://www.theguardian.com/education/2016/jan/02/ofsted-row-ministers-extent-teacher-shortages-michael-wilshaw.

21. Found at http://www.theguardian.com/education/2016/jan/11/teachers-unions-unite-to-highlight-national-crisis-in-profession.

22. *Evening Standard,* June 3, 2016.

23. Judith Burns, "Teacher Shortages in England, Spending Watchdog Confirms," BBC News, February 10, 2016, www.bbc.co.uk/news/education-35531982.

24. S. Pope, "The Supply of Mathematics Teachers in Context," paper given at Symposium on Sustainable Schools, House of Lords, June 6, 2016.

25. Advisory Committee for Mathematics Educators (2014), report on mathematics teacher supply, available at http://www.acme-uk.org/media/20263/teachersofmaths.pdf (accessed July 29, 2016).

26. House of Commons Library (2019), briefing paper no. 7222, *Teacher Recruitment and Retention in England,* February 12, 2019, 4.

27. Anne Cockburn and Terry Haydn, *Recruiting and Retaining Teachers: Understanding Why Teachers Teach* (London: Routledge Falmer, 2004).

28. House of Commons Library (2019), briefing paper no. 7222, *Teacher Recruitment and Retention in England,* February 12, 2019, 34–39.

29. D. Northcott, Evidence to the House of Commons Education Select Committee on Teacher Shortages, 2015.

30. K. Courtney Evidence to the House of Commons Education Select Committee on Teacher Shortages, 2015.

31. N. Gibb Evidence to the House of Commons Education Select Committee on Teacher Shortages, 2015.

32. M. Donelan, Evidence to the House of Commons Education Select Committee on Teacher Shortages, 2015.

33. Department for Education, *Educational Excellence Everywhere* London: Department for Education (UK government department), 2016.

34. University and College Union, Parliamentary briefing on teacher training implications of the Department for Education's *Educational Excellence Everywhere* white paper, 2016.

35. House of Commons Library, briefing paper no. 7222, *Teacher Recruitment and Retention in England,* February 12, 2019.

36. Department for Education, *Strengthening Qualified Teacher Status and Improving Career Progression for Teachers: Government Consultation Response* (May 2018).

37. See https://www.gov.uk/government/publications/supporting-early-career-teachers (accessed April 4, 2019) and Department for Education, *Early Career Framework,* London: Department for Education (2019).

38. See https://www.theguardian.com/global-development/2016/sep/18/global-education-is-civil-rights-struggle-of-our-age-says-gordon-brown (accessed September 23, 2016).

CHAPTER SIX

Teacher Education in Finland
Persistent Efforts for High-Quality Teachers

HANNELE NIEMI AND JARI LAVONEN

Teacher education systems in different countries can vary greatly in terms of length, content, and structure.[1] Historical and political roots and contexts are factors that shape the background of these differences. The agency or actor that is responsible for organizing teachers' pre- and in-service training also varies. The amount of professional autonomy that teachers are allowed and the way in which they are prepared for their professional roles depend upon many systemwide factors, such as the aims and value basis of the education, the status of the teaching profession, and the general quality of teaching and learning in school. Many of these factors are consequences of earlier decisions during certain historical situations, including in the Finnish education system and teacher education. In this chapter, we reflect upon how and why the Finnish education structure and teacher education have been revised in the last decades and what processes and decisions have led to its current situation. The Finnish education system has received a great deal of international attention because of its students' high performance in international comparative studies.[2,3] Worldwide, Finland is also ranked at the top in terms of its adult population's competencies in literacy and numeracy, and in problem solving in technology-rich environments.[4] Many researchers have reported that the quality of teachers seems to be a factor in this success.[5–7] When analyzing how Finnish teachers have achieved such competencies and professional quality, one must examine the decisions made in the Finnish education system beginning in the late 1960s, almost 60 years ago.

This chapter provides an overview of how teacher education and teachers' professional roles have developed in the Finnish education system mainly since the 1980s (with some sections beginning in the late 1960s) until the present. The chapter begins with a historical summary of landmarks in Finnish education that have been essential for high-quality teachers and their professional roles. Thereafter, it introduces the main features of recent teacher education programs and concludes with a focus on a new national development project called Teacher Education Forum.

Education as a Basic Right for All since the Late 1960s

The Finnish education system is an internationally examined example of a high-performing education system that successfully combines high quality with widespread equity and social cohesion through reasonable public financing.[8,9] The path to this current state has been a long one. After the Second World War, the baby boom of the 1950s increased the number of pupils in Finland. At the same time, the concept of a welfare society emerged in Nordic countries, particularly in Sweden, which is a neighboring country to Finland. In this vision, the state played a key role in protecting and promoting the social and economic well-being of its citizens. It was based on the principles of equality of opportunity, equitable distribution of wealth, and public responsibility for those unable to avail themselves of the minimal provisions for a good life. In Finland, free education was a part of this vision; it was regarded as a basic right and service for all citizens. On a strategic level and also a more practical level, education became a key condition for the Finnish economy's survival, as the country's economy structure was changing from agriculture, farming, and forestry to industry.

Equal opportunities in education were not a reality in the Finnish society of the 1950s. There were large disparities among the population despite the common obligation to attend elementary school that was enacted in 1921. In the 1950s, of the population older than 20 years, 29% had no education, and in rural areas this percentage reached 35%. Geographical differences were huge: in the southern part of Finland, the uneducated portion of the population (older than 20 years) was only 14%, but in northern rural areas of Finland, it was almost 48%.[10] In those days, Finland had a parallel education system; here, 10-year-old children had to choose their future careers. They had to seek entrance and pass examinations into academically oriented schools or choose a vocational track. If they selected the vocational route, they could not seek entrance to higher education. The education system placed individuals into one of two categories at a very early stage of their lives, thus creating a divided nation. The academic schools very often had tuition fees, which furthered the divide. Poor families and uneducated parents either could not see the value of schooling their children or could not afford to do so.

Moving from this parallel system toward a more comprehensive model was not easy. The head of the National Board of Education had proposed more equal comprehensive school as early as the 1930s, and educationalists and education administrators were working to change the education system in the 1950s. But, these claims and proposals did not lead to reforms.

Finally, in the 1960s, the ideology of social justice and education as contributing to a more equal society and democracy was gaining momentum in Scandinavian countries. In Finland, this was mainly within left-wing political parties as well as from some centrist groups. There were many political debates surrounding education, because right-wing party representatives and the earlier parallel education school teachers wanted to keep the old system. Finland's past livelihood was related to forestry and agriculture, and woodcutters and farmers had very low levels of education. However, all the parties understood that the labor market was in the process of changing. Finland was becoming an industrial country, and people's skills were lagging behind its development. Factories began to spring up in urban areas, and often, their workers had little or no education and often came from very poor families; social inequality increased. In the 1970s, the concept of lifelong learning also emerged, and it gradually overtook the earlier understanding that there were two separate groups of children: gifted academic children and those who were only practically oriented. As a small country, Finland would not achieve economic welfare if its overall level of education continued to be as low as it was. There was a wide consensus between politicians that the earlier system did not work. Finally, even though there were many different opinions about how to change the system, a new school model was planned. From 1965 to 1971, many committees of policy makers and experts made plans for a new school system, undertook explorative research and pilot studies in different parts of Finland and made plans for the implementation of school reform. Finally, Parliament passed the Comprehensive School Framework Law on May 24, 1968. The parallel system was abolished, and the comprehensive school model was born. Its main principles were as follows:[11,12]

- Basic education comprises nine years
- All citizens have an equal opportunity to receive basic education regardless of age, domicile, financial situation, sex, mother tongue, or residence
- School is free for everyone
- Municipalities are the local providers of education, and earlier state schools are placed under the control of local authorities

Implementation of the new law occurred from 1972 to 1978. The special strategy used to enact it was remarkable: the northern and eastern areas were the first to undergo these changes because they had the lowest level of education and the highest levels of inequality in education. The capital city area was the last to transform (from 1977 to 1978). The implementation was organized in such a way that there were coordinated national, regional, and local implementation plans. Concurrently, the Ministry of Education and the National Board of Education organized massive in-service training for all teachers. Teachers needed new competencies, as schools now contained entire age cohorts (range: 7- to 15-year-old students), not selected groups based on entrance examinations at 10 years of age. The task of teaching and motivating heterogeneous student groups was new to teachers. The new comprehensive school had two tiers: grades 1–6 as the primary level (7- to 12-year-old students) and grades 7–9 (13- to 15-year-old students) as the lower secondary level, and all students had a right and obligation to continue until the end of the 9th grade. Both levels had their own national curriculums. The new model was very centralized, and the national curriculum included detailed teaching content. In the mid-1980s, all public sector governance began moving toward a more decentralized model, and governance of the education system was part of this change. In addition to providing education, municipalities (which often means cities) also became responsible for a local curriculum and quality of education. Local education actors and the specific needs of local contexts became key factors for education and its functionality.

Grouping different students based on their skill levels was a polemical topic when Finland moved away from the parallel system based on student selection. In the beginning, the comprehensive schools used a tracking model in which students were sorted into low, intermediate, and high courses in math and languages within the comprehensive school. This was a concession to earlier academic secondary school teachers and business representatives who were afraid that Finland would lose its gifted children if they were placed in the same schools as the other children.[13] However, this principle was set into a new framework when students' paths to lifelong learning were assessed. The criteria for continuing to the next level of the educational system, particularly to upper secondary schools (high schools), demanded that students needed to complete at least the intermediate-level courses in the comprehensive school. The tracking system negated the lifelong learning paths, but the labor market and new occupations required students to continue their education after completing their basic education. The tracking system was completely abolished by the 1980s, and instead of segregation, schools were required to provide extra teaching hours and special needs support for weaker learners. Every student needed to have the skills to continue to the next level.

During the 1980s and 1990s, there were many political debates about the relevance of common comprehensive schools for all. Critical voices demanded more attention to gifted children. The comprehensive school had put many resources into helping children who had learning difficulties. These critical voices came from the business sector and right-wing party representatives. They were afraid that the common comprehensive schools did not provide enough inspiration, challenge, and support for gifted children. In spite of these debates, the comprehensive school model maintained its policy and the main national guidelines outlined that schools could have different local profiles and support students' individual qualities without separating them into different ability groups or schools.

Teachers were responsible for teaching an entire age cohort without dividing them into different competence profiles or school systems. The system also began to place a strong emphasis on inclusiveness, special needs education, and the students' holistic well-being; this trend continued and strengthened in the following decades. Understanding of learning had expanded, and differentiating based on students' personal learning needs and objectives within education had increased. It placed teachers as local actors in very high professional roles. Overall, systemic reform required a new pedagogical concept and an overhaul of teacher education.

Following the development through the decades, Niemi and Isopahkala-Bouret summarized the major features of the Finnish education system that have influenced teachers' work.[14] Their analysis reveals that the Finnish education policy has three main principles that have guided all activities throughout the education system for 40 years. These principles are *equity,* which means providing equal opportunities to all learners regardless of their social, ethnic, and economic background; *flexible educational structures,* which allow continuing one's education, even in the case of a failure; and a *high level of education* for the entire population.[15] The last principle means that lifelong learning is integrated with all levels of the system from early education to adult education.

Moreover, a fourth characteristic of Finnish education could be added: decentralization. It is related very much with the curriculum system and has been changed during the comprehensive school's lifetime. At the beginning, comprehensive schools were very centralized, but since 1985, the municipalities' freedom and responsibility were increased, as described earlier. Schools and teachers have become responsible for preparing a local curriculum and choosing learning materials and teaching methods.

Since 1994, the framework for basic education curriculum, prepared by the Finnish National Board of Education (since the 2017 National Agency of Education) has provided only very broad aims and content guidelines for teaching different subjects. The municipalities and, ultimately, the schools set up their own curricula based upon the national core curriculum. The national-level framework referred to as a core curriculum concerns all levels of the educational system: early education, preprimary, primary, lower (middle school), upper secondary (high school), vocational, and adult education. The National Agency of Education is responsible for revision processes, and curricula reforms are usually conducted every 10 years by inviting the teacher union, principals, parents' association, companies, teacher educators, and several experts to contribute to a new national core curriculum. The curriculum processes are interactive and participatory.[16,17]

Enhancement-Led Quality Assurance System for Improvements

The Finnish approach to quality assurance in education has been described as an enhancement/improvement-led evaluation.[18,19] Evaluation is performed for the sake of improvement, not ranking. This principle has also been implemented systematically in the entire educational system from early childhood until higher education and adult education. It concerns also the development of teacher education nationally and locally in different universities. An enhancement-led evaluation system also means that teachers' work is neither determined by high-stakes testing nor by standardized testing. The evaluation system aims to determine what types of improvements are needed for better learning outcomes. Local education providers (municipalities) are responsible for the quality of educational services and assessment methods. Teachers also implement enhancement-led evaluation in student learning. This means that formative evaluation methods are used to decide how to support various learners. Toom and Husu write: "Added to this, the task of assessment is to help pupils form a realistic image of their learning and development. It is also stated, that pupil assessment forms a whole, in which on-going feedback from the teacher plays an important part. With the help of assessment, the teacher guides the pupils in becoming aware of their thinking and actions and helps them understand what they are learning."[20]

Currently in Finland there is neither school inspection nor probationary time for new teachers as used to be the case for comprehensive schools. Nowadays, new teachers are fully licensed when they start their work in schools, after they graduate from teacher education programs. This has set high demands for such programs. Teachers have a high degree of professional responsibility as decision makers for all students' learning.

Teacher Education and Respect for Teachers

The big education system reform had a remarkable consequence for teacher education.[21,22] In the process, many important decisions had to be made. All teacher education was moved from the earlier colleges or seminars to eight traditional universities between 1971 and 1973. The major reason was that teachers needed new competencies in the comprehensive school. In 1973 the Teacher Education Committee drafted the outlines of new teacher education:

- Teacher education for basic and secondary schools should be academic, and given in universities.
- Teacher education should be unified. All colleges, seminars, and earlier normal schools should be affiliated with universities.
- Educational studies of teacher education should be rethought.
  - Teacher educational expertise should be increased.
  - Theory and practice should be integrated.
  - Pedagogical studies and academic subject studies should be combined better than earlier.
- Studies related to society and educational policy should be added to teacher education programs.

- Teacher education should be continuous and should ensure teachers' development throughout their careers.[23]

At the same time, Finnish higher education was undergoing changes. Degrees of social sciences, especially, were restructured; they all became four-year programs corresponding to a master's degree. Teacher education in universities had only one option: to provide MA-level programs. A new law of teacher education degrees was enacted in 1979. This was a big change, particularly for primary school teacher education, which was also increased to the master's degree level (five-year programs). Class/primary (grades 1–6) teachers had previously received their preservice teacher education in teacher training seminars or colleges. The programs varied from one to three years in length. A new model of studies provided the cultural, psychological, and pedagogical features of teaching and instruction. Almost one-fifth of the program is dedicated to research methodology studies, such as quantitative, qualitative, and mixed methods, in order to create a proper understanding of methodological issues in human sciences. A primary student teacher also carries out an extensive master's thesis as authentic research in educational sciences.

The secondary school (grades 7–12) teachers had previously studied their majors in universities to at least a bachelor's level; in many subjects they even had a master's degree, and after their degree they received one year's practicum in a teacher training school. A new teacher education provided all secondary school teachers with a master's degree, and the scope of their pedagogical studies was widened. Secondary teacher education is now organized into eight traditional universities in cooperation with the faculty of a specific subject, like the Faculty of Science, and the Faculty of Education / Department of Teacher Education. Studies are divided into two parts: the subject matter knowledge is studied at the department of the particular subject (e.g., physics) and the pedagogical studies at the Faculty of Education. These pedagogical studies give the student teachers the qualification necessary for teaching positions in all types of schools in their major and minor subjects. Since 1984, the secondary school student teachers have had pedagogical studies as a part of bachelor's- and master's-level studies. However, pedagogical studies can also be taken after the master's-level subject studies are completed. This is important in a country that always avoids dead ends in education: students and Finnish citizens in general have the option to continue their studies.

The aim was to unify different teacher categories and make all teachers familiar with the latest research in academic subject matter and pedagogy. Universities were seen as the most relevant place for teacher education because they provided the highest-quality research environments. The change made teacher education a part of the academic community. Educational sciences became a discipline that provided bachelor's, master's, and doctoral degrees. Teacher education degrees for primary teachers required a major in education with teaching practice and a minor in academic subjects, while secondary school teachers required a major in an academic subject and a minor in educational sciences, which also included teaching practice.

All university degrees were at that time very strictly defined programs. The centralized system led to a high degree of uniformity throughout the country's teacher education institutions. In the middle of the 1980s, a strong movement toward decentralization was implemented in all of Finland's public administrations, which also concerned education and higher education, including teacher education. Teacher education departments now had more freedom to organize their own degrees and connect teacher education to their university's profiles. However, they also had to produce teachers who had the qualification of a master's degree.

The teacher education degrees have been updated in different phases, depending on changes in the educational system. One of the recent teacher education reforms is linked with the European Bologna Process. This reform was carried out in 2004–2006 in all Finnish universities.[24] Teacher education was structured into three-year bachelor's and two-year master's degrees, but teacher qualification still required both degrees. The traditional distinction between class teachers and subject teachers was retained, but the structures of the respective degree programs allowed them to take flexible routes to include both in the same program or to permit a later qualification in either direction.

In Finland, the Bologna Process was implemented in educational sciences and teacher education interactively, both at a national level and also within the universities, through a national teacher education project during the years 2004 through 2006.[25] Nationally, all teacher education departments and other academic departments that had responsibilities in teacher education were invited to cooperate in making the draft recommendations for teacher education (TE) degrees. During that process, there were also many meetings and discussions with labor market representatives about teacher qualification. The common opinion was that teachers should have a master's degree. However, teacher education departments wanted to create some common guidelines, although it was emphasized that Finnish universities would remain autonomous.[26] It was decided that these guidelines could work as recommendations for how to combine degrees and also give a basis for quality assurance. Consequently, several main recommendations were agreed upon.

The teacher education curriculum should include the following components: (a) the latest scientific knowledge of subject matter and studies and how to transfer this knowledge into pedagogical content knowledge; (b) a research-based knowledge of pedagogy and subject matters; (c) research-informed professional skills and the competencies required to guide and support different learners; (d) an understanding of the social and cultural dimensions of education, which allows teachers to respond to the needs of individual learners in an inclusive way; and (e) studies that open the student teachers' awareness of teachers' roles as representatives of a moral profession and as public intellectuals in educational issues.[27]

The teacher qualification requires 300 ECTS units (a BA requires 180 ECTS, an MA requires 120 ECTS).[28] In the Bologna Process, credits were defined as ECTS (European Credit Transfer System) units (a unit consists of 28 hours of all students' studying, including contact hours and independent work with different types of assignments). Portions of various fields of teacher education studies can be summarized in the following way:[29,30]

- *Academic disciplines* (approximately 30% to 40 % of 300). Academic studies include a major or minors depending on the qualification being sought. Class teachers have a major in educational sciences and minors in other disciplines. Secondary school teachers have whatever disciplines are taught in schools or educational institutions.
- *Research studies* (approximately 20% of 300) consist of methodological studies, a bachelor's thesis, and a master's thesis.
- *Pedagogical studies* (minimum 60 ECTS) are obligatory for all teachers, and should also include teaching practice (approximately 33% of 60). The aim of 60 credits in pedagogical studies means the new teachers are able to:
  - integrate subject matter knowledge, knowledge about teaching and learning, and school practice into their own personal pedagogical view;
  - become aware of the different dimensions of the teacher profession: the social, philosophical, psychological, sociological, and historical basis of education;

- to collaborate in different networks and partnerships;
- to reflect on their own personal pedagogical "theory/view" (reflection for, in, and on action);
- act as autonomous professionals in planning, implementing, and assessing teaching and learning;
- develop potentials for lifelong professional development through research orientation.

- Finnish teacher education has aimed toward the integration of practice and theory.[31,32] The leading principle has been that teachers are educated to fill an autonomous professional role. This is the reason why pedagogical studies also include several phases of *teaching practicums*. All teacher education departments have teacher training schools. These schools are parts of universities and are specialized in supporting the student teachers' professional development. They also have commitments to develop teaching and learning by creating and applying new methods in learning environments. Practicum is divided into different phases. (a) The pedagogical studies begin with an orientation phase that allows the student teachers to observe and analyze students and schools from a teachers' perspective, after being a student for most of their lives. (b) The second phase is an intermediate practice during which the student teachers start to plan lessons and take on teachers' responsibilities in the classroom, and which also allows them to gradually widen their professional work. (c) The last phase is called advanced practicum, where the student teachers deepen and widen their competencies. This can happen in local, affiliated schools or in teacher training schools. It is worth noting that teacher training schools play an important role in the Finnish teacher education system.
- *Communication, language, and information and communication technology (ICT)* studies are obligatory (approximately 10–30 ECTS of 300).
- *Optional studies* may cover a variety of different courses through which students seek to profile their studies and qualifications (depending on other choices).

Teacher education programs in Finland are based on the assumption that evidence does not only grow from systematic research. It can also grow from observations and experiences of experts, policy makers, and practitioners in their own fields.[33,34] If teachers are expected to work as professionals who have the freedom and autonomy to make decisions in changing contexts, then they must also be in a position to evaluate what works and what does not. This kind of capability starts already in preservice teacher education, and the task of research studies is to prepare them to become critical professionals.

Research-Informed and Research-Based Teacher Education

The research component is an essential part of Finnish teacher education programs.[35–38] It makes up approximately 20% of the whole of TE studies for both elementary (who major in education) and secondary school teachers (who major in an academic subject). Research-oriented studies include research methodological courses, research seminars, and writing both bachelor's and master's theses.

It can be asked why Finnish teacher education emphasizes research-based orientation. In international literature there is often tension related to the concept of research-based education and a confusion between several closely related concepts: research-based, research-informed, research-led, evidence-based, and evidence-informed policy and practice.[39,40] Many researchers warn that education is one of the most difficult fields for research- and/or evidence-based policy and practice.[41–45] The major problem is who has ownership of knowledge and knowledge creation. Is it coming from academic or policy-level communities, outside practitioners' work, or are teachers themselves knowledge creators in their own profession? Berliner and Ozga see that education is a contextual activity.[46,47] It is very difficult to provide recommendations based only on experiments or data collected outside the practitioners' own field. Elliot has for a long time proposed action research as a tool for teachers' professional development, and there is a wealth of literature on how action research and design-based research can work in schools.[48–50]

In Finnish teacher education, the concepts above are complementary. "Research-based" means that teacher education is grounded in continuous research-based inquiry in academic disciplines, including educational sciences, and this provides a basis for the improvement of the curriculum in teacher education. Teacher educators in university departments and teacher training schools are seen as teachers and researchers. The basic qualification for a teacher educator is a PhD. Teachers in schools may also work as research-based professionals when they use scientific inquiry and methods in their work or conduct action research projects or small-case studies in classrooms or school communities. However, research-based, research-informed, or research-led concepts mean that knowledge from the scientific communities or practitioners' own inquiry-based communities is used in teaching and when selecting materials and methods for different learners. Teachers need knowledge about learners' development, recent scientific results in subject matters, and information about why some pupils learn and some don't. Teachers need scientific literacy as well as their practice-based evidence in order to understand on what grounds they can build their work. Teacher education must lead student teachers to this kind of culture. Even though educational research cannot provide direct applications to teachers, there are many ways it can inform or lead teachers' work. Design-based approaches in which practitioners and researchers work together in teachers' in-service training provide many options for practitioners to create a basis for their own work.[51] Prospective teachers must learn how knowledge is constructed and how they can use different sources of evidence in their work.

In-service training is necessary for maintaining teachers' high-quality competence. Contrary to preservice teacher education, the in-service education or professional development of teachers is the responsibility of the municipalities/cities in Finland. Therefore, municipalities should also have organized short in-service courses and professional development projects (PDPs) for teachers. Moreover, special centers have been established in many municipalities to coordinate local development efforts and in-service training. Some projects have substantially benefited from local and national networking. Moreover, teachers' pedagogical associations organize in-service training for teachers. For example, the Finnish Association of Teachers of Mathematics, Physics and Chemistry has annually organized in-service days for science teachers.

The Finnish National Board of Education (FNBE) is responsible for national-level implementation of educational programs and strategies (e.g., ICT strategies) and for financing ICT tools and long-term in-service training programs for teachers. For example, in 2016 the FNBE opened a call for projects emphasizing the development of innovative learning environments in basic and upper secondary education and training of teachers in these environments. Finnish teachers, in general, have a positive attitude toward in-service training, and they participate in the training voluntarily.

Different Approaches to Teacher Professionalism and Professional Autonomy

To understand a Finnish teacher's role and education, we have to see that teacher professionalism is a complex concept, and it has been defined in several ways. Other terms, such as *effective, competent, expert, quality, ideal,* or *respectful*, are used to describe a professional teacher.[52,53] The professionalism and effectiveness of a teacher is typically approached through analyzing: (a) the knowledge base of a professional teacher (input approach); (b) the process or the interaction that occurs in the classroom between the teacher and students (process approach); or (c) the outcomes of the teaching and learning process, such as students' learning outcomes measured by national tests or graduation rates (output approach).[54] The Finnish understanding of a professional teacher is close to the input approach. According to this approach, a professional teacher should have a versatile knowledge base, allowing him or her to act as an autonomous professional. The term *knowledge* is interpreted broadly in this context and is close to *competence* or *skill*. This knowledge base supports the broad planning, organization, and evaluation of teachers' own instructional practices and students' learning and learning outcomes. Broad planning encompasses the planning of the local curriculum down to the planning of a single lesson.

Teacher professionalism in the context of the input approach does not refer only to an individual teacher's competence but also to the status or appreciation of teachers.[55] In the Finnish context, the nature of leadership, a collaboration culture, and the structure of networks and school-society-family partnerships are important school-level factors that support teacher professionalism at the school level. Moreover, cultural and education policy factors, like trusting teachers without relying on heavy inspection or testing support teacher professionalism.[56,57]

From the very beginning of the current system of teacher education for the comprehensive school the objective has been to educate teachers, whose expertise is high-level. Programs need to ensure that their graduates are capable of professional, collaborative, and autonomous planning, implementing and assessing their own work, and planning local level curriculum. This kind of professional role has made teaching careers very attractive and desirable among applicants who seek entrance to teacher education programs in universities. In fact, they are among the most popular academic options in universities.

Decentralization has made schools more autonomous. It has assigned new responsibilities to principals and teachers. The curricula now must be drawn up by taking into account the schools' operating environments, local value choices, and special resources. Education providers in practice cities may decide about the implementation of a curriculum in cooperation with interest groups. The aim is to ensure a high standard of general education.

As it concerns pupil welfare and home-school cooperation, the curriculum must be drafted in collaboration with authorities charged with tasks that are part of the implementation of the local authority's social and health services.[58,59] Consequently, teachers are responsible for much more than simply providing teaching contents. Students must be ready to continue studying at the next level of education and learn new skills, and schools must support their personal growth.[60] Teachers must make a huge number of pedagogical decisions every day, and they must communicate students' learning problems to parents, special needs teachers, social workers, and nurses. Finnish teachers must also act as partners in multiprofessional groups for their students' well-being. Finnish schools are inclusive, and special needs students participate in normal classes with several support systems.

Consequently, quality work is distributed at the teacher level. Over the past several decades, research studies have indicated that local curriculum processes have inspired and empowered teachers and principals to develop the local curriculum and their own work and, moreover, increase the quality of education.[61–63] Education authorities and national-level education policy makers trust professional teachers, who together with principals, headmasters, and parents, know how to provide the best education for children and adolescents in a specific district.[64]

The teaching profession is very demanding everywhere in the world because of the complexity of many new needs of teaching and learning for the future. This is also the case in Finland, which is becoming a more multicultural society as well as a knowledge-based and technology-rich society; all of its people need high competencies for work and lifelong learning. The new trends of the national core curriculum emphasize that schools are learning communities in which all partners are members. In a recent analysis, Finnish teachers felt that initial teacher education did not provide enough preparation for collaboration between home and school, multiprofessional cooperation, or managing challenging students' needs.[65,66] The Finnish educational system requires much from teachers because of mixed-ability groups in teaching, high inclusiveness of education, and teachers' responsibility for modifying the national core curriculum to local needs. Even though teachers are under high pressure in developing teaching and learning environments, most teachers in the analysis felt that they were able to influence factors that promote students' learning.

At a classroom and student level, most challenges have focused on a trend of students' decreasing engagement in learning, especially in mathematics and science. Another discussion related to twenty-first-century competencies involves the challenges linked to the impact and use of new technologies in and out of school situations.[67,68] For responding to the urgent need to improve all students' learning outcomes and their engagement in learning, and also for supporting teachers' professional development, several national projects have been launched by the Ministry of Education and Culture in Finland since 2012, such as "future primary and secondary education" and a national project aiming to renew upper secondary education and teacher education.[69] They all aim to provide both teachers and students with twenty-first-century competencies. Preparation of national core curricula for pre-primary, basic, and upper secondary education belong to these endeavors.

New national-level core curricula for basic and upper secondary education were prepared in close collaboration with teachers, teacher educators, and providers of education (municipalities) during 2012–2015, and schools started with their own local curricula in 2016.[70,71] Both curricula emphasize the twenty-first-century competencies, and they support teachers in analyzing key education questions, such as: What will education mean in the future? How can education prepare all young people for the future? What types of competencies will be needed in everyday and working-life situations? And what kind of learning environments and practices or teaching methods would best produce the desired education and learning?[72] Therefore, the new curricula outline the need for broadly scoped competencies that align with twenty-first-century competencies, such as critical and creative thinking and an ability to use a wide range of tools, such as sociocultural (language) and digital (technological) tools. The curricula processes have continued during 2015–2016 at the local level. The Finnish National Agency for Education established the Majakka network (in English it means "Lighthouse") for supporting the local curriculum work at the municipality level. This network has meetings and a web platform. This second cycle has engaged teachers in analyzing the twenty-first-century competencies needed by all students. The national- and local-level curriculum processes will crystallize the vision of education for the future and the necessary know-how needed in Finnish society. The importance of these processes is not limited to the description of what should happen in Finnish classrooms, schools, and municipalities, but it will also highlight the values and efforts to be taken this time.[73]

As a part of education-related key projects in the current Finnish government program, a Finnish Teacher Education Forum was established by the

Ministry of Education in February 2016 aiming to foster the renewal of teacher education as part of a national reform program. The aims of the Teacher Education Forum are to prepare a development program for teachers' pre- and in-service education (lifelong professional development), to support the implementation of the program, and, moreover, to create the conditions for the renewal of Finnish teacher education through development projects. The forum consists of almost 100 teacher educators, teachers, and other stakeholders, including experts from municipalities and from the teacher and student unions. The forum has organized several meetings, both of the whole forum and of the smaller thematic groups. The forum has analyzed the research outcomes related to teacher education, benchmarked strategies and policy documents in other countries and organizations, and organized a national web-based brainstorming platform related to the renewal of teacher education. The forum published the reform program, *Development Program for Teachers Pre- and In-service Education* (lifelong professional development), in the beginning of October 2016. This program describes what kind of teacher education and continuous professional development of teachers are necessary to ensure that teachers are able to support students in the classroom to learn the competencies (knowledge, skill, and attitude) needed today, tomorrow, and in the future.

According to the forum program, Finnish future teachers are broad-based experts who create new pedagogical innovations and diversely utilize new learning environments. They are constantly developing their own competencies and their working communities. Second, teachers have in-depth knowledge of their field, pedagogical aptitude, and knowledge of values. Teachers have the courage to develop and experiment with things. They have the ability to apply new teaching innovations and the skill to change their own actions. Third, teachers use the latest research and evaluations in developing themselves, their working communities, and their educational institutions.

The teacher education development program also introduces six main actions for the development of teacher education. Finnish universities are conducting development projects under these actions during 2017–2019. The key actions are:

1. *Holistic view of teacher education*
    To identify what is common in teachers' pedagogical competence throughout the educational system from kindergarten to vocational training,

more closely connect pre- and in-service education, and develop a well-functioning induction phase.
2. *Selection and anticipation*
   To forecast demands of teachers and balance the number of teachers needed and educated in all areas and levels of the educational system.
3. *Supporting the development of competencies needed in generating novel ideas and innovations*
   To renew teacher education programs and their teaching and learning culture toward twenty-first-century competencies and to strengthen leadership, networks, and development operations for and together with local school sites.
4. *Collaboration culture and networks*
   To promote and strengthen cooperation between all teacher education actors in universities: subject departments, departments of teacher education, and teacher training schools; and further, to ensure cooperation between different teacher education programs: kindergarten, primary, secondary, and vocational teacher education.
5. *Supportive leadership*
   To promote schools as learning communities with high-quality pedagogical leadership: goal orientation and interaction, strategic planning, and quality culture.
6. *Research-based teacher education*
   To enhance teacher education programs and teaching practices and to ensure that they are based on research and that student teachers learn to (a) research skills and research orientation, (b) assess their practices, and (c) reflect on professional tasks and development independently and collaboratively.

These aims are very much in line with the earlier teacher education objectives of several decades ago. In changing contexts, the TE programs must be updated from a perspective of future needs and ensure that teachers have the competencies needed in schools and society today and in the coming years.

In addition to teacher education preservice revisions, teachers' in-service training is also under a cultural change toward more collaborative whole school programs.[74] In earlier years, Finnish in-service training was based on training days and short courses. These types of courses are still being offered to teachers, but the trend is toward a more holistic and integrated approach.

This trend is to see teachers as developers in the whole school community. Teachers have research-based orientation in preservice teacher education, and this should be used as a resource. It makes teachers capable of designing school-based projects and also teachers' own professional development as it relates to school development. Collaboration within the school community as well as with external partners, especially parents, is part of teachers' professional development, and they need support for that, especially in the beginning of their careers. Teachers' work is becoming more and more complicated, and working in multiprofessional cooperation is important, especially when students need special education.

Conclusions

The Finnish education context is challenging for teachers, because they are required to perform a variety of duties, such as planning the local curriculum and organizing assessments, engaging in networks at the school and city levels, partnering with families and participating in quality assurance processes. Thus, primary and secondary school teachers are educated in master's programs at eight Finnish universities. According to national- and university-level strategies, teacher education is based on scientific research and professional practices in the field. In Finland, the teacher education degree and the law of teacher qualifications require five years of university studies (for both BA and MA degrees) as a mandatory condition.[75] The program of study provides student teachers with the knowledge and skills they need to operate independently as academic professionals and to develop their fields.[76–78] Teaching is one of the most desirable academic fields in Finland. Revisions in the educational system, a systematic development toward a high profession status of teachers, trust in teachers, and high professional autonomy have made the profession very popular. An emphasis on research is an essential characteristic of the programs that educate primary and secondary school teachers in Finland.[79] Pedagogical studies are a core element of the educational programs for both primary and secondary school teachers. During their pedagogical studies, students learn to combine educational theories, subject knowledge, and their personal histories and to integrate subject matter knowledge, as well as knowledge about teaching and learning and school practice, into their own personal pedagogical view.[80]

Finnish teacher education has grown in the political and historical context in which equity and lifelong learning have been leading educational principles, and teachers' high-standard professional roles have been seen as the main factors in achieving these goals. These have been continuously upheld in the national educational agenda. It has not supported the status quo; instead it has been more or less a continuous process in which enhancement-led quality assurance, decentralization of the educational system, and teacher education programs are in mutual interaction. Decentralization is implemented in the Finnish education system in several ways: local providers of education (municipalities) and local teachers prepare the local curriculum and, consequently, localize the aims and content of the curriculum. The educational ecosystem requires that educational provisions also be in close cooperation with other sectors of society, especially with social and health care.

Finnish educational ideology has put a strong emphasis on inclusiveness and promotion of all students' learning.[81,82] Teachers are key players in taking care of different learners and promoting their holistic well-being. In addition to student-related competence, teachers are also responsible for the whole school development. They are decision makers, and they need to work in cooperation with several partners in education and society. This kind of teacher leadership requires high-quality teacher education and continuous, persistent work.

Preconditions for the Finnish decentralized education system, which aims to provide high-quality education and equal opportunities for all learners, to be successful, are: (a) common, national-level, long-term strategic aims must be established, and local level plans, such as a curriculum and an equity plan, must be prepared and implemented; (b) quality work, student assessment, and continuous improvement of learning environments and practices must be implemented at the local level; and (c) professional teachers must be educated to collaborate, engage in broad planning, and assess their own teaching abilities and their students' learning outcomes.

NOTES

1. See Darling-Hammond, D., & Lieberman, A. (Eds.) (2012). *Teacher education around the world. Changing policies and practices.* New York: Routledge.

2. Organisation for Economic Co-operation and Development (OECD). (2010). *PISA 2009 results: What students know and can do—Student performance in reading, mathematics and science. (Volume I).* Paris: OECD.

3. OECD. (2014a). *PISA 2012 results: (Volume V).* Paris: OECD. Retrieved from http://www.oecd.org/pisa/keyfindings/pisa-2012-results-volume-v.htm.

4. OECD. (2016). *Skills matter: Further results from the survey of adult skills.* OECD Publishing, Paris. http://dx.doi.org/10.1787/9789264258051-en.

5. E.g., Sahlberg, P. (2012). The most wanted: Teachers and teacher education in Fin-

land. In D. Darling-Hammond & A. Lieberman (Eds.) (2012). *Teacher education around the world. Changing policies and practices* (pp. 1–21). New York: Routledge.

6. E.g., Simola, H. (2005). The Finnish miracle of PISA: Historical and sociological remarks on teaching and teacher education. *Comparative Education, 41*(4), 455–470.

7. Välijärvi, J., & Sulkunen, S. (2016). Finnish school in international comparison. In H. Niemi, A. Toom, & A. Kallioniemi (Eds.). *Miracle of education: The principles and practices of teaching and learning in Finnish schools* (2nd ed.) (pp. 3–22). Rotterdam: Sense Publishers.

8. Sahlberg, P. (2011). *Finnish lessons: What can the world learn from educational change in Finland?* New York: Teachers College Press.

9. Niemi, H., Toom, A., & Kallioniemi, A. (Eds.), (2016). *Miracle of education: The principles and practices of teaching and learning in Finnish schools* (2nd ed.). Rotterdam: Sense Publishers.

10. Sarjala, J. (2005). Reforms from current perspectives. (Only in Finnish: Uudistukset nykypäivän näkökulmasta). In K. Hämäläinen, A. Lindrstöm, & J. Puhakka (Eds.), Yhtenäisen peruskoulun menestystarina (the name in English: A success story of the unified comprehensive school), Palmenia series, 36–40. Helsinki University Press.

11. E.g., Sarjala, J. (2005). Reforms from current perspectives. (Only in Finnish: Uudistukset nykypäivän näkökulmasta). In K. Hämäläinen, A. Lindrstöm, & J. Puhakka (Eds.), Yhtenäisen peruskoulun menestystarina (the name in English: A success story of the unified comprehensive school), Palmenia series, 36–40. Helsinki University Press.

12. E.g., Itälä, J. (2005). The change of the economic structure sealed the school reform. (Only in Finnish: Elinkeinorakenteen muutos ratkaisi koulu-uudistuksen). In K. Hämäläinen, A. Lindrstöm, & J. Puhakka (Eds.), Yhtenäisen peruskoulun menestystarina (the name in English: A success story of the unified comprehensive school), Palmenia series, 47–53. Helsinki University Press.

13. Purhonen, K. (2005). South Strand for comprehensive and private schools. (Only in Finnish Eteläranta peruskoulun ja yksityiskoulujen puolesta). In K. Hämäläinen, A. Lindrstöm, & J. Puhakka (Eds.), Yhtenäisen peruskoulun menestystarina (the name in English: A success story of the unified comprehensive school), Palmenia series, 61–65. Helsinki University Press.

14. Niemi, H. & Isopahkala-Bouret, U. (2012). Lifelong learning in Finnish society—An analysis of national policy documents. *International Journal of Continuing Education and Lifelong Learning, 5*(1), 43–63.

15. OECD. (2006). *Equity in education. Thematic Review. Finland Country Note.* Retrieved from http://www.oecd.org/education/school/36376641.pdf.

16. Halinen, I., & Holappa, A.-S. (2013). Curricular balance based on dialogue, cooperation and trust—The case of Finland. In W. Kuiper & J. Berkvens (Eds.), Balancing curriculum regulation and freedom across Europe. CIDREE Yearbook 2013, 39–62. Enschede: SLO Netherlands Institute for Curriculum.

17. Vahtivuori-Hänninen, S., Halinen, I., Niemi, H., Lavonen, J., & Lipponen, L. (2014). A new Finnish national core curriculum for basic education and technology as an integrated tool for learning. In H. Niemi, J. Multisilta, L. Lipponen, & M. Vivitsou (Eds.), *Finnish innovations & technologies in schools: Towards new ecosystems of learning* (pp. 21–32). Rotterdam: Sense Publishers.

18. Kumpulainen, K., & Lankinen. T. (2016). Striving for educational equity and ex-

cellence: Evaluation and assessment in Finnish basic education. In H. Niemi, A. Toom, & A. Kallioniemi (Eds.), *Miracle of education: The principles and practices of teaching and learning in Finnish schools* (2nd ed.) (pp. 71–82). Rotterdam: Sense Publishers.

19. Niemi, H., & Lavonen, J. (2012). Evaluation for improvements in Finnish teacher education. In J. Harford, B. Hudson, & H. Niemi (Eds.), *Quality assurance and teacher education: International challenges and expectations 6*, 159–186.

20. Toom, A. & Husu, J. (2016). Finnish teachers as "makers of the many": Balancing between broad pedagogical freedom and responsibility. In H. Niemi, A. Toom, & A. Kallioniemi (Eds.), *Miracle of education: The principles and practices of teaching and learning in Finnish schools* (2nd ed.) (pp. 40–46, p. 46). Rotterdam/Boston/Taipei: Sense Publishers.

21. Sahlberg, P. (2011). *Finnish lessons: What can the world learn from educational change in Finland?* New York: Teachers College Press.

22. Niemi, H. (2016). The societal factors contributing to education and schooling in Finland. In H. Niemi, A. Kallioniemi, & A. Toom (Eds.). *Miracle of education: The principles and practices of teaching and learning in Finnish schools* (2nd ed.) (pp. 24–40). Rotterdam: Sense Publishers.

23. Teacher Education Committee (1975). The committee report from the committee of teacher education of the year 1973. Series 1975:75. Helsinki: The Ministry of Education.

24. Jakku-Sihvonen, R., & Niemi, H. (Eds.). (2006). *Research-based teacher education in Finland—Reflections by Finnish teacher educators*. Research in Educational Sciences 25. Turku: Finnish Educational Research Association.

25. Jakku-Sihvonen, R., & Niemi, H. (Eds.). (2006). *Research-based teacher education in Finland—Reflections by Finnish teacher educators*. Research in Educational Sciences 25. Turku: Finnish Educational Research Association.

26. Jakku-Sihvonen, R., & Niemi, H. (Eds.). (2006). *Research-based teacher education in Finland—Reflections by Finnish teacher educators*. Research in Educational Sciences 25. Turku: Finnish Educational Research Association.

27. Niemi, H. (2016). The societal factors contributing to education and schooling in Finland. In H. Niemi, A. Kallioniemi, & A. Toom (Eds.) *Miracle of education: The principles and practices of teaching and learning in Finnish schools* (2nd ed.) (pp. 24–40). Rotterdam: Sense Publishers.

28. Jakku-Sihvonen, R., & Niemi, H. (Eds.). (2006). *Research-based teacher education in Finland—Reflections by Finnish teacher educators*. Research in Educational Sciences 25. Turku: Finnish Educational Research Association.

29. Niemi, H. (2016). The societal factors contributing to education and schooling in Finland. In H. Niemi, A. Kallioniemi, & A. Toom (Eds.). *Miracle of education: The principles and practices of teaching and learning in Finnish schools* (2nd ed.) (pp. 24–40). Rotterdam: Sense Publishers.

30. Lavonen, J., Krzywacki-Vainio, H., Aksela, M., Krokfors, L., Oikkonen, J. & Saarikko, H. (2007). Pre-service teacher education in chemistry, mathematics and physics. In E. Pehkonen, M. Ahtee, & J. Lavonen (Eds.), *How Finns learn mathematics and science*. Rotterdam: Sense Publishers.

31. E.g., Issitt, M., and Spence, J. (2005). Practitioner knowledge and evidence based research policy and practice. *Youth and policy, 88,* 63–82.

32. Jyrhämä, R. (2006). The function of practical studies in teacher education. In R. Jakku-Sihvonen and H. Niemi (Eds.), *Research-based teacher education in Finland: Re-*

flections by Finnish teacher educators (pp. 51–70). Turku: Finnish Educational Research Association.

33. E.g., Issitt, M., and Spence, J. (2005). Practitioner knowledge and evidence based research policy and practice. *Youth and policy, 88,* 63–82.

34. Jyrhämä, R. (2006). The function of practical studies in teacher education. In R. Jakku-Sihvonen and H. Niemi (Eds.), *Research-based teacher education in Finland: Reflections by Finnish teacher educators* (pp. 51–70). Turku: Finnish Educational Research Association.

35. Jyrhämä, R. (2006). The function of practical studies in teacher education. In R. Jakku-Sihvonen and H. Niemi (Eds.), *Research-based teacher education in Finland: Reflections by Finnish teacher educators* (pp. 51–70). Turku: Finnish Educational Research Association.

36. Jyrhämä, R., & Maaranen, R. (2016). Research orientation in teachers' work. In H. Niemi, A. Toom & A. Kallioniemi (Eds.), *Miracle of education: The principles and practices of teaching and learning in Finnish schools* (2nd ed.) (pp. 91–108). Rotterdam: Sense Publishers.

37. Niemi, H. & Nevgi, A. (2014). Research studies and active learning promoting professional competences in Finnish teacher education, *Teaching and Teacher Education, 43,* 131–142.

38. Niemi, H., & Jakku-Sihvonen, R. (2006). Research-based teacher education. In R. Jakku-Sihvonen & H. Niemi (Eds.), *Research-based teacher education in Finland— reflections by Finnish teacher educators* (pp. 31–50) Turku: Finnish Educational Research Association.

39. Biesta, G. (2007). Why "what works" won't work: Evidence-based practice and the democratic deficit in educational research. *Educational Theory, 57,* 1–22.

40. Boaz, A., Ashby, D., & Young, K. (2002). What have they got to offer evidence based policy and practice? Working paper 2. Systematic reviews: ESRC UK Centre for Evidence Based Policy and Practice. Queen Mary. University of London.

41. Biesta, G. (2007). Why "what works" won't work: Evidence-based practice and the democratic deficit in educational research. *Educational Theory, 57,* 1–22.

42. Boaz, A., Ashby, D., & Young, K. (2002). What have they got to offer evidence based policy and practice? Working paper 2. Systematic reviews: ESRC UK Centre for Evidence Based Policy and Practice. Queen Mary. University of London.

43. E.g., Berliner, D. (2002). Educational research: The hardest science of all. *Educational Researcher, 31*(8), 18–20.

44. E.g., Hammersley, M. (2004). Some questions about evidence-based practice in education. In G. Thomas and R. Prong (Eds.), *Evidence based practice in education.* Maidenhead: OUP/McGraw-Hill.

45. E.g., McCormick, R. (2003). Reliable evidence for policy making in complex settings. Paper presented to the EMINENT IV Conference, Geneva, 9–10 October 2003.

46. E.g., Berliner, D. (2002). Educational research: The hardest science of all. *Educational Researcher, 31*(8), 18–20.

47. Ozga, J. (2000). *Policy research in educational settings. Contested terrain.* Buckingham: Open University Press.

48. Borko, H. (2004). Professional development and teacher learning: Mapping the terrain. *Educational Researcher, 38*(8), 3–15.

49. Elliott, J. (2001) Making evidence-based practice educational. *British Educational Journal, 27*(5), 555–574.
50. Issitt, M., and Spence, J. (2005). Practitioner knowledge and evidence based research policy and practice. *Youth and policy, 88,* 63–82.
51. E.g., Korhonen, T., Lavonen, J., Kukkonen, M., Sormunen, K., & Juuti, K. (2014). The innovative school as an environment for the design of educational innovations. In H. Niemi, J. Multisilta, L. Lipponen, & M. Vivitsou (Eds.), *Finnish innovations & technologies in schools: Towards new ecosystems of learning* (pp. 38–56). Rotterdam, NL: Sense Publishers.
52. Cruickshank, D. R., & Haefele, D. (2001). Good teachers, plural. *Educational Leadership, 58*(5), 26–30.
53. Stronge, J. H., & Hindman, J. (2003). Hiring the best teachers. *Educational Leadership, 60*(8), 48–52.
54. Goe, L., Bell, C., & Little, O. (2008). *Approaches to evaluating teacher effectiveness: A research synthesis.* Washington, DC: National Comprehensive Center for Teacher Quality.
55. Müller, J., Norrie, C., Hernández, F., & Goodson, I. (2010). Restructuring teachers' work-lives and knowledge in England and Spain. *Compare, 40*(3), 265–277.
56. Lavonen, J., Korhonen, T., Kukkonen, M., & Sormunen, K. (2014). Rajaton luokkahuone [Boundless classroom]. In H. Niemi, & J. Multisilta (Eds.), *Innovatiivinen koulu* (pp. 86–113). Jyväskylä: PS-kustannus.
57. Lavonen, J., & Korhonen, T. (2017). Towards twenty-first century education: Success factors, challenges, and the renewal of Finnish education. In S. Choo, D. Sawch, A. Willanueva, R. Vinz (Eds.), *Educating for the 21st century: Perspectives, policies and practicies from around the world* (pp. 243–264). Singapore: Springer.
58. Finnish National Board of Education (FNBE). (2014). *The national core curriculum for basic education.* Helsinki: Finnish National Board of Education. Retrieved from http://www.oph.fi/ops2016.
59. Finnish National Board of Education (FNBE). (2015). *The national core curriculum for upper secondary education.* Helsinki: Finnish National Board of Education. Retrieved from https://verkkokauppa.oph.fi/EN/page/national-core-curricula-for-education/.
60. Niemi, H., & Isopahkala-Bouret, U. (2012). Lifelong learning in Finnish society—An analysis of national policy documents. *International Journal of Continuing Education and Lifelong Learning, 5*(1), 43–63.
61. Atjonen, P. (1993). Kunnan opetussuunnitelman koulun hallinnollisen ja pedagogisen kehittämisen kohteena ja välineenä [Local level curriculum as a target and tool for the development of school administration (management and leadership)]. *Acta Universitatis Ouluensis, series E.* Oulun yliopisto, Kasvatustieteiden tiedekunta.
62. Jauhiainen, P. (1995). Opetussuunnitelmatyö koulussa. Muuttuuko yläasteen opettajan työ ja ammatinkuva? [Preparation of a local curriculum. How do teacher profession and identity change?]. *Tutkimuksia 154. Helsingin yliopiston opettajankoulutuslaitos.*
63. Holappa, A.-S. (2007). Perusopetuksen opetussuunnitelma 2000-luvulla—uudistus paikallisina prosesseina kahdessa kaupungissa [The curriculum of basic education in the twenty-first century—a reform of local processes in two cities]. *Acta Universitatis Ouluensis, series E 94.* University of Oulu, Faculty of Education.
64. Simola, H. (2005). The Finnish miracle of PISA: Historical and sociological remarks on teaching and teacher education. *Comparative Education, 41*(4), 455–470.

65. OECD. (2014b). *TALIS 2013, Results: An international perspective on teaching and learning,* TALIS. OECD Publishing.

66. Johnson, L., Adams Becker, S., Estrada, V., and Freeman, A. (2014). NMC Horizon Report: 2014 K–12 Edition. Austin, Texas: The New Media Consortium. https://www.scribd.com/doc/243496936/2014-nmc-horizon-report-k12-en.

67. Hietajärvi, L., Tuominen-Soini, H., Hakkarainen, K., Salmela-Aro, K., & Lonka, K. (2015). Is student motivation related to socio-digital participation? A person-oriented approach, *Procedia—Social and Behavioral Sciences, 171,* 1156–1167. https://doi.org/10.1016/j.sbspro.2015.01.226.

68. Hakkarainen, K., Hietajärvi, L., Alho, K., Lonka, K., & Salmela-Aro, K. (2015). What engages digital natives. In J. Eccles and K. Salmela-Aro (Eds.), International Encyclopedia of the Social & Behavioral Sciences, Elsevier.

69. Press release (2014). Kiuru: Broad-based project to develop future primary and secondary education. Ministry of Education. http://www.minedu.fi/OPM/Tiedotteet/2014/02/perusopetus.html?lang=en.

70. Finnish National Board of Education (FNBE). (2014). *The national core curriculum for basic education.* Helsinki: Finnish National Board of Education. Retrieved from http://www.oph.fi/ops2016.

71. Finnish National Board of Education (FNBE). (2015). *The national core curriculum for upper secondary education.* Helsinki: Finnish National Board of Education. Retrieved from http://www.oph.fi/download/172121_lukion_opetussuunnitelman_perusteet_2015.docx.

72. Vahtivuori-Hänninen, S., Halinen, I., Niemi, H., Lavonen, J., & Lipponen, L. (2014). A new Finnish national core curriculum for basic education and technology as an integrated tool for learning. In H. Niemi, J. Multisilta, L. Lipponen, & M. Vivitsou (Eds.), *Finnish innovations & technologies in schools: Towards new ecosystems of learning* (pp. 21–32). Rotterdam: Sense Publishers.

73. Finnish National Board of Education (FNBE). (2014). *The national core curriculum for basic education.* Helsinki: Finnish National Board of Education. Retrieved from http://www.oph.fi/ops2016.

74. Niemi, H. (2015). Teacher professional development in Finland: Towards a more holistic approach. *Psychology, Society & Education, 7*(3), 279–294.

75. Niemi, H., & Nevgi, A. (2014). Research studies and active learning promoting professional competences in Finnish teacher education, *Teaching and Teacher Education, 43,* 131–142.

76. Cf. Cruickshank, D. R., & Haefele, D. (2001). Good teachers, plural. *Educational Leadership, 58*(5), 26–30.

77. Stronge, J. H., & Hindman, J. (2003). Hiring the best teachers. *Educational Leadership, 60*(8), 48–52.

78. Müller, J., Norrie, C., Hernández, F., & Goodson, I. (2010). Restructuring teachers' work-lives and knowledge in England and Spain. *Compare, 40*(3), 265–277.

79. Jakku-Sihvonen, R., & Niemi, H. (Eds.). (2006). *Research-based teacher education in Finland—Reflections by Finnish teacher educators.* Research in Educational Sciences 25. Turku: Finnish Educational Research Association.

80. Lavonen, J., Krzywacki-Vainio, H., Aksela, M., Krokfors, L., Oikkonen, J., & Saarikko, H. (2007). Pre-service teacher education in chemistry, mathematics and physics.

In E. Pehkonen, M. Ahtee, & J. Lavonen (Eds.), *How Finns learn mathematics and science*. Rotterdam: Sense Publishers.

81. Halinen, I., & Järvinen, R. (2008). Towards inclusive education: The case of Finland. *Prospects, 145, 38*(1), 77–97. UNESCO.

82. Laukkanen, R. (2007). Finnish strategy for high-level education for all. In N. C. Sognel & P. Jaccard (Eds.), *Governance and performance of education systems*. Dordrecht, NL: Springer.

CHAPTER SEVEN

Transforming Teacher Preparation and Development in Ghana

Progress and Prospects

KWAME AKYEAMPONG

Recent history of teacher education reforms in Ghana can be grouped under three main periods. The first came under the 1986 education reforms, which produced a restructured education system and rapidly improved access to basic education (primary and lower secondary), while simultaneously producing a decline in the quality of basic education that coincided with an exodus of trained teachers to find better-paid work in other countries.[1] Unqualified teachers were recruited to fill the vacancies that had been created by the exodus. On teacher education, the 1986 reforms raised entry qualifications for teacher trainees and initiated a program to replace unqualified teachers with trained teachers.[2,3] The Free Compulsory Universal Basic Education (FCUBE) and decentralization reforms in 1995 were introduced partly to address the decline in quality education that had resulted from the rapid increase in access to basic education, following the 1986 education reforms. Under FCUBE, the curriculum of preservice teacher education was reviewed to emphasize learner-centered pedagogy as part of other measures to improve teacher quality. Policy makers also raised the importance of professional development and linked it to the training of headteachers, who were in turn to train teachers at the local school level. Teacher education again came under the spotlight, after the Ghana Education Service produced a set of guidelines for the implementation of a new teacher education policy in 2000. The guidelines signaled a major shift in teacher preparation policy in Ghana and laid the foundation for another period of teacher education reforms ushered in by the Pre-Tertiary Professional Teacher Development and Management (PTPDM) policy framework in 2017.

In this chapter, I shall discuss the significance of each of these policy periods and how they have each contributed to a transformation of teacher preparation in response to imperatives to improve the quality of basic education in Ghana. The chapter is organized as follows—the first section discusses the 1986 and 1995 FCUBE education reforms and how they triggered initial reforms in teacher education for basic school teachers. Next, I discuss the 2000 teacher education policy guidelines, which laid the foundations for a new direction in teacher preparation in Ghana. The third section examines the PTPDM policy framework, how it extended the 2000 policy guidelines, and how it is continuing to shape teacher preparation for Ghanaian basic school teachers. In the fourth and concluding section, I reflect on the progress that has been made, and I highlight the significance and prospects for the future of teacher preparation in Ghana, as well as its implications for future research.

The 1986 Education and FCUBE Reforms

The year 1986 could be described as a significant time of change in Ghana's education system, as it marked a concerted effort to implement earlier proposals from nine education reform commissions from independence in 1957 to the mid-1980s.[4] The 1986 education reform occurred after a time of prolonged economic decline that had devastating consequences on the education system and teaching profession. From 1979 to 1983, total economic output in the country declined by 14% and real per capita income fell by 23%. The index of real monthly earnings in the formal sector dropped from 315 to 62.[5] Years of economic decline led to low investment in education, with most of the recurrent expenditure on education spent entirely on wages of teachers and non-teaching staff. Government spending on education dropped from 6.4% of GDP in 1976 to just 1.5% by 1984.[6] School enrollments declined, and facilities and infrastructure deteriorated and left the teaching force demoralized. Many Ghanaian teachers left for Nigeria in search of better pay and working conditions. The mass exodus of teachers meant that more than 50% of teachers of primary and middle schools had to be replaced by untrained teachers.[7]

The 1986 education reforms were initiated as part of the government's efforts to restructure the economy and ensure that education provided skills for self-employment and the labor market. The restructured education system replaced the six-year primary school, four-year middle school, and seven-year secondary school with a 6,6,3 system, and in effect, reduced pre-university education by five years; sought improvements in teaching and learning in basic schools by increasing school hours and teacher quality by phasing out the recruitment of untrained teachers; and intensified professional development of teachers.[8] The overall effect was a significant improvement in access to primary education, but under a climate of poor economic performance, the expectation that teacher performance would improve to impact learning outcomes did not materialize.[9] The reforms introduced a cascade model of training, in which headteachers were trained and expected to train teachers in their schools. However, much of the headteacher training was not directed at weaknesses in teachers' pedagogical skills. Instead, it focused much more on improving school organization and management. Besides, the reforms failed to address the overloaded school curriculum and the inadequate instructional facilities in basic schools.[10,11]

In 1994, eight years after the inception of the New Education Reform Program in 1986, the results of poor performance of pupils in nationwide criterion reference tests at age 12 led to the setting up of another Education Review Committee to review the performance of the basic education system.[12] The committee recommended a further reform, the Free Compulsory Universal Basic Education Programme (FCUBE), which was initiated in 1995, with massive donor assistance led by the World Bank. The increasing concern about the poor quality of teaching and learning in basic schools brought teacher education to the attention of reformers. In 1996, the Ministry of Education introduced a program of continuous professional development for teachers in which student-centered instructional practices and assessment techniques were emphasized.[13]

On teacher education, the FCUBE policy document stressed that "the implementation of the FCUBE program will require the services of a large number of well qualified teachers in the shortest possible time. The teachers should be well-versed in teaching, particularly in primary methodology," and "teacher development will be more 'school based' so that emphasis can be placed on hands-on-training activities in schools.'"[14]

The Education Review Committee felt strongly that teacher education was overly theoretical and not aligned closely, in content and design, with the primary school curriculum and the needs of real classroom teaching.

FCUBE reformers signaled the importance of school-based training as key to improving teacher quality. But, they also argued that by "reviewing and revising teaching materials in line with a revised, and more focused, syllabus and introducing new measures on teacher incentives including teacher prizes and teaching housing in rural areas, and a shift to in-service teacher training using distance learning materials," this would bring about the improvements in quality education that the 1986 reforms had failed to produce.[15] However, the FCUBE reforms did not tackle fundamental weaknesses in the approach to teacher preparation, which was theory-based. Even though it recognized the value of school-based training, nothing was done to change the three-year residential training program to include school-based elements. Basically, the three-year training program at the time consisted of a general education component (30%), academic education (30%), and professional studies (40%). The general education comprised eight "core" subjects: basic mathematics, basic science, English language, Ghanaian languages, physical education, cultural studies, general education, and agricultural studies. For academic education, trainees were offered two electives chosen from science or vocational-based subjects. Professional studies focused on the methods of teaching school subjects. Over the three-year program, trainees were expected to spend eight weeks on teaching practice in basic schools, although the actual time spent was often much less, typically between five to six weeks.[16] Instead, the revitalization of quality education was linked to an emphasis on material inputs, such as textbooks and school buildings.[17] Also, effective strategies were not introduced to improve teacher recruitment and training to match the increasing student intake in schools. By 2005, the student to trained teacher ratio had increased from 43:1 in 1996 to 63:1, and the number of untrained teachers, far from shrinking, had doubled for both primary and lower secondary schools.[18] Besides, as noted by Kadingdi,[19] FCUBE "policymakers appeared not to take into consideration . . . the need for change in teachers' practices rather than simply a change in their curriculum materials."

Official policy at the time of FCUBE reforms was to eliminate "pupil-teachers" (i.e., untrained teachers) and replace them with newly trained teachers from government teacher training colleges. By the time of the FCUBE reforms, Ghana had 38 teacher training colleges, with the first opened in 1848 by the German Basel Missionaries to train teachers for their schools. By the 1940s 10 new government colleges had been added.[20] After independence in 1957 and with a strong commitment to increase human resources for development, the government opened more teacher training colleges to cater to the expansion in school enrollment. By 1978, the number of teacher training colleges had increased to 38, offering a three-year residential postsecondary training for a teacher qualification called certificate A.[21] Total annual output of trained teachers from the 38 colleges has been between 5,500 and 6,000 since 1995.[22] All 38 colleges train teachers for both primary and lower secondary schools.

With the introduction of the three-year certificate A program, the number of trained teachers in the 1990s increased, although this upward trend started to reverse in the early to mid-2000s.[23] The government's policy to rely on in-service training using distance learning materials to develop teachers' skills also had limited impact: "only 3 percent of teachers receive[d] such training on a regular basis."[24] Teacher quality as measured by the use of improved teaching methods such as student-centered learning approaches had improved but could not be "described as widespread as they were used by a minority of teachers."[25]

There are two key points to note about the 1986 education reforms and the 1995 FCUBE reforms that impacted teachers in Ghana. First, the 1986 education reforms produced rapid expansion of access that increased the workload of an already demoralized and underpaid teacher workforce that had seen the real value of their wages drop as a result of economic decline in the 1970s.[26] Teacher morale was low, and "in 2003 nearly 13 percent of teachers had been absent in the past month for reasons other than sickness."[27] No serious attempt was made to undertake a fundamental review and restructuring of the teacher education program in the 38 teacher training colleges to prepare teachers for the challenges arising from the demands of the FCUBE program. On teachers, FCUBE investment focused largely on teacher management and incentives to reduce teacher absenteeism without addressing the deteriorating working environment and the quality of the preservice teacher education program for basic school teachers.[28,29]

There was, however, one key initiative to improve the preservice teacher education curriculum for training basic school teachers. In the late 1980s, Ghana received technical assistance from the British Department for International Development (DFID), at the time, known as the British Overseas Development Agency (ODA) to reform the preservice teacher education curriculum.

The pre-reform curriculum had an even stronger theoretical focus. The first-year program focused on strengthening the academic background knowledge of trainees before pedagogic knowledge and skills training in the remaining two years. The second-year curriculum introduced the methods of teaching school subjects and on-campus teaching practice. The emphasis at this stage was on "the use of professional knowledge in teaching and learning, as opposed to classroom teaching and learning situations providing the context for developing appropriate teaching and learning strategies."[30] The third year of training centered on Foundations of Education, curriculum studies and methodology, and included eight weeks of teaching practice in basic schools.

The reform of the curriculum under the DFID funded the Junior Secondary School Teacher Education Project (JuSSTEP), focused mainly on embedding learner-centered pedagogy in the teacher education curriculum. Improved teacher preparation was conceptualized mainly in terms of teachers' ability to adopt learner-centered pedagogy in classroom teaching.[31] But, after four years of the JuSSTEP reforms, evaluators concluded that structural constraints in the teacher education colleges, such as high trainee-tutor ratios, summative examinations system, and lack of training facilities, had rendered superficial and unsustainable the widespread adoption of learner-centered approaches that it was seeking to promote.[32] The approach adopted by JuSSTEP reformers assumed that by placing more emphasis on developing learner-centered instructional approaches, the quality of teachers would improve. The idea that, by making school-based training an integral part of learning to teach, this would produce more effective teachers able to address learning needs in real classrooms was recognized, but it was not taken forward in terms of making school-based training the fulcrum of teacher preparation.

Reconceptualizing Teacher Preparation and Development—The 2010 Basic Teacher Education Policy

In August 2000, the Teacher Education Division (TED) of the Ghana Education Service (GES) published a policy document setting out a new direction for preservice teacher education to improve the quality of basic school teachers.[33] The policy document outlined two main proposals that marked a significant change in the governance and content of teacher preparation in Ghana. First, it recommended upgrading the 38 government teacher education colleges to tertiary institutions. The proposals argued that to improve teacher quality for basic schools, it was necessary for preservice teacher education college curriculum to be upgraded to tertiary teacher education standards, and for programs to be accredited through a National Accreditation Board (NAB). The NAB would certify that teacher education colleges had the facilities and resources to offer a course of study for teachers and also determine whether the quality of programs measured up to approved standards. Second, it recommended the establishment of a National Teaching Council (NTC) through an Act of Parliament, which would act on behalf of the NAB to inspect college programs before they received accreditation.

On the content of teacher preparation programs, the policy document specified five core areas that should be targeted to produce a competent teacher:

- Knowledge and understanding of the development and nature of learners at the basic school level, the principles and processes of different kinds of learning for children at the basic level, individual differences and the psychology of adjustment;
- An understanding of the skills in implementing learning as a process through which behavior can be changed;
- Capability of using the local language in teaching at the lower primary classes;
- A high level of competence in using evaluative techniques and materials in such ways as to encourage children to learn and enhance their growth in meaningful ways;
- Competence in action research methods, suitable for the advancement of knowledge in the field of teaching and education in general.[34]

These areas pointed to a shift in the philosophy of teacher preparation in Ghana, which could be described as a "shift from teaching behaviours to learning opportunities."[35] In other words, the teacher preparation process should lead to teachers who focus on creating learning opportunities to maximize the impact on student learning. By stressing competence in action research, teachers were to become researchers of their own practice, using the knowledge and insights gained to improve the quality of their teaching. This new direction was consistent with another important change that the policy proposed, the introduction of school-based training; the argument was that "school-based practical training related to the realities of the classroom" and "opportunities for qualitative learning through self-study and self-learning" would transform the quality of basic school teachers.[36] To achieve this goal, it proposed a restructured three-year preservice teacher education program, where teacher trainees would spend the first two years on the college campus and the third year in school-based training learning to teach on the job. This became known as the "IN-IN-OUT" teacher education system and would lead to a new teacher qualification for all basic school teachers—the Diploma in Basic Education (DBE). Overall, about 75% of teachers were to be trained through this system and about 25% of untrained teachers in schools were to be trained through distance teacher education.

These proposals were justified as a response to increasing stakeholder concerns about the quality of basic school teachers in Ghana.[37] By the late 1990s, there was a growing feeling that teacher preparation for basic school teachers needed to focus on school-based training and move away from the continued emphasis on the academic knowledge of trainees.[38] The proposed "OUT" internship, or on-the-job training year, was viewed as offering the opportunity to use school-based training to reemphasize professional knowledge and practice. This, it was argued, would offer direct links with practical problems of teaching that were critical for the production of quality basic school teachers. This was to be achieved through:

- Support for trainees during the "OUT" internship year in the form of distance learning materials;
- Supervision of the trainees during the "OUT" internship year carried out by experienced teachers and headteachers acting as mentors and;
- Self-assessment instruments and the use of diaries to record field experiences. Additionally, assessment of trainees soon after the "OUT" internship would focus on "performance assessment," where trainees demonstrate an appreciation of the match between quality teaching and learning.[39]

The idea of using distance learning materials, mentors, and practical assessment instruments was to produce a more reflective teacher. To signal the importance of on-the-job learning in the teacher preparation process, teacher certification was to recognize and include experiences from the early years of a teacher's career. It proposed a two-stage licensing process. The first license would be a Provisional Teacher's License (PTL) issued to all trainees who completed formal training and would be held for two years. After this period, trainees would enter a probationary phase for a minimum of one year to a maximum of two years before they would be issued a Professional Teacher's Certificate (PTC). While these proposals were being developed, the colleges generally produced about 7,000 teachers a year. If all completed the PTL, then this same number would enter the probationary phase. Those who satisfied probation conditions would be issued a PTC. However, no details were provided on implementation, and also the policy proposals were silent on performance standards and criteria for earning a professional teacher license.

These policy proposals were the first to put forward the idea of raising the qualification of public basic school teachers from a postsecondary certificate to a university-level diploma certificate. The proposals reemphasized the importance of school-based learning in teacher preparation but this time using the early career probation period to develop and demonstrate practical knowledge and skills of teaching before earning a professional teacher license. Altogether, the 2000 basic teacher education policy proposals marked the most significant rethinking of teacher preparation in Ghana since independence in 1957. But, it took another four years before some elements of these policy proposals were incorporated in changes to the structure of teacher education for basic school teachers.

In 2004, the traditional three-year residential teacher preparation program, which had been in operation since the late 1970s, was restructured along the lines of the proposed IN-IN-OUT model but with some modifications (see fig. 7.1). Currently, it consists of three phases over six semesters. Phase one (year 1) is designed to support trainee teachers' foundation knowledge in core subjects (mathematics, science, English). This was introduced to strengthen the academic background knowledge of trainee teachers, since most teacher applicants entered training with weak subject knowledge backgrounds.[40,41] In the second phase (year 2), college coursework focuses mainly on curriculum studies, methods of teaching school subjects, and school visits. The second year, therefore, offers trainee teachers opportunities to apply the theories and methods of teaching in on-campus peer microteaching practice and school visits to observe and learn from the experience of regular teachers. The third year, spent in schools as off-campus teaching practice (practicum) has been split into two semesters, with the first semester used for on-campus teaching practice and the second semester devoted to off-campus teaching practice (practicum). The argument for introducing on-campus teaching practice was that it would offer trainees opportunities to practice instructional techniques acquired in the college classroom environment before the off-campus practicum.[42]

This model of teacher preparation could be described as the "applied science model," because it assumes that "if teachers first learn about principles [of teaching]; then they will be able to apply them in their classrooms. So a

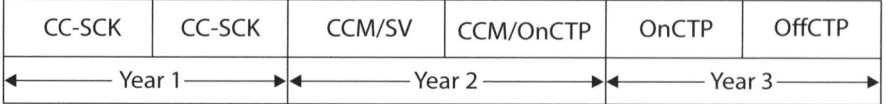

Figure 7.1. The restructured "IN-IN-OUT" pre-tertiary teacher education program in Ghana. *CC-SCK* = coursework in college–subject content knowledge; *CCM/SV* = coursework in college (methods of teaching) and school visits; *OnCTP* = on-campus teaching practice. *OffCTP* = off-campus teaching practice (practicum).

programme based on this model usually puts the student teachers first into a college or university and then sends them out for 'teaching practice' at a later stage. The emphasis is on acquiring theoretical knowledge which is to be applied later, rather than classroom skills. The personal, emotional aspects of teaching are often given less attention."[43] Thus, the "OUT" program did not reflect sufficiently the philosophy of school-based training as espoused in the 2000 policy proposals—which argued for knowledge *of* practice integrated with studying in a college.

The restructured three-year program qualification was upgraded from a postsecondary certificate to a DBE in 2004. In 2008, the 38 government teacher training colleges were also redesignated as Colleges of Education (COEs) to run a revised three-year six-semester DBE program as a step toward becoming tertiary institutions. All the colleges were affiliated with the Institute of Education of the University of Cape Coast which was responsible for designing the DBE program and conducting examinations leading to the DBE teacher qualification. A general objective of the program was to produce "teachers with a clear grasp of intended outcomes of their teaching activities, who are skilled in monitoring, diagnosing and providing equal opportunities for all pupils to learn."[44] It reaffirmed the assumption that effective teaching had predetermined outcomes produced by applying prescribed teaching methods in any classroom environment. Thus, the practicum in school-based environments was seen as only offering trainees the opportunity to demonstrate knowledge and skills acquired in teacher colleges.

Over the years, Ghana has produced basic school teachers with different qualifications and also recruited a large number of untrained teachers who needed formal training. The DBE program, therefore, was offered through three routes to ensure all basic school teachers had the same qualification. First, is the three-year "IN-IN-OUT" program for trainees, who entered training straight after completing secondary education. This provided training for about 40% of the existing trained basic school teachers. Second, is the four-year nonresidential program offered to an additional 30% of teachers who are themselves people who left middle school and secondary school prior to graduation and are without formal training and are thus teaching in schools as untrained teachers. This program, called the Untrained Teachers Diploma in Basic Education (UTDBE), started in 2004, with these teachers enrolled studying by using distance teacher education learning materials and periodic face-to-face instruction in teacher training colleges. Third, is the two-year sandwich program, which started in August 2007. Popularly called "top-up," the program was run as a fully residential program during the basic school vacation periods, by 16 colleges of education. This program was aimed at all the existing postsecondary trained teachers in basic schools with a certificate A qualification.[45]

Also, the move toward a DBE teacher preparation program reduced the length of time it previously took for a trainee straight out of secondary school to become a trained basic school teacher with a diploma qualification. A postsecondary trainee who entered teacher training prior to 2004 would have spent at least five years in full-time residential training—three years in a residential teacher education college and two years in a university teacher education program—to obtain a diploma qualification.[46] But more importantly, the DBE, while still predominantly college-based, had come to recognize the role that mentors in schools could play in socializing trainees into professional norms. Mentors' input into teacher preparation, however, was not given formal validation since their input was not included in the assessment and evaluation of trainees.

The 2000 teacher education proposals for basic schools firmly indicated the importance of multiple measures of performance under different contexts (college and school level) before a trained teacher could be classified as qualified. Implicit in the policy proposals was also the idea that improving teachers should be about improving teaching quality and the influence teachers can have on learning outcomes through intelligent engagement with learners and their classroom environments. This resonates with Kennedy's[47] argument that teacher education institutions should shift their focus away from teaching "discrete techniques" to integrating and practice, and in Ghana, the 2000 basic teacher education policy positioned the future of teacher preparation in this direction. These were changes that *if* fully implemented were going to influence the way in which basic school teachers studied to become qualified teachers. Certainly, the introduction of school-based elements in teacher preparation announced the importance of classroom contexts and the role experienced teachers could play in the teacher preparation process. Although the evidential basis for inclusion of classroom contexts and mentors in teacher preparation have been established in international research and implemented in many teacher preparation systems in developed countries,[48] these elements did not take firm roots in the DBE teacher preparation program in Ghana.

A New Policy Framework for Teacher Preparation and Development—The Pre-Tertiary Professional Development and Management Policy (PTPDM)

One of the tragedies of teacher education polices in many African countries is the inability to translate policy proposals into real changes on the ground. Often the scale of recommended changes and the resources required, plus the lack of a strong legal framework, makes it difficult to carry through with the reforms. Policy ambitions often outrun resources. The Ghana Education Service's 2000 basic teacher education policy proposals suffered a similar fate. Basically, the proposals required new legal and legislative instruments to ensure that the institutional and structural changes that were being recommended had the force of power to back them. The 2000 policy proposals did not feature in national official discourse on how to improve the performance of teachers and the quality of education in basic schools.

In 2010, the Ghana Education Service, through its Teacher Education Division, started a process of consultations and planning to introduce a new policy framework for teacher preparation, but this time drawing on new and relevant Ghanaian laws to give the new policy more power to introduce changes. It also got noticed in national education improvement discourse and strategic plans. The new policy, known as the Pre-Tertiary Professional Development and Management policy (PTPDM), was launched in 2012 by the Ministry of Education and framed in the context of the Education Act of 2008 (Act 778). Framers of the policy included statements from the Act to signal its relevance and legitimacy:

- The policy *draws its legitimacy* from the Education Act of 2008 (Act 778) in which the government stated the aims of producing well balanced individuals with the requisite knowledge, skill, value, aptitude and attitude which would be the basis of improving teacher quality and teaching and learning.
- Education Act 2008 (Act 778) calls for the establishment of a National Teach-

ing Council (NTC) with responsibility for setting professional standards and code of practice for professional development, registration and licensing of teachers. Section 10 of the Act stipulates that the NTC shall be responsible for establishing: (a) the framework for employment of teachers, (b) (framework for) in-service education and training (INSET), (c) and the periodic review of professional practice and ethical standards for teachers and teaching. *The PTPDM Policy defines the areas and principles for achieving these goals as outlined in the Act 778.*

- The Education Act 2008 (Act 778) also calls for the NTC to work with the Ghana Education Service (GES), Teacher Training Institutions, development partners and other accredited institutions *to implement the teacher professional development components of the Policy* (emphasis added).[49]

Furthermore, the document noted that "after the Education Law 2017 is passed, the relevant section of this policy should be identified and amended to facilitate implementation" (p. 3). Why did the framers of the new policy feel it was necessary to include these statements? From a historical perspective, the policy recommendations amounted to substantial changes to the teacher preparation and certification process that would lead to a reconceptualization of teacher quality in Ghana. The importance and intentions of the PTPDM policy is clearly captured in the introductory statement of the 2018 updated version:

> Over the years, Ghana has reformed and restructured its teacher education system in response to new challenges and aspirations of its education system. What has been missing in this entire process is a comprehensive policy framework that can guide the development and management of teachers in ways that commit them and the education establishment to the highest standards of professional practice. To fill this gap, the Ministry of Education designed and launched the "Pre-Tertiary Teacher Professional Development and Management Policy in Ghana" (referred to as PTPDM Policy 2012) as a policy instrument to guide the institutionalization of Continuous Professional Development (CPD) programs and the setting of the minimum standards, called as "The Pre-Tertiary Teachers' Standards for Ghana" 2018 (PTTSG) to guide the enhancement of teachers' professional values and attitudes, professional knowledge and professional practice.[50]

The policy emphasizes preservice teacher education and continuous professional development (in-service) as an integral part of the teacher preparation process, and it recognizes the importance of evidencing professional

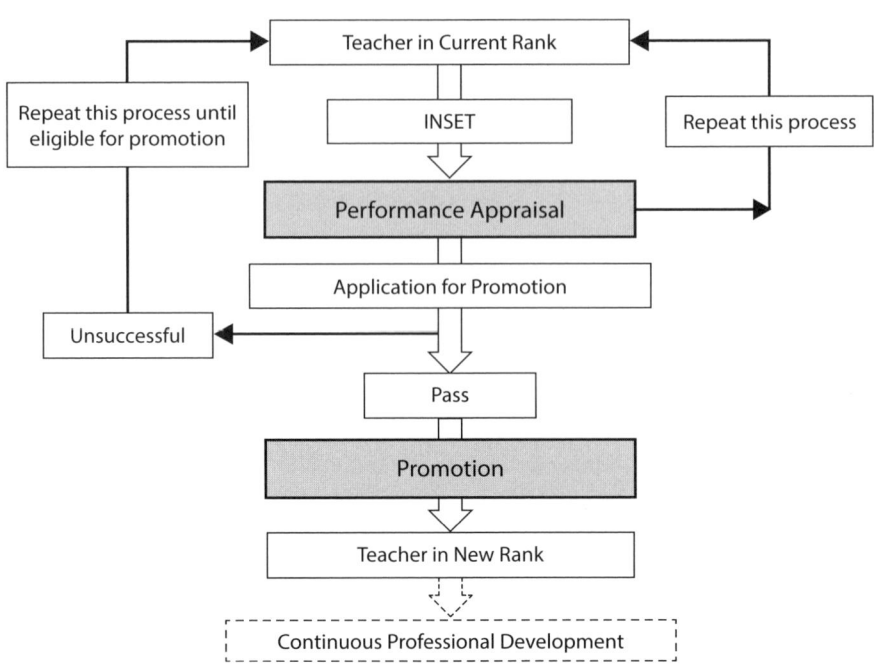

Figure 7.2. The PTPDM teacher professional development and promotion pathway. (Source: Ministry of Education / Ghana Education Service. PTPDM Policy: Guidelines for the Induction Programme for Beginning Teachers. Accra: Ministry of Education, 2017.)

growth and using it as a basis for promotion and career advancement. According to the policy, in-service training as a form of teacher professional development should play a key role in performance appraisal and the promotion process. This policy would apply to about 70% of basic school teachers. Until this policy takes effect, all teachers in Ghana are promoted simply on the basis of years of experience on the job and only go through an interview process for promotion to senior management positions.

As shown in figure 7.2, the new policy replaces this automatic promotion with a system that requires teachers to commit themselves to continuous professional development (INSET) and performance appraisal and to use evidence of professional growth as part of their application promotion. The policy also stipulates that "appraisal shall be used to identify areas where a teacher might need support for professional growth. It shall also be used to recognize and record their achievements."[51] Although the PTPDM policy incorporates key elements of the 2000 teacher education policy proposals, it was also influenced by international ideas on teacher preparation. The Japanese International Co-operation Agency (JICA) provided the funding and some of the technical assistance for its development using experts from Japan and the United Kingdom.

The concept of teacher licensing is new to teacher preparation in Ghana and is set to replace the current system of certification after trainee teachers have completed the DBE program. The PTPDM policy distinguishes the three stages of the licensing process: provisional/short-term teaching license; conditional license; and finally the teaching license. The provisional teaching license is to be a probationary license issued to beginning trained teachers on probation. This license would allow beginning trained teachers to teach in schools without a full teaching license. It is provisional because of the requirement for holders of this license to complete a program of induction and in-service training within the first year before a full professional license is issued. The conditional teaching license is a temporary teaching license, which is to be issued to any teacher without preservice training and prior to completing professional training. The policy makes it clear that the conditional license will be revoked if the holder fails to obtain the minimum required training within four years. Finally, the teaching license will be issued to all teachers who have received formal training as proof of professional qualification in Ghana. Professional teachers would, however, be required to "keep on developing their professionalism and competencies through INSET to renew their teaching license within a period of time as determined by the NTC and GES. The Teaching License shall be revoked if the holders neglect their duty of Continuous Professional Development (CPD) within the stated periods."[52]

What is striking is the message the licensing process sends about the importance and role of continuous professional development in becoming a professionally licensed teacher. Teacher preparation is presented as a lifelong learning process that starts from the preservice teacher preparation stage, through the early years of a teacher's career, and continues through the requirement to renew the teaching license at specific periods of a teacher's career. Also, "under the PTPDM Policy, two teacher standards have been developed to promote competency based on professional practice: (a) National Teachers' Standards 2017 (for teachers in training); (b) The Pre-Tertiary Teachers' Standards for Ghana 2018 (for in-service teachers)."[53]

It will not be an understatement to say that the PTPDM policy represents the most radical set of proposals for teacher preparation in the Ghanaian context. What is different from earlier attempts to reform teacher preparation are the laws and institutional structures and mechanisms that this time, have been introduced to back them. The NTC has been established and resourced and a database created to serve as the "sole repository of teacher information / data including all administrative transactions on every teacher in the country while in service. *It is designed to support evidence-based decisions on teachers by authorized stakeholders*" (emphasis added).[54] The policy has also introduced a new career structure that reflects the new philosophy of teacher preparation as one that is evidenced-based and requires teachers to commit to lifelong professional learning and development. Teacher data are also seen as important because of the potential to use such data to support evidence-based decisions about teachers' performance and achievements.

Recently, teacher preparation in Ghana has moved another step forward, and in September 2018, all colleges of education will offer a four-year degree in education under the modified IN-IN-OUT program design. In effect, teacher qualification has moved from a certificate A to a diploma in education and now a bachelor of education qualification. It has fulfilled an important ambition of the 2000 basic school teacher education policy proposal, which called for preservice teacher training to be upgraded to tertiary teacher education standards.

Summary and Conclusion

Ghanaian teacher preparation reforms in the 1980s and 1990s targeted the preservice curriculum to improve its influence on classroom practice. The aim was to introduce a model of teacher preparation using interactive pedagogies and activity-based materials in college-based training contexts to improve the quality of teachers in basic schools. Stakeholder concerns that teacher preparation was not providing enough opportunities for trainee teachers to learn teaching in real classrooms and, therefore, was limiting the impact of training on classroom practices was used to justify reforms to increase school-based training. Examining the changes through the lens of education reforms from the 1980s to the current teacher preparation reforms shows an increase in the actors (school teachers / headteachers acting as mentors) and sites (schools and teacher education colleges) involved in teacher preparation. It is a recognition that college-based teacher education, although important, has to include prolonged periods in school environments to portray teacher preparation as a continuing process of teacher development.

In early 2000, research into teacher colleges in five countries, including Ghana, reported that "professional links with school systems were often fragile or non-existent and practicing primary teachers were conspicuous by their general absence from activities organised in colleges." The researchers recommended that colleges need to establish closer relationships with schools.[55] It is clear in the case of Ghana, that the PTPDM policy reforms have moved the system of teacher preparation to reflect this recommendation. Also, shifting some of the responsibilities of learning to teach to trainees through self-assessment methods and investigation of classroom practice has signaled a departure from the traditional teacher education pedagogies, which placed an emphasis on prescribed methods or practices for trainees to adopt.[56] As to whether these changes will improve the quality of teacher preparation and teachers for basic school teachers in Ghana is too early to know. The effectiveness of the changes will depend on the quality of teacher educators and their capacity to work both within and outside the teacher education colleges in creative and innovative ways. It will also depend on the extent to which opportunities are offered to school mentors to work alongside teacher educators to achieve a common goal.[57] How well new governing bodies, such as the NTC and NAB are resourced and their capacities enhanced will also be critical. But, what these changes do is to bring teacher preparation in Ghana closer to global trends and practices.[58]

Another important element in the change is the move to link continuous professional development, much closer to preservice training. By requiring teachers to renew their teacher's license on a periodic basis, on evidence that they have been attending INSET regularly to improve their professional practice, recasts teacher preparation and development as a continuing journey of lifelong learning. But, a major challenge is how INSET will be financed to ensure that every teacher has access to equitable and quality INSET at the school and district level. INSET is not financed in the same way as preservice teacher education, which is funded from a central budget. The PTPDM policy expects that "Regional/District and School education budgets shall include budgets to cater for INSET, specifically for training INSET facilitators, managing INSET activities, as well as sponsoring teachers where necessary to participate in INSET programmes."[59] Equitable and quality INSET will, therefore, depend on the ability and willingness of regions, districts, and schools to allocate funds for INSET and the incentive for them to locate enough resources to support INSET activities.

The system of teacher preparation for basic school teachers in Ghana has come a long way, from the period where it was solely college-based to a more diversified approach supported by institutions and structures that commit the teacher to lifelong professional learning and development. It is both an exciting and challenging time for learning to become a teacher in Ghana. Looking ahead, research on the impact of new institutional arrangements and actors on the production of teacher quality and instruction will be critical to understand what further changes may be required, or which new directions teacher reforms should take to improve the quality of teacher preparation in Ghana.

NOTES

1. World Bank, *Basic Education Sector Improvement Program: Staff Appraisal Report* (Washington, DC: World Bank, 1996).

2. Department for International Development (UK) [DFID], *Ghana Education Sector Support* (Ghana: Department for International Development, UK, 1998).

3. World Bank, *Basic Education Sector Improvement Program*.

4. Howard White, *Books, Buildings, and Learning Outcomes: An Impact Evaluation of World Bank Support to Basic Education in Ghana* (Washington, DC: World Bank, 2004).

5. Kwame Akyeampong, "Revisiting Free Compulsory Universal Basic Education (FCUBE) in Ghana," *Comparative Education* 45, no. 2 (2009): 175–195.

6. World Bank, *Basic Education Sector Improvement Project (BESIP). Sector, Thematic and Global Evaluation Operations Evaluation Department* (Washington, DC: World Bank, 2004).

7. Kwame Asante, "Restructuring Education in Ghana," paper presented on Education, Accra, Ghana, 1988.

8. White, *Books, Buildings, and Learning Outcomes*, 8.

9. White, *Books, Buildings, and Learning Outcomes*, 8.

10. Ministry of Education, *Report of the Education Commission on Teacher Education* (Accra: Ministry of Education Ghana, 1993).

11. Peter Darvas and David Balwanz, *Towards Learning for All: Basic Education in Ghana to the Year 2000* (Accra: Ministry of Education Ghana, 1994).

12. Stanislaus Kadingdi, "Policy Initiatives for Change and Innovation in Basic Education Programmes in Ghana," *Educate—Journal of Doctoral Research in Education* 4 no 2 (2004).

13. Kadingdi, "Policy Initiatives."

14. Ministry of Education, *Basic Education Sector Improvement Programme Policy Document; Free Compulsory Universal Basic Education by The Year 2005* (Accra: Ministry of Education Ghana, 1996).

15. White, *Books, Buildings, and Learning Outcomes*, 9.

16. Kwame Akyeampong and Dominic Furlong, *Ghana: A Baseline Study of the Teacher Education System: The Multi-Site Teacher Education Research Project (MUSTER) Discussion Paper 7* (Brighton, UK: Centre for International Education, University of Sussex, 2000).

17. Kadingdi, "Policy Initiatives."

18. Akyeampong, "Revisiting Free Compulsory Universal Basic Education (FCUBE) in Ghana," 175–195.

19. Kadingdi, "Policy Initiatives," 8.

20. H. O. A. McWilliam and M. A. Kwamena-Poh, *The Development of Education in Ghana: An Outline* (London, England: Longman Group, 1975).

21. Akyeampong and Furlong, *Ghana*.

22. Kwame Akyeampong, Dominic Furlong, and Keith Lewin, *The Costs and Financing of Teacher Education in Ghana. The Multi-Site Teacher Education Research Project (MUSTER) Discussion Paper No. 18* (Brighton, UK: Centre for International Education, University of Sussex, 2000).

23. Kwame Akyeampong, "Government Policy and Teacher Education in Ghana," in *Education and Social Change—Connecting Local and Global Perspectives,* eds. Geoffrey Elliott, Chahid Fourali, and Sally Issler (London: Continuum, 2010), 162–174.

24. White, *Books, Buildings, and Learning Outcomes.*

25. White, *Books, Buildings, and Learning Outcomes,* 91.

26. Akyeampong, "Revisiting Free Compulsory Universal Basic Education (FCUBE) in Ghana," 175–195.

27. White, *Books, Buildings, and Learning Outcomes,* 15.

28. Kwame Akyeampong, *Teacher Training in Ghana: Does It Count? Research the Issues* (London: Department for International Development, UK, 2003).

29. White, *Books, Buildings, and Learning Outcomes,* 15.

30. Akyeampong and Furlong, *Ghana*.

31. Kwame Akyeampong, "Teacher Educators' Practice and Vision of Good Teaching in Teacher Education Reform Context in Ghana," *Educational Researcher* 46 no. 4 (2017), 194–203.

32. Ghana Education Service [GES] / Teacher Education Service [TES], *Junior Secondary School Teacher Education Project (JUSSTEP)* (Accra: GES/TES, 1993).

33. Ghana Education Service [GES], *Direction for Basic Teacher Education,* vol. 2: *Guidelines for Implementation of Basic Teacher Education Policy* (Accra: GES, 2000), 6.

34. GES, *Direction for Basic Teacher Education,* vol. 2: 6.

35. James Stigler and James Hiebert, "The Culture of Teaching: A Global Perspective," in *International Handbook of Teacher Quality and Policy,* eds. Motoko Akiba and Gerald LeTendre (London: Routledge, 2018), 162–174.

36. GES, *Direction for Basic Teacher Education,* vol. 2: 7.

37. GES, *Direction for Basic Teacher Education,* vol. 2: 7.

38. Kwabena Awuku, *Executive Summary of Proposals on Teacher Education Policy* (Accra: Ministry of Education, 1998).

39. GES, *Direction for Basic Teacher Education,* vol. 2: 18.

40. Christine Adu-Yeboah, *Learning to Teach Reading and Mathematics and Its Influence on Practice in Ghana, Draft Country Report. Teacher Preparation in Africa (TPA) Research Project* (Brighton: Centre for International Education, University of Sussex, 2012).

41. Akyeampong, *Teacher Training in Ghana.*

42. Ministry of Education, *Teaching Syllabus for English Language, Curriculum, Research and Development Division (CRDD)* (Accra: Ministry of Education, 2007).

43. Janet Stuart, Kwame Akyeampong, and Alison Croft, *Key Issues in Teacher Education—A Sourcebook for Teacher Educators in Developing Countries* (Basingstoke: MacMillan, 2009), 8.

44. Institute of Education *Three-Year Diploma in Basic Education: Course Structure* (Accra: University of Cape Coast, Ghana, 2005), 2.

45. Adu-Yeboah, *Learning to Teach.*

46. Kwame Akyeampong, "Government Policy and Teacher Education in Ghana," in *Education and Social Change—Connecting Local and Global Perspectives,* eds. Geoffrey Elliott, Chahid Fourali, Sally Issler (London: Continuum, 2010), 162–174.

47. Mary Kennedy, "Parsing the Practice of Teaching," *Journal of Teacher Education* 67, no. 1 (2016): 6–17.

48. Motoko Akiba and Gerald LeTendre, "Introduction: Conceptualizing Teacher Quality and Policy in a Global Context," in *International Handbook of Teacher Quality and Policy,* eds. Motoko Akiba and Gerald LeTendre (London: Routledge, 2018), 1–22.

49. Ministry of Education, *Pre-Tertiary Teacher Development and Management Policy,* 3.

50. Ministry of Education, *Pre-Tertiary Teacher Development and Management Policy,* 1.

51. Ministry of Education, *Pre-Tertiary Teacher Development and Management Policy,* 12.

52. Ministry of Education, *Pre-Tertiary Teacher Development and Management Policy,* 12.

53. Ministry of Education, *Pre-Tertiary Teacher Development and Management Policy,* 8.

54. Ministry of Education, *Pre-Tertiary Teacher Development and Management Policy,* 14.

55. Keith Lewin and Janet Stuart, *Researching Teacher Education: New Perspectives on Practice, Performance and Policy.* (London: Department for International Education, 2003), 188.

56. Akyeampong, "Teacher Educators' Practice and Vision," 194–203.

57. Akyeampong, "Teacher Educators' Practice and Vision," 194–203.

58. Motoko Akiba and Gerald LeTendre, "Introduction," 1–22.

59. Ministry of Education, *Pre-Tertiary Teacher Development and Management Policy,* 14.

CHAPTER EIGHT

From Traditional to Dialogical-Reflective Teacher Training
The Case of Teacher Education in Israel

ARIE KIZEL AND LILY ORLAND-BARAK

This chapter reviews and analyzes the major teacher training developments in Israel, in particular the teacher preparation offered from the 1980s to the present. This period was characterized by pervasive reports that new teachers and school heads did not feel that novice teachers were well prepared for working in a school at the end of their training. This issue and the disparity between the content of academic teacher education courses and school practicums has prompted a series of changes in recent decades, designed to improve teacher education programs and ensure that they answer the needs of the educational field. This chapter examines three teacher education models that developed as a result of the shifts undergone in the discourse of teacher education in Israel in terms of purposes, processes, and desired outcomes: (a) PDS (Professional Development School) dialogical-reflective teacher-training pedagogy introduced in order to bring academic content into closer alignment with practical and experiential requirements toward better teacher preparation for schools; (b) the Teach First Israel program, designed to attract outstanding students who would not otherwise have chosen teaching as their profession; and (c) the Academia-Class program, which incorporates elements from the other two schemes. The chapter critically examines each of the models in detail, outlining their innovative aspects with reference to one of the main goals of education in Israel: narrowing educational gaps and reducing socioeconomic gaps.

As in other countries across the world, the preparation of teachers to meet the challenges they face in the complex and dynamic school setting has been a subject of debate in Israel for over 30 years. Such concern is even more acute given the fact that Israel currently ranks high on the list of nations with great socioeconomic disparities and relatively low on international-exam level standards.[1] To this end, for years, teacher education in Israel has been under public, governmental, and pedagogic attack by top-ranking Ministry of Education officials, school heads, and students who feel unprepared for the field. As in other countries, teaching is regarded as an important profession, imparting knowledge that must be mastered in order to ensure equal opportunity for all students.[2]

Examining the policy and practice of teacher education from the perspective of enlistment, training, absorption, long-term profession development, and the collective enhancement of praxis, Darling-Hammond and colleagues[3] compared the approaches adopted in countries such as Australia, Canada, Finland, and Singapore with those prevalent in the United States, assessing the challenges posed by the introduction of changes into these systems.[4]

Israel is grappling with just the same challenges—the need to subsidize and fund quality students so that they can attend quality teacher education programs; increase novice teachers' salaries; link theory and practice more closely by offering courses that incorporate high-standard clinical experience into a better teacher-supportive framework; prepare students for professional practice while paying close attention to the learning and evaluation of knowledge, skills, and execution; introduce teacher-assessment systems based on professional standards that link student learning with classroom teaching; establish absorption models that support novice teachers via experienced mentors; engage in collaborative planning and a reduction of the teaching load to enable time for school learning; create a repertoire of teaching modes and support for/of professional development that allows teachers to study regularly with peers and colleagues within and across schools/teacher-training institutions; enhance broad professional capacities in order to facilitate strategies for broad cooperation in research; and support good teaching that recognizes successful forms of school and classroom teaching and enables specialist teachers and heads to run the system as a whole.

The Major Challenges of Teacher Education in Israel

One of the major challenges the Israeli education system faces is based on data from across the board—students, school heads, and education system officials—which indicate that teacher-education graduates feel unprepared to enter the teaching profession upon graduation.[5] These studies and reports relate to various dimensions, such as a lack of professional capacity in the field of knowledge, a lack of dialogical skills in teacher-student relations, a lack of sufficient classroom and lesson management skills, and above all, a lack of professional durability.

From a broader institutional and policy perspective, another challenge resides in the historic division that gained prominence over the years between university schools of education and teacher education colleges. Whereas the former have been traditionally perceived as preserving a more traditional curriculum that stresses theoretical aspects of learning to teach, often separated from practical learning in the school setting, the latter are commonly associated with more clinical and participatory orientations to teacher preparation[6] for which they are strongly supported financially by the Ministry of Education. The gradual prioritizing of budget allotted to clinical practice in colleges of teacher education over universities by the Ministry of Education was intensified as a result of the expansion of Israeli higher education, in the early 1990s, which brought to a growing funding[7] that was directed and distributed by the Parliament's Committee for Planning and Budgeting.[8] The funding model for resources' distribution amongst higher education institutions is based on two components: research (46%) and teaching (54%).[9] The funding model excludes clinical experience altogether, which is integral to professional higher education studies. Yet, along with forces pushing higher education toward basic research and applied knowledge models, there is also a widespread recognition of the added value of creating meaningful connections between schools and universities.[10] The need to strengthen connections between university courses and clinical experiences is strongly evident in student teachers' evaluation of their training, voicing the importance of enhancing opportunities for learning at the workplace in the context of preservice education.[11]

The above concerns and tensions had become pressing issues in the discourse of education already at the outset of the twenty-first century, prompting the minister of education at the time, Yossi Sarid, to appoint a committee to examine the teacher education process in Israel headed by Prof. Miriam Ben-Peretz, of the Faculty of Education in the University of Haifa. This was inter alia a response to requests from higher-education institutions in Israel not mandated to offer teacher-education programs for permission to do so, a lack of teacher-education students, a protracted and severe drop in the status of the teaching profession, and the need to train pupils for twenty-first-century skills. Above all, the committee reported that the current teacher-training programs in the various institutions—universities (primarily in the high school tracks), colleges of education (which train teachers for elementary and middle school teaching), and Orthodox seminaries (for the Jewish Orthodox communities)—do not equip teachers for educational praxis.

In this chapter, we review and analyze the Israeli education system's attempts to improve teacher-training by instituting a series of programs that seek to bring theoretical study in academic institutions providing teacher education into line with school practicums in order to create a long-term professional dialogue between the training institution and the school/kindergarten.

The Israeli Education System: A Diverse Cultural Tapestry

Israeli education is a complex system. Generally, the state is the owner and supervisor of public state education from kindergarten (ages 5–6) to the 9th grade. The state also supervises high schools (10th to 12th grade), which are usually owned by municipalities, foundations, and other entities.

The state's supervision of education is carried out as part of the State Education Law and is divided into several sectors: general Jewish sector, Jewish-religious sector, Arab sector (which encompasses the Christian and Muslim population), and the Druze and Circassians sector. The non-Jewish sectors conduct their studies in Arabic. Both their textbooks and the matriculation exams are in Arabic, and they teach Hebrew as a second language. In addition, there is an Ultra-Orthodox Haredi Jewish sector (called "independent education") which is mostly religious and has only little, if any, general studies depending on the type of the Ultra-Orthodox Jewish faction.

All the public-state sectors are subjected to a curriculum that is generally unified with room for some modifications. The Jewish Public-State Religious Sector will conduct prayers at school and will heighten religious studies, while the Arab and Druze sector will give more extensive room to the history of the Arabs under the supervision of the Ministry of Education. The Ultra-Orthodox Jewish schools are not committed to the full curriculum of the state and are independent in choosing the content they will learn. Many of them do not require their students to take the matriculation exams. In all the sectors there are children who learn in special education frameworks (either in separate schools or in special classrooms within regular schools).

According to the Taub Report (2017) the budget of the Ministry of Education in 2016 was 36 billion NIS. The education system employed 161,000 teachers in 4,733 classrooms and had 1,694,000 students.[12]

Teacher training in Israel is carried out in universities and state colleges of education, both for the Jewish and Arab sectors. In Arab colleges the language of instruction is Arabic, and there are also a few special colleges geared for the Jewish-religious or Jewish Ultra-Orthodox sectors. Students choose which training system they wish to learn in. There are no significant differences in the trajectory of teacher training in Israel between the sectors. The trajectory is determined by the Council for Higher Education, to which the teacher-training institutes are subjected.

This chapter focuses mainly on teacher education in the Jewish sector and, specifically, within the borders of the State of Israel (1967 borders). Our discussion, therefore, does not consider the teacher education system within the Palestinian Authority.

The Traditional Teacher Training Model: Developments and Challenges

In the mid-1980s, the Israeli teaching-training model was based mainly on a strict division between theoretical courses taught in academic institutions and practical school experience, confining the latter to one day a week over the period of studies. Herein, students were closely accompanied by a mentor from whom they were expected to learn professional skills, primarily via observation and some actual classroom teaching. As Zilbershtein, Ben-Peretz, and Greenfeld note,[13] "Teacher trainers and scholars at colleges and universities felt during this period that the traditional form of teacher-training programmes were not doing a good job."[14] There were no clear links between the various learning units, in particular between the psycho-educational and discipline-based units, the methods for teaching these disciplines, and so on. As in other countries, novice teachers in Israel were frustrated by this dichotomy.[15] The expectation that the novice teacher entering the multichallenge classroom is the one who will integrate the various study units and will connect them effectively has been proven to be unrealistic.[16]

During the 1980s, voices of open dissatisfaction with the education system began to be heard in Israel. One of the main voices was that of the progressive education representatives who established the first Democratic School in Hadera in 1987. The group was led by Dr. Yaakov Hecht, who claimed that the Israeli education system does not allow the teachers, students, and parents a dialogic and authentic expression. With regard to teachers, these parents claimed that the hierarchical nature of the Israeli education system hinders teachers' professional development and the ambient freedom and dialogue as is expressed in the philosophy of John Dewey, Martin Buber, and others. The first Israeli Democratic School put its emphasis on the students and the educational vision that heightens their need for freedom as a catalyst for development. This opened an educational discussion regarding the need for a different kind of teacher training, one that emphasizes teachers' ability to develop their professional identity and their personal vision, thus empowering them.

The outcomes of these progressive voices were the establishment of dozens of Democratic Schools in Israel, with teachers who had not necessarily been trained in the regular teacher training frameworks. Some of them didn't even have a teaching diploma but were tested according to students' and parents' satisfaction, as well as their collaboration among the school staff. These schools were only partially supervised by the Ministry of Education and were partially funded by the parents. At the same time other schools were established in Israel under the title of "open-dialogic schools"; the most prominent one was Meitar School in the Carmel Forests near Haifa. This school emphasized the personal development of students but also of teachers. It contested the conventional "industrial" system of teacher training and went against its authoritative and antidialogic conceptions. In his book *Meitar: Education in a Dialogical Spirit* (1998), Dan Lasri, the school's principal, criticizes teacher training in Israel: "In the day-to-day process of education it is easy to fall back upon prejudice, upon habits we acquired from our environment and from global fashions quite mechanically. We seek to take responsibility out of dissatisfaction with the state of the world today and our state within this world."[17]

In one of his articles on his website The Dialogical Academy, Lasri expressed a strong criticism made by many parents at the time: "Judging according to its distribution, the familiar teaching array is highly successful. All over the world we find almost the same framework: a teacher standing in the front of the classroom, students sitting behind him, he speaks most of the time and they are mostly silent. Do we learn like this? Probably not, but perhaps 'learning,' to begin with, is not the issue, and is not why the array has become so successful. This array contains many aspects of foreign work—a place where matter consumes the spirit, form takes over the essence and people lose their courage."[18] This criticism contained much outrage on teacher training becoming "a teaching factory" instead of it being a space for the development of teachers who are responsible also for the spiritual development of students.

Following these trends during the late 1980s the Democratic Institution in the Seminar Hakibutzim College in Tel Aviv was established. The institute placed much emphasis on programs such as "educational greenhouse," which sought to move the center of power from a centralistic teacher training to the empowering of the teacher and the groups of teachers while stressing the development of a personal initiative and personal freedom for creativity. This plan's vision underscored that the greenhouse for social-educational entrepreneurship is a program aimed at training educators who operate out of democratic values and worldview, who are critical thinkers, whose educational identity is evolving, and seeking to create a change in the educational sphere.[19]

The progressive voices in the educational sphere during the 1980s sought to move the emphasis in teacher training from the "training of a teacher" (who transfers materials, who reaches educational achievements and success in exams as preparation to the future) to "the development of teachers who are social entrepreneurs, activists, who have a clear identity on change-generators and leaders," as can be seen in the words of Hadas Leket, a humanities and democratic education student in Seminar Hakibutzim, that appears in the college website.

Unlike parents from the progressive and open-dialogic education (and those who supported home schooling in Israel) other communities of parents began to rise and to express dissatisfaction from the education system, claiming it was old-fashioned, outdated, neither innovative nor groundbreaking, and not technologically enhanced. These parents expressed dissatisfaction with the low scholarly achievements of students in Israel, as they surfaced in international examinations. As a result, the Israeli Association of Community Centers founded a division for community schools whose purpose was to create a stronger partnership between parents and teachers in order to better the dialogue between them. The model chosen to sound these voices was called "Parent Leadership." The dialogue led by these parents was intended to change the dialogue with the teachers from being an "oppositional defiance" to an "active collaboration seeking to initiate a change." Schools' parent leaderships, and class parent leaderships, aimed to give a voice to those parents who wanted to make a change amongst the existing teachers. These parents also voiced their dissatisfaction with the Ministry of Education and demanded change in teacher training in order to make the teachers a significant social force within the Israeli society, mainly with regard to scholarly achievements.

According to Anat Geffen-Sarig, these initiatives serve those parents with a high level of educational consciousness, who wish to educate their children in a unique framework as they see fit. The uniqueness, be it pedagogical or ideological, is the basis for the establishment of the school and what gives it legitimacy.[20]

Miriam Ben-Peretz summarizes the voices that were expressed by the Israeli public at the time, demanding a transformative success amongst students through a change in teacher training programs. She claimed that the twenty-first century brought with it changes in the perception of teaching, which now takes into consideration its transformative outcome. According to her, there is a need for teachers who will function as guides, who will be able to examine students' understanding and the amount of aid needed; therefore, there is a need for teacher training that will not only focus on knowledge but on understanding, mainly the understanding of the underlying significance of the material, discussion of ideas, and challenging standards of learning.[21]

In the 1990s, traditional teacher training programs based on academic learning were increasingly called upon by scholars and practitioners to offer students greater practical school experience.[22] This approach was predicated on the belief that teacher-training students must learn and gain experience of subject matter (knowledge) and themselves (their individual needs as worlds unto themselves).[23] Practical classroom experience under the guidance of experienced teachers and academic experts thus became an integral part of the teacher-training curriculum.[24] As Lucas[25] observes: "What is needed . . . is supervised practice, trial and error and repeated effort . . . it is as improbable that a novice can become a good teacher by enrolling in education courses as it is that an aspiring artist will attain proficiency as a painter or musician by attending lectures on art or music theory."[26]

The Shift to a Dialogue and Reflection-Based Pedagogy

The above-mentioned sources of tension called for serious rethinking amongst faculty members in the teaching department at the University of Haifa regarding the need to create a more meaningful and coherent teacher training curriculum that establishes tight and dialectical links between the university and the schools. The implementation of a partnership model in the context of university teacher training is, therefore, novel to university teacher training in the country. As such, it breaks with the traditional, applied university model by strengthening connections between academic learning and the real-life setting of teaching.

As part of the vision of the pedagogy of dialogical reflection, communities of multicultural students have been established. The groups are also composed of teacher-trainees specializing in various fields—history, civics, language, literature, English, communication, and so on. Here, too, the groups comprise diverse and pluralistic professional communities that promote generic discursive dialogue across divergent fields of knowledge with respect to their structure, curriculum, and method of instruction.

The communities of students seek to establish a broad dialogic culture in the teacher-training program in order to encourage creativity and self-reflective thinking. They emphasize two dialogic dimensions—dialogic organization and the dialogic classroom—on the basis of five premises (respect, listen, suspend judgment, free yourself, and communicate one's reasoning process). The content is tightly linked to dialogue and reflection. Throughout the day, these two axes are highlighted from both a practical and philosophical perspective with the aim of educating teachers to be continually engaged in classroom dialogue with their students, in organizational dialogue with the school administration and staff, and committed to reflection throughout their work in order to implement the necessary changes, accomplish the desired achievements, and encourage others to act in the same way in order to improve the school as a whole.

The learning day generally begins with a dialogical-reflective group conversation guided by the group leader. The discourse is attentive to the principles of dialogue and reflection, both formally and substantively. The students raise pedagogic and educational cases they have experienced in their practice, reviewing the dialogue they held with their mentors, the class they taught, and their views of the teaching profession. Opinions regarding pedagogy they witnessed and experienced are constructed, and issues such as organization within the classroom, the order of the meeting, classroom power relations, the school architecture, and so on are discussed. Diverse aspects relating to the teachers' classroom leadership and the ability to become agents of change dedicated to reflection, transcendence, and cognitive and political changes in the school reality are also examined. Some of the schools are challenging because they are located in middle- or low-class neighborhoods, the features of the student population constituting a key element in the teachers' work and the difficulties they face.

The group serves as a safe place that seeks to foster an atmosphere of security by enabling the participants to identify the basic views and concepts underlying the teaching-learning process in an open fashion and by linking the ideas to school reality, dilemmas, social, environmental, and material problems and the personal/emotional challenges that teachers will face when they become fully fledged.

The discourse group session is followed by a period during which the students observe lessons taught by their school mentor. The students then engage in another open discourse with the latter around the subjects that arose in the classroom that posed pedagogic and educational challenges, the mentor sharing his or her thoughts about the work process and in most cases also allowing room for feedback from the student. Herein, the teacher involves the student in her/his thoughts and deliberations regarding what had occurred and, the practices s/he had adopted taking a critical stance. This process constitutes a personal example for reflection as part of a revelatory dialogue, whereby the mentor turns from "knower" to "hesitator" and even sometimes to "not-knower." This reversal of roles gives the student an opportunity to experience, imagine, and envision him/herself as engaging in such a dialogue when s/he becomes a teacher.

During the day, the students also teach a class, or part of one. This may be a full or half class, a one-on-one lesson with three to five pupils, a group of students working on a project in a specific area, or preparing a lesson unit with the help of pupils. They also observe classes taught by their peers, sitting in the class and then discussing it afterward with the PDS coordinator and mentor. The latter activity contains a reflective dimension in which the students analyze their performance and receive feedback from the mentor, coordinator, and their peers. They also conduct a class dialogue designed to examine their pedagogic, educational, ethical, and philosophical performance in the classroom while observing the mentor (or other teachers), during extracurricular activities, and their own taking of a class.

The second form of dialogue they conduct is an organizational dialogue, which occurs in a series of circles. In the first, students observe and interview school staff, being made a partner to their difficulties and challenges. In the second, they meet with various school staff, from the principal to subject teachers. The goal of each organizational dialogical circle is to foreground the education system's obligations to the new teacher and give her as full access to the professional community as possible in order to enable her to understand the structure, performance, roles, and challenges that face the school and the teacher working as part of a team.

In contrast to student visits to schools designed to boost PR for the schools, showcase their curriculum and educational projects, and present their outward appearance, organizational dialogue seeks to train teachers to share their professional difficulties, concentrating in particular on helping those in authority engage in disclosure and reflection.

Thus, the University of Haifa was the first university in Israel to move from traditional teacher-training pedagogy to the dialogical reflective professional development school model (DRPDS).[27] Based on the pedagogy of reflection exemplified by a community of students studying in a network of Jewish and Arab schools, this is guided by the PDS approach first propounded by the Holmes Group.[28] Cochran-Smith[29] divides the complex teacher training institutes and training schools relationship into three models: consensus, critical dissonance, and collaborative resonance. The University of Haifa sought to cultivate trainees' ability to integrate various types of knowledge—practical and theoretical—within the framework of a learning community composed of teacher-training faculty and educational teams from field-training schools. Teaching being perceived as a practical-reflective profession, students were encouraged to regard the school as a place of learning and affirm its value based on their recognition of the contribution assignments make to their own development and society in general.[30]

Enriched by the pedagogy of reflection, the educational-intellectual atmosphere in such an environment can develop into a vibrant and dynamic space fostering intellectual tension and the sense of innovation and creativity so necessary for the educational task. As Copas[31] observes, this enhanced role includes guidance, personal support, direction, and mentoring. The pedagogy of reflection in a dialogical community further expands the mentoring teacher's role, making teacher-trainees part of a community of school teachers who are intimately involved in their training and ongoing education. The express intent is to make them part of their specific community and the education system in general.

In contrast to the traditional Israeli model, the PDS approach focuses on both the learning of material and the learner, while taking the individual needs of each student into consideration.[32] With students being exposed to a discourse that integrates disciplinary studies, pedagogy, and didactics during their field experience, they can prepare and initiate teaching-learning situations based on insights from various fields of knowledge on the one hand and find opportunities to study how to teach on the other.

The DRPDS model holds that proper reflective teacher-student dialogue rests on three pillars. The first is the legitimization of the personal view of each of the partners combined with sensitivity to difference, empathy, mutual respect, and openness. The University of Haifa model, based on the American model, for example, evinces that teacher-trainees and their teachers openly and nonjudgmentally share their views regarding their strengths and weaknesses with one another. This principle plays an important role in the accord between students and teachers regarding the level of the former's knowledge of their behavior as a launching point for future improvement, the real and imagined influence of the factors that interfere with their learning processes, and the ways to discern these and reduce their influence.

The second pillar is joint analysis of the possible ways of coping with a specific situation, choosing options, and focusing on solutions and outcome. This promotes student commitment to adopting successful methods and their consequent achievements and teacher/school system undertaking to provide feedback in a priori defined periods of time in order to help the students improve their work habits and results. For example, students and teachers analyze together different situations taken from the teaching-learning processes in class and suggesting different options for an inquiry of the circumstances. This joint process enables expanding both parties' viewpoints on the situation.

The third pillar is the use of metacognitive thought, at the heart of which lies student thinking about their thought processes. This is predicated upon the belief that the more aware students are of the various elements that influence their understanding, the better they will be at identifying and monitoring successful strategies, thereby increasing their knowledge and improving their ability to solve problems. The metacognitive approach is thus designed to contribute to enhancing students' personal responsibility, autonomy as learners, and awareness of the improvement process.

For example, during the group discussions after academic classes—guided by their mentors—they are asked to perform a metacognitive analysis of processes, be it observing a class or teaching it. As part of this framework they are asked questions such as: What is the strategy for solving a certain problem? When should a particular strategy be employed? How to employ it? Furthermore, they are asked to analyze the goals they set for the lesson, how they were ordered, the allocation of resources to a specific cognitive task, and monitoring the thought processes that were used, as well as assessing their effectiveness. The purpose of this metacognitive process is to enable students leaning toward an in-depth and comprehensive understanding and actively apply the knowledge they acquire in their learning process to a new context.

Reflective pedagogy adds a further component to this approach, placing at its center a process constructed in a community of learners whose members engage in reflective dialogue when confronted with an educational text presented during class discourse or the teacher-training group.

To gain evidence on the impact of the new model of student teachers' perceptions of the newly developed model, a multiyear study conducted over seven years (2010–2016) of student teachers' evaluation of their practice teaching in the context of the DRPDS model accompanied the program.[33] Seven to nine partnerships participated each year, depending on the number of teacher trainees and budgetary considerations. Each DRPDS partnership consisted of 10 to 20 student teachers from various teaching disciplines, who met on a weekly basis throughout the academic training period in a middle or high school (according to the cultural sector to which they belong, Hebrew- or Arabic-speaking). The overall purpose of the multiyear evaluation study was to gain insight into how student teachers evaluate the contribution of the DRPDS-model components in their studies. Specifically, the study examined the following research questions: How do student teachers evaluate the contribution of each of the components of the university-school partnership model for their learning? How do student teachers in each of the nine partnerships evaluate the contribution of each of the components of the model for their learning? And what kind of correlations can be identified between student teachers' evaluations of the different components of the model across all partnerships? To address these questions, a quantitative measures' questionnaire was developed that aimed at eliciting evaluations of the contribution of the five components of the university-school partnership model: the contribution of the university coordinators; the contribution of the school mentors; the contribution of the groups of students/colleagues; the contribution of the learning communities; and the contribution of the collaborative features of the university-school partnership model. One hundred nineteen students responded to a questionnaire, which included a 59-item self-report designed to evaluate, on a five-point Likert scale, the contribution of each of the components of the university-school partnership model to different aspects of learning to teach such as: fostering a positive attitude toward teaching, gaining professional support, encouraging critical thinking, connecting between theory and practice, applying new methods and techniques, and fostering independent learning. The questionnaire was divided into five sections, each referring to a different component in the partnership, as elaborated in the previous section. The questionnaire included items geared toward surfacing participants' attributions to the value of different forms of support in learning to teach. For example:

- "The university coordinator fostered a positive attitude towards teaching."
- "The university coordinator expanded my subject matter knowledge."
- "The school mentor contributed to my professional development as a team member."
- "The school mentor connected between theory and practice."
- "The group of student-colleagues was essential for my preparation as a teacher."
- "The learning-community expanded my knowledge about the curriculum."
- "The practice teaching collaborative model helped me to understand the school system."
- "The practice teaching collaborative model fostered the development of independent learning skills."

The questionnaire was delivered to the students taking part in the PDS program at the end of each academic year. The trainee participation rate in the evaluation study was 87% (table 8.1).

Three levels of evaluation were examined: (1) single students in each year; (2) all the students in each DRPDS partnership in each year; (3) all the students in all the DRPDS partnerships in the same year.*

---

*On level 3, a study of the multiyear evaluation of all the students in all the DRPDS partnerships was conducted. See D. Maskit and L. Orland-Barak, "University-School Partnerships: Student Teachers' Evaluations across Nine Partnerships in Israel," *Journal of Education for Teaching* 41, no. 3 (2015): 285–306.

TABLE 8.1
Multiyear student teacher participation rate in the evaluation study, 2010–2016

Year	Students in the annual program	Respondents to the annual questionnaire	Percentage of annual-questionnaire respondents
2010	141	126	89%
2011	128	118	92%
2012	163	134	82%
2013	135	111	82%
2014	108	105	97%
2015	122	102	84%
2016	97	85	88%
Total	894	781	87%

Overall, the findings show that the student teachers evaluated the contribution of the DRPDS components to their learning of teaching in the first year of the partnership (2010) as moderate to high on all four evaluation levels across all the statements. The program having begun in this year, the primary concern was to understand the nature and structure of the partnership.

Across the study time span, the teacher trainees evaluated the contribution of all partnership components to their studies as high. The average scores range lay between 3.85 and 4.53 (ignoring 2010).

The research indicates the strengths of training. The school practicums and mentors facilitated the students' training and entry into the teaching profession, the development of their professional responsibility as teachers, the deepening of their knowledge of the subject matter and familiarity with the curricula, their cultivation of class management skills, assessment, and individualized work with pupils.

These findings are important because they relate to practice, a central aspect of teacher training based on the premise that teaching knowledge is acquired and enhanced through practical training.

The multiyear research findings give evidence that students across the various disciplines acting as learning communities and their weekly meetings scored highly during the partnership years. This component contributes to the trainee teachers' entry into the teaching profession, the fostering of new thinking processes regarding the teaching profession, the development of teamwork, reflective thinking regarding the practicum, greater familiarity with the school system and role-holders in the school, and the development of school-integration and class-management skills.

The highest evaluation over all the years was of the university coordinator. This figure facilitates teacher-training studies and entry into the teaching profession, the development of professional identity and responsibility, knowledge of the school system and the role-holders in the school, the honing of teamwork, integration, and class-management skills, the cultivation of reflective abilities—a significant component of the practicum—and critical thinking.

The statements addressing the contribution the DRPDS model makes to the linkage between academic theory studied and practice in the field deserve special attention, the findings obtained being medial and the lowest scoring of all the statements in all the partnerships across all years. Although it was hoped that the partnership would bridge academic and school culture, the integration of theory and practice constituting one of the primary weaknesses of the traditional teacher-training model, the findings indicate that this topic continued to challenge the partnerships.

The Professional Development School (PDS) model was originally established in Israel between teacher training colleges (also known as colleges of education) and (middle and elementary) schools. The idea was to promote relevant links between the two cultures, through the design of teacher learner communities that foster praxical connections between theoretical understandings and practical-pedagogical teacher knowledge "in situ." While Israeli universities have, for many years, clung conservatively to the traditional model of the teacher-as-trainer, the University of Haifa was the first to develop a model of teacher-trainer-as-educator, through the establishment of school-university partnerships as integral to the preparation of prospective high school teachers. The Haifa teacher-education pedagogical model was envisioned and structured around two complementary dialogical and reflective curricular axes. In the course of the years, other universities in Israel joined in the implementation of the DRPDS model in diverse ways, which was eventually adopted (as will be described in the last part of this chapter), as a national program for teacher education in Israel.

Teach First Israel as an Alternative Teacher-Training Program

One of the other goals of the Israeli teacher-training programs instituted in the mid-1980s was to attract outstanding students to the profession in an attempt to reduce learning-achievement and socioeconomic gaps by means of education. In this framework, an alternative teacher training program entitled HOTAM—Teach First Israel—was introduced. Based on an international concept for the improvement of educational personnel, this forms part of Teach for All, a worldwide network of independent social organizations that seek to expand equal educational opportunities across the globe.

HOTAM began in Israel in 2010 as a partnership between the Education Ministry, the University of Haifa, Beit Berl College of Education, and other bodies. After the first four years, two other colleges of education—Oranim and Levinsky—took over the running of the program.

The Teach First Israel (TFI) program was brought to Israel by a series of entrepreneurs such as the JDC Israel, the Naomi Foundation, and the "Hakol Hinuch" (All is Education) campaign, an Israeli movement that sought to influence education in Israel. The declarative aim for the founding of Teach First Israel was "promoting equal-opportunities in Israeli education, according to a vision that every child will be able to choose his future regardless of his background."[34]

JDC Israel supported the program for several reasons, among them, the need of JDC Israel to put more emphasis on education in Israel. Furthermore, JDC is an organization that enables entrepreneurship and development, meaning it is not an operational organization but one that actively develops social initiatives to benefit both individuals and disadvantaged populations. Hence, Teach First Israel as a new initiative suited the JDC program until it could stand on its own two feet. Finally, there was a desire in the JDC to focus on underprivileged populations and areas.

The Naomi Foundation aids in financing Teach First Israel's training program called "Hotam Naomi" and in operating the entire program in memory of Dr. Naomi Kadar, who was an educator, lecturer, and researcher.

Hakol Hinuch, a public movement, decided to create an active program that will emphasize the quality of teachers, given the need for equal opportunities in education. Inspired by Teach for All and Teach First, the Hakol Hinuch movement decided to establish a similar program in Israel.

The Ministry of Education in Israel supported the joint initiative that brought forth the first tender for operating the academic program in the Faculty of Education in the University of Haifa (which by then had gained a significant reputation in operating a model for training a model DRPDS) and Beit Berl Academic College (one of the leading colleges in teacher education). The program did not confront any resistance in Israel, since the ministry's desire was to draw young, accomplished people to the field of education in any way. The budget for the operation of the program, with an investment of millions of NIS came from all the founding entities alongside the Ministry of Education.

While the program occupies only a small niche in Israel—the first class consisting of 66 students, with around 200 now participating in it (in the high school and primary school track)—it attracts high-quality students by providing financial funding and free scholarships for those seeking to earn a teaching diploma or even an MA. It thus meets a major teacher-training challenge in Israel—tightening the tie between theoretical studies and practical training.

TFI is based on the solutions to specific factors and conditions presented by the academic preparation program. One of these is the need for change in Israeli society and the Israeli educational system. While the latter has witnessed two reforms addressing teachers and time distribution (for elementary and high schools), the system has been slow to change, failing to take developments in Israeli society into account. In Israel, national identity and multiculturalism are still hot issues, with ideologically and ethnically divided groups interpreting reality divergently, the growing economic, social, cultural, and educational gaps influencing their way of life and experience. Thousands of children are also at varying degrees of risk. The resulting lack of solidarity prevents the education system from adopting an agreed-upon curriculum and providing solutions for the crisis of values.[35]

TFI seeks to integrate theory and practice and to implement a unique practical model closely linked to the school culture on the one hand and promote systemic cooperation between the training institutions, accompanying bodies, and educators in the schools on the other. Teachers within it target students from challenged populations or lower/middle socioeconomic classes, inculcating learning values such as persistence and respect for knowledge and the steps whereby they are acquired as well as the principles of access, aspiration, and achievement.

The teachers, who are meticulously selected, are trained on the basis of three values: choice ("I chose to be a TFI teacher"), commitment ("I am committed to my students"), and responsibility ("I am responsible for my students' progress"). The program's goals are aligned with these values. While initially a training program revolving around academic courses, evaluation following the first year suggested it should become holistic and integrative rather than a series of courses grounded upon a group of bodies of knowledge. Students spend most of their first year in training rather than preservice preparation, so the program must be structured around the principles of flexibility and creativity.

The philosophy at the heart of TFI has been described as a kind of "rescue pedagogy"[36]—that is, the idea that students from the geographical and social peripheries can escape their circumstances only through education. Seeking to link quality academic education with economic success, it works toward producing academically bright, socially sensitive teachers committed to its religiously overtoned social mission. During the first weeks of the summer semester, much of the content studied is in fact imbued with a sense of "mission" or "holy work," the teacher being represented as bringing the gospel of advancement or promise of success down from the "Mountain of the Knowledgeable" to the weak (known in Israel as "depressed") communities. This recruitment to the task of success is defined in many of the workshops as a "pioneering" task.

However, rescue pedagogy is slightly blind regarding new teachers' hardships. During recruitment to the program, the "rescuing" student makes a commitment to take upon herself/himself the vision of the "rescue church" and to become an "agent for change." Therefore, the program rests mainly (if not solely) on the strength of the teachers who are supposed to change their students or the reality in which their students operate. In TFI's document, "Goals and Strategies of the Summer Training," it states: "We at TFI develop teacher/leaders who are agents for change and who operate from having internalized the state of inequality in Israeli education" or "we act out of a sense of community and responsibility for ourselves and others and out of recognition of difference." Another version states: "TFI graduates act out of an aspiration for professionalism and continuous learning in order to maximize their influence on their students." The program's vision is therefore "development of self-efficacy, belief in the ability to experience change and to initiate change and in the ability of the students to experience change" (from the announcement of the implementation of the TFI program, published November 2013).

The attempt to transform rescue pedagogy into educational practice in Israel has encountered numerous difficulties, some deriving from the responsibility novice teachers feel for acting as agents of change. In this sense, they face many of the same challenges as their counterparts outside the program.[37] TFI hoped that academic preparation would overcome these difficulties, moving students directly to the third stage (influence) immediately upon arriving at the school after the short five-week summer training period.

The principal tensions between the program leaders and academic institutions relate to the possibility of skipping the problems of the entry phase. On the one hand, academia seeks to respond to the new teachers' needs and equip them with the most effective tools; on the other hand, alternative teacher training does not guarantee any shortcuts. Rescue pedagogy then adds organizational demands such as making teacher training faster, more condensed, and committed to a philosophy that seeks to inculcate change from the first minute the "agent-for-change" teacher takes his or her place in the school.

During the first four years, it quickly became apparent that rescue pedagogy was blind to some of the new teachers' difficulties. The program not only suffers from conceptual ambiguity but also serves the hegemonic discourse and its essentially neoliberal purposes rather than focusing upon or intensifying the call for social justice. Instead of explaining to future teachers how social gaps are the result of long-term social structuring, it concentrates on liberating students from their oppressive circumstances. The new teachers also enter schools in which the customary discourse is authoritarian rather than participatory.

Despite the challenges TFI poses to its participants, it is still regarded as a prestigious (albeit small) program. Its success in raising the teaching profession's reputation and imparting a sense of ambassadorship and solidarity to the students is due in large part to the circles of support it provides novice teachers upon their arrival in the school, where they are integrated as a group that receives close didactic and pedagogic mentoring, and the feeling of community it instills—together with the financial support it offers.

Academia-Class: A National Program for Dialogical-Reflective Pedagogy Based on Greater Field Training

The positive effect of the two models—DRPDS-based dialogical-reflective pedagogy and the TFI campaign to attract outstanding candidates and reduce the learning and economic gaps in Israel—upon teacher training is significant not only because it has prompted recognition of the need for change in the teacher-training programs and the introduction of dynamic elements but also because the Israeli discourse continues to insist that, even if it has improved, the education system still falls short of international levels of academic and learning achievements.

In this section, we shall examine the final model that has been introduced in order to improve teacher-training programs in Israel. In 2015, the

Ministry of Education adopted a national plan for teaching practice in schools entitled Academia-Class. Based primarily on DRPDS principles, this has led a national trend toward dialogue between the academic institutions offering teacher-education courses (universities and colleges of education). Mentoring schools were also selected by the Ministry of Education to serve as educational communities that would take students while they were studying, thereby constituting a type of "field academia."

This program increases the practicum to two or three days a week in order to provide the teacher-students with greater exposure to the educational establishment, its educational and pedagogic life, and school year schedule. The Ministry of Education in turn began offering significant funding and scholarships to those who participated in it in order to enhance the teaching profession's reputation. In parallel, the school mentors also received, for the first time in Israel, greater financial compensation, forming a leading elite within the schools. Academic institutions, schools, and the state thus all came to share a common goal.

Seeking to institute the DRPDS model, the student practicum was designed to expose the teacher trainees to a series of steps intended not only to familiarize them with the school but also afford them diverse teaching opportunities—inter alia, independent teaching of a large class, paired teaching with a senior teacher in a large class, small-class teaching, and individual tutoring. The mentoring teachers in effect also become field teachers, engaged in constant dialogue with the students in preparing lessons, after-class analysis, and during the professional development processes. The students were also asked to take part in the life of the staffroom in order to get to know the routine awaiting them, as well as trips, professional team sessions, school management meetings, grading sessions, parent-teacher meetings, and parents' days.

The new program expected the mentoring teachers to be involved in student training at all work levels in which they were involved—lesson planning, implementation, professional analysis, and after-class reflection. The goal here was to ensure as continuous a learning process as possible, integrating advanced technology and up-to-date knowledge. It was also decided that the universities and colleges would aid the school educational teams in their professional development in order to tighten the professional ties between the two and create parallels between the content studied in the training institute and that learned in the field via the offering of jointly taught courses.

Beginning its third year in the academic year 2017–2018, the program expanded to schools in diverse sectors of the Israeli education system and a greater age range. During the 2017–2018 academic year 2,000 teacher-students (out of 12,500 teacher-students in Israel) participated in the program. During the 2018–2019 academic year it is expected that 3,000 students will participate in the program.

The first year was evaluated in 2016 by RAMA (the Israeli National Authority for Measurement and Evaluation in Education), the study being conducted following a preliminary qualitative study carried out by means of observation and in-depth interviews with the various parties—teachers, students, heads, leading factors, and pupil focus groups. The research was based primarily on the collection of quantitative data from the participants.[38]

Although the principal findings are exploratory, they point to positive trends amongst all the participants. The student teachers, for example, worked closely in tandem with the mentoring teachers, establishing good interpersonal relations. A high number of student teachers and professional teachers also reported collaboration in planning lessons, albeit slightly lower than the other parameters (also being lower amongst the teachers than the teacher-students). A large number of student teachers stated that they were capable of taking a large class on their own and teaching in pairs. Despite the fact that many teachers did not receive any training as mentors prior to their participation in the program, they believed themselves to be adequate for the task. The number of students, teachers, and heads who felt that the students benefited from the program was very high (90%–95%) in all the age groups at which the novices began teaching. The teacher-students reported that the program had made a significant contribution in all the areas evaluated.

As noted above, this assessment related to the first year of the program. It is thus too early to draw far-reaching conclusions, certainly not in respect to the improvement of the level of teaching in Israel or the raising of learning-achievement levels due to a reduction in the learning and economic gaps in Israeli society. It nonetheless already represents vital thought regarding the dynamics required for teacher education and teacher training, adopting more positive principles than its predecessors.

One of the major challenges of a new national program is its multipartner nature—academic institutions, schools, district administration, professional-development centers, mentors, and classroom/specialist teachers. These all demand a complex collaboration that impinges upon the program's implementation. The formation of an Academia-Class headquarters in the Ministry of Education that also coordinates the learning community of all these partners will enable the pooling of all the resources and future research knowledge.

Putting It All Together

Since the 1980s, Israel has faced serious challenges in properly preparing teacher-students to work in schools in preservice frameworks. These local challenges are also true for teacher education across contexts and countries, in an effort to create tighter alignments between academic institutions and the school as a workplace environment through partnerships and reciprocal collaborations between the two.[39] As described earlier, there is a rich body of knowledge already established on collaborations between schools and universities. Teacher educators, however, are still being called to better understand how the notion of partnership and its implementation in various forms and modalities is manifested in different educational contexts and higher education cultures, as suggested by the Blue Ribbon Report of the National Council for Accreditation of Teacher Education (NCATE).[40] The shifts undergone in teacher education in Israel, and especially in universities, toward partnership models guided by reflective, clinical, and situated approaches to professional education align with the broader, global call for universities to become more relevant to the local needs of society.

This chapter has examined three programs that have adopted organizational, pedagogic, and educational steps designed to address the above pressing issues. The DRPDS model has sought to replace the ideal of the single teacher-mentor with a community of learners in the context of promoting a culture of broad dialogue between teacher-students, teachers, and pupils. To this end, it has advocated the use of dialogical and reflective tools and the close alignment of academic studies and school practicums. The TFI set itself the goal of reducing socioeconomic and learning-achievement gaps in Israeli society by attracting outstanding teacher-students committed to rescue pedagogy and working with students from marginalized communities in Israel. It also encourages professional pride, giving greater weight to the practicum in the workplace, and it offers scholarships and financial benefits to its participants. The new national Academia-Class program incorporates elements from the other two models in order to bring academic studies as closely into line as possible with school practicums while increasing the amount of time spent and the learning space in the school prior to the novice teacher's entry into the profession. This program also offers a scholarship to its participants and financial payments to its teacher-mentors.

NOTES

1. A. Weinreb and N. Blass, "Pupil Trajectories from First to Eighth Grade: Differences between Sectors": http://taubcenter.org.il/pupil-trajectories-from-first-to-eighth-grade-differences-between-sectors-2 (2017).

2. J. MacBeath, *Future of the Teaching Profession* (Brussels, 2012).

3. L. Darling-Hammond, D. Burns, C. Campbell, A. L. Goodwin, K. Hammerness, E. L. Low, A. McIntyre, M. Sato, and K. Zeichner, *Empowered Educators: How High-Performing Systems Shape Teaching Quality around the World* (San Francisco, CA, 2017).

4. L. Darling-Hammond and A. Lieberman, *Teacher Education around the World: Changing Policies and Practices.* New York, NY (2012); see note 3.

5. D. Kfir, S. Avdor, and R. Reingold, *Preliminary Training and Teacher Professional Development: A Continuum,* Research report 1 (Tel Aviv, 2006); Y. Dror, "The Policy of Teacher Education in Israel: What Can We Learn from Reports in the Past and Towards the Future? In D. Kfir and T. Ariav, eds., *The Crisis in Teacher Education: Reasons, Problems and Possible Solutions* (Tel Aviv / Jerusalem, 2009), 56–92; E. Weisblay, *The Status of the Teacher in Israel and the OECD Nations: Training, Agreements, Salaries, and Working Conditions* (Jerusalem, 2013); M. Ben-Peretz, "Teacher Education in Israel over the Course of Time: Report of the Committee for Examining Teacher Education in Israel" 34 (2002), 222–225; M. Ben-Peretz, *Position Paper on "The status of Teachers: New Directions"* (2009); T. Ariav, *Outline Guides for Teacher-Training in Higher-Education Institutions in Israel: Report of the Ariav Committee* (Jerusalem, 2006).

6. T. Ariav and D. Emanuel, *How Mentor Teachers in Professional Development Schools (PDS) Perceive Their Professional Growth: Barriers and Opportunities.* Paper presented at the annual meeting of the American Educational Research Association, Chicago, April 9–13 (2007); I. Margolin, "A Coterminous Collaborative Learning Model: Interconnectivity of Leadership and Learning," *Brock Education* 21, no. 2 (2012): 70–87; M. Zellermayer and I. Margolin, "Teacher Educators' Professional Learning Described through the Lens of Complexity Theory," *Teachers College Record* 107, no. 6 (2005): 1275–1304.

7. Organisation for Economic Co-operation and Development (OECD) Education at a Glance: OECD Indicators 2006, Paris, France. Retrieved on March 12, 2017 from http://www.oecd.org/document/52/0,3343,en_2649_34515_37328564_1_1_1_1,00.html (2006).

8. Position paper for the Public Committee of Tuition Policy in Higher Education Institutions, in *A Report by the Public Committee of Tuition Policy and Aid Projects for Students in Higher Education Institutions, 1991–1996,* chaired by Supreme Court judge (retired), Yaacob Meletz (1996).

9. Higher Education Council, Guiding Outlines for Initial Teacher Education in Higher Education Institutions (Jerusalem, Israel, 2006).

10. BERA-RSA (British Educational Research Association, Action and Research Centre), *Research and the Teaching Profession: Building the Capacity for a Self-Improving Educa-*

tion System (BERA, 2014); P. Sorensen, J. Twidle, and A. Childs, "Collaborative Approaches in Initial Teacher Education: Lessons from Approaches to Developing Student Teachers' Use of the Internet in Science Teaching," *Teacher Development* 18, no. 1 (2014): 107–123; K. Zeichner, "Rethinking the Connections between Campus Courses and Field Experiences in College- and University-Based Teacher Education," *Journal of Teacher Education* 61, nos. 1–2 (2010): 89–99.

11. T. Ariav and D. Emanuel, "The Professional Development School System between the Junior High School Track and the 'Sharett' and 'Dror' Mentoring Schools in 2004: Modified Evaluation Stressing Student Teachers," *Research and Evaluation Unit* (2004); R. Moore, *Teacher Leaders Advise on Clinical Preparation,* retrieved on March 12, 2017: http://www.ncate.org/LinkClick.aspx?fileticket=h6o66KQ1Vdw%3D&tabid=715 (2010); K. Waege and O. K. Haugalokken, "Research-Based Hands-On Practical Teacher Education: An Attempt to Combine the Two," *Journal of Education for Teaching* 39 no. 2 (2013): 235–249.

12. N. Balass and Y. Shavit, "The Education System in Israel in Recent Years: An Overview," Taub Center for Social Policy Studies in Israel (2017).

13. M. Zilbershtein, M. Ben-Peretz, and N. Greenfeld, eds., *New Trends in the Training Programs of Teachers: Partnership between Colleges and Schools—The Israeli Story* (Tel Aviv, 2006).

14. Zilbershtein, Ben-Peretz, and Greenfeld, *New Trends in the Training Programs of Teachers,* 12.

15. T. Ariav, "Training for Teaching: A Picture of the Situation in the World and in Israel and a Look to the Future," in D. Kfir and T. Ariav, eds., *The Crisis in Teacher Education,* 19–55.

16. S. Beck, "Two Views of College-Field Relations," discussion paper 6 (Tel Aviv, 2001); T. Ariav, *Training Teachers and Schools: A Different Relationship, Responses, and Thoughts,* Discussion paper 6 (Tel Aviv, 2001); M. Zilbershtein, R. Panvevsky, and E. Goz, *The Triangle of Instruction: Pedagogical Instructor-Student-Mentor Teacher—A Recipe for Success or Failure?* (Tel Aviv, 2005).

17. D. Lasri, "Meitar: Education in a Dialogical Spirit," Center for Futurism in Education, Ben Gurion University, in the Negev (Beer Sheva, Israel, 1998), 28 (Hebrew).

18. D. Lasri, "The Dialogical Academy" (Hebrew), http://www.dialogit.org/archives/1559.

19. From the greenhouse website (Hebrew): http://www.democratic.co.il/%D7%AA%D7%97%D7%95%D7%9E%D7%99-%D7%A4%D7%A2%D7%99%D7%9C%D7%95%D7%AA/%D7%9E%D7%A1%D7%9C%D7%95%D7%9C%D7%99%D7%9D%D7%90%D7%A7%D7%93%D7%9E%D7%99%D7%99%D7%9D/%D7%94%D7%97%D7%9E%D7%9E%D7%94%D7%9C%D7%99%D7%96%D7%9E%D7%95%D7%AA-%D7%97%D7%99%D7%A0%D7%95%D7%9B%D7%99%D7%AA/.

20. A. Geffen-Sarig, "Do It Yourself: Civic Entrepreneurship as a Strategy for Innovation in Israeli Education Policy" (The Hebrew University in Jerusalem, Israel, 2004), 4 (Hebrew).

21. M. Ben-Peretz, "Policy Making in Education: A Holistic Approach in Response to Global Changes" (Tel Aviv, Israel, 2011), 90 (Hebrew).

22. Carnegie Forum on Education and Economy, *A Nation Prepared: Teachers for the Twenty-First Century* (New York: Author, 1986); Holmes Group, *Tomorrow's Teachers* (East

Lansing, MI: Author, 1986); Holmes Group, *Tomorrow's Schools: Principles for the Design of Professional Development Schools* (East Lansing, MI: Author, 1990).

23. L. Darling-Hammond and M. W. McLaughlin, "Policies That Support Professional Development in an Era of Reform," *Phi Delta Kappan* 76, no. 8 (1995): 597–609.

24. S. Thompson and D. Sopko, "Empowered through Experience: Preservice Teaching and Learning in Professional Development Schools," *Professional Educator* 22, no. 2 (2000): 65–77.

25. C. J. Lucas, *Teacher Education in America: Reform Agendas for the Twenty-First Century* (New York, 1999).

26. Lucas, *Teacher Education in America,* 271.

27. A. Kizel, "Pedagogies of Reflection: Dialogical Professional-Development Schools in Israel," in C. J. Craig and L. Orland-Barak, eds., *International Teacher Education: Promising Pedagogies. Part A—Advances in Research on Teaching 22* (Bingley, UK, 2014), 113–136.

28. M. Copas, "Critical Requirements for Cooperating Teachers," *Journal of Teacher Education* 35 (1984): 49–54.

29. M. Cochran-Smith, "Reinventing Student Teaching," *Journal of Teacher Education* 42, no. 2 (1991): 104–119.

30. H. Marshall and H. Beyond, "The Work Place Metaphor: The Classroom as a Learning Setting," *Theory in Practice* 29 (1990): 94–100.

31. Copas, "Critical Requirements for Cooperating Teachers," *Journal of Teacher Education* 35 (1984): 49–54.

32. Darling-Hammond and McLaughlin, "Policies That Support Professional Development in an Era of Reform," 597–609.

33. N. Bar, *Research Report—Internal Summary of the Professional Development School Program for the years 2010–2016* (Haifa: University of Haifa, Faculty of Education, Department of Learning, Instruction and Teacher Education, 2016); D. Maskit and L. Orland-Barak, "University-School Partnerships: Student Teachers' Evaluations across Nine Partnerships in Israel," *Journal of Education for Teaching* 41, no. 3 (2015): 285–306. See also M. Rachamim and L. Orland-Barak, "Constructing Meaning in a Community of Learners: The 'Star' Pattern of Talk," *Oxford Review of Education* 42, no. 4 (2016): 475–490, https://doi.org/10.1080/03054985.2016.1200022.

34. From Teach First Israel website: http://tfi.org.il/.

35. N. Dagan-Buzaglo, *Aspects of Privatization in the Education System in Israel* (Tel Aviv, 2010).

36. A. Kizel, "'Rescue Pedagogy': The Educational Philosophy of Teach First Israel as a Test Case for the Internationalization of Teacher Training," in P. M. Rabensteiner, ed., *Internationalization in Teacher Education* (Baltmannsweiler, DE: Schneider, 2014), 78–90.

37. F. F. Fuller and O. H. Brown, "Becoming a Teacher," in K. Ryan, ed., *Teacher Education: The 74th Yearbook of the National Society for the Study of Education,* part II (Chicago, 1975), 25–52.

38. RAMA (National Authority for Measurement and Evaluation in Education in Israel), *Evaluation Report on Academia-Class Program* (Jerusalem, Israel, 2016).

39. I. Menter, M. Hulme, D. Elliot, and J. Lewin, et al., "Education and Lifelong Learning: Literature Review on Teacher Education in the 21st Century," retrieved on August 19, 2018: https://www.gov.scot/resource/doc/325663/0105011.pdf (2010).

40. N. L. Zimpher and D. D. Jones, *Transforming Teacher Education through Clinical Practice: A National Strategy to Prepare Effective Teachers.* Report of the Blue Ribbon Panel on Clinical Preparation and Partnerships for Improved Student Learning (Washington, DC: National Council for Accreditation of Teacher Education [NCATE], 2010).

CHAPTER NINE

Teacher Education for a Knowledge-Based Economy
The Singaporean Case

JASON LOH AND GUANGWEI HU

Singapore's Educational Achievements: An Overview

A report by the Organisation for Economic Co-operation and Development (OECD), entitled *The Knowledge-Based Economy,* announces that "the OECD economies are increasingly based on knowledge and information. Knowledge is now recognised as the driver of productivity and economic growth, leading to a new focus on the role of information, technology and learning in economic performance. The term 'knowledge-based economy' stems from this fuller recognition of the place of knowledge and technology in modern OECD economies . . . The need for workers to acquire a range of skills and to continuously adapt these skills underlies the 'learning economy.'"[1]

The same report defines "knowledge-based economies" (KBE) as "economies which are directly based on the production, distribution and use of knowledge and information."[2] Since the publication of the OECD report, many nations, particularly the economically developed ones, have emphasized the development of a KBE as a response to globalization, especially since low-cost manufacturing jobs have largely moved to developing countries. This economic policy shift has engendered an ever growing focus on the education, reeducation, and higher education of the affected populations simply because "in the knowledge-based economy we now inhabit, the future of our country rests on our ability, as individuals and as a nation, to learn much more powerfully on a wide scale."[3]

The import and significance of a KBE was brought to the fore for Singapore during the 1997/98 Asian financial crisis. In its 1998 report, the Committee on Singapore's Competitiveness believed that Singapore had lost its competitiveness vis-à-vis the other regional economies, whose currencies were devalued sharply.[4] Its recommended vision to the government was "for Singapore to develop into an advanced and globally competitive knowledge economy,"[5] and one of its key recommendations was that Singapore would need "to develop a world class workforce, comprising domestic and foreign talent, which is motivated, cost-competitive and with outstanding capabilities. This is crucial to our transition to a knowledge economy. This developmental process needs to be comprehensive. It should start with schools, where the young are taught new skills and their creativity talent nurtured. The process should continue at the workplace in a life-long learning environment. It should include the development of entrepreneurship."[6]

This milestone report has helped to set the tone for Singapore's economic orientation. The emphasis on developing its human capital was reiterated in 2005 by the then senior minister of state for information, communications and the arts and health: "Another key component in facilitating a knowledge-based economy is nurturing talent, or investing in human capital."[7] Most recently, the importance of this education-economy relationship has been reemphasized by Ong Ye Kung, the minister for education: "The education system that prepares students for the previous economic strategy will need to adjust to prepare them for this new economic strategy. Thus the education system is undergoing transformation, to better align with this new economic environment and trajectory."[8]

Throughout Singapore's postcolonial history, the government has emphasized the fundamental role of education in Singapore's economy. As Senior Minister Sadasivan pointed out, "Education has always been a priority of Singapore's policy planning."[9] The value of education is also clearly revealed in Singapore's social imaginary[10] characterized by its drive toward the acquisition of knowledge and pursuit of educational excellence. Over the past decade, Singapore has done consistently well in all the international benchmark studies, such as the *Progress in International Reading Literacy Study* (PIRLS), the *Programme for International Student Assessment* (PISA), and the *Trends in International Mathematics and Science Study* (TIMSS). In the 2006 PIRLS, Singapore was the top-performing country in the English language, had the largest percentage (19%) of students reaching the PIRLS Advanced International Benchmark (international median: 7%), and had the third highest percentage (58%) of students reaching the PIRLS High International Benchmark (international median: 41%).[11] Five years later, Singapore did even better in the 2011 PIRLS. It continued to be the top-performing country in the English language (the other three top-performing countries were assessed in other languages: Hong Kong SAR in Chinese, the Russian Federation in Russian, Finland in Finnish and Swedish). In addition, Singapore had the largest percentage (24%) of students reaching the PIRLS Advanced International Benchmark (international median: 8%), and the fourth highest (62%) reaching the PIRLS High International Benchmark (international median: 44%). It was one of the six countries that had shown improvements at all four international benchmarks over the last decade.[12]

Similarly, when Singapore took part in the OECD's PISA survey for the first time in 2009, it was one of the top-performing countries, ranking fifth in reading out of the 65 participating countries and economies, and boasting the second highest proportion (12.3%, as compared with the average 4.1% for the OECD countries) of students who were top performers in all the three subjects of reading, mathematics, and science.[13] It also topped the first PISA problem-solving test, together with South Korea.[14] In the latest PISA survey held in 2015, Singapore topped the global ranking,[15] taking first place in all the three subjects of reading, mathematics, and science.[16] Other than the international benchmark assessments, Singapore has also led the Asia-Pacific region in the International Baccalaureate (IB) diploma exams for seven consecutive years.[17] Notably, 57 (i.e., 60.6%) of the 94 students from across the world who obtained a perfect score of 45 points in 2017 came from Singapore. This was comparable to the 59% in 2015 and 61% in 2016.[18] In addition, the average score (i.e., 38.27) of the Singaporean students was markedly higher than the global average of 29.21 points.[19]

This high standard of educational achievement has been attributed in part to the work of Singapore's teachers by Low Khah Gek, the deputy director–general of education.[20] This key factor (i.e., quality of teaching) was also underscored by Professor Lee Sing Kong, former vice-president of Nanyang Technological University (NTU), which houses the National Institute of Education (NIE), Singapore's sole teacher education institute. As pointed out by Professor Lee, "Singapore invested heavily in a quality teaching force—to raise up the prestige and status of teaching and to attract the best graduates."[21] The role of teachers in ensuring high academic achievement has been recognized widely.[22] It is acknowledged in the OECD's report on Singapore, which notes that "teachers are the pillars of Singapore's education system."[23]

Singapore's educational success testifies to what the Holmes Group's (1986) report, focusing on the reform of teacher education in the United States, argues—that the training of teachers is "a highly significant part of the making of the nation."[24] For a tiny island–city-state with a land area of 719.9 km² devoid of natural resources, a resident population of 3,965,800, but a literacy rate of 98.8%,[25] its teachers have truly played a significant role in its outstanding achievements. As the people are the only resource that Singapore has, the government has consistently devoted huge proportions of its annual budgets to education, ranging from 16.05% to 22.50% since 2012.[26] The educational share of the budget has been second only to the defense expenditure. As a case in point, in the 2013 budget, S$5.89 billion (about US$4.29 billion) was allotted to primary schools, special education schools, secondary schools, independent schools, centralized institutes and junior colleges, and S$2.93 billion (about US$2.14 billion) was earmarked for the university sector. From the university budget, S$113,901,200 (about US $83 million) was given to NIE, which had 3,793 enrolled students in 2013.[27] This emphasis on education in general and teacher education specifically has helped Singapore make enormous progress in academic achievement since its independence in 1965.

As Singapore's only teacher education provider, NIE has played a key role in the nation's educational success. Though now an autonomous institute parked within a research university (i.e., Nanyang Technological University), it started out as the Teachers Training College (TTC) and transitioned to the Institute of Education (IE), before becoming NIE in 1991. In the beginning, it provided part-time on-the-job training to meet the huge demands for trained teachers. When the nation no longer had severe shortages of teachers, it became a provider of full-time teacher education. It is now also a provider of quality postgraduate education for the nation and the region. In the recent QS World University Ranking, NIE is ranked No. 16 for the Subject of Education in the world.[28] This is a remarkable achievement for an institute that once depended on the director of the London Institute of Education for advice on improving teacher preparation.[29] Much has been written about Singapore's teacher education over the years,[30] and it is beyond the scope of this chapter to cover this extensive literature on Singapore's teacher education and its development over the past five decades.[31] As such, in this chapter, we will focus on three main themes: (1) cooperation with the Ministry of Education (MOE) for teacher education and professional development (PD); (2) collaboration with schools for teacher education; and (3) coherence of educational research. Our aim in choosing these themes is to focus on both what is unique to Singapore's teacher education landscape and what has found parallels with other nations' teacher education history. Before moving on to the three themes, we will present a condensed historical overview of teacher education development since Singapore's independence in 1965.

Singapore's Teacher Education: A Brief History
The Teacher Training College Years: Ensuring Adequate Supply
Prior to the establishment of TTC in 1950, there was no designated institution providing comprehensive training to (prospective) teachers. There was a pupilage system in late nineteenth-century colonial Singapore, where some pupils were selected by the managers of the English-medium schools to be "pupil teachers."[32] The pupilage system was generally an informal system. It was only in 1906 that the Raffles Institution, Singapore's first school, started formalized training for in-service teachers at the primary level. In 1928, when the Raffles College was set up, teachers at the middle/secondary levels were also trained. The non-English medium schools were left to their own devices, prior to World War II. In the post–World War II years, there was some effort to train these teachers; however, the training was largely informal, in-service, and not systematic in scope or plan.[33] Teacher training was only formally institutionalized in 1950, with the establishment of TTC.

As a result of the postwar baby boom, which coincided with Singapore's winning of its self-governance status in 1959 and its independence in 1965, there was a massive expansion of the primary and secondary education sectors. Enrollment in both sectors rose to 518,000 in 1967, making up 27% of the total Singaporean population of 1,956,000.[34] This created an enormous demand for teachers; as such, there was a need to train large numbers of teachers within a relatively short period of time. Hence, a part-time in-service teacher-in-training scheme was adopted, in which student teachers were attached to schools to teach for half a day and drew a stipend during the training. As a result, the teaching force almost doubled, from 10,500 in 1959 to over 19,000 by 1968.[35]

Full-time training formally commenced in 1966, after the demand for primary school teachers stabilized. The part-time training scheme still continued, as there was still a huge backlog of untrained teachers. The hiring of so many untrained teachers was due to the increasing demand for teachers in the growing primary and secondary education sectors; the only feasible way to provide training to such a big pool of untrained teachers was through the part-time in-service model. Such part-time in-service training, though "criticized to some extent at that time," was deemed indispensable—that is, "accepted as a necessary evil"—because it was "an exigency of prevailing circumstances to sacrifice in some measure quality for quantity,"[36] due to the need to educate the young people in a young state that aimed to have universal education.

The Institute of Education Years: Upgrading the Teacher Supply
In November 1970, the Parliament passed the Institute of Education Act to convert TTC to the Institute of Education (IE). Prior to this Act, TTC was managed and directed as a government department; with this Act, it became a Statutory Board with the autonomy to hire from outside the civil service and to raise the academic standing of teacher education. The intent of the Act was to raise the quality of teacher education. The initial plan was for IE to confer bachelor's of education and master's of education degrees. However, there was a reconsideration of whether it was feasible for such a small nation like Singapore to set up a body solely to confer education degrees. Consequently, the establishment of IE was delayed. It was only on April 1, 1973, that IE was established to take over the functions of TTC, the former School of Education of the University of Singapore (the predecessor of the National University of Singapore), and the Research Unit of MOE.

The School of Education at the then University of Singapore encountered difficulties in recruiting enough students for it to be a feasible teacher training facility. Most applicants preferred to study at TTC, because they would earn a stipend during training; there was a high financial cost if they studied full-time at the university. As a result of this situation, and with the establishment of IE, the School of Education was closed and teacher education came under one sole provider.

IE took over the Diploma in Education (a program for graduate teachers) from the University of Singapore, and the part-time in-service training model inherited from the early years was to be phased out. However, due to the projected shortfall in secondary school teachers in the 1970s, the part-time in-service model continued. In August 1979, MOE reviewed the scheme and decided that it would be phased out by the time the July semester started in the following year and that full-time training would replace the part-time scheme completely. Concomitantly, the Teacher-in-Training Scheme was introduced in 1979 to replace the part-time Teaching Cadetship Scheme; this was a significant change, even though the duration and requirement of training were unchanged. The status was upgraded from a cadet to that of a teacher-in-training: as teaching cadets, the students would be teaching two-thirds of a regular teacher's workload, while receiving allowances pegged to two-thirds of a trained teacher's salary; with the change in status, the teacher-in-training would be given a formal appointment in the Education Service and paid a full salary pegged to the government's Executive and Clerical Services, while undergoing training.[37] This change was intended to make the teaching service more attractive to better candidates. In that same year, a Certificate in Education (preprimary and lower primary) was introduced to train teachers to implement the new preprimary education programs introduced by MOE in a number of primary schools.

In 1981, the one-year full-time Further Professional Certificate in Education (FPCE) was started to upgrade all nongraduate primary school teachers and thus give them a two-increment salary advantage.[38] This move to upgrade the primary school teachers (who were trained in the nongraduate Certificate in Education program) was in part influenced by MOE's plan to hire only graduate teachers for the secondary sector. A few years later, in 1984, the College of Physical Education (CPE) was established to offer a two-year Diploma in Physical Education for teachers who specialized in physical education, and during this same period, the one-year full-time Diploma in Educational Administration (DEA) was initiated for school leaders, that is, principals and vice-principals. With this program, the influence of IE on the schools was strengthened.

In the same year when the FPCE was started, IE moved to a bigger campus, which provided a 30% increase in its teaching and office space. With the increase in stature and autonomy in hiring, as well as an increasing emphasis on research, the profile of the IE academic staff changed significantly (see table 9.1).

From 1983, there was a strengthening of research and training linkages at IE. Three strategies were adopted: (1) the "formal recognition of research as a crucial criterion for staff recruitment, promotion and development" and the use of "explicit statements pertaining to research and publications" in the recruitment advertisement and promotion guidelines;[39] (2) the requirement that senior management officers in IE had to demonstrate an "active

TABLE 9.1
Profile of IE academic staff

Highest qualifications	No. of academic staff	
	April 1975	November 1982
PhD	5 (4.8%)	19 (12.0%)
Masters	34 (32.7%)	88 (55.3%)
Honours	8 (7.7%)	12 (7.6%)
Pass Degree	15 (14.4%)	15 (9.4%)
Nongraduate	42 (40.4%)	25 (15.7%)
Total	104 (100%)	159 (100%)

Source: Chor-Yee Lun and Weng-Cheong Chan, "A Brief Survey of Teacher Education in Singapore," in *IEXperience: The First Ten Years,* ed. Chor-Yee Lun and Dudley de Souza (Singapore: Institute of Education, 1983), 14.

interest and involvement in research,"[40] so as to lead by example and encourage the rest of the IE staff to follow suit; and (3) to incorporate research or "at least some investigatory work" in the major preservice and in-service programs. These strategies were deployed to encourage the next generation of teachers to perceive research as "a potentially useful professional ally rather than the esoteric tool for ivory tower residents."[41] The Educational Research Association (ERA) was founded in 1987 to encourage a research-oriented culture, and the Educational Research Unit (ERU) was set up in early 1988 to promote and develop the ideals and understandings of educational research in general and in teacher education, and also to articulate a formal research agenda for IE.

This emphasis on research led to an increasing interest in the Master in Education (MEd) program offered by IE: about 200 applications for its MEd program were received, even though only 20 places were available.[42] Up to this point, IE's diploma and postgraduate degrees were conferred by another body—the University of Singapore (prior to 1980) and the National University of Singapore (after 1980).

The National Institute of Education Years: Refining Teacher Education
In 1986, the Holmes and Carnegie reports on teacher education that were issued in the United States advocated universitization of teacher education as a strategy for improving schools and hence the national economy.[43] A few years later, in January 1990, the then minister of state for education presented her report entitled "Teacher Training in the 1990s: Issues and Strategies" to the then minister for education. Two issues focused on in this report were the need to merge IE and CPE, and the necessity to upgrade primary

teacher education. The report argued that it was necessary to restructure and upgrade the teacher education sector, "which had last undergone a major change in 1973, when the Institute of Education was established."[44] A committee headed by the minister of state for education conducted a survey and analysis of primary teacher training programs in 11 selected countries/jurisdictions (including Australia, Canada, Japan, South Korea, the United Kingdom, the United States, and Taiwan). The committee concluded that the establishment of degree programs for primary teacher education recognized the primary teacher's job as requiring "adequate mastery of a wide range of subjects (substantive content knowledge) . . . , a rich repertoire of pedagogical knowledge and skills to successfully handle children with different abilities and interests and at different stages of development," and "the ability to transfer knowledge in such a manner that children at different cognitive levels can learn effectively."[45] The three most significant of the 14 key recommendations of the committee were: (1) the introduction of a four-year degree program for the training of primary school teachers; (2) the merger of IE and CPE to form the National Institute of Education (NIE); and (3) the incorporation of NIE as an independent institute of the proposed Nanyang Technological University (NTU), "with its own Board of Management."[46] The affiliation to a university would also raise the stature of teacher education and make it easier to recruit "high-calibre" future teachers.[47]

The committee's report and recommendations were accepted by MOE, and on July 1, 1991, IE and CPE were merged to become NIE, which was concomitantly established as an independent specialized institute, with its own Board of Management, within the newly formed NTU. NIE started with four schools—the Schools of Arts, Science, Education, and Physical Education—and a Centre for Applied Research in Education (CARE). It introduced the four-year degree programs, bachelor of arts/bachelor of science with diploma in education, for training both primary and secondary school teachers, and upgraded existing certificate and diploma teacher training programs to diploma and postgraduate levels, respectively. It offered three routes into teaching: the one-year Postgraduate Diploma in Education (PGDE) for both primary and secondary teachers, the four-year bachelor of arts/science (BA/BSc) programs for both primary and secondary teachers, and the two-year Diploma in Education program for primary teachers.

In 2000, NIE moved into its new 16-ha premises on the NTU main campus, following one of the key recommendations put forward in the Seet Report.[48] With this move, NIE began offering more postgraduate programs at master's and doctoral levels through NTU; developed a new Framework of Desired Attributes of a Beginning Teacher, in which Values, Skills, and Knowledge (VSK) were emphasized; repositioned and renamed the BA and BSc with diploma in education programs to the bachelor of arts (education) and bachelor of science (education) programs, respectively; and established the Centre for Research in Pedagogy and Practice (CRPP) in 2003. Concomitantly, there was a significant increase in enrollments in initial teacher preparation programs (10.6% increase) and teacher professional development (in-service) programs (250% increase) during this period.[49]

Even in the 2000s, NIE had to ensure that there was an ample supply of fully trained teachers. In 2004, the then minister for education started an initiative "to provide schools with more teachers,"[50] which would translate to MOE's recruitment of about 2,000 teachers every year. Two years later, MOE wanted to "boost the size of the teaching workforce to 30,000 by 2010,"[51] and when it reached the target, it set a new target of 33,000 by 2015.[52] In response, NIE increased its hiring and formalized its secondment scheme with MOE to bring in experienced teachers to help teach in the preservice programs.

In 2005, NIE introduced the Professional Development Continuum Model (PDCM) to provide alternative options for graduate teachers to embark on and pursue postgraduate qualifications. This was in response to the increased options for serving teachers to seek higher academic certification on a modular basis. In 2007, it launched the first dual-degree Doctor of Education program offered jointly by NIE and IOE—the Institute of Education, formerly of the University of London (and since December 2014, University College of London Institute of Education). The collaboration was a result of NIE's desire to learn from IOE, which is well recognized internationally (e.g., international recognition for its educational research, experience in offering doctoral programs) and NIE's lack of experience in offering an EdD program. Furthermore, by drawing on NIE's strengths (e.g., knowledge and research relevant to the local context), the program will provide its doctoral students with a diversity of educational experience from complementary perspectives.[53] These were moves anticipating a possible push for a total graduate teaching force, which was announced by the then minister for education with the intent of raising the standards of education in Singapore's primary schools.[54]

In 2009, NIE launched its Model of Teacher Education for the 21st Century (TE21) as a response to the needs of the twenty-first-century learner.

Six broad recommendations were put forward: an emphasis on the internal qualities of the teacher (VSK); an explicit articulation of the competencies expected of any NIE graduand; a strengthening of the theory-practice nexus through emphasis on reflection and inquiry-based projects; an extension of the pedagogical repertoire for the teachers; introduction and use of an assessment framework for twenty-first-century teaching and learning; and an enhanced pathway for professional development.[55]

In the year of 2012, when the minister for education announced that the target of 33,000 teachers was met ahead of schedule,[56] the director of NIE, in his annual address to the NIE faculty, acknowledged that the meeting of the target meant declining preservice intakes, but he exhorted the faculty to seize the opportunity "to build up our professional development programmes to cater to the advanced learning needs of serving teachers and school leaders."[57] Against this backdrop, NIE reviewed its existing teacher education programs and launched the NTU-NIE Teaching Scholars Programme (NTU-NIE TSP). This signature program was designed to offer the new generation of future teachers "a unique opportunity for both personal development and international exposure in interdisciplinary training through seminars, conference presentations, research assignments and mentorships, internships, and overseas programmes," and its revamped curriculum aimed to help these scholars "acquire practical experience from industry and thought leaders on best practices and management insights globally as well as to sharpen analytical skills and develop their research expertise."[58] Concomitant with the creation of the TSP, NIE made structural changes to its four-year degree programs to enhance the design and delivery to allow student teachers to undertake both educational and content research in their third and fourth year, respectively. Furthermore, those who are in the TSP are given extensive opportunities to go for overseas practicum and semester exchanges with NIE's network of partner universities in Europe, North America, and Asia, including Linkoping University, Sweden; Stanford University, United States; UCL Institute of Education, United Kingdom; University of Melbourne, Australia; and Seoul National University, South Korea (see https://www.nie.edu.sg/about-us/global-connections). The TSP students are also fully sponsored to present papers at international conferences.[59]

With this turn, NIE has moved from training and educating large numbers of teachers in its early years and recent history to focusing on building a distinctive "core group of high-calibre and deeply passionate beginning teachers with intellectual rigour, strong leadership qualities, global perspectives and a keen desire to make significant contributions to education."[60]

Cooperation with MOE for Teacher Education and Professional Development

By virtue of the fact that NIE (and formerly IE) is the sole provider of teacher education in Singapore, it has a close symbiotic relationship with MOE. Under the Institute of Education Act of 1970, the Council of IE (i.e., the governing body of the institute) consisted of the chairman (usually director of education) and 13 other members, with four representatives from the government and three from IE.[61] About 36% of the council came from MOE, which meant a strong MOE influence on the council's decision making for IE. Even now, of the 11 total members in the NIE Council, five (i.e., 45.5%) are from MOE, with the permanent secretary (education) and the director-general of education acting as the chairperson and the vice-chairperson, respectively.[62] The benefit of having such a close symbiotic relationship with MOE is that NIE is always entrusted with the mission of meeting the demands of MOE and its school system. One of NIE's key roles is to ensure that there is always an adequate supply of teachers for the education system. After all, the "overall purpose of any system of teacher preparation is to ensure a numerically adequate supply of appropriately qualified teachers for the schools, and to maintain and enhance the knowledge and expertise of the existing teaching force."[63] NIE has fulfilled such a role throughout the years of its existence.

In addition to ensuring that there is an adequate supply of teachers, the close relationship between IE/NIE and MOE/the school system has helped to ensure that the quality of the teachers trained are in "greater likelihood of meeting (school) needs with a higher satisfaction,"[64] since MOE is the employer of teachers and the schools are the consumers of the IE/NIE "products."[65] This fact was accentuated by the then director of IE: "So long as it is IE's business to serve its main customer, the schools, IE will be committed unavoidably to adjusting its supply of teachers according to the quantitative and qualitative demands of the schools . . . IE can only be a successful leader if it follows closely what its customers need and want."[66]

Even now, one of the ways to achieve NIE's vision as an Institute of Distinction is to: "meet the needs of its key stakeholders through the education of highly trained and motivated teachers, with the competence to prepare young Singaporeans for the challenges of the twenty-first-century workplace. In meeting the needs of its stakeholders, NIE has to ensure that both its initial teacher preparatory programmes and professional development courses keep pace with developments in the educational landscape, both locally and globally. Locally, NIE's major stakeholder and partner remains the Ministry of Education."[67]

As such, the different Academic Groups (AGs) of NIE have worked closely with their counterparts in MOE in deciding what content is to be taught to the student teachers.[68] The student teachers need to be cognizant of what needs to be taught at the different levels of education (e.g., primary, secondary, and junior college). Although the academic content for the bachelor programs is comparable to that of other noneducation arts and science programs in other universities, the AGs must also ensure that the content covered gives the student teachers a good grounding and understanding of content they will need to teach as teachers. Hence, whenever there is a syllabus review of the different school subjects, the academic faculty of NIE AGs are called upon as curriculum consultants. This ensures that both NIE and MOE have inputs for the school syllabi, and NIE is aware of the changes that are taking place in real time, so that the content of its teacher education programs can be adjusted and updated with the changes in mind. Therefore, graduates from NIE are always ready to teach the content required in the classrooms.

The cooperation with MOE and the schools has also influenced NIE's in-service professional development (PD) programs for teachers. MOE launched the Teacher Growth Model (TGM) in 2012, a "professional development model which encourages Singapore teachers to engage in continual learning and become student-centric professionals who take ownership of their growth."[69] To ensure that its PD offerings would stay relevant to the needs of MOE, NIE adjusted its PD programs to align with the objectives laid out in the TGM; this was attested to by the senior parliamentary secretary for MOE.[70] NIE has also customized many of its offerings to meet the needs of the individual schools, which has ensured the relevancy of NIE's PD courses and contributed to its vision as "an institute of distinction: leading the future of education" (NIE's corporate vision).[71]

Collaboration with Schools for Teacher Education

Traditionally, student teachers are sent out to schools for their teaching practicums. During these stints, student teachers are expected to apply what they have learned in their teacher education courses. This university-based "learn and then apply" teacher education model has been often criticized for creating a theory-practice gap. To bridge the gap, NIE has regularly reviewed its programs. Fully cognizant of the government's plan to "prepare [its] citizens for the knowledge-economy" and the role "placed on education institutions to meet the challenges brought about by this new landscape,"[72] NIE has taken the initiative to embark on its own Programme Review and Enhancement, and the TE21 Report[73] is the result of that review and it presents a teacher education model for the twenty-first century.

The TE21 Report makes a number of recommendations for building closer links with schools. One of the recommendations is highlighted by Stanford University professor Linda Darling-Hammond in her foreword for the report: "A particularly important step is the NIE's plan to deepen the theory practice nexus by strengthening the role of mentorship in the clinical school experience."[74] This theory-practice nexus is a key focus in the TE21 Report. School-based inquiry or research projects have been incorporated as part of the BA/BSc programs. Specifically, in year three, the BA/BSc students are required to embark on an educational research project, which provides an excellent opportunity for them to develop an intimate understanding of the school system and find out what schools are currently doing. In addition, pedagogical tools such as analyses of lesson scripts and videos of classroom lessons have provided the student teachers an "important induction into the world of teaching."[75] Another recommendation of the TE21 Report is to incorporate experiential learning, which includes "fieldwork, microteaching, teaching activities in schools, service learning and field trips."[76] These have since been incorporated into the different courses in NIE. There is also a Structured Mentorship Preparation Programme to guide the schools' mentors on how to mentor the student teachers when they are doing their Teaching Practicum, and how to organize and facilitate Professional Learning Inquiries before, during, and after the Teaching Practicum, among other skills. There has also been an increase in the secondment of practitioners from schools to NIE to "facilitate the development of a shared professional language with academics."[77] In the words of A. Lin Goodwin, then Evenden Professor of Education and Vice Dean at Teachers College, Columbia University, "TE21 marks a new era of teacher preparation at NIE and Singapore and undoubtedly will sharpen, improve, extend, and enrich the impressive work Singaporean educators have accomplished in their definition of and deliberately rapid progress toward quality and qualified teachers."[78]

Coherence of Educational Research

Enshrined in the Institute of Education Act enacted in 1970 is "the promotion of research in education."[79] However, as the sole institute entrusted with the task of training large numbers of teachers for Singapore's school system, IE gave priority to preparing teachers rather than to conducting research. As Taylor noted, a limited amount of research had been done since the establishment of IE in 1973, due to the need to prepare an adequate number of teachers in the primary and secondary sectors. Due to the lack of time and the pressure of numbers, IE staff members were "forced to draw on the findings of research carried out in the United States and Great Britain rather than those based on the problems and progress of children and schools in Singapore."[80] The preceding quotation from the then permanent secretary and director of education should not be taken to suggest that Singapore no longer valued its links to IOE or research done in Great Britain and the United States, but it indicated a desire to complement research findings from those places with research conducted in the context of Singapore because such research would address Singapore-specific educational issues and thus have greater local relevance. It was also believed that IE faculty's engagement in research would yield firsthand insights into and deepen their understanding of the educational issues they lectured about, improving the relevance and quality of their teaching. For this reason, the then MOE director of education, who was also the chairman of the IE Council, felt that research should be an essential part of IE: "A lecturer who, in his research, has worked with slow learners, would give a more practical, relevant and credible lecture than one whose only experience with slow learners was through his textbooks."[81]

However, teacher education research at IE did not take off until 1982, when a deliberate effort was made to set up four related teacher education research projects, prior to the 1983 Conference on Research and Teacher Education held at IE.[82] The then director of IE was of the opinion that "each lecturer at IE should be able to provide a tentative answer to the problem, not from intellectual guesswork nor from studies conducted elsewhere but as far as possible from actual investigations by the lecturer or by a team involving the lecturer concerned. For example, if a lecturer advocates a particular method as the most worthwhile one for teachers to use, his suggestion should preferably come from his own research study rather than from reading certain textbooks or journal articles."[83]

This emphasis on research was reiterated in the recommendation put forth by the then minister of state for education, when she stated that the way forward for NIE would be for it to "pay great emphasis" on its research, because there was "much scope for studies on educational matters in Singapore and the region which need to be validated locally rather than being based on Western norms."[84] With the perceived importance of research and because of NTU's corporatization as a research intensive university in 2006, NIE was able to establish itself as an important contributor to teacher education research on the international scene in the first decade of the twenty-first century. Prior to the corporatization of NTU, NIE set up the Centre for Research in Pedagogy and Practice (CRPP) in 2003 to embark on research for the purposes of studying and improving teacher educational practices. Each year, there have been quite a number of research projects approved and funded by MOE. These projects have focused on a wide variety of issues pertaining to curriculum, instruction, assessment, teachers' professional development, and students' characteristics.[85] The Centre has helped to coordinate and allocate research funding for the academic faculty at NIE, filling the void of a "body responsible for funding relevant work, either in Ministry, IE or elsewhere" highlighted in Taylor.[86] Two years later, in 2005, the Learning Sciences Laboratory (LSL) was established to study and enhance the use of technology in teaching and learning, serving in a complementary role to CRPP's research foci.

A key strategy for accomplishing NIE's vision of becoming an Institute of Distinction is to achieve international recognition through high-quality educational research. This is articulated in the Strategic Plan provided to all NIE faculty members. Specifically, the Strategic Plan promulgates the synergy of NIE's teaching and research roles, recognizing that "excellence in teaching rests upon a foundation of relevant, high-calibre research" and that an "appropriate balance between the two roles will therefore contribute to NIE's international standing."[87] With this push toward research excellence, NIE managed to rise to the 10th position in the QS ranking of Universities by Subject (Education) in 2015.

Since 2008, MOE has provided NIE with a pool of research funds under the NIE Education Research Funding Programme (ERFP), which is open to NIE faculty members, MOE staff, and other institutes of higher learning in Singapore. ERFP has been administered by the Office of Education Research, which oversees NIE's research centers—CRPP and CRCD (Centre for Research in Child Development). While ERFP welcomes research proposals in all subject disciplines, it has strategic areas of priority in each request for research proposals. This has created a systematic coherence of research for the NIE faculty, focusing on the key educational areas. To date, there have been 340 approved ERFP projects from 2008 to 2017.

Some Current Issues

Darling-Hammond, in her paper on the need for teacher education in the United States to reform, points out that "no amount of coursework can, by itself, counteract the powerful experiential lessons that shape what teachers actually do. It is impractical to expect to prepare teachers for schools as they should be if teachers are constrained to learn in settings that typify the problems of schools as they have been—where isolated teachers provide examples of idiosyncratic, usually atheoretical practice that rarely exhibits a diagnostic approach and infrequently offers access to carefully selected strategies designed to teach a wide range of learners well."[88]

This is true of teacher education in Singapore as well. Even though much has been done to ensure a successful education of the future teachers, when they start teaching in a school system heavily influenced by neoliberal discourse, they will be subjected to all kinds of normative pressures.[89] As a result of these neoliberal pressures, some teachers have left the service.[90] Hence, it is crucial for NIE to identify and work with school sites "where state-of-the-art practice is the norm"[91] to provide its student teachers with meaningful practicum and school-based experiences. However, finding such sites is difficult because high-quality practice tends to be enacted by individual cooperating teachers, rather than a school as a whole. All along, NIE has not had any official partner professional development schools. If indeed "creating high-quality professional development schools" is "critical to transforming teaching,"[92] then this is something that NIE should explore. NIE's senior management did acknowledge the problem, or the challenge: "We do not believe that there is sufficient pedagogical capacity across the system to support this model of professional learning," where student teachers engage in "the key tasks of teaching in authentic classroom settings under the tutelage of expert teachers."[93] It is probably time for NIE to take up the challenge and consider what it can do to help like-minded schools develop into sites of pedagogical excellence where NIE's student teachers can acquire enriched learning experience and benefit from the mentoring of model practitioners.

Another issue facing NIE concerns the development of its graduates' ability to cater to different learning needs. In NIE, the teacher education curriculum focuses on preparing its student teachers to teach the mainstream, middle-ability students. This is due to the fact that NIE's graduates are most likely to teach this segment of the larger student population. As such, when they have in their classrooms students who have special needs or who are much slower in progress, they tend to encounter difficulties. In this regard, Singapore may learn from the practice of Finland, where "teacher training emphasizes learning how to teach students who learn in different ways—including those with special education needs," because the "egalitarian Finns reasoned that if teachers learn to help students who struggle, they would be able to teach all students more effectively and would indeed leave no child behind."[94] Taking a leaf from Finland's book, NIE needs to explore how in-depth knowledge, skills, and understanding of the varying needs of diverse learners can be woven into its existing teacher education curriculum. NIE has the expertise to do more along this line because one of its AGs specializes in special needs education.

NIE's work is not done. To achieve its vision of being an Institute of Distinction and leading in the Future of Education, it needs to seriously consider the two above-mentioned issues. Without professional development partner schools to demonstrate the state-of-the-art practice, it is quite difficult for student teachers to transform education and resist the onslaught of educational neoliberalism. Without a special needs component in their teacher education program, future Singaporean teachers are likely to fall short of the ability to meet the learning needs of every student. With a strong foundation laid over the years in both teaching and research, and the flexibility that a smaller enrollment in the preservice programs affords, NIE has again found itself at a historic crossroads, where challenges and opportunities exist side by side.

NOTES

1. OECD, *The Knowledge-Based Economy* (Paris, France: OECD, 1996), 3.
2. OECD, *The Knowledge-Based Economy,* 7.
3. Linda Darling-Hammond, "Teacher Education and the American Future," *Journal of Teacher Education* 61, no. 1–2 (January 2010): 35.
4. Ministry of Information and the Arts, Singapore, "Press Release of the Report of the Committee on Singapore's Competitiveness," http://www.nas.gov.sg/archivesonline/speeches/view-html?filename=19981111o2.htm (November 11, 1998).
5. Ministry of Information and the Arts, Singapore, "Press Release," para. 8.
6. Ministry of Information and the Arts, Singapore, "Press Release," para. 15.
7. Balaji Sadasivan, "Singapore's Commitment to Innovation for Knowledge-Based

Economy," speech by Dr Balaji Sadasivan, Senior Minister of State for Information, Communications and the Arts, and Health, at the "Celebrating Knowledge: The Power and Potential" Conference Organised by the National Library Board, https://www.mci.gov.sg/pressroom/news-and-stories/pressroom/2005/11/singapores-commitment-to-innovation-for-knowledgebased-economy (November 14, 2005), para.14.

8. Ye Kung, Ong, "The Constants and Variables of the Singapore Formula," Opening Remarks by Mr Ong Ye Kung, Minister for Education (Higher Education and Skills) at dinner hosted by the Singapore Chamber of Commerce (Hong Kong), https://www.moe.gov.sg/news/speeches/opening-remarks-by-mr-ong-ye-kung—minister-for-education-higher-education-and-skills-at-dinner-hosted by-the-singapore-chamber-of-commerce-hong-kong (April 23, 2018), para.32.

9. Sadasivan, "Singapore's Commitment to Innovation for Knowledge-Based Economy," para. 14.

10. Charles Taylor, *Modern Social Imaginaries* (Durham, NC: Duke University Press, 2003).

11. Ina V. S. Mullis, Michael O. Martin, Ann M. Kennedy, and Pierre Foy, *PIRLS 2006 International Report* (Chestnut Hill, MA: TIMSS & PIRLS International Study Center, Boston College, 2007), http://timssandpirls.bc.edu/PDF/P06_IR_Ch2.pdf.

12. Ina V. S. Mullis, Michael O. Martin, Pierre Foy, and Kathleen T. Drucker, *The PIRLS 2011 International Results in Reading* (Chestnut Hill, MA: TIMSS & PIRLS International Study Center, Boston College, 2012), https://timssandpirls.bc.edu/pirls2011/downloads/P11_IR_FullBook.pdf (December 2012).

13. Ministry of Education, Singapore, *International OECD Study Affirms the High Quality of Singapore's Education System,* http://www.nas.gov.sg/archivesonline/data/pdfdoc/20101214001/pisa_2009_press_release_moe_final.pdf (December 2010); OECD, *PISA 2009 rankings,* http://www.oecd.org/pisa/46643496.pdf (2010).

14. OECD, *Singapore and Korea Top OECD's First PISA Problem-Solving Test,* http://www.oecd.org/pisa/singapore-and-korea-top-first-oecd-pisa-problem-solving-test.htm (April 2014).

15. OECD, *Singapore Tops Latest OECD PISA Global Education Survey,* http://www.oecd.org/education/singapore-tops-latest-oecd-pisa-global-education-survey.htm (December 2016).

16. Sean Coughlan, "Pisa Tests: Singapore Top in Global Education Rankings," BBC, December 6, 2016, https://www.bbc.com/news/education-38212070 (December 2016); Sandra Davie, "Singapore Students Top in Maths, Science and Reading in Pisa International Benchmarking Test," *The Straits Times,* December 6, 2016, http://www.straitstimes.com/singapore/education/singapore-students-top-in-maths-science-and-reading-in-international.

17. Yuen Sin, "Singapore Tops Asia-Pac Region in IB Exams Again," *The Straits Times,* January 5, 2017, http://www.straitstimes.com/singapore/education/singapore-tops-asia-pac-region-in-ib-exams-again.

18. Sin, "Singapore Tops Asia-Pac Region."

19. Channel News Asia, "More than 60% of Perfect IB Scores from Singapore," *Channel NewsAsia,* January 4, 2017, https://www.channelnewsasia.com/news/singapore/more-than-60-of-perfect-ib-scores-from-singapore-7537270.

20. Davie, "Singapore Students Top."
21. Coughlan, "Pisa Tests," para. 34.
22. Linda Darling-Hammond, "Teacher Quality and Student Achievement: A Review of State Policy Evidence," *Education Policy Analysis Archives* 8, no. 1 (January 2000): 1–50; Linda Darling-Hammond, "Teacher Education and the American Future," *Journal of Teacher Education* 61, no. 1–2 (January/February 2010): 35–47; Anne Lin Goodwin, "Quality Teachers, Singapore Style," in *Teacher Education around the World,* eds. Linda Darling-Hammond and Ann Lieberman (NY: Taylor & Francis, 2012), 22–43; Mullis, Martin, Foy, & Drucker, *The PIRLS 2011 International Results in Reading; OECD, Building a High-Quality Teaching Profession: Lessons from around the World,* http://www.oecd.org/site/eduistp13/Building%20a%20High-Quality%20%20teaching%20profession.pdf (November 2011); Andreas Schleicher, *Preparing Teachers and Developing School Leaders for the 21st Century: Lessons from around the World,* https://www.oecd.org/site/eduistp2012/49850576.pdf *(June 2012).*
23. OECD, *Profile of Singapore,* https://www.oecd.org/pisa/PISA-2015-singapore.pdf (2016), 3.
24. Holmes Group, *Tomorrow's Teachers: A Report of the Holmes Group* (East Lansing, MI: Holmes Group, 1986), 24.
25. Department of Statistics, Singapore, *Singapore in Figures 2018,* https://www.singstat.gov.sg/sif (2018).
26. Ministry of Finance, Singapore, *Analysis of Revenue and Expenditure,* https://www.singaporebudget.gov.sg/budget_2018/BudgetSpeech/RevenueExpenditure (2018).
27. Ministry of Finance, Singapore, *Budget 2014: Revenue and Expenditure Estimates,* https://www.singaporebudget.gov.sg/budget_2014/RevenueandExpenditure (2014).
28. Quacquarelli Symonds Limited, "QS World University Rankings by Subject 2018—Education," https://www.topuniversities.com/university-rankings/university-subject-rankings/2018/education-training (accessed October 1, 2018).
29. William Taylor, *Teacher Education in Singapore 1980: The Role of the Institute of Education* (Singapore: National Institute of Education Library, 1980); William Taylor, *Teacher Education in Singapore: Report of a Follow-Up visit, 7th to 13th March 1981* (Singapore: National Institute of Education Library, 1981).
30. Ai-Yen Chen and Siew-Luan Koay, *Transforming Teaching, Inspiring Learning: 60 Years of Teacher Education in Singapore, 1950–2010* (Singapore: National Institute of Education, 2010); Suat-Khoh Lim-Teo, "Pre-Service Preparation of Mathematics Teachers in the Singapore Education System," *International Journal of Educational Research* 37, no. 2 (December 2002): 131–143; Leslie Sharpe and Saravanan Gopinathan, "Universitisation and the Reform of Teacher Education: The Case of Britain and Singapore," *Research in Education* 50, no. 1 (November 1993): 5–16; John Yip and Wong-Kooi Sim, *Evolution of Educational Excellence: 25 Years of Education in the Republic of Singapore* (Singapore: Longman, 1994).
31. A detailed treatment of the history of teacher education in Singapore can be found in Chen and Koay, *Transforming Teaching, Inspiring Learning.*
32. Chor-Yee Lun and Weng-Cheong Chan, "A Brief Survey of Teacher Education in Singapore," in *IEXperience: The First Ten Years,* eds. Chor-Yee Lun and Dudley de Souza (Singapore: Institute of Education, 1983), 3–17.

33. Lun and Chan, "A Brief Survey," 3–17.
34. Lun and Chan, "A Brief Survey," 3–17.
35. Mona Mourshed, Chinezi Chijioke, and Michael Barber, *How the World's Most Improved School Systems Keep Getting Better* (London: McKinsey & Co., 2010).
36. Lun and Chan, "A Brief Survey," 10.
37. Lun and Chan, "A Brief Survey."
38. Taylor, *Teacher Education in Singapore: Report of a Follow-Up Visit*.
39. Wong-Kooi Sim, "National Case Study of Teacher Education in Singapore," in *Teacher Education in Singapore: Change and Continuity in Curricular Perspectives*, ed. Wah-Kam Ho (Singapore: Institute of Education, 1990), 57.
40. Sim, "National Case Study," 58.
41. Sim, "National Case Study," 58.
42. Lun and Chan, "A Brief Survey."
43. Carnegie Commission, *A Nation Prepared: Teachers for the Twenty-First Century* (New York: Carnegie Forum on Education and the Economy, 1986); Holmes Group, *Tomorrow's Teachers*.
44. Sharpe and Gopinathan, "Universitisation and the Reform of Teacher Education," 10.
45. Ai-Mee Seet, *Teacher Training in the 1990s: Issues and Strategies* (Singapore: National Institute of Education Library, 1990), 3.
46. Seet, *Teacher Training in the 1990s*, i–ii.
47. Sharpe and Gopinathan, "Universitisation and the Reform of Teacher Education."
48. Seet, *Teacher Training in the 1990s*.
49. National Institute of Education, *333 Roadmap 2007–2012* (Singapore: National Institute of Education, 2007).
50. Shanmugaratnam, Tharman. Speech by Mr. Tharman Shanmugaratnam, Minister for Education, at the MOE Workplan Seminar, Ministry of Education, September 29, 2004, http://www.nas.gov.sg/archivesonline/speeches/view-html?filename=2004092902.htm.
51. Ministry of Education, Singapore, *MOE Unveils $250m Plan to Boost the Teaching Profession*, http://www.getforme.com/previous2006/040906_moeunveilssgd250millionplantoboostteachingprofession_more.htm (September 2006), para. 13.
52. S. Iswaran, Speech by Mr S. Iswaran, Senior Minister of State, Ministry of Trade & Industry, Ministry of Education, at the 2010 MOE promotion ceremony on 9 April 2010, http://www.nas.gov.sg/archivesonline/data/pdfdoc/20110427001/2011_seo_1_promotion_ceremony__apr_sms_iswaran.pdf (April 2010).
53. Anneliese Kramer-Dahl, "First EdD Cohort Embarks on Dual Programme," *NIE News*, October 2007, https://www.nie.edu.sg/docs/default-source/nie-files/nie-news/nie_news_oct_07_1.pdf?sfvrsn=2, p. 5.
54. Eng-Hen Ng, Speech by Dr Ng Eng Hen, Minister for Education and Second Minister for Defence, at the MOE Work Plan Seminar 2008 (September 2008).
55. National Institute of Education, *TE21 Implementation Report—NIE's Journey from Concept to Realization*, https://repository.nie.edu.sg/bitstream/10497/15503/1/TE21%20Implementation%20Report.pdf (2012).
56. Swee-Keat Heng, Keynote address by Mr Heng Swee Keat, Minister for Education, at the Ministry of Education Work Plan Seminar, https://www.moe.gov.sg/news/speeches/keynote-address-by-mr-heng-swee-keat—minister-for-education—at-the-ministry-of

-education-work-plan-seminar—on-wednesday—12-september-2012-at-920-am-at-ngee-ann-polytechnic-convention-centre (September 2012).

57. Joy Camille Atienza, "Director NIE Launches New 5-Year Strategy Plan: 3:3:3 Roadmap Charts the Course to 2017," *NIE News,* December 2012, http://www.nie.edu.sg/nienews/dec12/08–01.html, para. 3.

58. "Welcome Message," Teaching Scholars Programme, accessed October 1, 2018, http://tsp.nie.edu.sg/message.htm, para. 3–4.

59. National Institute of Education, *Institutional Profile,* www.nie.edu.sg/docs/default-source/nie-files/office-of-strategic-planning-academic-quality/nie-corp-slides-2015-feb_update.pdf (February 2015).

60. National Institute of Education, *Institutional Profile,* 37.

61. Taylor, *Teacher Education in Singapore 1980.*

62. "NIE Council," National Institute of Education, accessed October 1, 2018, https://www.nie.edu.sg/about-us/corporate-information/nie-council.

63. Taylor, *Teacher Education in Singapore: Report of a Follow-Up Visit,* 88.

64. S. P. Eng, "Teacher Education: The Singapore Model and Beyond," in *Teacher Education in Singapore: Change and Continuity in Curricular Perspectives,* ed. Wah-Kam Ho (Singapore: Institute of Education, 1990), 69.

65. Long-Fay Chin and G. D. Balakrishnan, "Teacher Education Programmes in Transition," in *IEXperience: The First Ten Years,* 21–40.

66. Wong-Kooi Sim, "IExamining and IExpanding IExperience: Delineating IE's present and future roles," in *IEXperience: The First Ten Years,* 100.

67. National Institute of Education, *333 Roadmap 2007–2012,* 29.

68. For more details about NIE's Academic Groups, see https://www.nie.edu.sg/our-people/academic-groups.

69. Ministry of Education, Singapore, *New Model for Teachers' Professional Development Launched,* www.nas.gov.sg/archivesonline/data/pdfdoc/20120607003/press_release_tgm.pdf (May 2012), para. 2.

70. Ann Sim, Speech by Ms Sim Ann, Senior Parliamentary Secretary, Ministry of Education and Ministry of Law at the NIE Teachers' Investiture Ceremony, https://www.moe.gov.sg/news/speeches/speech-by-ms-sim-ann—senior-parliamentary-secretary—ministry-of-education-and-ministry-of-law-at-the-nie-teachers—investiture-ceremony-at-930am-on-wednesday—11-july-2012—at-the-nanyang-auditorium—nanyang-technological-university (July 2012).

71. For more details of NIE's PD offerings, see https://www.nie.edu.sg/professional-and-leadership-development/professional-development-catalogue.

72. National Institute of Education, *A Teacher Education Model for the 21st Century Report* (Singapore: Strategic Planning & Corporate Services, 2009), 10.

73. National Institute of Education, *A Teacher Education Model.*

74. National Institute of Education, *A Teacher Education Model,* 7.

75. National Institute of Education, *A Teacher Education Model,* 65.

76. National Institute of Education, *A Teacher Education Model,* 66.

77. National Institute of Education, *A Teacher Education Model,* 70.

78. Goodwin, "Quality Teachers, Singapore Style," 42–43.

79. Kim-Leong Goh, "Preface," in in *IEXperience: The First Ten Years,* v.

80. Taylor, *Teacher Education in Singapore 1980,* 1.

81. Goh, "Preface," vi.
82. Wah-Kam Ho, *All Things Considered: A Review of the Research in Teacher Education in Singapore (1968–1988)* (Singapore: Institute of Education Library, 1989).
83. Sim, "IExamining and IExpanding IExperience," 105.
84. Seet, *Teacher Training in the 1990s*, 12.
85. "About Us," Centre for Research in Pedagogy and Practice, accessed October 1, 2018, https://www.nie.edu.sg/research/research-offices/office-of-education-research/centre-for-research-in-pedagogy-and-practice-crpp.
86. Taylor, *Teacher Education in Singapore 1980*, 57.
87. National Institute of Education, *333 Roadmap 2007–2012*, 29.
88. Darling-Hammond, "Teacher Education and the American Future," 42.
89. Zongyi Deng and Saravanan Gopinathan, "PISA and High-Performing Education Systems: Explaining Singapore's Education Success," *Comparative Education* 52, no. 4 (September 2016): 449–472; Jason Loh, "From Fantasy to Depression: A Beginning Teacher's Encounter with Performativity," *AsTEN Journal* 1, no. 1 (2016): 17–28; Jason Loh and Guangwei Hu, "Subdued by the System: Neoliberalism and the Beginning Teacher," *Teaching and Teacher Education* 41 (July 2014): 13–21.
90. Calvin Yang, "5,000 Teachers Leave Service over Five Years, http://www.straitstimes.com/singapore/education/5000-teachers-leave-service-over-five-years (October 2016).
91. Darling-Hammond, "Teacher Education and the American Future," 43.
92. Darling-Hammond, "Teacher Education and the American Future," 43.
93. David Hogan and Saravanan Gopinathan, "Knowledge Management, Sustainable Innovation, and Pre-Service Teacher Education in Singapore," *Teachers and Teaching: Theory and Practice* 14, no. 4 (September 2008): 378.
94. Darling-Hammond, "Teacher Education and the American Future," 45.

CHAPTER TEN

Reforming South Africa's Teaching
The Difficult Dilemmas of Teacher Education Policy Reform Post-1994

AZEEM BADROODIEN AND CAROL ANNE SPREEN

Debates about teachers, their preparation, work, and professional responsibilities are widespread in the international literature. These dimensions of teaching are often placed alongside comparisons of pupil achievement where teachers and their quality are the focus of widespread policy debates.[1] The 2005 OECD report, *Teachers Matter,* fueled international conversations on teacher professionalism, norms and standards, and the impact of globalization on teaching. Aptly named, *Teachers Matter* summarized the vast research on determinants of student learning, suggesting that "though the largest variation in outcomes is attributable to social background and student abilities, the most important influence, potentially open to policy influence, is teaching, especially teacher quality."[2]

The growing attention on international comparative assessments of student achievement has also once again brought teachers to the forefront of the global education policy agenda. Having grown significantly over the last decade, this increased attention on teachers and improving teaching is mainly due to pressure by global and external actors on governments to meet global goals and targets set in UNESCO's *Education for All Global Monitoring Reports* and most recently the United Nations' Sustainable Development Goals (SDGs). In 2015, the United Nations launched the SDGs, which are meant to serve as a blueprint for global aid and development policy over the next fifteen years. Goal 4 of the SDGs not only broadens the scope of the earlier policy priorities to expand schooling access and enrollment but includes wider goals regarding "inclusive, quality education for all" and specific target aims that address gender disparities and improving teaching and learning.[3] Within this SDG Goal 4 there is a specific call to increase the number of qualified teachers, and to prioritize this through national teacher development and support programs. It is a shift that signals policy maker recognition of the importance of fully trained and prepared teachers in addressing the quality of education, and the increasing need to involve teachers and teacher educators in the design and implementation of new approaches to reach the SDG Goal 4 targets. There is a realization that working together and building a unified front may substantially improve education quality and help increase learning outcomes.

Yet, while global consensus over the importance of teachers might suggest that governments wanting to improve education are keen to pour vast resources and greater innovation into teacher education, worldwide reform efforts appear to be more centered on privatization and increased accountability, pushing for more effective managerial structures and accountability mechanisms that regulate teachers' work and education and that secure compliance with globally determined standards of quality, outcomes, and efficiency.[4]

A number of scholars caution about the overreliance on insufficient data and decontextualized conclusions drawn from international comparisons to make national policy decisions, particularly those policies regarding teaching and teacher preparation.[5] They point out that neoliberal ideologies urging "new accountability" and "new professionalism" (as promoted by international agencies such as the OECD and the World Bank) have already significantly altered the shape and form of the teaching profession.[6] The impact of these neoliberal ideologies are most visible in the development of national standards for recruiting and selecting teachers; the redesign of teacher education curriculums; new systems of accreditation and certification; incentives and rewards linked to performance (often measured by student test scores); and the emphasis on subjects considered essential to compete in the global market (e.g., STEM).

South Africa is no exception to this new managerialist trend, where teacher accountability and concerns over teacher capacity dominate current public debates over the education crisis. While South Africa has been recognized the world over for postapartheid policies designed to promote an equitable and democratic transformation of society, it remains to be seen whether and how these have been put into place, or if they have brought about actual, meaningful change.[7] In this chapter we show that despite numerous proposals and policy attempts to confront the challenges of transforming a vastly unequal education system over the last two decades, South Africa still remains one of the most unequal societies in the world and its schools and its teachers continue to be largely rooted in the historical apartheid legacy of extreme inequality and overall poor performance. We argue that the postapartheid policies aimed at building a new national curriculum and its strong emphasis on access and increased resource distribution, have overlooked the critical role of teachers in bringing about change and addressing issues of poverty in classrooms, and more specifically failed to address what kinds of support and preparation teachers need to be able to do so in a complex and changing education system. Most postapartheid policy reforms vis-à-vis teachers have largely ignored the different contexts of poverty and inequality, particularly with regard to how these play out in the social, cultural, and linguistic lives of the majority of learners, and how these affect the teachers who teach them.

We describe in the chapter how over the last two decades South Africa has overseen the construction of an imposing new apparatus of provision, certification, and regulation of teachers, including the particular definition of norms and standards for teachers, and we argue that this has had a significant impact on the form of teacher education delivery. A key concern is that many of the above policies, specifically directed at teaching and learning, were crafted in committee meetings within the halls of the government capital, with very little sense of the different needs and variations in the socioeconomic contexts that needed to be shifted for any significant change to take hold. Restructuring from a distance has failed to understand or engage with real issues on the ground in the majority of schools, or to build on the understandings and capacities of the majority of the country's teachers.

We will show that despite the progressive postapartheid policy rhetoric that reenvisioned teachers to play different roles after 1994 and that attempted to better professionalize the teaching force, radical transformation of teacher education remains dormant, and further, has failed to build on teachers' professional capacities. Given the particular historical construction and treatment of teachers (particularly the majority black teachers) as technicians and implementers of apartheid state thinking, most South African teacher policy reforms have tended to emphasize increased control over teachers' work and performance via a teacher-proof curriculum (as in the current Curriculum Assessment Policy Statements—CAPS incarnation). This has left little room to promote the professionalization and increased capabilities of teachers.

Our main challenge is to grapple with what is meant by a "well-prepared teacher" in South Africa and teacher education reform, and how quality teaching can be fostered in contexts where the local, historical, and political dimensions that shape teachers' lives, work, and identities are given serious consideration. We place our discussion of postapartheid teacher-related policy reforms in South Africa within the multiplicity of forces unleashed by the global context of neoliberal education reform. However, we also emphasize that a set of *specific* historical, economic, political, cultural, and institutional contexts have shaped current ideas and understandings about teaching and teachers in South Africa. Importantly, we underscore how political and economic shifts in South Africa's macroeconomic restructuring[8] from 1996 have had a profound impact on the level and type of provisioning and delivery of teacher training, and was forcefully shaped by the consolidation of teacher education institutions across the country from 1998.[9] Ultimately, issues of economic restructuring (informed by the consolidation of universities) and failed attempts at social and economic redress and redistributive policies, along with the lingering effects of racial constructions of teacher identities and abilities,[10] combined to undermine teacher development initiatives and ultimately teacher quality.

While more research must be undertaken to understand how teacher learning can be connected with improvements in pupil learning, we caution against preoccupations that mainly look at teachers' work as a "value-add" provided by teachers preoccupied with learner achievement. The regulatory and global accountability mechanisms that are emerging in South Africa to control the teaching profession (and teacher education providers) include, for example, standard setting, teacher testing, and evaluation and accreditation of teacher preparation centers, and it is these processes that must be scrutinized and critiqued for their ability (or inability) to address the contextual needs and the diverse realities across South African schools. At first glance accountability tools may be intentioned to increase the quality of teachers and teacher preparation, but there are inevitable de facto consequences when teachers are prepared based on market principles or to mainly teach in globally competitive ways. We point instead to the specific needs and challenges of South African schools, learners, and teachers, and we would seek to understand what knowledge, skills, and attitudes teachers require to help learners learn and thrive in different contexts.

A Brief Review of Key Shifts in Teacher Education Provision in South Africa

Both before and under apartheid, national and provincial authorities shared responsibility for South African teacher education. During this time provincial teacher training colleges trained primary school teachers whilst universities trained secondary school teachers. This situation coexisted alongside an inequality of programs and services across South African provinces and racially separated departments of education. Parker observes that "by the end of the apartheid era South Africa had nineteen different governance systems controlling colleges of education, together with 32 partially autonomous universities and technikons that were providing teacher education."[11] This created a state of affairs that bedeviled national planning after 1994 and prompted huge concern about the variable quality, cost, and coordination of teacher education.[12]

Throughout the apartheid period education commissions and reports made direct reference to the challenges tied to joint central and provincial government control of education. They highlighted in particular the uneasy location of teacher education halfway between higher education and general education, with frequent recommendations made to locate teacher education largely or even solely at the university level.

From as early as 1910 teacher training in South Africa had always been understood to be a facet of higher education and thus under the control of the central Union Government. However, due to differences in how provinces spatially organized provision for its constituent populations and, given that white teacher training was already differently located under the control of the four provinces, it was agreed that all different teacher training colleges would operate under the auspices of the four Provincial Education Departments.[13] By 1935 there were a total of 30 teacher training colleges in South Africa for which the provinces had direct authority—with as many as 3,540 student teachers.[14] This number of teacher training colleges increased to roughly 49 over the period 1935 to 1990. Given the focus of apartheid policy on separate development, these were provided in the form of 18 colleges for white teachers, 16 colleges for coloured teachers, 2 colleges for Indian teachers, and 13 colleges for African teachers that fell under the

Department of Bantu Education (later renamed Department of Education and Training) within white South Africa—with all separately and differently spread out over the four provinces.[15]

Rose and Tunmer observe that a number of minority and dissenting reports did challenge provincially vested interests in retaining control of teacher education, with many revealing deep concern about quality, cost, and curriculum coordination.[16] However, because the main thrust of teacher training colleges by that time was to create different pathways to teacher education predicated along race and ethnicity lines, the provincial location of teacher training colleges continued to be the preferred approach until the end of apartheid.

Notably, teacher education also continued to be provided within the universities during the above period. At universities student teachers could achieve a secondary teacher's diploma after they completed their bachelor's degree, which allowed them to teach specific school subjects at high schools, or a four-year professional/academic bachelor of education degree that allowed them to focus on primary school teaching. Both offerings could be accessed at different universities that were themselves organized according to the separate university education regulations for different racial groups.

The main difference between the offerings of teacher training colleges and those of the universities was related to teacher qualifications and the assumed pedagogical orientation of qualified teachers. Universities believed that their offerings equipped student teachers with a strong disciplinary knowledge base, while teacher training colleges insisted on a greater focus on practice when inducting teachers into the profession. Colleges were deeply skeptical of an overly academic emphasis during teacher education preparation.[17] For both forms of provision and delivery, however, trained teachers were posted and allocated to particular racially and ethnically segregated schools, with each type of teacher training college and university preparing teachers for specifically designated schools.[18] This meant that the supply and demand for teachers (and thus the shape and form of teacher education) before 1994 was mainly organized to maintain racial division and separation and was not based on national need.

In South Africa a key consequence of the above system was that until 1994 teacher education produced different kinds of teachers with different kinds of expectations of what they could provide in their classrooms. Within the black education sector, students could thus qualify as teachers with standard eight school leaving certificates, while by contrast students in the white education sector needed matriculation certificates to enter teaching training.[19] This meant that newly qualified teachers entering the schooling system in 1994 arrived there via different providers, with different content and curriculum, and with differing qualifications and performance expectations. A huge problem was that most graduates from black teacher training colleges were mainly trained in subjects such as religious studies and history and were underdeveloped to teach mathematics, science, and technology.

After the first democratic elections in 1994, the national Department of Education sought to seriously modify and take control of both the governance and curricula of teacher education in order to shift the ways qualifications and entry requirements were being structured. It set about doing so by determining national norms and standards for education planning, provision, governance, monitoring, and evaluation for the education system, as well as for the reconfiguration of teacher education providers.[20]

This process began with the National Teacher Education Audit of 1995 and was followed by a number of further investigations such as the National Commission on Higher Education (NCHE) of 1996, all focused on the goal of making the teacher education system more integrated, efficient, and service-based.[21] Over the period 1994 to 2000 a unified central system of national teacher education was put in place, with all teacher education providers absorbed into universities and the higher education system. This led to about 104 teacher education providers after 1994 either being incorporated into universities, closed, or used as premises for other provincial services (technical colleges, teacher development institutes, or provincial administration offices). The main reasoning for the closure of the teacher training colleges was that these were seen to be producing an excess of primary school teachers, they were regarded as too authority-based and content-centered with a lack of integration of theory and practice, and were seen as inefficient due to their size and their wastage of human resources.[22]

The reconfiguration of teacher education providers was further shaped by the merging of higher education institutions in 1999, whereby 32 existing South African universities and technikons were realigned to form 23 universities and universities of technology. This led to the shrinking of the postapartheid teacher education landscape to 21 providers of initial teacher education (ITE) programs, which it was felt would presumably resolve previous duplication in the system and ensure greater quality and equity across providers (and student populations).[23]

The nine established provincial Departments of Education after 1994 were thereafter made responsible for implementing education programs aligned with the above national goals, including the allocation of funds and the employment of teachers. Teachers became fully certified through public higher education institutions from 2004, which became the primary providers of formal, accredited teacher education and development programs. To resolve previous inequities, it had been determined via constitutional decree that all colleges of education would close to "bring the number and quality of teachers being trained more closely into line with the needs of the provinces in whose schools they are to teach," and to "reduce duplications and inefficiencies."[24] The aim was to establish a teacher education system that prepared teachers from across South African society to *uniformly* teach in all schools in the various provinces.

A key corresponding development after 1994 that also led to teacher education's absorption into universities was that the teaching profession was arguably seen as more unattractive or unprestigious than before, and it was felt that if ITE programs were located in higher education it would better serve the development and expansion of teacher education. Welch and Gultig observe, however, that the shift ironically had the opposite effect, with teacher education instead becoming a "stepchild" of higher education rather than a high-priority field in its own right.[25] Furthermore, this was not helped by a funding formula for universities that placed teacher education in the lowest possible category (within universities) and where teacher education was not prioritized.[26]

In the above process (the shift of teacher education to universities) primacy had also mainly been given to clarifying technical and administrative procedures within universities, developing communication channels across higher education institution (HEI) campuses, and aligning institutional and faculty policies.[27] Little focus was given to the academic implications of the mergers for teacher education development, or to issues of delivery. For example, clarity was not provided on which students could get access to which universities and which schooling communities different teacher education providers would serve. In a sector that had previously served particular communities and racial populations and produced teachers for particular kinds of schools, little attention was given to how a "new set of institutions" would be able to develop alternative and inclusive institutional cultures, organizational structures, academic offerings, and approaches to pedagogy and knowledge production for teachers meant to serve different geographical locations.

In the end, HEI teacher education providers struggled to overcome technicist approaches to institutional change post-2000, or to reorientate or establish themselves as an established and equitable sector across the different HEIs.[28] For the most part different universities incorporated teacher education departments into their normal functioning, which in some instances forced departments to conform to the particular educational markets in which their universities operated.

For example, in most universities of technology teacher education departments were made up of previous teacher training colleges, early learning centers, and foundation phase training facilities, with little access and few links to the overall schooling system. For these departments after 2004 it was often easier to organize programs in ways that drew on the main practices and knowledge bases of universities of technology rather than to mirror teacher education programs of traditional universities. In such instances this invariably meant a stronger focus on teaching practice induction, and less on bridging practice and theory. For many it also entailed adopting managerial approaches that prioritized increased specialization and instrumental responses about how to address broader social and economic contexts and realities in the majority of schools, and to understand the conditions under which most of their prospective teachers would work. In such cases student teachers were rarely academically and intellectually prepared at universities of technology to grapple with the bigger challenges inherent in the education system. This meant that depending on the perceived context under which prospective teachers would teach, and based on the traditional offerings that different universities offered, teacher education programs varied in significant ways across institutions. Such differences are particularly evident in a recent 2019 book by Sayed, Carrim, Badroodien, McDonald, and Singh in which they examine student encounters with initial teacher education (at the foundation phase level) at five different institutions in South Africa.[29] These and other challenges within the South African teacher education landscape are also addressed in a forthcoming 2019 book by Linda Chisholm, particularly in her chapter "Dismantling and Reconfiguring the System, 1994–2018."[30]

Most interestingly, in the period after 2011, managerial approaches that have prioritized increased specialization and instrumental responses to address broader social and economic school contexts and realities have, ironically, created a scenario where the students who choose to enroll at different HEIs for teacher education programs based on their socioeconomic status and the fee structures of individual universities, have actually hardened older boundaries and teacher education approaches.

A final point about teacher education's struggle to find traction and to fortify itself (teacher education) as a national and critical priority is that the discord was not only apparent within HEIs after 2004. Institutional bodies like departments of education and national education councils were also ill prepared administratively to address many changes that were needed. For example, in the national Department of Education (DoE) most matters related to teacher education and development after 2004 were spread across a variety of sections/divisions that often worked in isolation from one another. Invariably these sections adopted very technical managerial approaches to address educational matters. This meant that teacher development activities could feature within curriculum units of the national DoE but could also be features of specialized units within those dealing with education leadership and management, inclusive education, rural education, and others, without the different officials overseeing the different units ever meaningfully engaging with each other about what each division was doing.

To compound matters even further, after 2011 formal, qualification-based teacher education and development programs were shifted to a branch of the newly established national Department of Higher Education and Training (DHET), which dealt primarily with higher education matters. Given that teacher education within HEIs was already regarded as the "lowest-status discipline" within South African universities, it was perhaps inevitable that the new DHET branch (upon its establishment) would not provide much oversight or direction to teacher education development and its overall purpose. This shift added to the confusion around teacher education in South Africa, with little alignment between the oversights and regulations of this branch of the national DHET and that of the Chief Directorate for Teacher Education and Development within the national Department of Basic Education.[31]

The Debate and Misinformation over Teacher Supply and Demand

Teacher salaries are normally the single most important investment and budget line item in public expenditure, with teacher costs normally constituting some 75% of education budgets, and some often reaching as high as 80% to 90%. Especially at times of constrained fiscal austerity (as was the case in the 1990s), it is little surprise that debates on returns on investment almost always take teachers and their work into account.

The reconfiguration of the spatially and institutionally fragmented teacher education system in the late 1990s and its full incorporation into a downsized higher education system from 2001 meant that an entirely new governance platform, focused on efficiency, rationalization, and tighter managerial and fiscal control, became attached to the preparation and support of teachers after 2000. The national audit report of 1995 argued that consolidating initial teacher education programs into universities would streamline teacher education provision, avoid duplication in the system, address the varying ITE offerings in different spaces, and ensure greater quality and equity.[32] This national audit report position was reinforced by a plethora of international consultants at the time (mainly from the World Bank and USAID) that advised on the "generally high cost and low quality of the colleges of education in South Africa in particular, and of the university sector more generally."[33] Hofmeyr and Hall had also described the teacher training colleges before 1994 "as probably the most expensive form of post-school education or teacher training," prompting, many would argue, the subsequent rationalization of teachers in South Africa.[34]

One of the main aims of the teacher rationalization program of the late 1990s, it was claimed, was to achieve a more equitable distribution of teachers across schools and provinces and to create a more equitable learner-educator ratio (LER). It had been found at the end of apartheid that the LER was between 1:20 and 1:30 for white learners, while between 1:40 and 1:70 for African learners. This problem in African classrooms was exacerbated by only 54% African teachers being qualified—as compared to white teachers (99%), Indian teachers (93%), and coloured teachers (71%)—and left African learners significantly more disadvantaged.[35]

On the one hand, the rationalization program led to some 30,000 teachers being redeployed across the school system, and about 16,000 teachers being given voluntary severance packages.[36] On the other hand, it led to a decline in the number of employed teachers between 1999 and 2004, from 365,447 teachers to 362,042 teachers, as well as a stagnation in the number of young teachers entering the schooling system.

In the period between 1994 and 2000, there had also already been a substantial decline in ITE enrollments (from 71,000 to 10,000 teachers) due to the reconfiguration of the teacher college system and its incorporation within universities. According to Fiske and Ladd, by 2001 the number of newly qualified graduates across South Africa had shrunk to about 5,000, and was expected to drop even further to below 3,400 after 2004.[37]

In the above regard, the *Preliminary Report to the Teacher Development Steering Committee* noted in August 2009 that while there were 384,938 state-employed teachers (including relief, permanent, probationary, and temporary teachers and part-time teachers) in public schools at that time, with a stable teacher attrition rate of around 5%-6% per annum from 1994 and a low increase in public school enrollments (less than 1% per annum), between 19,250 and 23,000 state-employed teachers would need to be replaced each year. It further noted that due to increased enrollments in Grade R, Early Childhood Development (ECD) and secondary school, it would bring another 900,000 learners into the system by 2014, meaning that an additional 28,000 teachers were required.[38]

Chisholm, Soudien, Vally, and Gilmour have detailed the political and economic impetus around teacher rationalization policies in the late 1990s, noting that policy makers proceeded with the rationalization program despite clear evidence that revealed an enormous need for more teachers in rural and high-needs classrooms.[39] But the push to reduce the national teacher salary bill meant that skilled and experienced teachers were incentivized to leave the profession. As such, the rationalization program contributed to and helped create a dearth of qualified teachers in South Africa.

Ironically, the closure of teacher colleges and incorporation into HEIs as well as the rationalization program in the 1990s occurred at a time when greater access to education was being promised and guaranteed. It was presumed that this meant that more teachers would be required in the system. Sayed et al. describe this expected teacher demand to have come from a "combination of growth in learner enrolment and the replacement of teachers who terminated their services in the 1990s. It was also tied to increased demand linked to population growth, high repetition rates, policy changes such as the lowering of learner-education ratios (LERs) and decreasing class sizes, and enhanced education access to previously marginalized groups."[40]

A concerted teacher recruitment campaign subsequently began in 2008 that tried to reverse previous trends and stimulate interest in teaching as a career. It was a direct response to the drop in teacher numbers in the period between 1999 and 2007. However, this push to recruit teachers after 2008 was not prioritized as a national demand, nor were alternative or new pathways provided that could accelerate this requirement.

Rather, the focus on recruitment tended to highlight various dimensions within the teacher shortage problem and focused on how to address these. For example, in the teacher graduate cohorts of 2009 only 168 (13%) of the

1,275 teacher cohort had an African language as their mother tongue. With the mother tongue of most learners in South Africa being an African language, this was identified as representing a significant mismatch between the entry of ITE graduates into schools and their ability to address, understand, and communicate with the learning needs of the majority of marginalized and poor learners. The mismatch was made even more apparent at the provincial level where, of the 168 ITE graduates, 124 graduated in Kwazulu-Natal and would most likely teach in that province. This meant that only 44 graduates with an African language as their mother tongue were produced in the rest of South Africa in 2009.[41]

Such developments suggested that recruitment processes needed to expand their reach and ambition, and with more funding being made available by the DHET to programmatically address the new challenges, teacher education providers were thus asked to also design programs when addressing the teacher shortage problem. Providers were asked to design recruitment approaches in ways that intersected with other challenges associated with language, schooling phase, and subject, as well as urban-rural disparities. As such, teacher education providers were expected to recruit more students, produce teachers across the various phases with adequate expertise and knowledge, as well as prepare them for teaching in contexts like rural schools with associated skills to teach in mother tongue languages, and in priority subjects like mathematics. They were asked to do this without any significant further governmental assistance.

In the end, it was approaches and initiatives to teacher education until 2010, as well as to the conditions of teachers within schools, that significantly demotivated and discouraged preservice and in-service teachers from the profession. Added to this, many qualified teachers were also inefficiently utilized due to poor school- and provincial-level management, sluggish and cumbersome recruitment and employment processes, individual teachers' resistance to being redeployed, and difficulties in replacing or transferring ineffective teachers.[42] It is this static teacher supply, as Van Broekhuizen notes, that has posed the most serious challenges to the South African schooling system, even more so given that the current school population of 12.4 million is expected to rise by another one million learners by 2023.[43]

Since 2011 there has been a concerted effort to overcome key weaknesses in the teacher education system, particularly with regard to improving access to education, providing better school infrastructures and teaching contexts, providing learning and teaching support materials, increasing teacher numbers, and improving their skills. A key goal in the Department of Basic Education's *Action Plan to 2014* and the *Action Plan to 2019* has been to target teacher redeployment and placement and devise a model that better utilizes information about teacher recruitment, attrition, exit, and migration to inform provincial planning and resourcing of teacher workforces. Efforts have focused on providing "the right quality and quantity of teachers and support staff with the right qualifications and competencies in the right position at the right time."[44] Disconcertingly, however, recent approaches to teacher education reform have been mainly operationalized as a revision of *costing models* rather than deep-changing policy formulations geared toward redress or productively engaging with older institutional legacies. There is also little in recent teacher education reform that privileges and supports the agentic roles of teachers in contributing to classroom change and meaningful learning experiences.

The Impact of Higher Education Restructuring on Teacher Education
Over a 10-year period from 1994 to 2004 teacher education providers in South Africa were reduced from over 150 institutions to just 21 providers located in 23 HEIs. This restructuring process and confinement of teacher education to HEIs had a variety of quite overt consequences for the schooling and teaching sector, as noted by the Commission on Higher Education (CHE) in 2010, and revisited below. These include:

- A significant decline in the number of institutions that offered teacher education in South Africa in the 1990s, at a time when teaching as a profession had a declining attractiveness worldwide, and where there was a serious decline in enrollments in higher education itself.
- A new set of ITE institutions that was thought to be of better quality and that would systemically produce teachers more cheaply for the state, but that transferred greater direct learning costs onto enrolling individuals, with fees that were significantly higher than at colleges and were now the students' burden to carry.
- The loss of control of the training of teachers that was instead placed solely in the hands of HEIs. While HEIs were better resourced, a key challenge was that HEIs were allowed a degree of autonomy that was substantial enough for them to reinterpret and sometimes deflect key government policy mechanisms meant to ensure that a national resource like teachers was regularly and consistently reproduced. In a South Afri-

can tertiary sector that continues to serve different student communities according to their differentiated schooling results and ability to pay fees, university autonomy allowed for the reinforcement of previous inequities between teachers in different schools and thereby contribute to a reinforced dual system of education.

- The opportunity for some HEIs to thwart national teacher education aims based on their individual financial needs. With some HEIs struggling to find new revenue streams to offset diminishing government subsidies, and given their complicated institutional restructuring exercises, many HEIs often focused on developing lucrative, short-term teacher upgrading programs rather than focusing on meaningful longer-term initial teacher preparation.

- An inversion of a previous systemic challenge where more primary school teachers rather than secondary school teachers were produced by the teacher college system. With the shift to HEIs, teacher education providers tended to concentrate on the traditional strength of HEIs in preparing secondary school teachers especially at the FET (Further Education Training) level, to the neglect of primary school (Foundation and Intermediate Phase) and ECD teachers. The DHET, for example, has funded the introduction of a number of such programs at different universities since 2011, focusing both on the required teacher educator human resources and the necessary associated infrastructure at universities that would make such programs sustainable.

- The disadvantaging of opportunities and decreased access for prospective teachers from rural areas, where their distance from and access to HEIs meant that their enrollment in ITE programs came at a significant cost. With the geographical concentration of HEI teacher education provisioning mainly in urban areas, this meant that potential teachers from rural areas, particularly if they were poor or otherwise historically disadvantaged, had to bear substantial travel costs to HEIs. This greatly reduced access and increased costs for the neediest prospective teachers.[45] Essop observes in this regard that "cost was probably the major reason for the rationalisation of the colleges of education" in the 1990s.[46] In the past the cost to the state for funding a student in previous colleges of education would previously have cost R40,000 per student, with negligible individual costs for individual teacher education students. From 2000, in the interests of economic viability, the per capita cost for funding a teacher education student through a university only cost the state R10,000. This was accomplished by transferring the main costs of teacher education studies onto individual learners.

- It is ironic that the shift and consolidation of teacher education within HEIs and the closing of teacher colleges in the period between 1994 and 2004 in most instances reduced the teacher preparation opportunities of teachers in rural areas. Whereas they were able to access some form of teacher training (even when of low quality) in previous colleges, the switch to universities added a further educational challenge for teachers in rural areas at the very time when larger numbers of rural learners were getting access to schooling and education for the first time.[47]
- The shift of teacher education providers to urban centers that were often far removed from rural communities, where teacher training, new teacher graduates, and the up-skilling of current teachers were needed most, was subsequently followed by many urban universities that previously served the needs of township communities being swallowed up by "flagship" (majority white universities) interests when delivering teacher education programs.

Furthermore, after 1994 postapartheid policy makers have not only focused on the physical transformation of the teacher education sector but have also set about bringing uniformity across ITE program curricula and qualifying teachers in the various institutions in ways that deliver one national school curriculum predicated on particular values or goals. Two policy interventions stand out in this regard.

The first major intervention that sought to frame initial teacher education programs tried to embed a particular set of values within all teachers (as captured in teacher education programs at universities). Tied to the particular demands of the curriculum of that time (outcomes based education), the Norms and Standards for Educators policy of 2000 focused on what an ideal teacher should look like, and it listed three competencies that universities needed to develop amongst all teachers, namely, practical competence, foundational competence, and reflexive competence. It also sketched seven main roles that all teachers needed to fulfill, that is, (1) learning mediator; (2) interpreter and designer of learning programs and materials; (3) leader, administrator, and manager; (4) scholar, researcher, and lifelong learner; (5) community, citizenship, and pastoral role; (6) assessor; and (7) learning area / subject specialist.[48] These attributes highlighted the different roles teachers were expected to play in schools as well as their commitment to further developing themselves and their skills for the benefit of their learners.[49] By presenting a national vision of what an ideal teacher was, this approach in 2000 seemingly sketched the broad outlines and left it to teacher education providers to determine how to incorporate the various roles and competencies within their various programs and modules.

The second intervention occurred in 2011, with a shift away from what kinds of teachers were required (as in Norms and Standards for Educators) to a greater focus on the content and focus of initial teacher education programs. The release of the Minimum Requirements for Teacher Education Qualifications (MRTEQ) policy in 2011, while supposedly adding to the seven roles highlighted in NSE, provided a firm description of what knowledges teachers needed to be equipped with prior to becoming teachers. The goal thus was to give particular expression to the seven roles of teachers by tying this to a particular curriculum (CAPS) and providing teacher education providers with clear guidelines with regard to the development of Higher Education Qualification Framework (HEQF)–aligned qualifications and teacher education programs.[50] In so doing MRTEQ sought to emphasize and shape what happens within providers with regard to the content and conceptual knowledge generated amongst student teachers, and the kinds of academic skills and knowledge forms that they exited with. With more attention on knowledge and learning, MRTEQ has represented since 2011 a significant shift within teacher education provision and attempted to embed a standard, formulaic, common curriculum that all teacher education university programs have to cover in terms of knowledge and practices. As such, its narrowing of ITE curricula can be seen as a tightening and specification of what happens in teacher education in South Africa, with a greater focus on what constitutes program content and the assessment therein.

Indeed, with the constant changing of the national school curriculum—from outcomes based education (OBE) in 1994 to the national curriculum statement (NCS) to the renewed national curriculum (RNC) to the curriculum and assessment policy (CAPS) in 2011—and the introduction of the Norms and Standards for Educators policy (NSE) and the shift to MRTEQ, together they have required a substantial alignment of teacher education with what constitutes quality benchmarks at various times. This has reshaped how teacher education providers have developed their programs. Recognizing the need for dramatic transformation in teaching and new visions for teachers, government committees and national summits have assembled a set of norms and standards for teachers that hope to shape the avenues that provide training outreach and services for teachers and the content knowledge they acquire.

A final challenge attached to teacher education provision shifting to HEIs has been that a range of organizations, including HEIs, provincial structures, NGOs, and unions, now provide for the continuing professional development of teachers. This is one area that continues to need greater clarification and formalization and that remains on the periphery of policy attention. At the provincial and district level, several dozen teacher development institutes and education resource centers provide accessible physical spaces for educators, education officials, and community members to meet, engage in professional development, access facilities and services, and disseminate information. However, there remain wide variations in infrastructural capacity, distance to/from these facilities and schools, equipment, numbers and training of staff, and funding and monitoring between these structures, and the kinds of programs and partnerships they currently offer are limited and irregular and are in need of structural improvement.

South Africa's Ongoing and Pervasive Schooling Inequality and the Role of Teachers in Reforming the System

As noted earlier, with the end of apartheid in 1994 South Africa had to radically transform its education system from a racially separate and unequal system to a more centralized system that equitably redistributed resources and services. A new school curriculum was developed after 1994 to address vast and prevalent social and economic inequalities, followed over the next 25 years by a flurry of policy activity as a way of meeting goals focused on structural improvement, changing the content of the curriculum, integrating schools, and linking communities to schools through more effective local governance. Amidst all these sweeping policy reforms, how to train, support, and increase *teacher capacity* to address the vast inequalities that remained as a legacy of apartheid was, it has been argued, almost an afterthought.

In the first instance, policies didn't seem to approach the *relation* between teachers and the schools in which they taught as needing to influence their practice or their capacity to add value to learner development. Schools in the past, embedded as they were in colonial and apartheid organizational forms, were instrumental in perpetuating inequalities and reproducing social fragmentations, which led to the allocation of resources and access to (and quality in) schools varying quite widely. The new government after

1994 was confronted by a system of mass inequality that needed to be reformed, and it stood to reason that the years 1994–1999 would be the most significant period in terms of policy reform and that new frameworks would be developed that would restructure the education sector completely.

Twenty-odd years after 1994, however, most schools in South Africa continue to struggle with structural factors that militate against schools being equal anytime soon. In that regard, the Department of Basic Education (DBE) earmarked infrastructure as a key nonnegotiable goal for 2020, with minimum norms and standards for public school expenditure that became legally binding in 2013. This provided for every school to have water, electricity, internet, working toilets, safe classrooms with a maximum of 40 learners per classroom, good security, libraries, laboratories, and sports facilities.[51] From data drawn from the National Education Infrastructure Management system (NEIMS) report however, as well as from the DBE report of 2015, severe disparities continue. For example, out of a total of 24,703 schools in South Africa in 2011 about 4,348 still did not have electricity (or a reliable electricity source), 5,013 still did not have running water (or a reliable source), 913 had no ablution facilities, and 11,450 only pit latrine toilets, 22,938 had no libraries (with 19,541 without even a possible space for libraries), 21,021 had no laboratory facilities, 2,703 had no fencing at all, and 19,037 had no school computer centers (with a further 3,267 having computer rooms but with no computers).[52]

When further disaggregated, the data (albeit based on previous conditions) in a 2014 report reveal the majority of schools that were privileged under apartheid to have very minimal infrastructure gaps. In these previously advantaged schools few have problems with electricity (0.6%), water (0.2%), toilets (2.2%), or libraries (29%), and the average number of learners per class remains roughly around 15. When compared to the majority of disadvantaged schools without electricity (22.1%), water (14.8%), toilets (53.3%), or libraries (92.1%), and with learners per class over 35.2, eliminating backlogs in school infrastructural development remains a fundamental educational priority in South Africa[53] and continues to serve as a key impediment to quality learning.

In the second instance, the infrastructural challenges outlined above invariably militate against adequate access to quality education, and they affect the quality of teaching and learning that can take place, as well as the motivation of teachers to remain in such environments.[54] It has remained a truism that teachers who are well trained and equipped to cope with the challenges facing South African schools are probably better placed to ensure that quality learning takes place.

As such, where historic inequalities, untransformed spatial and structural landscapes, and cross-sections of race, class, and geography continue to shape the educational possibilities of previously disadvantaged learners, the preparation at the tertiary institutional level of teachers with key strengths and knowledge forms can arguably influence the greater access of learners to quality learning, attainment, and school performance. Sayed et al. note that "comprising the greatest expense of the education system, and situated at the coalface of the learning experience,"[55] it is teachers equipped with key strengths and knowledge forms that can become the most important and effective resource in resolving equity- and quality-related challenges. "We need to therefore ensure that we promote and nurture their professional agency as agents of change and quality."

In 2013 there were 24,136 public schools in South Africa, with 391,829 teachers servicing some 11,975,844 learners.[56] Within this large number of teachers there exists a range of different teacher qualifications and limited teacher experience with, or exposure to, new and different teaching environments and methods.[57] It was found in 2016, for example, that most well-qualified teachers in South Africa still mainly teach in well-resourced, urban, safe, professionally and academically supportive environments, while it is the less-qualified teachers who are generally exposed to schooling contexts characterized by daily deprivation, violence, socioeconomic challenges, and weak managerial capacity. In teacher terms this has created a "dual system of education" that ensures a maldistribution across the schooling system, with more highly qualified and higher-paid teachers tending to work in wealthier, previously advantaged schools, while a shortage of formally qualified teachers (often in specific skill areas) remains in the poorer schools.[58] A grating irony in this maldistribution is that it enables wealthier schools to continue to further maximize their overall schooling performance.

With 13,000 of just over 25,000 schools in South Africa located in rural areas and accounting for more than 50% of ordinary public schools and 30% of learners, it is rural schools that, ironically, are more likely to have large numbers of underqualified or less experienced qualified teachers whilst also being the most difficult environments to teach in.[59] Findings from a recent study by Moletsane et al. suggest that teachers in rural contexts face multiple deprivations, experience high stress and dissatisfaction levels, and are more likely to take frequent leave and leave classes unattended, and that this definitively and negatively affects teaching and learning.[60]

In the third instance, the focus on school integration and empowering local school governing bodies (SGBs) to enhance school organization post-1994, has barely addressed the capacities of teachers to contribute to change via robust assessment processes and delivering bilingual or dual language teaching in the majority of South African schools. On the one hand, most teachers in the neediest schools often have the lowest qualifications and the least number of years of postschool training and, given their contextual struggles at their individual schools, struggle to keep themselves up to date with curriculum reforms and new practices determined at the provincial or national level. On the other hand, many teachers in rural schools are predominantly taught in their mother tongue, which is not English (or Afrikaans). Having to teach in English (or translate English materials into their mother tongue) then puts both teachers and their learners at a significant disadvantage. Furthermore, not only does the learning that takes place often not meet the particular demands of the curriculum, but any future promise of mother-tongue-based bi/multilingual education is undermined by an educational knowledge project that prioritizes predetermined instructional tools and teacher support systems that are misaligned with the linguistic resources of the majority of children and their instructional contexts.[61] The challenge for teacher education providers in various contexts is how to prepare teachers with the required linguistic techniques and tools, as well as provide a sociohistorical understanding of how to approach this challenge.[62]

In all three above (and many other) respects, neither policy reforms nor teacher education institutions from 1994 were substantially redesigned to anticipate or address the protracted socioeconomic challenges that most learners face despite twenty years of democratic transformation. Spreen and Vally have previously argued that policy reforms can't ignore contextual factors of continuing inequality and protracted poverty, conceding that many policies post-1994 have sought to address structural issues like access and redistribution and have tried to better prepare and connect learners to skills for joining the global marketplace.[63] We add here, however, that a key challenge has been that none of these policies have explicitly set out to address poverty head on (especially with regard to the more than two-thirds of children in South Africa who live in the poorest 40% of households or grapple with the kinds of spatial apartheid that has continued to shape key learning outcomes.[64] In this, the national project of integrating schools in South

Africa, "taking the ghetto out of schools and schools out of the ghetto," addressing the distances that learners have to travel to get to school, their lack of transport to access schools, and counteracting other gatekeeping and hidden mechanisms such as school fees and high education costs, has remained largely stillborn.[65]

In this context, we suggest that teachers (as well as teacher educators) are too easily (and unfairly) blamed for not being able to address ongoing learner performance and other gaps in South African schools. Given the pervasive socioeconomic and contextual challenges that continue to plague most schooling contexts, it is little surprise that teacher abilities and capacities to influence their classrooms have remained limited.

New Managerialism and the Impact on Teacher Education and Work in South Africa

In South Africa as well as elsewhere, the increasing importance of the global market and "new managerialism" has had several effects on formal schooling, in particular for teachers and for teacher education. For example, teacher's autonomy, independence, and control over their work have been greatly reduced, while workplace knowledge and control have increasingly been placed in the hands of administrators, government committees, or worse, for-profit private industries.[66] This has operated alongside an increased focus on goals, targets, and indicators as part of a global development framework (SDGs) that claims to concentrate more ambitiously on eradicating poverty, promoting inclusion and equity, and facilitating access to quality education. It has also sought mainly to quantify outcomes and achievements without a firm plan on how to eradicate persistent inequalities within the different school contexts in which teachers practice.[67] As such, within current accountability measures and constant monitoring and surveillance, it is difficult to see how teachers, and teacher education providers, can be expected to exhibit any real agency in addressing the multiple and conflicting demands that they are confronted with in regard to the difficult everyday contexts of schools.

Like elsewhere in the world, the increasing allure of technology as the silver bullet to delivering "world-class curricula," and the use of technology to implement scripted "teacher-proof" curricula to compensate for poor teacher quality, has gained considerable resonance. These will undoubtedly have considerable influence on the kinds of teacher education programs that are provided in the future and the ways in which student teachers are inducted into school practices.

The critical element, however, in the development of the above narrative of managerialism, intervention, and closer monitoring of teachers is the way in which teachers and their teacher preparation are constantly demonized and how this has been tied to their supposed failure to improve education outcomes in schools. It could be argued that this discourse was already apparent in early policy debates in South Africa, with teacher quality described early on as the "actual effects of teachers on learning." Already with the newly drafted White Paper of 1995, concern was expressed about what was termed poor teacher quality and "poor educational performance" at many colleges of education.[68] Using language such as "poor subject knowledge" and "lack of professional confidence" and a "cycle of mediocrity," the White Paper voiced concern that these would be perpetuated in the classrooms in which most teachers found themselves.[69]

This kind of discourse was followed in the 2000s by a persistent focus on a perceived "poor quality of teaching and learning in the country" and what was regarded as a pool of teachers poorly qualified and competent to teach certain subjects, or in specific phases (especially the Foundation Phase and Grade R, but also the Intermediate and Senior Phase), or in specific languages (African languages in particular), or in special schools, or in rural and remote schools.[70] In that regard, the consequence of constantly reverting to a narrative of poorly trained teachers is that any reconfiguration of teacher education provision has limited appeal and effect. Teacher education is both about the creation of quality education and quality teachers (within programs) and about ensuring that the teaching of graduates is effective in the learning and lives of school participants. However, while the term "teachers matter" has often been used within policy thinking post-1994, policy developments haven't necessarily shown how this is best recognized or how teacher quality can be secured and improved for quality education.[71]

There has instead been a strident focus by national bodies and departments on transforming the content and specification of what constitutes initial teacher education within university programs. The narrative of "teachers matter" in that respect has mainly focused on the instrumental elements of teacher professional development and preparation and how they contribute to a more effectively run educational system. This is further evident in the ways in which teacher education policies since 2000 have prioritized the creation of qualified teachers who are able to deliver a national school curriculum predicated on equality and democracy but have narrowed this to a very specific set of skills. In the latter regard, the DoE initiated a framework for ITE programs in 2000, with the promulgation of the Norms and Standards for Educators policy (as discussed previously), to deliver on particular kinds of teachers required.[72]

Notably, in the first attempt (by the DoE) to conceptualize what the expression "good teacher" entailed, the Norms and Standards for Educators (NSE) listed particular competencies and roles but was not overly prescriptive. For many, especially those who wanted a more managerialist approach to education policy, the key problem with the NSE was that by not making it part of everyone's training, many teachers found it difficult to realize in practice the vast variety of competencies and roles.[73] However, in subsequent iterations, teacher education policy increasingly shifted away from a focus on what "kinds of teachers were needed" or "what a good teacher entailed" to a focus on the content of initial teacher education preparation programs within HEIs.

To this end, the MRTEQ policy of 2011 started defining particular knowledges that all prospective teachers needed to be equipped with prior to becoming teachers and specifying for HEIs what ideal teacher education curricula should look like to produce "the ideal teacher."[74] In that respect, the focus of teacher education policy after 2011 sought to reconstitute the discourse of teacher education by defining what needed to happen within provider programs and what a commonly accepted curriculum should constitute in knowledge and practice terms.[75] By narrowing for providers what curricula needed to look like, the focus turned to specifying more deliberatively both what ITE needed to achieve and to increasing the emphasis on particular kinds of content and assessment.

This policy turn fitted neatly with the grip of the "new managerialist" mindset on policy thinking at the time. The shifting governance landscape of teacher education within HEIs post-1994, and the tighter definition of what constituted ITE within HEI provision, also seemed to logically fit with the kinds of responsibilities being given to professional bodies and attending role players such as SACE, DBE, and the EDTP SETA (Education, Training and Development Practices and Training Authority) in this period, in setting particular standards and specifying how teacher education programs needed to become better aligned with the policy requirements for teacher education qualifications.[76]

As such, in the above policy shifts within teacher education, the drive to ensure uniformity and consistency within ITE programs aligned to CAPS and MRTEQ has tended to overshadow programmatic attempts to critically address and eradicate the inequities that persist in school contexts in which prospective ITE teachers will teach.

Conclusion

The history of teacher education provision in South Africa since 1994 offers a number of important lessons about policy approaches and practices that focus on equity and transformation. It also reveals how such approaches may have promoted further inequality and institutional confusion. Ultimately, meaningful policy processes result from positive relationships between governance and institutional legitimacies.

It is common knowledge that in most cases where there are low levels of initial state capacity, weaker systems of teacher governance emerge. A widespread consequence is that teacher education institutions prepare teachers who are daily concerned and confronted with fragmented recruitment and management approaches, concerns about teacher attrition rates, low levels of pay and retention, and reports of reinforced forms of localized deployment based on patronage. These invariably erode perceptions of systemic legitimacy and discourage teachers from staying within the schooling system. Over the long term this erodes the capacity of teacher education providers to attract prospective teachers.

In contexts where deep divisions and recurring conflicts over race, class, culture, and language continue to underscore the need to build a common and inclusive national identity, there is a desperate need to foster greater teacher agency in local South African classrooms. However, what teachers do in the classroom has to be nurtured in meaningful teacher education programs both at the ITE level and in further teacher development programs. Notably, there are a number of international trends that could assist, reinforce, or caution policy developments in South Africa. We suggest considering some of the following:

- Initial teacher education and continuing professional development is a continuum that tends to be serviced through one integrated institutional system.
- Initial teacher education tends to be a national responsibility that is located in the higher education sector.

- The general trend internationally is to treat teaching as a graduate profession.
- Worldwide, there are a variety of institutions involved in the delivery of initial teacher education. These include colleges of teacher education, institutes of teacher education, and faculties of education at universities.
- Normally, formal, qualification-based continuing professional development programs are delivered through accredited higher education institutions, while informal programs are delivered by a variety of institutions and organizations.
- Teacher education can be made more accessible through nested, integrated, holistic networks of delivery institutions at national, provincial, regional, district, and school levels.
- There is a trend to locate the school-practice component of initial teacher education within professional practice schools, a process that is organically and symbiotically connected to both delivery institutions and schools.
- Locating management and budget responsibility for continuing professional development at more local levels is increasingly being preferred.
- A number of countries show a recent preference for specialized, purpose-built local teacher development centers from which teacher development is being coordinated.

Teacher education reforms are especially needed for contexts where self-serving and parochial systems of patronage and vested provincial interests make accountable governance systems and democratic policy development difficult to embed. With the growing demand for more, better-distributed, and more competent and qualified teachers, there has to be a simultaneous commitment to establishing teaching contexts in which meaningful learning can take place. Reforming and reconfiguring a teacher education system that is in constant conversation with other policies, both within and without the education sector, to ensure schooling contexts that have more profound outcomes for learners, is a difficult and uneven process. But it is necessary if equity in the quality of teachers and teaching is to be experienced across the various schools that make up the South African education landscape.

NOTES

1. Lewin, Keith M., and Janet S. Stuart, "Researching Teacher Education: New Perspectives on Practice, Performance and Policy" (2003), *Multi-Site Teacher Education Re-*

search Project (MUSTER): Synthesis Report (London: Department for International Development, United Kingdom, 2003); Tatto, Maria Teresa, et. al., "The Challenges and Tensions in Reconstructing Teacher-Parent Relations in the Context of School Reform: A Case Study," *Teachers and Teaching* 7, no. 3 (2001): 315–333; Tatto, Maria Teresa, "Developing Teachers and Teaching Practice: International Research Perspectives," *Comparative Education Review* 47, no. 4 (November 2003): 504–506.

2. Organisation for Economic Co-operation and Development, Paulo Santiago, and Source OECD, *Teachers Matter: Attracting, Developing and Retaining Effective Teachers* (Organisation for Economic Co-operation and Development, 2005).

3. United Nations Department of Economic and Social Affairs (2015). *Transforming Our World: The 2030 Agenda for Sustainable Development*. Retrieved from https://sustainable development.un.org/content/documents/21252030%20Agenda%20for%20Sustainable%20 Development%20web.pdf.

4. Tatto, Maria Teresa, "Education Reform and the Global Regulation of Teachers' Education, Development and Work: A Cross-Cultural Analysis," *International Journal of Educational Research* 45, no. 4–5 (2006): 231–241; Anderson, Gary, and Kathryn Herr, "New Public Management and the New Professionalism in Education: Framing the Issue," *Education Policy Analysis Archives* 23 (2015): 84; Connell, Raewyn, "The Neoliberal Cascade and Education: An Essay on the Market Agenda and Its Consequences," *Critical Studies in Education* 54, no. 2 (2013): 99–112; Connell, Raewyn, "Good Teachers on Dangerous Ground: Towards a New View of Teacher Quality and Professionalism," *Critical Studies in Education* 50, no. 3 (2009): 213–229.

5. Connell, "Good Teachers on Dangerous Ground, 213–229; Spreen, C., and J. J. Knapczyk, "Measuring Quality Beyond Test Scores: The Impact of Regional Context on Curriculum Implementation (in Northern Uganda)," *FIRE: Forum for International Research in Education* 4, no. 1 (2017), http://dx.doi.org/10.18275/fire201704011110; Verger, Antoni, Christopher Lubienski, and Gita Steiner-Khamsi, "The Emergence and Structuring of the Global Education Industry: Towards an Analytical Framework," in *World Yearbook of Education 2016*, 23–44 (Routledge, 2016; Education International [EI]); *Teachers Assessing Education for All—Perspectives from the Classroom* (Education International: Brussels, 2015).

6. Anderson, and Herr, "New Public Management," 84, 1–9; Anderson, Gary, and Michael Cohen, "Redesigning the Identities of Teachers and Leaders: A Framework for Studying New Professionalism and Educator Resistance," *Education Policy Analysis Archives* 23 (2015): 85.

7. Spreen, Carol Anne, and Salim Vally, "Education Rights, Education Policies and Inequality in South Africa," *International Journal of Educational Development* 26, no. 4 (2006): 352–362.

8. South Africa's economy did not, as expected, rebound after 1994 with the overthrow of apartheid—especially in the period that it was being dismantled. And even when some investment did return after 1994, postapartheid South Africa struggled to address how to reintegrate the previously disenfranchised and oppressed majority into the economy. Initially starting with an economic plan entitled the Reconstruction and Development Programme (RDP), this was replaced in 1996 by a five-year Growth, Employment, and Redistribution (GEAR) plan that favored some forms of privatization and the removal of exchange controls that would supposedly lay the foundation for sustained growth, a mea-

sure of industrial self-sufficiency, and future economic progress. The goal was arguably both to improve the living conditions of the impoverished black population and to address the demands for economic liberalization from business interests and Western governments. Importantly, the economic climate led to a number of educational decisions that undermined meaningful transformation and institutional reform.

9. The main manifestation of the system of apartheid was the rigid separation of people in South Africa according to racial classification, allied to the introduction of separate educational institutions for all learners that included the establishment of separate teacher training colleges for the training of teachers for the different sets of schools. A key challenge after 1994 was to disentangle the system of separate education provision across all fronts. How this pertained to teacher education is addressed further on in the chapter.

10. From its origins in the 1700s the nature and form of teacher education in South Africa was shaped by the levels of education that different groups were allowed to access. Kallaway traces the origins of teacher training to 1737 in South Africa at Genadendal (Baviaanskloof) in the Cape Province, where Khoikhoi assistants were first trained to help with the teaching of black children in the mission schools of the Moravian Mission Society. Peter Kallaway, *Apartheid and Education* (Johannesburg, 1984). By the nineteenth century, however, formal teacher training focused only on preparing teachers for schools that served white learners. In the beginning this focused on the preparation of monitors (older learners in the schools), who served alongside the imported teachers that staffed most schools for white learners at that time, and required them to have spent at least five years in assisting in the infant classes. It was extended and formalized into a state-aided normal college in 1878 that trained white teachers in secondary departments of schools, and was followed by the establishment of three more such institutions after 1893 for the training of white elementary teachers. One institution was established to train a small number of coloured teachers in the early 1890s, but no dedicated institutions were provided for African teachers until after the 1940s—with these confined mainly to the "homelands." The attitude adopted in the training of African teachers for much of this time was that the secondary schooling of African teachers was enough to constitute their teacher training. Council on Higher Education, "*Report on the National Review of Academic and Professional Programmes in Education*" (Council on Higher Education, 2010).

11. Parker, Ben, *Roles and Responsibilities, Institutional Landscapes and Curriculum Mindscapes: A Partial View of Teacher Education Policy in South Africa, 1990–2000* (Centre for International Education, University of Sussex, 2002), 5.

12. Sayed, Yusuf, "Changing Forms of Teacher Education in South Africa: A Case Study of Policy Change," *International Journal of Educational Development* 22 (2002): 381–383; Council on Higher Education, *Report on the National Review*, 7–11; Chisholm, Linda, "Apartheid Education Legacies and New Directions in Post-Apartheid South Africa," *Storia delle donne* 8, no. 1 (2012): 81–103.

13. Council on Higher Education, *Report on the National Review*, 7; Rose, Brian, and Raymond Tunmer, *Documents in South African Education* (Johannesburg: Donker, 1975), 281.

14. Kallaway, Peter, *The History of Colleges of Education* unpublished paper developed for the Higher Education Quality Committee (HEQC) (2008).

15. Hofmeyr, Jane, and Graham Hall, *The National Teacher Education Audit: Synthesis Report* (Department of Education, 1996). There were also about 78 teacher training colleges

for African teachers that were established within the variously created (apartheid) homelands from the 1960s.

16. Rose and Tunmer, *Documents in South African Education*, 290–310; Sayed, "Changing Forms of Teacher Education," 381–383; Council on Higher Education, *Report on the National Review*, 7–11; Chisholm, "Apartheid Education Legacies," 81–103.

17. Council on Higher Education, *Report on the National Review*, 8.

18. Sayed, "Changing Forms of Teacher Education," 382.

19. Of the 11,931 primary school teachers who were in service in the Transkei homeland in 1977, almost 94% were teaching with qualifications lower than matric. Council on Higher Education, *Report on the National Review*, 9. Within white South Africa, as noted by Christie, 62% of African teachers had the equivalent of a matriculation and 32% having a lower qualification. Only 5% of African teachers had a university degree, compared to 32% of white teachers with university degrees (and none with qualifications lower than matric). Pam Christie, "Changing Regimes: Governmentality and Education Policy in Post-Apartheid South Africa," *International Journal of Educational Development* 26, no. 4 (2006): 373–381.

20. In addressing the issue of teacher education, the national government in 1994 drew heavily upon the research of the 1992 National Education Policy Investigation (NEPI), whose teacher education report proposed three models by which colleges of education could be managed post-1994. It was this NEPI report that initially influenced the ANC's Policy Framework for Education and Training in 1994 and that suggested that "the entire system of teacher preparation and development needed to be reconstructed—given the lack of uniformity and the absence of planning across the teacher education sector, coupled with the uneven quality of inputs and outputs, the under-utilisation of many college facilities, undemocratic governance, and a stifling and uncritical ethos." African National Congress, *The Reconstruction and Development Programme (RDP): A Policy Framework* (African National Congress, 1994), 48–50.

21. Council on Higher Education, *Report on the National Review*, 9.

22. Council on Higher Education. *Report on the National Review*, 10; Sayed, Yusuf, Azeem Badroodien, Yunus Omar, Lorna Balie, Zahraa McDonald, et al., *Engaging Teachers in Peacebuilding in Post-Conflict Contexts: Evaluating Education Interventions in South Africa*, report produced for and funded by the ESRC/DFID Joint Fund for Poverty Alleviation (Cape Town: Centre for International Teacher Education, CPUT, 2017), 228.

23. Department of Basic Education & Department of Higher Education and Training, *Integrated Strategic Planning Framework for Teacher Education and Development in South Africa 2011–2025,"* Department of Basic Education & Department of Higher Education and Training(Pretoria: DBE & DHET, 2011), 21.

24. Council on Higher Education, *Report on the National Review*, 10–11.

25. Welch, Tessa, and John Gultig, *Becoming Competent: Initiatives for the Improvement of Teacher Education in South Africa, 1995–2002,* Paper presented to Pan-Commonwealth Conference, Durban, South Africa, July 2002. http://citeseerx.ist.psu.edu/viewdoc/download?doi=10.1.1.458.9640&rep=rep1&type=pdf (accessed on August 5, 2018).

26. Council on Higher Education, *Report on the National Review*, 14.

27. Gordon, Adele, "Cutting and Pasting: Changing the Fabric of Teacher Educators' Work at CPUT," *Opportunities & Challenges for Teacher Education Curriculum in South Africa* (2009).

28. Gordon, "Cutting and Pasting;" Sayed, "Changing Forms of Teacher Education."

29. Sayed, Yusuf, Nazir Carrim, Azeem Badroodien, McDonald, Zahraa, and Marcina Singh, *Learning to Teach in Post-Apartheid South Africa: Student Encounters with Initial Teacher Education* (Cape Town: SunPress, 2019).

30. Chisholm, Linda, *Teacher Preparation in South Africa: History, Policy and Future Directions* (Bingley, UK: Emerald Publishing, forthcoming).

31. Sayed, Yusuf, Azeem Badroodien, and Nimi Hoffman, *Teacher Professionalism and Accountability in South Africa: A Review of Literature* (Cape Town: Centre for International Teacher Education, 2016).

32. Hofmeyr and Hall, *The National Teacher Education Audit*, 52.

33. Crouch, Luis, "Public Education Equity and Efficiency in South Africa: Lessons for Other Countries," *Economics of Education Review* 15, no. 2 (1996): 125–137.

34. Hofmeyr and Hall, *The National Teacher Education Audit*, 52, 93.

35. Sayed, Badroodien, Omar, Balie, McDonald, et al., *Engaging Teachers in Peacebuilding*, 133.

36. Jansen, Jonathan, and Nick Taylor, *Educational Change in South Africa 1994–2003: Case Studies in Large Scale Education Reform* (Washington, DC: World Bank, 2003).

37. Fiske, Edward B., and Helen Ladd, *Elusive Equity: Education Reform in Post-Apartheid South Africa* (Cape Town: HSRC Press, 2004), 198.

38. Cape Peninsula University of Technology, *Preliminary Report to the Teacher Development Steering Committee on Progress Made and Emerging Recommendations on a New, Strengthened, Integrated Plan for Teacher Education and Development in South Africa* (Cape Peninsula University of Technology, 2010).

39. Chisholm, Linda, Crain Soudien, Salim Vally, and Dave Gilmour, "Teachers and Structural Adjustment in South Africa," *Educational Policy* 13, no. 3 (1999): 386–401.

40. Sayed, Badroodien, Omar, Balie, McDonald, et al., *Engaging Teachers in Peacebuilding*, 133.

41. Department of Basic Education & Department of Higher Education and Training, *Integrated Strategic Planning Framework*.

42. Sayed, Badroodien, Omar, Balie, McDonald, et al., *Engaging Teachers in Peacebuilding*, 136.

43. Van Broekhuizen, Hendrik. "Teacher Supply in South Africa: A focus on Initial Teacher Education Graduate Production," *Stellenbosch: Stellenbosch University Department of Economics Working Paper* 7 (2015): 15.

44. Department of Basic Education, *Draft Strategy on Recruitment and Deployment of Educators: Towards Improvement of Recruitment and Deployment of Educators by 2014/15* (Pretoria: Directorate of Educator Human Resource Planning, 2015).

45. Sayed, Badroodien, and Hoffman, *Teacher Professionalism and Accountability in South Africa*.

46. Essop, Ahmad, *The Incorporation of Colleges of Education into Higher Education: A Brief Synopsis* (Pretoria: Department of Education, 2008).

47. Council on Higher Education, *Report on the National Review*.

48. Department of Education, Norms and Standards for Educators, *Government Gazette* 415, no. 20844 (Pretoria: Department of Education, 2000).

49. Department of Education, Norms and Standards for Educators, 30.

50. Department of Higher Education and Training, Minimum Requirements for Teacher

Education Qualifications (MRTEQ), *Government Gazette* 553, no. 34467 (Pretoria: DHET, 2011), 9; Department of Higher Education and Training, National Qualifications Framework Act 2008 (Act No. 67 of 2008): Revised Policy on The Minimum Requirements for Teacher Education Qualifications, *Government Gazette,* no. 38487 (February19) (Pretoria: DHET, 2015).

51. Sayed, Badroodien, Omar, Balie, McDonald, et al., *Engaging Teachers in Peacebuilding,* 115; Equal Education, "School Infrastructure" (2015), available at: http://www.equaleducation.org.za/campaigns/minimum-norms-and-standards (accessed July 1, 2018).

52. Department of Basic Education, *National Education Infrastructure Management System (NEIMS) Report* (Pretoria: DBE, 2011); Department of Basic Education, *Draft Strategy on Recruitment and Deployment of Educators,* cited in Sayed, Badroodien, Omar, Balie, McDonald, et al., *Engaging Teachers in Peacebuilding,* 116.

53. Rakabe, Eddie, *Equitable Resourcing of Schools for Better Outcomes,* vol. 16 Technical Report: Submission for the Division of Revenue 2015, 2014: 119.

54. South African Council of Educators (SACE), *Code of Professional Ethics* (Pretoria: SACE, 2010).

55. Sayed, Yusuf, E. Mokgalane, Sarah Gravett, and Tarryn De Kock, *Observations on the Impact of Education Laws and Policies of the Past 20 Years and Policy Options for the Future: Outcomes of the Public Education Policy Dialogue Series, March to June 2017,* Thematic Area Three: Teachers, in National Education Collaboration Trust (NECT) (Midrand: NECT, 2017), 118.

56. Department of Basic Education, *Draft Strategy on Recruitment and Deployment of Educators.*

57. Department of Basic Education, *Action Plan 2014: Towards the Realisation of Schooling 2025"* (Pretoria: DBE, 2012).

58. Sayed, Badroodien, Omar, Balie, McDonald, et al., *Engaging Teachers in Peacebuilding.*

59. Sayed, Badroodien, Omar, Balie, McDonald, et al., *Engaging Teachers in Peacebuilding,* 138–141.

60. Moletsane, Relebohile, Andrea Juan, Cas Prinsloo, and Vijay Reddy, "Managing Teacher Leave and Absence in South African Rural Schools: Implications for Supporting Schools in Contexts of Multiple-Deprivation," *Educational Management Administration & Leadership* 43, no. 3 (2015).

61. Ramadiro, Brian,and Kim Porteus, "Foundation Phase Matters: Language and Learning in South African Rural Classrooms" (East London: Magic Classroom Collective Press, 2017).

62. Based on hegemonic views of English as the vehicle for greater social class mobility, many local school governing bodies often push and overwhelmingly vote for English to be the main language of instruction. This predilection for a particular language invariably informs which preferred teachers are appointed in the different schools, and it creates a situation where there is no pressure on teacher education providers at different universities to reconfigure the shape and form of their programs.

63. Spreen and Vally, "Education Rights, Education Policies and Inequality in South Africa," 352–362.

64. Statistics South Africa, *General Household Survey 2015* (Pretoria: Stats SA, 2016).

65. Alexander, Neville, "Schooling in and for the New South Africa," *Focus* 56 (2010):

7–13; Soudien, Crain, "'Constituting the Class': An Analysis of the Process of 'Integration' in South African Schools," in Linda Chisholm ed., *Changing Class: Education and Social Change in Post-Apartheid South Africa* (Cape Town, 2004), 89–114; Motala, Shireen, and Kim Porteus, "School Reform in South Africa: Surviving or Subverting the System" in *45th Annual Conference of the Comparative International Education Society* (Washington, DC: 2001).

66. Tatto, Maria Teresa, "Education Reform and the Global Regulation of Teachers' Education, Development and Work: A Cross-Cultural Analysis," *International Journal of Educational Research* 45, no. 4–5 (2006): 231–241; Anderson and Herr, "New Public Management," 84, 1–9; Anderson and Cohen, "Redesigning the Identities of Teachers and Leaders"; Spreen and Vally, "Education Rights, Education Policies and Inequality in South Africa," 352–362.

67. United Nations Department of Economic and Social Affairs, *Transforming Our World: The 2030 Agenda for Sustainable Development* (2015), retrieved from https://sustainabledevelopment.un.org/content/documents/21252030%20Agenda%20for%20Sustainable%20Development%20web.pdf.

68. Republic of South Africa, *White Paper on Education and Training. Notice No.196 of 1995*, WPJ. Pretoria: DoE, ch.4, para. 9, March 1995.

69. Republic of South Africa. *White Paper on Education and Training. Notice No.196 of 1995*, WPJ. Pretoria: DoE, ch.5, para. 49, March 1995.

70. Cape Peninsula University of Technology, *Preliminary Report to the Teacher Development Steering Committee*.

71. Department of Basic Education, *Draft Strategy on Recruitment and Deployment of Educators*.

72. Department of Education, Norms and Standards for Educators.

73. Chisholm, Linda, Shireen Motala, and Salim Vally, "*South African Education Policy Review: 1993–2000*" (Wits University, 2003).

74. Department of Higher Education and Training, Minimum Requirements for Teacher Education Qualifications (MRTEQ), 9.

75. Department of Basic Education, *Draft Strategy on Recruitment and Deployment of Educators*.

76. Department of Basic Education, *Draft Strategy on Recruitment and Deployment of Educators*, 8; Sayed, Badroodien, Omar, Balie, McDonald, et al., *Engaging Teachers in Peacebuilding*.

CHAPTER ELEVEN

Changing Paths and Enduring Debates in US American Teacher Education

LAUREN LEFTY AND JAMES W. FRASER

The three decades spanning the new millennium witnessed a sea change in teacher education in the United States. In 1990, if an American wanted to become a school teacher, he or she needed to obtain a bachelor's or graduate level degree in education from a college or university. Fast forward to 2020, and somewhere between 20% to 30% of the nation's teaching force enters the profession through a nontraditional pathway.[1] Prospective educators now face a dizzying array of preparation options: four-year undergraduate degrees, one- and two-year master's level degrees, alternative certification programs with a few weeks of summer training, online for- and not-for-profit certifiers, and school district–based residencies.

This dramatic transformation in the way American teachers are prepared resulted from a variety of factors. For one, the teacher education policy landscape in the United States, as around the world, reflected the changing political sensibilities of the era, particularly the embrace of neoliberalism beginning in the 1980s and continuing for three decades. Consequently, market forces and nonstate actors were believed by both major political parties to be solutions to a perceived crisis in education broadly and a failure of teacher education specifically. As a result, when alternative routes to teaching began to appear in the United States in the 1980s, they found surprising levels of support in terms of state policies, financial donations, and public support. Second, action and in too many cases inaction from within traditional teacher education programs also contributed to this change. While some university programs provided and continue to provide excellent professional preparation, many programs in the highly decentralized US system did not reform in the wake of critiques and provided an admittedly low-quality education to aspiring teachers, opening the door to complaints about an industry of mediocrity and new outsider models. And finally, what we term a "revolt of the superintendents"—a loss of faith in education schools alternative providers by school-based leaders who hire teachers—led some superintendents to decide they could do it better on their own.[2]

The following chapter will provide a brief overview of the history of teacher preparation in the United States from the founding of the republic to the 1980s, then discuss the reasons for and implications of the dramatic shift in teacher preparation at the close of the twentieth century, and conclude by considering the enduring dilemmas and challenges faced by teacher educators in the United States today. For example, what do teachers need to know and be able to do before entering the classroom? What type of preparation will make them ready for effectively addressing the challenges of the classroom, and what institutional setting is appropriate for that preparation? How can the profession attract high-quality individuals while remaining a low-status, fairly low-paid career? And who exactly should be the teachers for an increasingly diverse student body? While the United States is indeed a unique nation—in size, demographics, history, and political structure—it also possesses an oversized global influence, and we will also briefly touch on the role of the United States in teacher preparation around the world during the era under study.

A Brief 210-Year History of Teacher Education in the United States, 1776–1986

What perhaps makes the United States unique in terms of teacher preparation are the themes of decentralization and diversity. As opposed to centralized and standardized systems in other parts of the world, the tradition of federalism in the United States has meant that the federal government has not played a particularly powerful role in influencing policy for teacher education, and it really only assumed that role in the 1960s, and even then to a highly limited degree. Rather, national trends in teacher preparation have happened through state-level actions and policy convergences brought about by education reform networks, foundation influence, accreditation agencies, and intellectual trends more than top-down mandates. There are also over 1,200 institutions that prepare teachers across the country, and each one sets its own curriculum, despite having to abide by state-level requirements and accreditation guidelines across fifty states, each with its own certification laws.

This decentralized hodgepodge can be traced to the earliest days of the American experience. In the early republic, teachers had no formal training and were considered qualified to teach by the mere possession of an education greater than their pupils, if even by a few years. Teaching primary school was often an inglorious career held for a few years by young men on their way to other professions, such as law or ministry. The monitorial method was used in the early nineteenth century, in the United States and around the world (see the introduction), which meant the most advanced older students taught younger pupils in a large, open classroom under the direction of one lead instructor. By the 1820s and 1830s, a movement for the expansion of the public school system gained steam (inspired by and in-line with similar global movements), led by liberal education reformers such as Horace Mann and Henry Barnard. These New England–based education leaders called for a public school system to serve the growing nation's young (white) pupils and provide them with a common education in basic literacy, arithmetic, Christian morality, and civic principles.[3]

During this time, reformers like Catharine Beecher also made the case that women were "naturally" suited to teaching and should assume the role of teachers for the new common schools as virtuous "republican mothers"— a strategic argument used to gain a foothold in the public sphere, where opportunities for women were limited, even if the strategy built on essentialist notions of females as nurturers.

This system of "common schools," as they were called, necessarily required more teachers, thus spurring a movement for more and better teacher preparation. The first normal schools in the United States, inspired by the French and Prussian models, appeared in Vermont and Massachusetts in the 1830s, followed by more on the East Coast and in the new midwestern states in the ensuing decades. These new two-year institutions, some public and some private, aimed to teach both content and pedagogy. As the boundaries of the United States spread westward in the nineteenth century (from the often-violent acquisition of indigenous and Mexican-controlled land), educational institutions also spread west, including a variety of normal schools, but also Teacher Institutes that provided summer or winter courses to educators to improve their teaching skills, and high school "normal" tracks.

By the last quarter of the nineteenth century, state normal schools had expanded dramatically, and feminized greatly; while there were only a few such schools in operation in 1839, by 1870 there were 39, and by 1910, 180 normal schools trained teachers across the country.[4] Notably, however, these institutions often reflected the racial segregation and hierarchies that plagued the nation. While free black Americans and white philanthropists had opened schools for black children in the North, they remained segregated, and only rarely were black and white teachers educated alongside one another until the mid-twentieth century. When slavery was abolished in 1865, opportunities for black Americans in the South grew somewhat, though they remained highly segregated and more limited than in the North. Native Americans and other nonwhite Americans faced discrimination from society's dominant institutions as well, and often trained in separate, segregated spaces.

American teacher education started to move into universities beginning in the early twentieth century but did not solidify its place in the academy until after the Second World War. In the first few decades of the twentieth century, research universities began opening departments of pedagogy or education, which began to produce research in the field of education but also trained some teachers. Normal schools continued to operate, though some morphed into degree-granting four-year teachers colleges. Then in mid-century at least three developments led to increased standards for teachers. First, the Great Depression of the 1930s allowed school boards to be much more selective than they were in the past as more people became unemployed and teaching a more sought-after career. By the end of the 1930s, most high school teachers held a college degree, as did a growing number of elementary school teachers, though that degree may have been from either a normal school, teachers college, or university. In the years immediately after World War II, the GI bill subsidized higher education for returning servicemen, and again increased the supply of university-trained aspiring teachers. And third, after the Soviet Union launched Sputnik in 1957, Cold War anxieties led to a greater effort to train high-quality teachers for the nation's schools. As a result, by the 1950s state after state began requiring a college degree—often specifically in the field of education—to be a public school teacher. Old normal schools were transformed first into teachers colleges, if they had not been already, then eventually comprehensive four-year colleges and universities—often branch campuses of the flagship state university—while they offered education degrees alongside other liberal arts and sciences majors. Teacher education programs expanded at more elite research universities in the postwar era as well, often serving as a low-prestige but income-generating field. The Ford Foundation became a particularly influential philanthropy devoted to encouraging and funding the move of teacher preparation into the university in the postwar era, from its pilot program in Arkansas to its national grant programs. By 1960, every state in the Union required a four-year baccalaureate degree for both primary and secondary teaching.[5]

Yet with the move of teacher education into the college and university setting, a few key former strengths of normal schools and teachers colleges were lost. In elite research universities, professors in the education departments often attempted to gain the esteem and prestige of their colleagues in the academy by appealing to the standards of disciplinary fields rather than the needs of schools. As Geraldine Clifford and James Guthrie described the fate of teacher educators in the university, "The more forcefully they have rowed toward the shores of scholarly research, the more distant they have become from the public schools they are duty bound to serve."[6] This meant education research became more theoretical and less applied, locating education research in a precarious position: devalued by many in the disciplines and deemed irrelevant by school-based practitioners. In former normal schools turned regional state universities, the education faculty became more and more divorced from disciplinary content even if they maintained better relationships with schools. Education faculty were left to teach only methods and pedagogy courses, as professors in content areas such as history and physics began assuming the teaching roles for those fields, but with little concern for what has been termed "pedagogical content knowledge," or how to teach a subject. As historian Jeffrey Mirel notes, "With this move, faculty members in the liberal arts and their colleagues in the School of Education were literally and intellectually separated. The once-collaborative approach to teacher education vanished."[7]

While many people in the United States assume teacher education always happened in universities and that anything different is a radical change, it must be admitted that university-based teacher preparation was the 30-year exception rather than the rule in the nation's history, and it came with both losses and gains. Starting in the 1980s, new ideas emerged about where teacher education could and should happen, fueled by critiques of the field from various constituencies—from liberal and left-leaning activists to centrist governors to conservative intellectuals. Yet themes of decentralization and diversity would continue to animate the discussion, as no one lever set teacher education policy, no two programs were alike, and the country itself became an increasingly diverse place.

A New Era: Challenging the University Model, Opening New Pathways, 1980–2020

Critiques of university-based teacher preparation and schools of education were far from novel in the 1980s, though they did gain steam and, more importantly, traction. As early as 1953, as teacher education was just solidifying its place in the American university, historian Arthur Bestor published a booked entitled *Educational Wastelands: The Retreat from Learning in Our Public Schools,* in which he blamed the education faculty at universities for the nation's poor academic performance.[8] Other commentators such as James D. Koerner and former Harvard president James Bryant Conant became two more voices in a loud choir decrying the low quality of pedagogy courses and schools of education in the following decade.[9] They often argued that education faculty were academically weak, that methods classes were lacking in rigor, and that education students represented the lowest academic performers on campus. By the '60s, the first alternative teacher certification experiment appeared that aimed to bypass schools of education completely. The National Teacher Corps, a Peace Corps–inspired program of the Lyndon Johnson years, brought the "best and the brightest" young college graduates without a degree in education into struggling low-income urban and rural schools. The program served as a precursor for the types of preparation programs to come and popularized the idea that traditional education-school graduates lacked the drive, innovative spirit, and academic prowess to be great teachers.[10]

By the '70s and '80s a new generation of critics arose, representing such varied constituencies as civil rights activists frustrated with the predominantly white university programs that were not serving students and teachers of color well; conservative intellectuals critical of regulation, bureaucracy, and liberal education faculty; and even those within education schools who recognized reform as necessary. With the rise of black and brown power movements in the late '60s, many communities of color believed traditional university-based programs to be lacking in sufficient diversity and culturally responsive pedagogy. And they were often right. A report released as late as 1996 found the teacher education professoriate to be majority male and 90% Anglo (non-Hispanic white).[11] Onerous certification requirements and the cost of degrees also had the effect of creating a predominantly white student body in most teacher education programs. Many people were therefore open to bringing teacher preparation closer to communities and making teaching a more accessible career to black and Latinx individuals, who had historically been discriminated against in American society. The New Left of the late '60s and '70s had also been highly critical of institutions and bureaucracy, which led to a critique of traditional teacher preparation from a variety of liberal to far left voices.

On the more conservative end of the political spectrum, the highly influential 1983 *Nation at Risk* report—issued by President Ronald Reagan's National Commission on Excellence in Education—also served as a clarion call for reform. In signaling the alarm bell of an educational "crisis" in the United States, it called for a number of reforms to the educational enterprise broadly, including teacher education specifically. Among many alarmist claims, the report stated, "The teacher preparation curriculum is weighted heavily with courses in 'educational methods' at the expense of courses in subjects to be taught," and it recommended that barriers be lowered for talented individuals to enter the field.[12] Around this time conservative economist Milton Friedman also began popularizing his ideas on markets and choice in books and a public television series called *Free to Choose,* which similarly critiqued theory-heavy university training and advocated alternative teacher licensure programs. Conservative think tanks and commentators backed these ideas enthusiastically, as did the media generally.[13]

New Jersey became the first state to experiment with an alternative certification program in 1983, causing much rancor and debate, but also serving as a model for many other states to follow.[14] Governors across the country, both Republicans and Democrats, embraced education as a leading cause, taking on teacher education reform as a politically low-hanging fruit that encountered little resistance, save from the education establishment. Just three years later, in 1986, an article in the popular publication *Education Week* ran a story entitled "Alternative Licensing Prevalent," and it noted that half of the fifty states were allowing alternative certification in some form or another.[15] As superintendents and principals struggled with teacher shortages, they welcomed these new programs, which seemed to promise a larger and higher-quality pool of potential teachers.

In the spring of 1986 two influential reports also arrived that focused specifically on improving the way teachers were prepared in the United States. *A Nation Prepared,* a report by the Carnegie Forum on Education and the Economy (spearheaded by the private Carnegie Corporation philanthropic organization) and *Tomorrow's Teachers,* the first of three reports from the Holmes Group of Education Deans (leaders of some of the nation's most prestigious education schools), both appeared almost simultaneously. These reports, which had surprisingly similar recommendations, sought to redefine teacher education in the United States. In looking at the national context, but also spurred by the specter of increasing global economic competition, Carnegie recommended the creation of a National Board for Professional Teaching Standards to establish what the best teachers needed to know and be able to do. Both reports recommended a hierarchy within the profession of teaching, headed by "Lead Teachers" and followed by a large number of "Professional Teachers" supported by aides and interns. And both reports recommended requiring a bachelor's degree in an arts and sciences discipline instead of an education major, professional development (PD) schools where students could gain school-based experience, and a new professional curriculum in graduate schools of education leading to a master of arts in teaching (MAT) degree based on systematic knowledge of teaching and residencies in schools.[16]

Many faculty and administrators in schools of education acknowledged that the range of issues raised by these reports warranted attention, from increasing admission standards to providing much more school-based "clinical" time for students, to fundamentally rethinking what was taught and how it was taught to students. On the other hand, there was also widespread resistance to the Holmes and Carnegie recommendations. While graduate programs grew and many new MAT degrees appeared in the '90s, far too many education faculty members took an attitude of "this too shall pass" and simply ignored the whole reform enterprise. Many university presidents, especially at elite research universities, also failed to support their education schools and teacher preparation programs as they came under attack. The Education Department at the University of Chicago, where John Dewey once taught, was closed outright by the administration, and many other schools of education faced uphill battles as they experienced funding cuts and little institutional backing. School-based administrators such as district superintendents and school principals, though often critical of education schools, also proved generally unwilling to implement many of the reports' recommendations that called for school-based restructuring or changes in the teaching profession.

What resulted was slow-moving and inconsistent reform from within universities and education schools during a time of increased experimentation and criticism of teacher education from the outside. Perhaps the most well-known non-university-based teacher preparation effort came from Wendy Kopp and her program Teach for America (TFA), which started in 1990 and expanded on the '60s Teacher Corps and New Jersey experiments but with a '90s-era neoliberal flair. It recruited top-flight graduates of elite universities, provided them five weeks of in-house summer training, and then sent them into the nation's most struggling schools as lead instructors for two-year stints aiming to close the nation's "achievement gap" between white and black and Latinx students. While TFA started as a small not-for-profit with 489 corps members in 1990, it grew to a giant movement educating over 55,000 teachers per year, and a multimillion-dollar organization that earned significant financial backing from major foundations, the federal government, corporations, and individual donors. While the percentage of TFA teachers was still fairly small nationwide (though larger in some districts, particularly low-income districts serving students of color), it was also a program that managed to alter the policy landscape by lobbying for changes in certification laws and producing a number of alumni who went on to serve in powerful education leadership positions across the country.[17]

Changes in state and federal laws allowed TFA to expand, but it also allowed similar and sometimes lower-quality offshoots to proliferate in the 1990s and early 2000s. Teaching fellows programs sprang up in cities and states as diverse as New York City and Kentucky, offering TFA-inspired summer boot camp training to recent college graduates and later-in-life career changers wishing to enter the classroom. In some highly deregulated states such as Texas, lower-quality options also appeared, providing poor training to anyone willing to pay for a credential. In 2001 when Congress passed the No Child Left Behind Act, the law called for a "highly qualified" teacher in every classroom, though "qualified" was not defined as needing a degree in education, thus opening the door to even more nontraditional programs to proliferate.*

Proponents of what became known as "alternative certification" lauded these programs as successfully bringing higher-quality and more diverse candidates into the teaching profession. Critics decried them as offensive to the very profession of teaching, lacking in the proper theoretical and in-service training required by teachers, and representing problematic class and race dynamics. As quickly prepared novice teachers were often sent into the highest-needs classrooms serving mostly students of color, middle- and upper-class white students were still largely taught by university-trained professional educators. These teachers, who came to the profession through alternative routes, also left the profession at high rates, often only after two or three years of teaching. TFA and programs like it became controversial lightning rods in the field of American education, spurring much research, rancor, and debate.

School-based personnel, faced with teacher shortages and lacking full faith in the training of their ed school graduates, generally supported the new state laws in the '80s and '90s, however. Superintendents across the country formed partnerships with TFA and teaching fellows programs, and principals kept hiring alternatively certified teachers (hiring and teacher placement is generally done at the school-based level in the United States, as opposed to some countries described in this book where teachers are assigned to schools by central offices). Some school districts also began attempting to prepare teachers themselves through a new model called district-based residencies, which brought teacher preparation under the control of local superintendents. The first such residency program appeared in Boston in 2003 and tried to rectify some of the acrimony in the teacher education wars by drawing on ideas from both the university and alternative certification camps.

The Boston Teacher Residency (BTR) drew on both teacher education research from universities and practices in alternative certification programs to produce a new hybrid model of teacher preparation. The one-year program consists of two months of summer coursework in partnership with the University of Massachusetts, Boston, after which residents spend one year

---

*"Highly Qualified" as designated by Title II of the No Child Left Behind Act called for teachers to (1) hold a bachelor's degree, (2) possess full state certification or licensure, as defined by the state, and (3) demonstrate competency, as defined by the state, in the subject they would teach. Source: "No Child Left Behind: A Toolkit for Teachers," US Department of Education, last modified August 13, 2009, https://www2.ed.gov/teachers/nclbguide/toolkit_pg6.html.

interning in district classrooms, slowly assuming teaching responsibilities under the supervision of an experienced teacher throughout the school year. Residents also complete master's-level coursework alongside this school-based training, and they participate in "clinical rounds" observations of various classrooms in the spirit of doctor-in-training residency rounds.[18] This type of district residency became a popular policy choice during the Obama years (2008–2016), supported by university-based teacher educators as well as proponents of alternative certification. It was also encouraged in President Obama's Race to the Top program, which awarded competitive grant money to states who were reforming their education systems, as well as by the 2015 Every Student Succeeds Act (ESSA), which replaced the Bush-era No Child Left Behind Act (NCLB) and devolved power back to the states. Residencies grew in cities such as Seattle and Denver as well as rural areas such as New Hampshire. While quick-prep alternative certification was the reform du jour in the '90s and '00s, year-long clinical teaching residencies have now assumed that position going into 2020 and operate as either district-run entities or as degree programs in universities that have also adopted the model.[19]

Following TFA, the early years of the millennium also saw new alternative certification models enter the field of teacher preparation. Alternative certification "2.0 programs" gained traction, such as Relay Graduate School of Education, which claims that title but is unaffiliated with a college or university and embraces an entrepreneurial ethos, a technical skills–based curriculum, and outcomes-oriented evaluation for its teacher candidates.[20] Perhaps not surprisingly, Relay's curriculum and test-score-based evaluation methods are criticized by many as being antiprofessional and neoliberal. Online for- and not-for-profit certification programs have also proliferated. On the more promising end of the spectrum, institutions like Western Governors University—a completely online university catering to nontraditional students—has developed a teacher education degree program that has received positive evaluations from the National Council on Teacher Quality (NCTQ) (though ranking systems are notoriously difficult to rely on). On the troubling side of the online universe, for-profit entities like the University of Phoenix are now one of the largest degree-granting institutions in the nation, but are also known for their predatory recruitment tactics, low graduation rates, and questionable quality. Charter school chains (independently run public schools and school-management organizations) are also starting to prepare teachers in their own residency programs as state-level laws allow, garnering opposition from the vocal anti–charter school movement, which tends to lean to the left on the political spectrum. The "Teaching Academy Stipulation" of the 2015 ESSA made it even easier for charter-chain teacher preparation programs to proliferate, though ultimately states control those laws.[21] And Silicon Valley–inspired tech entrepreneurs have entered the fray, proposing "disruptive" technologies to every realm of education, including teacher preparation.

Meanwhile, a cadre of professional teacher educators such as Stanford University's Linda Darling-Hammond, the University of Michigan's Bob Bain, and the University of Washington's Kenneth Zeichner, to name just a few, served as influential voices in the field of university-based teacher education during the most rancorous years of change. Throughout the 1990s and 2000s they produced meaningful research on effective practices in teacher education and helped reform their programs into leading models of high-quality professional education from their respective universities. Dr. Darling-Hammond's work has been particularly influential, both nationally and internationally, and her critiques of Teach for America and work outlining what a teacher needs to know and be able to do before entering the classroom laid the groundwork for a robust professionalization movement seen in many countries around the world, including several described in this volume.[22] Curriculum incorporating multicultural and culturally responsive practices, behavioral science and learning theory, pedagogical content knowledge, and improved student teaching experiences stood in marked contrast with the quick-prep, skills-based training of alternative certification programs, which came under increasing attack as TFA alums became vocal about their less-than-satisfactory five-week preparation and low-income communities criticized the prevalence of young and undertrained teachers in their schools. As earlier in the decade, however, in the highly decentralized US system, the quality of teacher education programs varied from university to university, and while stellar examples existed and still exist, from Stanford to the University of Wisconsin to former normal schools like Montclair State University, many more are not preparing teachers adequately for the challenges they face in the classroom.

Twenty years into the new millennium, the field of teacher preparation in the United States is vastly different than it was thirty years prior. The time period in which this volume concentrates, 1970–2020, was one of great upheaval, change, and debate. New actors, ideas, and voices entered the field of teacher preparation calling for new models—often outside of universities and in line with the standards, accountability, and choice models that characterized education reform more broadly. Yet many (though not all) professional teacher educators also responded with thoughtful critiques of these new programs and offered innovative preparation models from within the university, and ones that took learning theory, clinical practice, and culturally sensitive preparation seriously. To say that university-based educators caused this shift due to their failures is a mischaracterization, though too many ed schools sat idly by. A bipartisan embrace of neoliberal policies from the Reagan to the Obama years (1980s–2016), public support for alternative certification, and a "revolt of the superintendents" at the district and school level also led to this dramatic shift. At the writing of this chapter, it is unclear what the 2016 election of Donald J. Trump will mean for American teacher education, though the field does not seem to be a major priority and the federal government still holds a relatively weak role in the policy arena, as more control is devolved back to the states with the Every Student Succeeds Act.

The debate seems to be heading less in the direction of where preparation should happen—in or outside a university—and more toward what preparation should entail and how it should be evaluated, regardless of institutional configuration. More emphasis is also being placed on mentorship and retention once teachers enter the classroom, as many realize that teacher education is an ongoing process and should involve multiple stakeholders, continuing through the early years of a teacher's career. Despite the rapid proliferation of alternative certification programs, the percentage of teachers holding a postbaccalaureate degree has actually increased from 2000 to 2020, implying that American teachers are becoming more educated, though not necessarily in the field of education.[23] The next section will discuss in greater depth some of the leading dilemmas and challenges in American teacher education today but also consider what similarities and differences might exist with other nations around the world.

Twenty-First-Century Developments, Dilemmas, and Challenges to American Teacher Education

Scholars of American teacher education have noted that the field has long been plagued by a few key dilemmas since the common school days of the nineteenth century. For one, teaching is a high-demand and feminized field, a formula that has historically yielded a low-status and low-paid profession.[24] As of 2017, there were 3.6 million full-time public school teachers in the United States, and districts are often confronted with teacher shortages, leading to lower standards and a sentiment that "anyone can become a teacher." Around 77% of the teaching force identified as female, which in a patriarchal society has often meant low status.[25] Even within universities, teacher education is considered low-status as an applied rather than theoretical discipline.[26] The average salary for a school teacher also hovers around $55,000—a lower-middle-class income, and one on which many find it difficult to support a family. A 2018 study shocked many (though perhaps not teachers themselves) when it reported that one in five American teachers supplement their incomes with additional jobs to make ends meet.[27] Another 2019 study indicated that half of all teachers were seriously considering leaving the profession. For these reasons, it has been difficult to attract top-flight candidates to the classroom in terms of academic ability, as teaching is a less elite and lower-paid field than many other career paths in the country, particularly since the 1970s, when more career paths opened to women and people of color. Programs emphasizing the social justice aspects of the teaching profession, or organizations that have cultivated an elite image through competitive admissions standards, such as Teach for America and teaching fellows programs, have succeeded in overcoming some of these status issues, though teaching is generally still not a highly appealing field for young people.

Furthermore, teaching has long been caught between identities as a profession and a trade. Are teachers workers or professionals? Is teaching an art or a craft? While university-based teacher educators have attempted to codify a set of standards and create a unified curriculum for what a teacher should know and be able to do, those professional norms have been less widely accepted than in more prestigious fields such as law or medicine, or even in other pink-collar professions such as nursing or social work. Most recently, the Council for the Accreditation of Educator Preparation (CAEP) established the CAEP standards in 2013 in an attempt to define what makes a quality educator, as defined by teacher educators, teachers, parents, unions, and school leaders. The CAEP standards represent an impressive attempt to raise professional requirements, but studies have also shown that they may have the unintended effect of limiting diversity in the teacher candidate pool and causing teacher education programs to focus too much on documenting compliance and not enough time on thoughtful pedagogy.[28] Teacher strikes across various states in 2017–2018 reignited discussions over the idea of teachers as workers, and a growing number of teacher organizers have been aligning with anti-neoliberal and workers' rights organizations for better health care, working conditions, pensions, and funding for their schools. Yet the unique nature of teaching as what has been called a semiprofession still creates challenges, and teachers unions in the United States have been historically weak compared with other nations. These questions raise the issues of where teacher preparation can and should take place, what it should entail, and what effects on professional identity certification pathway engenders.

These queries relate to another challenge: we simply do not have conclusive evidence proving one preparation pathway or curriculum is better than another. Researchers have attempted to discern which teachers perform better, ones from traditional university-based programs or alternative routes like TFA. Yet different studies have yielded different results, and often they are conducted by individuals with clear political stances on which pathway they support, rendering their conclusions problematic or at least worthy of contextualization.[29] Evaluating a teacher preparation program is also inherently difficult because we have not come to a consensus on exactly what should be measured and how it should be measured. Should student test-score data be taken into account? Are principal surveys valuable? Who should be responsible for tracking retention data, and if a teacher quits is that the fault of the preparation program, the school district, or the teacher herself? Not to mention, education is a highly complex and multivariable phenomenon. Though "value-added measurements" tracking a teacher's impact on student achievement data became a trend in the 2010s, the validity of these conclusions was quickly challenged. Anyone familiar with teaching knows that a number of factors, from a teacher's skill in content delivery to the poverty levels of the child or a student's mood on a particular day impact academic performance. As Michael Feuer and his colleagues concluded in a 2013 National Academy of Education study entitled *Evaluation of Teacher Preparation Programs,* "Social science is still far from reaching a conclusive judgement about how to measure pedagogical skills, content knowledge, temperament, interpersonal styles, empathy, and understanding the meaning of the learning needs of children, and how those attributes, however they may be measured, combine to make the most difference in a teacher's effectiveness . . . by and large the knowledge base about essential qualities of teaching is still at a rudimentary stage, a reality that necessarily places limits on the design of valid measures for assessing TTP [Teacher Training Programs]."[30]

Many of these challenges in American teacher education are shared in countries across the world: low-status, low-pay, and difficulty in setting professional standards and evaluation methods, particularly given insufficient research on program efficacy; these dilemmas are not unique to teachers in the United States, as our other chapters show. Yet a few other challenges may be unique to the American context. For one, the cost of higher education is higher in the United States than anywhere else in the world. Since the 1980s, the cost of college has increased dramatically, and students have taken on increasing amounts of individual and family debt in order to obtain undergraduate and graduate degrees.[31] Given the relatively low salary of teachers, aspiring educators are often enticed by quick-preparation programs that provide a few weeks of training before they can begin earning salaries. Otherwise, a one-year MAT degree can cost upwards of $50,000, depending on the institution, while the average cost of an undergraduate teaching degree can range from $20,770 per year (the average for in-state public school tuition) to $46,950 (the average at private schools).[32] When the price of this credential leads to a starting salary in the range of $32,000–$45,000 depending on the state, many question the value of these programs and career path.[33] If the United States wants to improve teacher education and teaching more broadly, it must also discern how to make preparation affordable.

The United States is also the most diverse democracy on earth. Yet with this fact also comes a history of institutional racism toward nonwhite citizens. The demographics of the public school population is rapidly changing, with an increasing number of Latinx and Asian students especially. While the student population was 51% nonwhite in the 2016–2017 school year, the teaching force was 80% white.[34] Quality teacher preparation programs must both recruit a more diverse teaching force for the nation's schools—as studies show that all students perform better when they have a teacher of color leading the classroom—and prepare all teachers to teach all students well, whatever race, ethnicity, gender, sexual preference, or disability status they possess. At the moment, alternative certification programs are doing a slightly better job of recruiting more diverse cohorts of aspiring teachers along lines of race, ethnicity, and gender, though all programs need to improve.[35]

The United States also must be mindful of its historic and contemporary role in the world. For much of the twentieth century the United States served as a global power, as it does today, influencing economies, cultures, and political regimes around the globe. In the realm of education, US-based or US-influenced institutions have had a significant impact on the course of education policy, as has US-produced research. While sometimes these interactions are based on mutual cooperation and exchange, at other times policies have been more forcibly imposed on other nations, particularly in the context of Cold War–era intervention and regime change, neoliberal reforms known as the "Washington Consensus" backed by the IMF and World Bank, or "benevolent" aid, which also becomes the content of debates over neo-imperialism. US Americans should therefore be aware of this history, humble in its interactions with the world, and aware of its geopolitical power, even in areas of "soft power" such as education.

The United States has also historically looked to the world for inspiration in the realm of teacher education, as it continues to do today. The earliest models of professional teacher education in the American republic took inspiration from French, British, and Prussian models, and it stood in conversation with a global circulation of liberal education reformers. During the Progressive Era, famed American educational philosopher John Dewey, who still maintains a large presence in teacher education curriculums around the world, traveled extensively and was inspired by education reforms he observed in the Soviet Union, Mexico, Turkey, and China. In the postwar era, the United States participated in global conversations about teacher education through bodies like UNESCO and the World Bank, and by the '80s, when the Carnegie Corporation issued its recommendations in *A Nation Prepared: Teachers for the 21st Century,* it did so by studying other countries and their education systems. The most well-known teacher education researcher in the United States, Linda Darling-Hammond, has written about international models of teacher education, and programs in Finland, Japan, and Singapore have become well-known exemplars by which to judge the domestic scene in many places, the United States included. Going into the future, we hope that those interested in improving teacher education in the United States will continue to converse, humbly and openly, with teacher educators around the world to improve the preparation of all the world's teachers while still taking local context seriously.

NOTES

1. "Characteristics of Public School Teachers Who Completed Alternative Route to Certification Programs," National Center for Education Statistics, last updated May 2018, https://nces.ed.gov/programs/coe/indicator_tlc.asp.

2. This chapter (and argument) is based on more extensive research in James W. Fraser

and Lauren Lefty, *Teaching Teachers: Changing Paths and Enduring Debates* (Baltimore: Johns Hopkins University Press, 2018).

3. James W. Fraser, *Preparing America's Teachers: A History* (New York: Teachers College Press, 2007).

4. David Labaree, "An Uneasy Relationship: The History of Teacher Education in the University" 2008, https://web.stanford.edu/~dlabaree/publications/An_Uneasy_Relationship _Proofs.pdf; Christine A. Ogren, *The American State Normal School: "An Instrument of Great Good"* (New York: Palgrave Macmillan, 2005); John I. Goodlad, Roger Sodor, and Kenneth A. Sirotnik, eds., *Places Where Teachers Are Taught* (San Francisco: Jossey-Bass, 1990).

5. Fraser, *Preparing America's Teachers*.

6. Geraldine Clifford and James Guthrie, *Ed School: A Brief for Professional Education* (Chicago: University of Chicago Press, 1989): 3.

7. Jeffrey Mirel, "Bridging the Widest Street in the World: Reflections on the History of Teacher Education," *American Educator* (Summer 2011): 7.

8. Arthur Bestor, *Educational Wastelands: The Retreat from Learning in Our Public Schools* (Urbana: University of Illinois Press, 1953).

9. James D. Koerner, *The Miseducation of American Teachers* (Boston: Houghton Mifflin, 1963); James Bryant Conant, *The Education of American Teachers* (New York: McGraw-Hill, 1963).

10. Bethany Rogers, "'Better' People, Better Teaching': The Vision of the National Teacher Corps, 1965–68," *History of Education Quarterly* 49 (August 2009): 347–372; Dana Goldstein, *The Teacher Wars: A History of America's Most Embattled Profession* (New York: Random House, 2014).

11. Nancy Zimpher and Julie Sherrill, "Federal Policy and Teacher Education," in *Handbook on Research on Teacher Education,* John Sikula, ed. (New York: Macmillan, 1996).

12. *A Nation at Risk: The Imperative for Educational Reform,* The National Commission for Excellence on Education, April 1983, https://www2.ed.gov/pubs/NatAtRisk/risk.html.

13. Milton Friedman, "What's Wrong with Our Schools?" *Free to Choose* (Public Broadcasting Corporation, January 1980).

14. For two narrative accounts of the New Jersey Alternative Certification debates by involved actors from different perspectives, see Leo Klagholz, *Growing Better Teachers in the Garden State: New Jersey's "Alternate Route" to Teacher Certification* (Washington, DC: Thomas B. Fordham Foundation, 2000), and Ken Carlson, "The Teacher Certification Struggle in New Jersey," Paper Prepared for the National Commission for Excellence in Teacher Education, US Department of Education, 1984.

15. "Alternative Licensing Prevalent," *Education Week,* January 8, 1986.

16. *A Nation Prepared: Teachers for the 21st Century: The Report of the Task Force on Teaching as a Profession* (New York: Carnegie Forum on Education and the Economy, 1986); *Tomorrow's Teachers: A Report of the Holmes Group* (East Lansing, MI: Holmes Group, 1986).

17. Wendy Kopp, *One Day All Children: The Unlikely Triumph of Teach for America and What I Learned Along the Way* (New York: Public Affairs, 2003); Donna Foote, *Relentless Pursuit: A Year in the Trenches with Teach for America* (New York: Vintage, 2009); "Annual Lobbying for Teach for America," Center for Responsive Politics, http://www.opensecrets.org/lobby/clientsum.php?id=D000057438; Kerry Kretchmar, Beth Sondel, and Joseph J.

Ferrare, "The Power of the Network: Teach for America's Impact on the Deregulation of Teacher Education," *Educational Policy,* March 23, 2016, http://epx.sagepub.com/content/early/2016/03/22/0895904816637687.full.pdf+html.

18. Jesse Solomon, "The Boston Teacher Residency: District-Based Teacher Education," *Journal of Teacher Education* 60:5 (November/December 2009), http://jte.sagepub.com/content/60/5/478.full.pdf+html.

19. Tamara Azar and Sudipti Kumar, "Investing Up Front: The School-Based Approach to Teacher Prep," *The Huffington Post,* October 5, 2015, http://www.huffingtonpost.com/tamara-azar/investing-up-front-the-school_b_8223662.html. "The Residency Model" and "Mission & History," National Center for Teacher Residencies, https://nctresidencies.org/about/residency-model-teacher-mentor-programs/, accessed July 18, 2019.

20. "Our Institution," Relay Graduate School of Education, http://www.relay.edu/about/institution; June Kronholz, "A New Type of Ed School," *Education Next* 12:4 (Fall 2012); Angus Shiva Mungal, "Teach for America, Relay Graduate School, and the Charter School Networks: The Making of a Parallel Education Structure," *Education Policy Analysis Archives* 24:17 (February 8, 2016): 1–26.

21. US Department of Education Press Office, "Education Department Releases Final Teacher Preparation Regulations," USDOE, October 12, 2016, http://www.ed.gov/news/press-releases/education-department-releases-final-teacher-preparation-regulations?utm_content=&utm_medium=email&utm_name=&utm_source=govdelivery&utm_term=; Stephen Sawchuk, "ESEA-Rewrite Bill Includes Controversial New Teacher-Prep Provisions," *Education Week,* December 8, 2015, http://blogs.edweek.org/edweek/teacherbeat/2015/12/teacher-prep_provisions_in_ess.html; Lillian Mongeau, "In Search of High Quality Teachers, Charter Network Trains Its Own," The Hechinger Report, http://hechingerreport.org/in-search-of-high-quality-teachers-charter-network-trains-its-own/.

22. Marilyn Cochran-Smith and Kenneth M. Zeichner, eds., *Studying Teacher Education: The Report of the AERA Panel on Research and Teacher Education* (New York: Routledge, 2005); Linda Darling-Hammond and John Bransford, *Preparing Teachers for a Changing World: What Teachers Should Learn and Be Able to Do* (New York: John Wiley and Sons, Inc.: 2007); Ken Zeichner, "Reflections of a University-Based Teacher Educator on the Future of College- and University-Based Teacher Education," *Journal of Teacher Education* 57, no. 3 (May/June, 2006): 326–340.

23. "Characteristics of Public School Teachers," National Center for Education Statistics, last updated April 2018, https://nces.ed.gov/programs/coe/indicator_clr.asp.

24. David Labaree, *The Trouble with Ed Schools* (New Haven: Yale University Press, 2006); Fraser, *Preparing America's Teachers.*

25. "Fast Facts: Teacher Trends," National Center for Education Statistics, last updated April 2018, https://nces.ed.gov/fastfacts/display.asp?id=28.

26. Labaree, "An Uneasy Relationship."

27. Madeline Will, "To Make Ends Meet, 1 in 5 Teachers Have Second Jobs," *Education Week,* June 19, 2018.

28. Linda Darling-Hammond, "Teacher Preparation: Build on What Works," *Education Week,* March 16, 2011; Linda Darling-Hammond, "Constructing 21st-Century Teacher Education, *Journal of Teacher Education* 57, no. 10 (2006); M. Cochran-Smith, R. Stern, J. G. Sánchez, A. Miller, E. S. Keefe, M. B. Fernández, W. Chang, M. C. Carney, S. Burton, and M. Baker, *Holding Teacher Preparation Accountable: A Review of Claims and Evi-*

dence (Boulder, CO: National Education Policy Center, 2016), http://nepc.colorado.edu/publication/teacher-prep.

29. Linda Darling-Hammond, Deborah J. Holtzman, Su Jin Gatlin, and Julian Vasquez Heilig, "Does Teacher Preparation Matter? Evidence about Teacher Certification, Teach for America, and Teacher Effectiveness," *Education Policy Analysis Archives* (University of South Florida) 13 no. 42 (October 12, 2005); "Response to Recent Linda Darling-Hammond Study: Letter from Abigail Smith, Vice President of Research and Policy," Teach for America, www.tfanewsletter.teachforamerica.org; P. T. Decker, D. Mayer, and S. Glazerman, *The Effects of Teach For America on Students: Findings from a National Evaluation* (Washington, DC: Mathematica, 2004); Linda Darling-Hammond, *Educational Opportunity and Alternative Certification: New Evidence and New Questions* (Stanford: Stanford Center for Opportunity Policy in Education, 2009).

30. Michael J. Feuer, Robert E. Floden, Naomi Chudowsky, and Judie Ahn, *Evaluation of Teacher Preparation Programs: Purposes, Methods, and Policy Options* (Washington, DC: National Academy of Education, 2013), 1, 10.

31. Suzanne Mettler, *Degrees of Inequality: How the Politics of Higher Education Sabotoged the American Dream* (New York: Basic Books, 2014).

32. "Fast Facts: Teacher Trends."

33. "2017–2018 Average Starting Teacher Salaries by State," National Education Association, accessed August 9, 2019, http://www.nea.org/home/2017–2018-average-starting-teacher-salary.html.

34. "Indicator 6: Elementary and Secondary Enrollment," National Center for Education Statistics, last updated February 2019, https://nces.ed.gov/programs/raceindicators/indicator_rbb.asp.

35. "Compared to those who entered through a traditional route, a higher percentage of alternative route teachers were Black (13 vs. 5 percent), Hispanic (15 vs. 8 percent), of Two or more races (2 vs. 1 percent), and male (32 vs. 22 percent)." "Characteristics of Public School Teachers Who Completed Alternative Route to Certification Programs," updated May 2018, https://nces.ed.gov/programs/coe/indicator_tlc.asp.

A Concluding Word

LAUREN LEFTY AND JAMES W. FRASER

As we read the chapters of this volume we are struck by the similarities, but also the significant differences, in the ways teacher education has changed around the globe in the last 40 years. We believe that a volume that looks at teacher education in many different contexts—in highly industrialized societies with well-established systems of education and teacher education, in the Global South, where many nations have emerged from a more tightly managed colonial rule, and in other countries that do not fit either category—can provide key insight into the relationship between global trends and national or regional contexts. Despite their differences, legislatures, ministries of education, and nongovernmental authorities in all nations have taken a major interest in how aspiring teachers prepare to teach. We are more convinced than ever that a focus on only the nations that fit one pattern, or only on the Industrialized North or the Global South, misses important developments that cut across these divisions. At the same time, any generalizations are bound to be offset by the exceptions even in nations with similar histories. We would reiterate Maria Teresa Tatto's concern about "decontextualized conclusions."[1] Context matters, national history and culture matter, legacies of imperialism matter, and all of these dynamics impact policy. Some themes, and some influential ideas and organizations do appear again and again—perhaps embraced more strongly in some places than others—but with just enough difference to make nuance essential.

While we emphasize the particularity of national cases, in this conclusion we also do some of the work of connecting, comparing, and conceptualizing that is essential to a more globally minded history of teacher education, as discussed in the introduction. A few similarities between our case studies seem most common. Perhaps the most dominant theme is that, since the 1980s, it has been the case that in almost every context, governments seem to care about the preparation of teachers in a way that was not as true before that era. Since the end of World War II, many nations had been in the process of moving teacher education out of free-standing institutions such as normal schools and into comprehensive universities. Certainly that trend continued and accelerated, especially in places like China after the end of the Cultural Revolution, and also in Brazil and Ghana and places where many teachers still lack a higher education degree. On the other hand, since 1980 many countries have begun to move in the opposite direction intentionally supporting a more decentralized, some would say fragmented, system of teacher education in which alternative routes based either in school districts or independent agencies took the place of university programs. But such moves are far from universal. While England, Ghana, Brazil, Argentina, Israel, and the United States all have alternative routes to a teaching career that did not exist in 1980, other nations including Catalonia/Spain, Singapore, and Finland have maintained a strong historic commitment to the university preparation of teachers, and yet others—China and South Africa stand out—have moved toward ending independent programs in normal schools and toward ensuring that all teachers are prepared in a university setting.

Whatever the institutional home of teacher preparation, we have also found some relatively common curricular developments. Wherever a program to educate new teachers is found, there is close to universal agreement that the so-called theory-practice divide that was common in the enterprise was a mistake, and that the old methods courses needed to be reduced and replaced with school-based practicum experiences and strong content courses. While some efforts to blend theory and practice have been much more successful than others, no context seems to be without effort in that direction. Indeed, the move, seen dramatically in some places like the United States, to transition toward year-long teacher residencies rather than shorter-term student teaching has been gaining momentum as a commitment to practice-based preparation and has grown in popularity.

There is also a larger problem making the development of preparation difficult. As the authors of chapter one on teacher education in Argentina note, "As in other countries, teaching in Argentina is not organized around a research-based, categorized and shared corpus of knowledge that could support a reliable system of quality control as expected in other professions." This is a close to universal problem. Rarely is there an agreed-on knowledge base for teacher education in spite of the heroic efforts some have made to create one and build a consensus around it. In a few cases, again Finland comes to mind, there is general agreement about a research-based corpus of knowledge, but in most cases researchers differ, government agencies listen to different voices, and those seeking to deliver high-quality professional preparation for teachers are left in the midst of conflict rather than being able to base their work on a widely accepted research base.

As we read these case studies of teacher education in ten very different national contexts we are also struck by an interesting tension. On the one hand, the national context seems to define everything about teacher preparation. The fact that China was emerging from the Cultural Revolution, Singapore and Ghana were newly independent after centuries of colonial rule, and Argentina, Brazil, and South Africa were all emerging from different forms of right-wing dictatorships, shaped every aspect of what these nations wanted in a new generation of teachers and expected of those who prepared them. On the other hand, many ideas about what constitutes quality teacher preparation flow across national borders and through countries with radically different ideological approaches to schooling. Reports published by the Organisation for Economic Co-operation and Development (OECD), the United Nations (especially UNESCO), the World Bank, and the European Union such as the 1990 *World Declaration on Education for All* or the 2015 *Incheon Declaration "Education 2030,"* are cited again and again in chapters about countries with few other similarities. In the European Union, the 1999 Bologna Process, which required consistent standards for degrees across the EU, has had a huge impact from Spain to England to Finland. Certain scholars, perhaps most of all Stanford University's Linda Darling-Hammond, retain influence in widely differing nations. Institutional partnerships such as the partnership between Singapore's National Institute of Education and the Institute of Education at University College

London or the links between Beijing Normal University and Michigan State University cross many boundaries. In many cases ideas seem to flow from the United States and Europe to other parts of the globe, but as one probes more deeply the flow in the opposite direction is also clear.

There are a number of challenges that are beyond the scope of what is traditionally considered part of teacher preparation but that clearly impact the field. In many nations there are severe or predicted teacher shortages. The sometimes difficult conditions of teaching around the globe, the tendency for political and business leaders to criticize teachers, and the relatively low pay for teaching in many countries exacerbate this problem.[2] Especially in some fields that are well paid outside of teaching, most of all mathematics and the sciences, the shortages are close to universal. Perceptions of prestige matter, along with the realities of money. While in many nations, teaching was once about the highest-prestige job open to women, a worldwide feminist revolution has made that far less true in the decades under consideration here. For some, concerns about prestige have led women away from teaching. In other cases, a concern for prestige has influenced the kind of preparation new teachers have sought. In the case of countries like Argentina, the opportunity to move from low-prestige preparation in normal schools to a university-based program has made a significant difference. In other cases such as the United States, England, and Israel with its Teach First (a Teach for America–inspired program), the alternative routes outside of the university seem to sometimes have higher prestige than university education schools.

While it is difficult for teacher educators to address these problems, they are often blamed for them, and alternatives to the traditional routes to teaching are especially popular in times of shortages. Teacher shortages, and the needs for faster and easier preparation, are almost universal problems when it comes to teaching in rural or otherwise nonmetropolitan areas. Whether it is in rural England or rural South Africa or many other places, teachers who move to a metropolitan area for their university preparation do not want to leave, and more isolated areas find it very difficult to find and keep teachers. The rapid expansion of education systems in nations emerging from colonial rule and grappling with poverty in places like Africa and Latin America, or the fast-growing societies of Asia, has also meant a rapidly expanding demand for teachers: a demand that has been hard for institutional providers to meet and that has sometimes, as in the case of Brazil, led to a reduction in the standards for preparation.

Yet other global developments have impacted teacher education. The influence of neoliberal ideas and the growing trust by many national leaders in letting market forces handle all problems has had an impact on the regulation of and expectations for teacher preparation. This has certainly been a major issue in Argentina, Brazil, South Africa, and Ghana; but it is also discussed in the chapters on Singapore, England, Israel, China, and the United States. Sometimes countering the trust in letting market forces take their course, and sometimes not, the interest in governmental authorities in regulating teacher education has had its own impact. Some places, certainly in the well-known cases of Finland and Singapore but also in Catalonia/Spain and elsewhere, market forces have had virtually no impact on teacher preparation, as central authorities have sought to maintain a system that is considered excellent and protect it from undue outside influence, even if in some cases this has also meant protection from winds of change that could be productive. For some, Argentina comes to mind, centralization has sometimes been associated with past dictatorships or state abuses, and therefore there is great interest in decentralized models, both neoliberal and more autonomous left-leaning models, while in other cases, such as Finland, nationwide centralization has been seen as a vehicle for protecting democratic freedoms in education.

Ironically there have also been huge differences in the rationale for teacher preparation. Perhaps the most extreme differences illustrated in this volume are between those in South Africa, where many want teachers to be prepared to challenge the economic system as it exists, and Singapore, where the education of teachers is specifically tied to a national commitment to economic development. Of course, defining the purposes and practices of teacher preparation depends on whose voices are valued. Especially in the cases of Singapore and Finland, classroom teachers have a role along with administrators and policy makers in setting policy for the preparation of the next generation of practitioners. In other cases, South Africa for one, teachers tend to feel that policy is implemented from afar without their input or experience being valued. Just who should decide how teachers are prepared is as much a contested matter as any particular decision about how to prepare teachers or, indeed, what teachers need to know and be able to do. We expect that the contestation will continue, but we also hope that understanding the way the issues have played out in these many different contexts will add intelligence and insight to the conversation.

NOTES

1. Maria Teresa Tatto, "Introduction: International Comparisons and the Global Reform of Teaching" in Tatto, ed., *Reforming Teaching Globally* (Charlotte, NC: Information Age Publishing, 2009), 7.

2. Nelly P. Stromquest, *The Global Status of Teachers and the Teaching Profession* (Brussels: Education International, 2018).

CONTRIBUTORS

LAUREN LEFTY holds a PhD in the history of education from New York University. She is coauthor with James W. Fraser of *Teaching Teachers: Changing Paths and Enduring Debates*.

JAMES W. FRASER is a professor of history and education at New York University. He is the author or editor of twelve books, including *Between Church and State: Religion and Public Education in a Multicultural Society* and *Teach: A Question of Teaching*.

KWAME AKYEAMPONG is a professor of international education and development at the University of Sussex, United Kingdom.

RICHARD ANDREWS is a professor in education and head of the Moray House School of Education and Sport at the University of Edinburgh, Scotland.

AZEEM BADROODIEN is a professor of education and the deputy director of the School of Education at the University of Cape Town, South Africa.

GUSTAVO E. FISCHMAN is a professor of educational policy at the Mary Lou Fulton Teachers College at Arizona State University.

GUANGWEI HU is an associate professor and the deputy head of research in English language and literature at the National Institute of Education, Nanyang Technological University, Singapore (NIE/NTU).

ARIE KIZEL is head of the Pedagogical Development of Educational Systems Program in the department of Learning, Instruction and Teacher Education at the Faculty of Education, University of Haifa, Israel.

JARI LAVONEN is a professor of physics and chemistry education at the University of Helsinki, Finland, and a director of the National Teacher Education Forum.

WEI LIAO is an assistant professor of teacher education at Beijing Normal University.

JASON LOH is a senior lecturer in English language and literature and a teacher educator at the National Institute of Education, Nanyang Technological University, Singapore (NIE/NTU).

MARIA INÊS MARCONDES is a professor and researcher in the Department of Education at the Pontifical Catholic University (PUC-RIO) of Rio de Janeiro in Brazil.

SILVANA MESQUITA is a professor of teaching and curriculum in the Department of Education at the Pontifical Catholic University (PUC-RIO) of Rio de Janeiro in Brazil.

HANNELE NIEMI is a professor of education in the Faculty of Behavioral Sciences at the University of Helsinki, Finland.

LILY ORLAND-BARAK is a professor in the Department of Teaching, Instruction and Teacher Education at the University of Haifa, Israel.

PAULA RAZQUIN is a professor, researcher, and director of the School of Education at the University of San Andrés in Argentina.

CAROL ANNE SPREEN is an associate professor of international education in the Steinhardt School of Culture, Education, and Human Development at New York University.

EDUARD VALLORY, PhD, is the director of the Escola Nova 21 program and a board member of the Program for Improvement and Innovation in Teacher Training (MIF) for the Government of Catalonia, Spain.

YISU ZHOU is an assistant professor of educational policy at the University of Macau, China.

INDEX

Academia-Class program (Israel), 199, 218–21
academization, 141, 151n18
accountability ideology, 22, 250, 252; in England, 143, 144, 147
Afghanistan, 20
African Americans, 12, 16, 284
Akyeampong, Kwame, 179–98, 307
Alfonsín, Raúl, 39
Allende, Salvador, 22
Alliance for an Advanced Education System (Catalonia), 90
Alliance for Progress, 19
Alphabet of Jihad Literacy, 20
alternative certification programs, 24, 123, 135–40, 214–18, 281, 287–88, 290–91, 292–93, 296
Andrews, Richard, 132–52, 307
apartheid, 16, 253–55, 276n9, 277n19
applied science model, 187–88
Argentina, 36–53, 303, 305; decentralization in, 38–39, 40, 44; history of teacher education in, 38–39; and neoliberalism, 40–43; normal schools in, 7, 38, 43, 48, 58n49; professionalism discussion in, 37, 53; school enrollment in, 40, 47, 50; since mid-1980s, 39–47; socioeconomic factors in, 47–52; teacher salaries in, 39, 42, 46–47, 51–52, 58n49
ASEAN (Association of Southeast Asian Nations), 25–26
Association of Israeli Community Centers, 205–6
Australia, 11, 14

Bache, Alexander D., 7
Badroodien, Azeem, 249–80, 307
Bain, Bob, 292
Barcelona, Spain, 93–94
Barnard, Henry, 7, 283
Barretto, Elba, 72–73
Beecher, Catharine, 7, 9, 283
Beijing Normal University, 8, 120, 126, 304
Beit Berl Academic College, 215
Bell, Andrew, 5, 27
Bello, Andrés, 7
Belt and Road Initiative, 125
Ben-Peretz, Miriam, 202, 203, 206
Berliner, D., 164
Bestor, Arthur, 286
Bohla, H. S., 15
Bologna Process, 25, 109n14, 136, 303; and Finland, 161–62; and Spain, 99; and United Kingdom, 146–47, 149
Boston Teacher Residency (BTR), 290
Brazil, 61–85, 304; curriculum in, 79–82; military dictatorship in, 62, 65; private schools in, 64–65; professionalization narrative in, 16, 68, 70, 71, 79, 84–85; public policy initiatives in, 79–84; school enrollment in, 63–64, 69–70, 85n4, 86n16; secondary education in, 70–71, 72, 86n16; socioeconomic status in, 16, 72–73, 76; teacher formation structures in, 66–73; teacher recruitment in, 65, 66, 78, 85
Brexit, 133, 136
Buber, Martin, 204

Cai Hesen, 18
Canário, Rui, 77
CAPES (Coordination for the Improvement of Higher Level Personnel, Brazil), 81–84
Cardoso, Fernando Henrique, 62, 67–68
Carnegie Corporation, 21
Carnegie Forum on Education and the Economy, 233, 288, 297
Carrim, Nazir, 257
Catalan Education Act, 89
Catalonia/Spain, 89–108, 305; centralization and bureaucratization in, 91–93; curriculum in, 90, 91, 94–95, 102, 108; enhancing teacher training in, 102–7; Escola Nova 21 in, 89–90, 104–7, 110n22; Franco dictatorship in, 94, 97; history of teacher training in, 93–94; licensing and certification in, 99; limitations of teacher training in, 96–102; MIF program in, 89, 103–4, 107; secondary/primary school separation in, 98; university studies in, 98, 103, 109n13
Centre for Applied Research in Education (CARE, Singapore), 234
Centre for Research in Child Development (CRCD, Singapore), 241
Centre for Research in Pedagogy and Practice (CRPP, Singapore), 235, 241
certification. *See* licensing and certification
Charlot, Bernard, 76, 77
charter school chains, 291–92
Chile, 22–23
China, 21, 111–27; boosting economic growth in, 111, 115–21; Cultural Revolution in, 111, 114–15, 128n4; economy of, 112, 115, 118, 121–22; global agenda of, 111, 125–27; harmonizing society in, 111, 121–25; higher-education massification movement in, 118, 122, 123–24; literacy campaign in, 15; and national reconstruction, 111, 112–15; normal schools in, 8, 18, 113, 116, 117–18, 123, 124; rural areas of, 115, 122, 123, 124–25; teacher recruitment and shortages in, 114, 123, 124, 125; three-level teacher education in, 113–14; two-level of teacher education in, 115–16, 118–19

Chisholm, Linda, 257, 260
Chubb, John, 22
civil servants, 92, 94, 97, 99, 124, 231
classroom management, 77–78
Clifford, Geraldine, 285
clinical residency, 101–2, 103–4, 106, 108
Cochran-Smith, M., 209
Cockburn, Anne, 132, 143
Cold War, 19–20
Colegio Superior de Señoritas, 10
College of Physical Education (CPE, Singapore), 232
Columbia University, 13–14, 126
Commission on Higher Education (CHE, South Africa), 262–63
Committee on Singapore's Competitiveness, 227
common schools, 283, 293
community centers (Israel), 205–6
Comprehensive School Framework Law (Finland), 155–56
Compulsory Education Law (China), 114
Conectar Igualdad, 46
Conference on Research and Teacher Education (1983), 240
Confucianism, 114
"Constructing a Harmonious Society" (China), 122
contact zones, 22, 34n73
Continuous Professional Development (CPD), 149, 191, 193
Copas, M., 209
Cordero, Rafael and Celestina, 11–12
Council for the Accreditation of Educator Preparation (CAEP, US), 294
Cousin, Victor, 6
Cuba, 15
Cuban, Larry, 2, 3, 32n42
Cultural Revolution (China), 111, 114–15, 128n4
curriculum: in Argentina, 39, 41; in Brazil, 79–82; in Catalonia/Spain, 90, 91, 94–95, 102, 108; in Finland, 156, 158, 162, 163, 166–67, 168; in Ghana, 181, 182, 183–84, 187; in Israel, 201, 202–3, 216; in Singapore, 236, 238; in South Africa, 251, 265–66, 272; UNESCO/ILO recommendations on, 19; in US, 287, 292

curriculum and assessment policy (CAPS, South Africa), 265, 273

Darling-Hammond, Linda, ix–x, 200, 239, 242, 292, 297, 303
Dávila, Jerry, 16
decentralization, 179, 302, 305; in Argentina, 38–39, 40, 44; in Finland, 156, 158, 161, 166–67, 172; in US, 282, 283, 286, 292
decolonization, 20
Decroly, Ovide, 93
Delors, Jacques, 95
Democratic Schools (Israel), 204–5
democratization, educational, 39, 62
Deng Xioping, 112, 115
Department for International Development (DFID, Britain), 27, 183, 184
Department of Higher Education and Training (DHET, South Africa), 258
deprofessionalization, 143, 146
deregulation, 46, 146
Development Bank (US), 25
Development Program for Teachers Pre- and In-service Education, 169
Dewey, John, 13–14, 17, 91, 93, 204, 288–89, 297
dialogical professional development school model (DRPDS, Israel), 199, 209–14, 219, 221
dialogical reflection, 207–14
Dias, Amália, 70
Diploma in Basic Education (DBE, Ghana), 186, 188–89
Diploma in Educational Administration (DEA, Singapore), 232
Donaire, Ricardo, 49
Dubet, François, 76, 87n31
Dwight, Henry E., 7

East China Normal University, 126
École Normale Supérieure, 6
Education Act of 2008 (Ghana), 190–91
Educational Excellence Everywhere, 144
Educational Research Association (ERA, Singapore), 233
Educational Research Unit (ERU, Singapore), 233
Educational Wastelands (Bestor), 286

education and learning: competency-based, 101; experiential, 239, 242; Finnish philosophy of, 155, 157, 158, 167, 171; Ghanaian philosophy of, 185–86; lifelong, 155, 157, 158, 167, 171, 193–94, 227; by rote and memorization, 9, 13, 21, 90–92, 94, 95, 96, 97–98, 100–102, 108; student engagement in, 167–68, 189; students' lack of, 74–78; UNESCO and OECD reports on, 90–91, 95–96, 105
education budgets: in Ghana, 180, 195; in Israel, 201, 203, 216, 218; in Singapore, 229; in South Africa, 258. *See also* funding
education faculty, 8, 207; in Singapore, 236, 238, 240, 241–42; in US, 285, 286, 288
Education Research Funding Programme (ERFP, Singapore), 241–42
Education Week, 287–88
Elliott, J., 164
Émile, or On Education (Rousseau), 8
England, 132–52; accountability ideology in, 143, 144, 147; and Brexit, 133, 136; opportunities for teaching in, 145–49; regions in, 142, 147–49; routes into teaching in, 134–39; teacher recruitment in, 133–34, 140–41, 145; teacher retention in, 139, 142–43, 144–45, 150; teacher shortage in, 132–34, 139–45; types of schools in, 134
entrepreneurship, 145–46
Escola Nova 21 (Catalonia), 89–90, 104–7, 110n22
"Essay on the Education of Female Teachers for the United States, An" (Beecher), 9
Estonia, 102
European Higher Education Area, 104
Evaluation of Teacher Preparation Programs (Feuer et al.), 295
Every Student Succeeds Act (ESSA, US), 291, 292

Fanon, Franz, 20
Federal Council of Culture and Education (CFCyE, Argentina), 40, 41
Federal Education Law (Argentina, 1993), 40–41
feminization of teaching. *See* women in teaching
Ferrer i Guàrdia, Francesc, 93

Feuer, Michael, 295
Finland, 102, 153–72, 303, 305; curriculum in, 156, 158, 162, 163, 166–67, 168; decentralization in, 156, 158, 161, 166–67, 172; education as universal right in, 154–58; enhancement-led evaluation system in, 158–59; principles of education policy in, 158; professionalism discussion in, 165–71; research-based education in, 164–65; secondary school education in, 160–61; social disparities in, 154–55; teacher education reform in, 159–64; teacher qualification in, 159, 162–63, 171
Finn, Chester, Jr., 22
Finnish National Board of Education (FNBE), 165
Fischman, Gustavo E., 19–20, 36–60, 307
Fiske, Edward B., 259
Flores, Ruben, 17–18
Ford Foundation, 21, 285
Forten, Charlotte, 16
Foster, David, 145
Franco, Francisco, 94, 97
Fraser, James W., 281–300, 301–6, 307
Free Compulsory Universal Basic Education (FCUBE, Ghana), 179, 181–84
Freedman, S., 141
Free Teacher Education program (FTE, China), 123–25, 130n36
Free to Choose, 287
Freinet, Célestin, 93
Freire, Paulo, 15, 20, 78
Friedman, Milton, 22–23, 287
Froebel, Friedrich, 8–9
funding: in Brazil, 82, 83, 84; in England, 134; in Ghana, 184, 192–93, 195; in Israel, 201, 204, 218, 219; philanthropic, 12, 16, 21, 284, 285; in Singapore, 241; in South Africa, 256, 261, 263–64; in US, 16, 285, 289. *See also* education budgets
Further Professional Certificate in Education (FPCE, Singapore), 232

Galvão, Izabel, 77
Gatti, Bernadete, 68, 71, 72–73, 84
Geffen-Sarig, Anat, 206
Ghana, 179–96; Basic Teacher Education Policy of, 184–90; curriculum in, 181, 182, 183–84, 187; decolonization of, 21; economy of, 180–81, 183; education spending in, 180, 195; history of teacher education in, 182–83; licensing and certification in, 183, 186–87, 191, 193, 194, 195; PTPDM in, 190–94; reforms of 1986 in, 180–84; school-based training in, 182, 184, 185–86, 187, 188, 194; teacher recruitment in, 179, 181, 188
Gilmour, Dave, 260
globalization, 25–26, 226; and China, 125–27
Goodwin, Anne Lin, 239
Gorostiaga, Jorge, 44
"grammar of schooling," 12, 32n42
Greenfeld, N., 203
Gultig, John, 256
Guthrie, James, 285

Hakol Hinuch campaign (Israel), 215
Hall, Graham, 259
Harris, William T., 8
Haydn, Terry, 132, 143
Hecht, Yaakov, 204
Heckman, James, 101
Herbart, Johann, 8–9
Hess, Rick, 22
Higher Education Law (Argentina, 1995), 40–41
Higher Education Qualification Framework (HEQF, South Africa), 265
Hobsbawm, Eric, 12
Hofmeyr, Jane, 259
holistic approaches, 100, 105–6, 157, 169–70, 172, 216
Holmes Group of Education Teachers, 209, 229, 233, 288
Hostos, Eugenio María de, 7
How People Learn (National Research Council), 95
Howson, J., 140
Hu, Guangwei, 226–48, 307
Husu, J., 159
Hutchings, M., 141

immigration, 26, 133, 150n5
Incheon Declaration "Education 2030," 90, 303
Indonesia, 11

IN-IN-OUT system (Ghana), 186, 187, 188–89, 194
in-service education and training (INSET, Ghana), 191, 192, 193, 195
Institute of Education (IE, Singapore), 231–33, 240
Institute of Education Act of 1970 (Singapore), 231, 237, 240
International Labour Organization (ILO), 18–19
International Monetary Fund (IMF), 18, 22, 297
Isopahkala-Bouret, U., 157–58
Israel, 199–222; Academia-Class program in, 218–21; challenges of teacher education in, 201–2; curriculum in, 201, 202–3, 216; dialogical reflection pedagogy in, 207–14; education budgets in, 201, 203, 216, 218; education system in, 202–3; socioeconomic disparities in, 200; Teach First Israel in, 24, 199, 214–18; traditional teacher training model in, 203–7

Japan, 6, 8
Japanese International Co-operation Agency (JICA), 192–93
JDC Israel, 215
Judge, Harry, vii
Junior Secondary School Teacher Education Project (JuSSTEP, Ghana), 184

Kadar, Naomi, 215
Kadingdi, Stanislaus, 182
Kennedy, John F., 20
Kennedy, Mary, 189
Kirchner, Néstor, 43, 46
Kisilevsky, Marta, 51
Kizel, Arie, 199–225, 307
knowledge: Chinese conception of, 114; Finnish conception of, 166; UNESCO definition of, 100, 109n16
knowledge-based economies (KBE), 226–27
Knowledge-Based Economy (OECD report), 226, 229
Knowledge Transformation and Education Reform (Shi), 119–20
Koerner, James D., 286

Kopp, Wendy, 289
Kuenzer, Acacia Zeneida, 72

Ladd, Helen, 259
Lancaster, Joseph, 5
Lancaster-Bell system, 4, 5–6, 12
Lancaster Society, 5, 21
language of instruction, 185; in Israel, 202, 203; in South Africa, 261, 269, 279n62
Lasri, Dan, 204–5
Latin America, 6, 9–10; and globalization, 25–26; and neoliberalism, 22–23; US programs in, 19–20. *See also* Argentina; Brazil
Laubach, Frank, 15
Lavonen, Jari, 153–78, 307
learner-educator ratio (LER), 259, 260
Learning Sciences Laboratory (LSL, Singapore), 241
Learning: The Treasure Within (Delors), 95
Learning to Be: The World of Education Today and Tomorrow (UNESCO report), 94, 108–9n7
Lee Sing Kong, 228
Lefty, Lauren, 1–35, 281–300, 301–6, 307
Leket, Hadas, 205
Liao, Wei, 111–31, 307
licensing and certification, 13, 24, 25–26; alternative, 24, 281, 287–88, 290–91, 292–93, 296; in England, 136, 149; in Finland, 159, 162–63, 171; in Ghana, 183, 186–87, 191, 193, 194, 195; in Singapore, 232, 234; in South Africa, 254–55; in Spain, 99; in US, 283, 286, 287–88, 290–91, 292–93, 296
Lieberman, Ann, ix–x
literacy campaigns, 15
Liu, Liyan, 18, 21
LOGSE Act (General Organization of the Education System Organic Act, Spain), 94–95, 98
Loh, Jason, 226–48, 307
London, England, 142
London First, 138
London Institute of Education, 13–14, 235
Louzano, Paula, 67
Low Khah Gek, 228
Lucas, C. J., 206–7
Lula de Silva, Luis Inácio (Lula), 62, 68

Madras system, 4, 5
Majakka network (Finland), 168
managerialism, 250, 270–73
Mandela, Nelson, 11
Mann, Horace, 7, 283
Mao Zedong, 18, 128n4
Marcondes, Maria Inês, 61–88, 308
Margalida Comas Program for the Improvement of Teaching and Learning, 107
mathematics teachers, 142–43, 304
May, Theresa, 151n18
McDonald, Zahraa, 257
McKinsey & Co., 138
Meitar: Education in a Dialogical Spirit (Lasri), 204
Meitar School, 204
Menem, Carlos, 40
MERCOSUR, 25–26
Mesquita, Silvana, 61–88, 308
metacognitive approach, 210–11
Mexico, 17–18
Michigan State University, 126, 304
Minimum Requirements for Teacher Education Qualifications (MRTEQ, South Africa), 265, 272, 273
Ministry of Education (MOE, Singapore), 230, 232, 234, 235; NIE cooperation with, 237–38, 241; Research Unit of, 231
Mirel, Jeffrey, 285
Moe, Terry, 22
Moletsane, Relebohile, 268–69
Montessori, Maria, 13, 93
Montessori schools, 93
Moon, Bob, ix–x, 26
Mori, Arinori, 8
multi-academy trust (MAT), 141
multiculturalism, 26, 216, 292
multipurpose teachers, 66–70

Nanyang Technological University (NTU), 228, 229, 234–35, 241
Naomi Foundation, 215
National Accreditation Board (NAB, Ghana), 183, 195
National Association of Teachers (England), 143–44
National Commission on Higher Education (NCHE, South Africa), 255
National Council for Accreditation of Teacher Education (NCATE, Israel), 221
National Council on Teacher Quality (NCTQ, US), 291
National Curricular Guidelines for Initial and In-Service Teacher Education for Basic Education Professionals (Brazil), 79–82
national curriculum statement (NCS, South Africa), 265
National Education Law (Argentina 2006), 43–46, 56n29, 57n35
National Education Policy Investigation (NEPI, South Africa), 277n20
National Institute of Education (NIE, Singapore), 228, 229, 239, 241, 303–4; about, 233–37; current issues and challenges, 242–43; MOE cooperation with, 237–38
National Institute of Teacher Education (INFD, Argentina), 44–45
National Professional Development Plan (NPDP, China), 124–25
National Research Council (US), 95
National Teacher Corps (US), 286
National Teacher Education Audit (South Africa), 255
National Teaching Council (NTC, Ghana), 185, 190–91, 193–94, 195
National Union of Teachers (England), 144
National University of Ireland, 126
National University of Singapore, 231, 233
Nation Prepared, A (Carnegie Forum on Education and the Economy), 233, 288, 297
Native Americans, 16–17, 284
Nature of Learning, The (OECD report), 95–96
Nehru, Jawaharlal, 20
neoliberalism: and Argentina, 40–43; ideology of, 21–25, 250–51, 305; and Singapore, 242; and US, 291, 293. *See also* managerialism
new accountability, 250
New Education Reform Program (Ghana), 180–81
New Jersey, 287
new professionalism, 250

New School Movement, 93, 94. *See also* Escola Nova 21
New Zealand, 11
Niemi, Hannele, 153–78, 308
Nkrumah, Kwame, 20
No Child Left Behind Act (US), 289–90, 291
normal schools, 17, 23, 97, 302, 304; in Argentina, 7, 38, 43, 48, 58n49; in Brazil, 7, 66, 67, 68–70, 85n5; in China, 8, 18, 113, 116, 117–18, 123, 124; global rise of, 6–8, 12; as political hotbeds, 17, 20; in US, 7–8, 16, 283–85; women in, 9, 10
Normal Superior program (Brazil), 68, 85n5
Norms and Standards for Educators policy (South Africa), 264–65, 272
Northcott, D., 143–44
Nóvoa, António, 84
Now Teach, 139

Obama, Barack, 291
Okano, Kaori, 8
Oliveira, Romualdo Portela, 62
Olstein, Diego, 1–2
Ong Ye Kung, 227
Open University of Catalonia (UOC), 107
Organisation for Economic Co-operation and Development (OECD), 18, 27, 95, 132, 228, 303; *Knowledge-Based Economy*, 226, 229; *The Nature of Learning*, 95–96; *Teachers Matter: Attracting, Developing and Retaining Effective Teachers*, 25, 249
Orland-Barak, Lily, 199–225, 308
outcomes based education (OBE), 265
Overseas Development Agency (ODA, Britain), 183
Ozga, J., 164

Palmer, Steven, 9
Parent Leadership, 206
PARFOR (National Plan for the Training of Teachers in Basic Education, Brazil), 69
Parker, Ben, 253
Peace Corps, 19, 20
Pedagogy of the Oppressed (Freire), 20
Perazza, Roxana, 46
Permanent Federal Teacher Education Network (RFFDC, Argentina), 41
Pestalozzi, Johann, 8

PIBID (Government Grant Program for Initial Teacher Education, Brazil), 81–84
Pini, Mónica, 44
political pedagogical projects, 38–39, 46, 81, 87n44
Pompeu Fabra University (UPF), 107
Pope, S., 143
postgraduate certificate in education (PGCE, England), 136–37
Preliminary Report to the Teacher Development Steering Committee (South Africa), 260
Pre-Tertiary Professional Teacher Development and Management (PTPDM, Ghana), 180, 190–94, 195
Primo de Rivera, Miguel, 93
private schools, 38, 64–65, 75, 94, 296
privatization, 23, 40, 250, 275n8
Professional Development Continuum Model (PDCM, Singapore), 235
professional development projects (PDPs, Finland), 165
professionalism, 22; Argentina discussion of, 37, 53; Finland discussion of, 165–71; "new," 250
professionalization, 13, 14, 15, 292; Brazil narrative of, 16, 68, 70, 71, 79, 84–85; and feminization, 9; global calls for, 19, 22; and racial inequality, 16
Professional Standards for Preschool, Elementary and Secondary School Teachers (China), 126
Professional Teacher's Certificate (PTC, Ghana), 186–87
Program for Improvement and Innovation in Teacher Training (MIF, Catalonia), 89, 103–4, 107
Programme for International Student Assessment (PISA), 96, 227–28
Progress in International Reading Literacy Study (PIRLS), 227–28
ProUni (University for All Program, Brazil), 83
Provisional Teacher's License (PTL, Ghana), 186–87
pupilage system, 230

Race to the Top program (US), 291
Raffles Institution, 230
Ramsey, Paul, 7

Razquin, Paula, 19–20, 36–60, 308
Reagan, Ronald, 287
Recommendation Concerning the Status of Teachers (ILO/UNESCO report), 18–19
Reform and Open Door policy (China), 112
regionalism, 147–49
Relay Graduate School of Education, 291
religious orders, 11
rescue pedagogy, 217–18
Rethinking Education (UNESCO report), 90, 91, 96
Rockefeller Foundation, 21
Rojas Chaves, Gladys, 9
Roldan Vera, Eugenia, 6
Rose, Brian, 254
Rousseau, Jean-Jacques, 8
Roussef, Dilma, 68
rural areas, 17, 154, 291, 304; in China, 115, 122, 123, 124–25; in South Africa, 260, 263, 264, 268–69

Sadasivan, Balaji, 227
Sáenz, Moises, 17
Sarid, Yossi, 201–2
Sarmiento, Domingo Faustino, 7, 9–10, 38, 55n7
Sayed, Yusuf, 257, 268
school-based training, 182, 184, 185–86, 187, 188, 194
School-Centered Initial Teacher Training (SCITTs, England), 138, 141
School Direct (England), 137–38, 141
school enrollment: in Argentina, 40, 47, 50; in Brazil, 63–64, 69–70, 85n4, 86n16; in China, 112, 114; in Ghana, 180, 183; in Singapore, 229, 230, 235; in South Africa, 259–60
Shi, Zhongying, 119–20
Silicon Valley, 26, 292
Singapore, 226–43, 305; budget and funding in, 229, 241; curriculum in, 236, 238; educational research in, 240–42; history of teacher education in, 230–37; links with teacher education schools in, 238–39; MOE-NIE cooperation in, 237–38; school enrollment in, 229, 230, 235; teacher recruitment in, 234, 235
Singh, Marcina, 257

socioeconomic status: in Argentina, 47–52; in Brazil, 16, 72–73, 76; in Israel, 200, 214, 216, 221; in South Africa, 257–58, 269–70
Soudien, Crain, 260
South Africa, 249–74, 305; apartheid in, 16, 253–55, 276n9, 277n19; curriculum in, 251, 265–66, 272; economy of, 252, 275–76n8; funding in, 256, 263–64; higher education restructuring in, 262–66; history of teacher training in, 11, 253–55, 276n10; and new managerialism, 270–73; post-apartheid shifts in, 255–58; rural areas of, 260, 263, 264, 268–69; schooling inequality in, 266–70; socioeconomic status in, 257–58, 269–70; teacher rationalization program in, 259–60; teacher supply and demand in, 258–62
Southwest University (SWU, China), 118
Soviet Union, 15, 20
Spain. *See* Catalonia/Spain
specialization, 70–73, 99–100, 257
Special Teaching Position (STP, China), 122–23, 124
Sposito, Marília, 77
Spreen, Carol Anne, 249–80, 308
standardization, 73; in China, 126; and professionalization, 13, 14
standardized tests, 64, 158
Stowe, Calvin, 7
Structured Mentorship Preparation Programme (Singapore), 239
"Suggestions on the Adjustments of Distribution and Structure of Teacher Education Institutions" (China), 116
"Suggestions on the Reforms and Development of Teacher Education" (China), 116
Sustainable Development Goals (SDGs), 249–50, 270

Tatto, Maria Teresa, viii, 301
Taub Report, 203
Taylor, William, 240, 241
teacher demonization, 271
Teacher Education and the Challenge of Development (Moon, ed.), i–x
Teacher Education around the World (Darling-Hammond and Lieberman), ix–x

Teacher Education Curriculum Standards (China), 126
Teacher Education for the 21st Century (TE21, Singapore), 235–36, 239
Teacher Education Forum (Finland), 168–69
Teacher Education Program (*licentiate*, Brazil), 71–72, 73, 86n14
Teacher Education system (TEd, Argentina), 36–37, 38; institutionalization of, 36–37, 54n2; and neoliberal reforms, 40–43; socioeconomic profile of students in, 47–52; in 2005–2015, 43–47
Teacher Growth Model (TGM, Singapore), 238
teacher identity, 204, 205, 294
Teacher-in-Training Scheme (Singapore), 232
teacher morale, 143–44, 183
teacher rationalization, 259–60
teacher recruitment: in Brazil, 65, 66, 78, 85; in China, 123, 124; in England, 133–34, 140–41, 145; in Ghana, 179, 181, 188; in Israel, 217; in Singapore, 234, 235; in South Africa, 260–61; in US, 291, 296
Teacher Recruitment and Retention in England (Foster), 145
teacher retention, 273, 293; in England, 139, 142–43, 144–45, 150
teacher salaries: in Argentina, 39, 42, 46–47, 51–52, 58n49; in Brazil, 65, 78; in Catalonia/Spain, 97; in England, 141, 143, 150n7, 157; in Ghana, 183; in South Africa, 258
teachers as civil servants, 92, 94, 97, 99, 124, 231
teacher seniority, 92
teacher shortages, 268, 304; in China, 114, 123, 125; in England, 132–34, 139–45; in US, 288, 290, 294
Teachers Matter: Attracting, Developing and Retaining Effective Teachers (OECD report), 25, 249
"teachers matter" narrative, 271–72
teacher strikes, 39–40, 294
teachers' unions, 23, 101, 294–95; in Argentina, 46, 53; in England, 143–44
Teacher Training College (TTC, Singapore), 230–31
teacher workload, 78–79, 143, 145, 183, 232

Teach First (England), 24, 138–39, 141
Teach First Israel (TFI, HOTAM), 24, 199, 214–18
Teach for All network, 123, 138, 304
Teach for America (TFA), 24, 289, 290, 291, 295
Teach for China (TFC), 123
Teaching Chinese as a Foreign Language (TCFL), 125
Teaching Scholars Programme (TSP, Singapore), 236
technology, 26–27, 270–71
Tenti Fanfani, Emílio, 77
Terigi, Flavia, 45
Test Brazil, 74, 86n23
Thatcher, Margaret, 137
theory-practice nexus, 80, 81, 163, 216, 236, 239, 302
Thinking History Globally (Olstein), 1–2
Tinker Foundation, 25
Tomorrow's Teachers (Holmes Group), 288
Toom, A., 159
tracking system, 156–57
Transfer Law (Argentina, 1992), 40
Trends in International Mathematics and Science Study (TIMSS), 227
Troy Female Seminary, 10
Trump, Donald J., 293
Tschurenev, Jana, 4
Tsuchiya, Motonori, 8
Tunmer, Raymond, 254
Tyack, David, 2, 3, 32n42

UNESCO (United Nations Educational, Scientific and Cultural Organization), 18, 297, 303; *Education for All Global Monitoring Reports*, 249; Four Pillars of Learning of, 95, 105; knowledge definition of, 100, 109n16; *Learning: The Treasure Within*, 95; *Learning to Be: The World of Education Today and Tomorrow*, 94, 108–9n7; *Recommendation Concerning the Status of Teachers*, 18–19; *Rethinking Education*, 90, 91, 96
Union of Women Teachers (England), 143–44
United Kingdom. *See* England
United Nations, 18, 249–50, 303

United States, 281–305; alternative certification in, 281, 287–88, 290–91, 292–93, 296; cost of university degree in, 296; history of teacher education in, 5, 282–86; new pathways to teacher education in, 286–93; number of teachers in, 293–94; racial discrimination in, 16–17, 284; twenty-first-century challenges in, 293–97
University and College Union (England), 141–42, 144
University College London, 126, 146; Institute of Education at, 235, 303–4
university degrees, 19, 47, 118, 137, 194; in Brazil, 69, 71–73; in Catalonia/Spain, 97–102, 109n13; in Finland, 160, 161; in Singapore, 231, 233, 234, 235, 236; in South Africa, 254, 277n19; in US, 281, 284–85, 288, 293, 296
University of Chicago, 13–14, 288–89
University of Haifa, 207, 209, 210, 215
University of Phoenix, 291
University of Vic, 107
university partnerships, 126, 236, 303–4
Untrained Teachers Diploma in Basic Education (UTDBE, Ghana), 189
USAID (United States Agency for International Development), 19, 20, 259

Vallory, Eduard, 89–110, 308
Vally, Salim, 260, 269

Values, Skills, and Knowledge (VSK), 235, 236
Van Broekhuizen, Hendrik, 261
Vargas, Getúlio, 16, 70
Vick, Malcolm, 14
Vygotsky, Lev, 17

Washington Consensus, 23, 297
Welch, Tessa, 256
Western Governors University, 291
Whitehead, Alfred North, 91
Wigdorz, Brett, 138
women in teaching, 3, 9–10, 304; in Argentina, 38, 50; in Brazil, 66; in US, 293–94
Woodbridge, William Channing, 7
World Bank, 18, 22, 27, 259, 297, 303
World Declaration for Education for All, 22, 303

Xiao Zisheng, 18
Xi Jinping, 125

Yen, Y. C. James, 15

Zeichner, Kenneth, 292
Zhou, Jun, 114
Zhou, Yisu, 111–31, 308
Zilbershtein, M., 203
Zimmerman, Jonathan, 14